VICTIMS
Second edition
Reviews and praise for first edition

"Remarkably objective but uncompromising, she [the author] reveals the irony of the term 'criminal justice.'" — *Publishers Weekly*

"...recreates the emotions of the victim (and the secondary victim) with a directness and clarity that is impossible to ignore." —*Washington Post*

"The author takes a searching, compassionate look at victims of crime and provides much-needed insight into the complex, often devastating aftermath for victims, their families and their friends." —*Tampa Tribune*

"*Victims* will do for all crime victims what Brownmiller's book [*Against Our Will*] did for victims of rape." —Richard Quinney, Ph.D., criminologist

Featured on the *Today Show*
and in *People* magazine

Selected Other Books by Jan Yager, Ph.D.

Nonfiction
Essentials of Victimology:
Crime Victims, Theories, Controversies, and Victims' Rights
Looking Backward, Going Forward:
Reflections on a Writer's Life
Friendshifts: The Power of Friendship and How It Shapes Our Lives
When Friendship Hurts
Friendgevity
How to Finish Everything You Start
365 Daily Affirmations for Happiness
Road Signs on Life's Journey
Skills Building Workbook for College Students
time Management and Other Essential Skills for College Students
Effective Business and Nonfiction Writing
Productive Relationships
Work Less, Do More
125 Ways to Meet the Love of Your Life

Fiction
On the Run
The Pretty One
Untimely Death (with Fred Yager)
Just Your Everyday People (with Fred Yager)

VICTIMS

Second Edition

Jan Yager, Ph.D.

(a/k/a J.L. Barkas)

With a new introduction, overview, bibliography, resources, and updated statistics and selected updates in the original Scribner book

Stamford, Connecticut
Hannacroix Creek Books, Inc.

THIS BOOK IS DEDICATED TO MY OLDER BROTHER,
Seth Alan Barkas (1945-1969)

and to all crime victims, their families, friends, and those who help
victims

Cover design by Daniel Middleton

Published by: Hannacroix Creek Books, Inc.
1127 High Ridge Road, #110 Stamford, CT 06905 USA
https://www.hannacroixcreekbooks.com
e-book: hannacroix@aol.com

ISBN: 978-1-938998-62-1

Where anonymity was requested, to assure that anonymity, minor details were
changed in the interviews, stories, and letters that follow. However, care was taken
that no change would distort the meaning. Editing of all original material was
minimal and restricted to sequence and length. For anonymous cases, even if names are
fictitious, the cases are true.

This publication contains the opinions and ideas of its author and is designed to
provide useful information regarding the subject matter covered. It is sold with
the understanding that the author and publisher are not engaged in rendering
legal, psychological, or other professional services in this publication. Laws vary from state to state,
and if the reader requires expert assistance, therapy, or legal advice, a competent
professional should be consulted.

The author and publisher specifically disclaim any responsibility for any liability, loss, or
risk, personal or otherwise, which is incurred consequently, directly, or
indirectly, of the use and application of any of the contents of this book.

CONTENTS

Part One

Introduction to Second Edition
Including Updated Bibliography and Resources for
Getting Help

It has been forty-three years since I wrote and published the original hardcover edition of *Victims* by Scribner's in 1978 in the U.S. and Peel Press in 1979 in the U.K. It has been eight years since 2015 when I released this book as an e-book with an Overview about what had changed in the decades since the first edition of *Victims* was published. The 2015 additional material especially highlighted one brave woman's story in depth based on several phone interviews. That survivor is Debra Puglisi-Sharp, who was raped and kidnapped and held hostage for several days; her husband was killed by her attacker.

In this new introduction, I discuss some of the issues that crime victims, service providers, and experts have been addressing since 2015, namely the #metoo Movement; providing help for victims; DNA evidence; and consideration of such controversial individuals as Sue Klebold, mother of one of the Columbine high school killers, or Kerri Rawson and her brother and mother, the family of the BTK serial killer, as victims of crime, In this new introduction, I also share the results of a survey on crime victimization that I conducted, completed by 225 men and women throughout the U.S. You will find a poem I wrote as a tribute to the 32 victims of the Virginia Tech mass shooting on April 15, 2007, as well as updated major violent and property crime statistics.

In addition to the results of the new survey, this introduction is based on interviews I conducted with speakers in the Victimology class that I teach at John Jay College of Criminal Justice, which has included victims of rape, robbery, sexual assault, domestic violence, mass shootings, and the family of homicide victims as well as experts in forensic criminology, trauma therapy, crime victim behavior, investigative services, and more, as well as additional interviews with victims and service providers who answered my queries published in HARO (Help a Reporter Out) newsletter, requesting information..

Finally, this new introduction h a s an updated bibliography and resources for crime victims and their family and friends. It concludes with the addition in 2023 of suggested interview guidelines for law enforcement, contributed by Daniel King, who was a police officer in the Henderson, Nevada police department for 23.5 years.

#MeToo Movement

In the U.S. in 2018, there were 139,380 rapes based on the new definition, that includes male as well as female victims, and 101,151 rapes, according to the legacy definition. Please note: It is estimated that only 40% of rapes in the U.S. are reported to police so the actual number of rapes is probably much higher. Rape is a global problem with South Africa having the highest rate of rapes —132.40 per 100,000 compared to 28.60 per 100,000 for Australia, 27.30 per 100,000 for the United States, and a rate of just 1 per 100,000 for Japan.)

At the website for metoomvmt.org, 2006 is given as the start date for the Me-Too Movement by Tarana Burke, to get a national dialogue going about sexual violence. But most Americans only became familiar with the hashtag and term #metoo when the *New York Times* published an article on October 5, 2017 with accusations by actresses Rose McGowan and Ashley Judd of sexual harrassment by movie mogul Harvey Weinstein. Dozens more women came forward with similar allegations and over the next few years the accusations went from bad to worse with a trial beginning on January 20, 2020 leading to a conviction on February 24, 2020 of one count of criminal sexual assault in the first degree and one count of rape in the third degree. Weinstein was sentenced to 23 years in a state prison in New York.

Another high-profile celebrity rape accusation and conviction was in April 2018, the trial of TV mega-star Bill Cosby began. Then, on September 25, 2018, 81-year-old Cosby was found guilty of three counts of aggravated indecent assault and sentenced to three to ten years in a state prison in Pennsylvania, a fine, and prosecution cost repayment He had been found guilty of drugging and raping Andrea Constand at his home in 2004. But in June 2021, after serving 2+ years in prison, his conviction was overturned due to a legal issue.

"The #metoo movement has pretty much driven the discussion on crime victims in the last five years," says Leonard A. Sipes, Jr., a retired federal senior public affairs specialist and former senior specialist for crime prevention and victim services for the Department of Justice's clearinghouse.

As Carole Lieberman, M.D., M.P.H., a Beverly Hills-based forensic psychiatrist and expert witness confirms, "There is one employment case, for example, where the employee was alleging sexual harrassment by her supervisor, but her employer was not taking it very seriously, until the trial of Harvey Weinstein. When he saw how much attention such allegations can attract, he fired the man and took her complaint much more seriously."

Molly Blair Richardson credits age —she is now 43, living with her significant other, with two children in their early teens —as well as the #metoo movement with her increased willingness to share about what happened to her back in 1995, when she was a high school senior in New Orleans. What makes her story especially unusual is that she was raped along with her best friend Caroline (not her real name). Molly shares that even before the #metoo movement, she had been quite outspoken on social media, especially getting into arguments about gun violence since Molly always discloses, "Have you ever had a gun pointed at your head?"

Here is an edited version of my phone interview with Molly, who is now a photographer, as well as her e-mails to me about what happened to her and Caroline when they were 18 and 17-year-old high school seniors and juniors, respectively, and its short- and long-term aftermath:

> *Back in 1995, I was driving my best friend home after we watched a movie together at her house, and we were pulled over by a car with a blue flashing light. I assumed it was the police. Just as I realized it was not the police, but a group of kids about the same age as us impersonating the police, we had three males in hoodies with assault style semi-automatic weapons pressed up against us.*
>
> *I got pushed into the back seat and my friend was shoved in the front with other perps. They drove us to near the train tracks. We were both raped. We both had guns to our heads.*

When this was happening, all I could think about was, I don't want to be killed. Do whatever I have to do. I don't want to die tonight.

After the rapes were done, we were both naked and they took us and shoved us into the trunk of my car. I thought surely there were going to gun down the trunk and we're going to be dead.

I don't know how long we were in the trunk but after a few minutes, when we didn't hear anything —they must have been super quiet — when they drove away, we were trying to kick down the back seat of my car. But that didn't work.

Then I realized that I had a busted taillight on my car. We just needed that ventilation. Then I realized that I had an issue with the trunk of my car not opening so the car mechanic had walked me through unlocking the trunk of my car. So, I suddenly thought, "I can get us out of here." So, I unlocked the trunk.

We got out of the trunk and I grabbed my shirt and we got our clothes on and we went to a nearby popular bar. There were people there and I knew that if there's a bar, there's going to be a cop nearby. So, we found the detail cops and told them what happened. They ended up calling backup and the whole night till the next two months, we were involved in the investigation, starting with going to the hospital and having rape kits done.

We later found out that these kids were part of a gang, and while a couple of them were apprehended, some got away. We later learned that they had been on a crime spree that week and had killed a man the night before our rape at an ATM.

I ID'd one of the perpetrators from the photo I saw of him on the front page of the newspaper because he was arrested for murder. [But] my ID was not allowed because it was not made under protocol.

It wasn't until sixteen or seventeen years later, in 2011 or 2012, that a detective called me up saying that the man that I had believed raped me had been linked to my rape via DNA.

It turned out that the boy I identified in 1995 did indeed end up being the boy that held a gun to my head and raped me in the back seat of my car.

Caroline and I had huge issues with the way the case was handled in 1995, and I am still not sure what became of the detective in 2011 that contacted me or even what happened to the individual who raped me. I know he was in prison for another crime. The detective told me that she was trying to use the evidence in my crime to get him to talk about the other men involved that night that raped Caroline.

I carry this with me every day. But I do feel like I have still been able to live a normal life. In all honesty, the stress and anxiety of having a gun pointed to my head has brought more pain than the rape itself. I almost died that night by a kid my age. My best friend was 15 feet away being raped by a couple of men, and I could see her in my peripheral up against a fence. I know she dealt with the aftermath so much differently than me.

This experience has definitely made me a gun control advocate because I want people to understand that I would have died if I had a gun on me. I would have been shot in the head if I carried a weapon.

What Molly's best friend Caroline described to me about how she was handled by the police after the rape is what psychiatrist and crime victim expert Dr. Martin Symonds refers to as the "second injury." That is when the "system" handles a victim so ineffectively that it feels like a second victimization. In a nutshell, Caroline's reaction to what happened was to get angry, but the police were ill-prepared to deal with her strong emotions. Since she did not conform to their expectation that she would act like a traumatized victim who was breaking down from what she had just endured, they basically accused her of being involved. Says Caroline, "I wasn't behaving like a victim, then I must not have been a victim. I must have been involved." Her friend Molly, however, thinks the reason the police treated Caroline like a suspect was because she is mixed race; Molly is white. The perpetrators were black.

Caroline continues, "My experience from start to finish was that there was very little compassion from beginning to end with everything I was dealing with including taking the morning-after-pill before my parents, who were away, got back to town."

The rape occurred on March 31st. The next day, which happened to also be April fool's day, Caroline was supposed to fly to Washington, D.C. with her choral group. When she told her teacher that she was unable to go on the trip because she had been assaulted, her teacher replied. "That's not funny." Caroline repeated herself. "That's really not funny," her teacher said once again.

Caroline does not remember being judged by her classmates, who all suddenly knew what happened, but she does recall her biological father being critical of how she had handled herself. Says Caroline, "I do remember my biological father being obsessed that I had not fought back since I know martial arts and how to shoot guns. But in that moment, when I realized there's a semiautomatic weapon pointed at Molly's head, and someone's telling me to take my clothes off in the car, right now you decide, you could start screaming, or I could have thrown myself out of a moving vehicle since I did not have a gun to my head, but I wasn't going to leave Molly. Then I remembered the story my grandmother had told me about having a gun held to her head." Her grandmother told her that what mattered was just getting through it and that is what Molly did.

She told herself, "My job is not to be a hero. My job is not to abandon Molly."

Her father eventually realized he had been wrong. "Years later, my Dad said to me, apologetically, "You were right. Often people who go along survive better."

11

What Caroline learned, and what may be helpful to another potential victim, is that she did what she needed to do. She also realized that she had to make sure, while she was being raped, that she kept herself involved in what was happening so she could make her best choices. She fought off the tendency to shut down and instead she forced herself to stay alert. She kept telling herself, "This *is* happening. You'd better stay awake. You cannot pretend it's not happening. You can't be hysterical."

I asked 20-year-old Christina R. (not her real name) to share about how the #metoo movement has impacted her since she is a survivor of childhood sexual abuse. Between the ages of 4 and 11, her older cousin molested her. She finally reported it to her middle school advisor who immediately told the police. Her cousin was arrested, and he confessed. Christina and her parents soon learned that he had been molesting her older sister previously but stopped when she got to a certain age and began molesting Christina instead. Her cousin, who was 24 when his crimes were finally revealed, entered a plea bargain, and received a sentence of 10 years for each crime, with the sentences to run consecutively.

Here is what Christina shared about how the #metoo movement is impacting her:

> In regard to the #metoo movement, I think that I put up a guard to protect myself from being triggered when seeing it in the media all the time so I feel very separated from that movement. In not many instances that I saw were stories about family members, so I tended to detach myself from those strong survivors. A couple of times I questioned whether or not to speak out like they did but settled on the fact that I am not one to post or publish my story on Facebook, Instagram, etcetera. I and not sure why, but maybe it was to protect myself.
>
> I have also found myself in many situations where people I was with (acquaintances or friends of

friends) were making fun of the movement with jokes or even questioning the honesty of the survivors. I finally got the strength and courage to defend the survivors in a mature and educational way every time anyone made a joke or felt that the stories were made up.

I've always felt that my story is mine, and those I tell is my choice and I know it's safe wherever it goes. In short, the movement hasn't really changed the way I view myself or what happened to me, but it's made me gain the courage to speak up when people are mishandling the stories that they've seen.

Jennifer Storm is a survivor of rape at the age of 12 who openly speaks out about what happened to her, including her decline afterwards when she became addicted to alcohol followed by crack cocaine. She finally hit bottom, got into a 28-day recovery program that changed her life, and has been sober ever since. After running a local victim witness assistance program for 10 years, she became the victim advocate for the Commonwealth of Pennsylvania. The first edition of her book, *Blackout Girl*, was published in 2008; the second edition in 2020. In our interview, Jennifer, who is now 45 and the parent of a 5-year-old adopted son, shares how that rape at 12 was the beginning of a 10-year decline that included a suicide attempt. But it finally ended in 1997 when she entered a 28-day rehab program. Before the rape, Jennifer was a straight A student with perfect attendance, and a cheerleader. "I was a happy kid. I had two older brothers. We had a good middle-class home upbringing," Jennifer says.

She explained that her parents decided to let her go out alone that fateful night when she was 12 to a roller-skating rink. On the way to the roller-skating rink, she and her best friend stopped off at a quarry. She got into the car with a 28-year-old who proceeded to rape her.

When she got back to her house after the rape, the police were there because her parents had reported her missing since she had not returned home at the agreed-upon time. When she told her mother what happened, her response was to slap Jennifer across her face. Jennifer explains, "I spent Sunday morning having a rape kit done at the hospital.

It completely and totally shifted my life. We didn't have victim advocates. I didn't have anyone with me at the hospital. I had no idea what was going on with my body."

How did her parents deal with Jennifer's rape? Says Jennifer:

> *They pretended like it didn't happen. The man was arrested and charged with seven counts. I started a spiral downward. I had significant insomnia. I started skipping school and ended up turning to alcohol because I needed something to numb the pain. I had just turned thirteen, but it wasn't hard to access alcohol.*
>
> *I attempted to take my own life, but it wasn't really a suicide attempt as much as a cry for help. I wanted someone to see the pain I was in because I couldn't articulate it. I ended up spending that summer in a psych ward which was probably the last place they should have sent me.*
>
> *My junior and high school years with alcohol gave way to marijuana and cocaine. I became addicted to crack cocaine and was raped again when I was 17 at a friend's house. Raped by my friend's cousin. He was convicted and ended up going to jail.*

Fortunately, Jennifer was eventually able to heal as she records in *Blackout Girl* and its sequel, *Awakening Blackout Girl: A Survivor's Guide for Healing from Addiction and Sexual Trauma.*

The #metoo movement has helped to educate the public that sexual abuse and rape can happen to anyone, even boys and men. Ron Blake is the survivor of rape. "There were three men involved in my rape," explains Ron. "One man held me down and raped me. One of the other men was on the bed and watched n and laughed as it happened. I asked him to help and he would not. The other man came into the room after the rape. But he assaulted me and tried to stop me from calling the police after I told him I was raped."

Blake continues, sharing about the aftermath of the rape: "I struggled badly with PTSD for several years after the incident. I have bene through a lot of physical therapy. And I became dependent on prescription sleeping pills because of this trauma."

Derek Smith, of the multi-state firm, Derek Smith Law Group, PLLC. that handles sexual harrassment, hate crime, sexual assault, child sexual assault, and discrimination cases on the East and West Coasts, sees the positive and negative sides of the #metoo movement for victims. "The good side," says Derek Smith, "is that now women should feel more comfortable coming forward. At the same time, the bad side is that before, it would have elicited a gasp. It was considered a much more serious event. Now, it's so much in the media that sometimes these cases are not looked at seriously enough. People may feel that, 'Another person sexually harassed.' It's almost like the benefits and the negatives cross each other out at this point."

One of the clear developments from the #metoo movement is the public having a much stronger opinion about whether someone is telling the truth or not in allegations of sexual harrassment, abuse, assault, or rape. Says Derek Smith:

Victims should always have the benefit of the doubt. But that doesn't mean that what they're saying is true. But to not give the alleged victim the benefit of the doubt is unethical. But you have to give it a commonsense analysis and first you have to take a look and ask certain questions:

- *What motivation does this person have to lie?*
- *Why would this person say something that isn't true?*
- *What are the details?*
- *Does it make sense?*

That is why we have a court system to determine these things.

Diana Anzaldua, who treats sexual assault victims, is a licensed clinical therapist at the Austin Trauma Therapy Center that is based in Austin, Texas. She says this is the most important idea to share about sexual violence victimization: "We need to always be talking about this. Bringing awareness is important. Consent is everything. Young girls, young boys, need to know that if somebody is invading their private spaces, that's not okay. We need to be having these discussions." Diana recommends *Know My Name*, by Chantal Miller, the memoir by the young woman sexually assaulted in 2015 in California and whose 7,000 word victim impact statement went viral who, till her book's 2019 publication, was only known as "Emily Doe."

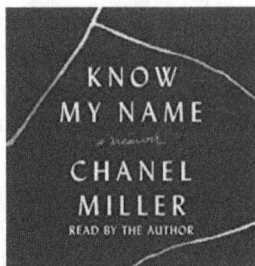

KNOW
MY NAME
a memoir
CHANEL
MILLER
READ BY THE AUTHOR

Survey results:
"Have you personally been the victim of a crime?"

In the United States, there are two primary sources of crime data currently available. The first is the Uniform Crime Report (UCR), which has been used as the way that crime data is collected in the U.S. since 1930 when it was introduced. The key crimes that the UCR tracks are the Part I index offenses which includes: murder and non-negligent manslaughter, rape. robbery. burglary, motor vehicle theft, larceny-theft, aggravated assault, and arson.

However, the UCR was replaced on January 1, 2021 with the NIBRS (National Incident-Based Reporting System). This system gathers more data on a bigger number of offenses--52-- including more victim-offender information. Like the UCR, the NIBRS is based only on reported crimes reported annually by local law enforcement to the FBI to collect and release to the public.

The second type of data that is regularly collected to try to figure out how much crime occurs in the United States is the National Crime Victimization Survey or NCVS. Started in 1972, a representative sample of households is interviewed twice a year with extensive questions asked about non-fatal victimization of anyone over the age of 12 in the household. The sample consists of approximately 90,000 households with an estimated 160,000 persons. That information has limitations too since it is only addressing victimization with the reference point of the last six months.

In my sample of 225 men and women, there was no limit on the time of the victimization that I was referring to, but you had to be 18 or older to participate.

What did I discover? *That nearly seven in ten respondents (68 percent) said they have been a victim of a crime whether or not it was reported.*

Twenty-eight percent of that 68% of crime victims had been victimized once. But 40% had been a victim of two or more crimes with 22 percent indicating *repeat victimization* three or more times.

Since there were so many who had been victims of multiple crimes, to find out more information about just one of those crimes, I asked the respondents to answer the next questions about their *most recent victimization.*

Of the 170 in my survey who answered that they had been victim of one or more crimes, their most recent victimization was the following, in order of frequency: theft (21.18%) followed by robbery (12.35%), next was domestic violence (10%), followed by cybercrime (7.06%), burglary (6.47%), with a tie for the next spot between motor vehicle theft (5.88%) and fraud (5.88%).

Reporting to the Police

The third question out of the ten questions that I asked that I think has the most significant was the respondents' answer as to whether they reported their most crime victimization It was almost a 50/50 split: of

17

those who answered: 44.83 percent did *not* report to the police, but 41.95 percent did.

In a follow-up question, those who answered that they did not report the crime to the police were asked to provide the reason. Here are the most popular reasons, in descending order:

Reasons for Not Reporting Most Recent Crime to Police

"I didn't think they would be able to do anything about it"	37.39%
"I didn't think they had enough information to Make an arrest so why bother reporting it"	16.52%
"I considered it a private, family matter"	9.57%
"I was worried about retaliation or repercussions of reporting it"	6.96%
"I was too upset to want to talk about it with anyone"	7.83%
"I was worried about what might happen if I reported it"	5.22%
"I didn't want to take the time to report it to the police"	5.22%

From these results it is obvious that the police need to educate the public about the benefits of reporting crime, even if they question whether anything could be done about it. The public need to know that by not reporting a crime to the police, information could be shared that might be useful in helping to solve another crime. I was reminded of that when I did a ride along years ago with the police through a precinct on the lower East Side of Manhattan. They finally caught a man who was accused of committed multiple rapes in the area. The police explained that they were hampered from solving the case sooner because too few of the victims came forward to share the details of the criminal's modus operandi. He had such a pattern to the rapes he committed that getting the word out about those behaviors could have avoided one or more women being victimized because it is likely the rapist could have been caught much sooner.

An even more dramatic example of the benefits of reporting a crime to the police was shared by Kerri Rawson, daughter of the BTK killer, who killed ten people, mostly women. I interviewed Kerri and ten days later, she was guest speaker for several of the classes I teach at John Jay College of Criminal Justice. Rawson, author of the bestselling memoir, *A Serial Killer's Daughter*, shared that during her freshman year, when she was away at college, when she returned home for dinner one time, her father tried to strangle her older brother. Her father had stopped killing by that point, but it is possible that an investigation into her brother's strangling might have linked her father to the BTK killer. Could it have closed the case sooner which had countless women and families in Kansas living in fear? Maybe. Maybe not.

As Kerri writes in her memoir, *A Serial Killer's Daughter*:

> *All families get into arguments, but what my father did was inexcusable. Yet, at the time, we dismissed it. It'd been that way as long as I could recall. Dad is under a lot of stress. He just lost control. He didn't mean it. He will apologize soon.*

> *On the exterior, our family looked like the American dream, and I'd grown up believing that very thing. I tucked away deep within me, this outburst of my father's, telling no one till he was arrested. What would have happened if we had called the police that night? Would they have done anything? Would they have questioned him enough to find decades-long terror hiding behind his rage? These questions still haunt me.*

Help for Victims

I interviewed Cecile Tucker, a registered clinical counselor, who provides counseling for victims through her British Columbia, Canada center, Cecile Tucker Counselling service. Cecile shared with me about the exemplary program she is part of in Canada, providing crime victims with 15 sessions of free counseling. The only requirement is that the crime was reported to the police but there is no statute of limitations on how recently the crime occurred, although most clients have been victimized recently. Says Cecile, "I recently had a client who was victimized in her teens, but she did not report it until she was in her 40s. But I still saw her."

Although extensions beyond the 15 sessions are feasible, if requested in writing, along with an explanation of why more treatment is necessary, Tucker finds that for most crime victims, the set number of sessions is enough to get them back on their feet. She finds the emotional help victims need following a crime falls into three distinct stages:

Stage 1 – Getting victim functioning again
Doing basic emotional management work. "I can't function." "I am feeling overwhelmed."

The goal during this stage is to get the victim functioning again.

Stage 2 - Processing what happened
Whether the client has a formal PTSD (Post Traumatic Stress Disorder) diagnosis or not, working through the memories of the crime.

Trying to understand what the victim went through.

Doing trauma work around the abuse or crime that they survived

Tucker explains: "In domestic violence cases, discussing the cycle of abuse and helping them find the balance between their role in it but recognizing that they are not to blame at all."

Stage 3 – What's next?

During this last stage, the counselor and victim work on, "Where do you go from here?"

If the victim was in an abusive relationship, discussing "What do I want my future relationships to look life? What steps can I take to achieve that?"

If the husband was the income earner, and the victim is no longer with her husband, what are her plans to be able to support herself and her children?

How long victims spend in each of these stages depends on the client. Some can start almost immediately at Stage Two while others may take ten First Stage sessions to work through their emotions so they can get to the next stage.

In the United States, depending on where you live, there may be free or sliding scale counseling individual or group sessions available for crime victims. Some services, even if direct programs are local, such as Safe Horizons in New York City, founded in 1978, offer support for all victims of violence and abuse through their toll-free national hotline: 1-800-621-HOPE. (See listing in Resources section.)

Ashleigh Diserio is a behavioral consultant who has 13 years of experience working with the U.S. government and private sector clients consulting on felony-level crimes that includes mass shootings, child abuse, homicide, and sexual assault. Diserio, who has a master's in forensic psychology, shares her key insights about helping victims:

1. *Until you have been the actual victim of that particular crime, or something similar, do not think you can fully understand what victims are feeling and going through.*

2. *A commonly known resource that victims can seek support form is therapists. A more obscure resource used to help victims grow, heal, and prosper is life coaches. Life coaches work with clients to examine where their client is at in the present moment and where they want to be in the future. The*

client and life coach work together to help identify the client's goals and to develop an actionable plan to achieve them. Seeking assistance from one or both resources is a positive step to dealing with the challenges that victims might be facing.

3. *Law enforcement agencies who implement evidence-based best practices when conducting interviews seem to gather more information and build better rapport with interviewees. I teach law enforcement the cognitive interview approach* which was developed by Dr. Ronald Fisher at Florida International University. My agency interviews victims, subjects, and witnesses using the same interview style, and we conduct all interviews in the same room. Some law enforcement would not think of conducting interviews of subjects in "soft rooms," which are typically used for victim interviews. "Soft rooms" have couches, chairs, comfy pillows, and calming artwork. It took years to get some law enforcement on board with conducting interviews using evidence-based best practices, but we have seen great results in the amount of information obtained with these techniques.*

4. *Help domestic violence victims to become more proactive in pressing charges before it is too late. Law enforcement often does not understand why victims become hesitant to press charges. We must be understanding about the reasons behind why these victims go back to abusive situations. Throw as many resources at them and keep showing up every time these victims seek help. Domestic violence victims typically try to leave abusive situations eight times before they leave for the final time.*

*Cognitive interviewing is a form of interviewing that suggests using all five senses for victims or witnesses to describe a crime scene and it even recommends looking at the crime scene from various perspectives including the criminal's.

What I have learned is that what most crime victims want, besides getting the medical, financial, and legal help they need, as well as justice, is to be listened to with empathy. You cannot generalize that all victims want their offenders to go to prison or even to be tried. For various reasons, some victims prefer not to report their victimization to the police which can mean they have eliminated the possibility of free counseling and other services by the government, but even if they do report the crime, they may decide they prefer not to be involved in testifying if the case goes forward. As a woman I will call Beverly shared with me, "I was sexually assaulted eight years ago. It was someone that I knew that I had previously dated. He kept on calling and texting and I finally agreed to meet him. It was at that point that he assaulted me."

Beverly called her friend after the rape happened and her friend called the police. She went to the hospital, had an examination and a rape kit was done. It took until 7 a.m. the next morning, and her college graduation was going to be at 9 a.m., so Beverly missed her graduation.

It turned out that her rapist had not disconnected his call to her, so the entire rape was recorded on Beverly's phone. The police and assistant district attorney could hear Beverly yelling during the assault, "Stop" and "What are you doing?"

There was so much evidence in her case she had been told that a plea-bargained guilty plea or even winning at trial would probably be a slam dunk. Initially Beverly cooperated with the assistant district attorney, but then she decided to withdraw her complaint. Without her testimony, the case did not go forward. Soon afterwards, Beverly changed her phone number, moved, and never saw the guy again.

Why did she change her mind about pursuing a case against her rapist?

"I'm Latino," Beverly shared with me. "My brother and my father have both been in prison for various reasons. So, I did not want to be responsible for taking away someone's freedom where they end up going to prison. I felt so bad about being that person who had some of that control. I decided I didn't want to do that."

Does she now regret her decision to withdraw her complaint?

"I'm in a different place in my life now. I wish I had done something to have a voice for myself and for other people who are survivors of sexual assault."

Domestic Abuse

Tracie Yamauchi of T and C Protection Firm in Fort Worth, Texas offers help to victims, especially domestic abuse victims, by facilitating a victim getting out of an abusive situation without a tragic outcome. Avoiding a tragic outcome in domestic abuse and divorce situations is the paramount goal. I saw the results of a breakup that had a tragic outcome when, in my early thirties, I attended the funeral of the 20-year-old younger sister of a woman I had befriended, the manager of the local photocopy shop in Manhattan near the apartment where I was living in at the time. Her sister had married an older man, in his 50s, but the marriage was over, and her sister had filed for divorce. Her estranged husband asked to stop by to pick up more of his things and my friend's sister agreed.

Tragically, her husband shot and killed her and then killed himself.

At that funeral there are no words to describe the loss that my friend and her family felt. Those who cared about her and her sister could only affirm the horror and senselessness of it all.

These are the kind of fatal situations that Tracie Yamauchi's firm seeks to avoid. Those of us who study crime victims, or work with domestic violence victims, know that the most dangerous time for these victims is after she or he has announced the decision to finally leave. The word *finally* is an important one since she or he may have tried to leave many times before, but this time it is really going to happen. "On average, it may take seven attempts to get away," says Tracie.

When the firm gets involved, they do something called a civil standby, and they arrange with the attorneys and law enforcement and courts so they can get the victim out of the situation "with a one-time shot." "We're able to get a protective order," says Tracie. Tracie continues, "We present that to the abuser as well as we offer the victim protection to get away. We also help them put a plan in place so we can get them somewhere safe. We coordinate with helping them to get away."

There may be no more than a three-minute window available to help clients to get away. "Often times they have small children with them," says Tracie. "She needs to have access to those children when we arrive or there is the fear that she might lose those children."

Disabled Victims

Another group of victims that needs to be addressed are the disabled who have a much greater likelihood of becoming a crime victim. Karin Willison, who has been in a wheelchair all her life due to cerebral palsy at birth, on November 28, 2014, she was attacked in her home in San Diego, California. She was and thrown out of her wheelchair by a masked intruder who turned out to be a former home caregiver and her boyfriend. They were both found guilty of this and other crimes and sent to prison. The crime and subsequent death threats sent by the perpetrators so terrified her, Karin packed up and moved to the Midwest.

Willison, who is a writer, has a website, FreewheelinTravel.org, where she writes about life and travel with a disability. She says that since people with disabilities are "set up to be victimized," she recommends being careful about who you hire to help you including these suggestions:

1. *Get referrals from trusted sources.*
2. *Before you hire someone, do an extensive background check.*

25

3. *Look up whoever you are considering employing and see who they live with.*
4. *Check the applicant's social media for any red flags.*

Domestic Emotional Abuse

If domestic violence included physical abuse, it might be included in the statistics for aggravated assault or even attempted murder. But if the abuse is only emotional, that is a victimization that is a lot harder to criminalize even though the emotional scares run deep. Mannette Morgan, author of *Finding Your Voice*, was such a domestic violence victim. She married her high school sweetheart and had two children by the time she was 23. "I was emotionally abused," says Mannette.

One day, when she was twenty-three, she was watching *Phil Donahue*, a TV show, and the person being interviewed talked about depression. The interview resonated with Mannette and she realized that she was in an extremely negative situation for her and her children. "Within six months, I was out of there." She moved in with a friend for two weeks as she figured out what she would do next.

Fortunately, Mannette landed on her feet, started a business and, years later, found love with a second husband who treated her in the way she learned she deserved to be treated. When he died nine years later, she eventually fell in love again and remarried a man who also treats her well. She never let herself be mistreated the way she had been in her first marriage.

Mannette shared with me that when she called up her first husband to let him know that she had written a book and that he was in it, although he was not named, "His comment was, 'I never beat you.'"

Her book, *Finding Your Voice*, and the accompanying workbook, *Finding Your Voice Workbook,* is her way of helping others to gain the courage to create the positive life that they are meant to have. Through her speeches, life coaching, and writing, she tells current victims, and those who have made the break, "I get you. You're worth so much more than the abuse you've experienced."

Help for Secondary Victims*

We usually associate secondary victimization with the family and friends of homicide victims. But there is an increasing awareness that family and friends of all crime victims including rape and sexual assault, robbery, burglary, and any major violent or property crime can suffer along with their loved ones, the primary victims. A student interview with a friend who was robbed highlighted this so powerfully when he shared in his transcript that the mother of his friend who was robbed said that she felt as if she too had been robbed.

I interviewed Rob Longley whose daughter was molested for 2-1/2 years by a trusted authority figure/teacher, along with 3 other girls. After 4 years and 48 court appearances, the offender was found guilty, served 2-1/2 years, and was released "on a technicality."

Rob, his wife, and their other daughter, who was two years younger, were impacted by his daughter's sexual abuse. The entire family, went into therapy after the abuse was revealed. Two-and-a-half years after he became aware of his daughter's sexual abuse, Rob's response was physical. He says: "I tend to internalize my stress and I actually developed an ulcer. I almost died as a result of bleeding internally and I didn't know it."

His other responses have been healthier ones. "I write about it," says Rob. He also has a coaching blog for parents who are dealing with their child's abuse: sexualabusecoaching.com. "I try to help others who are dealing with this as well. I built software that is used in victim services for case management where they used to use index cards." In 2015, he published a book to help other parents who are going through the same experience that he and his wife went through with their

*In my textbook, *Essentials of Victimology*, I define two additional victim categories: *tertiary victims*, those who help victims including police, EMTs, 911 operators, doctors, and nurses, and a fourth category that I originated, *quaternary victims*. They are the family, friends, or co-workers of the tertiary victims and even a local or broader community impacted by a specific crime or crime in general.

daughter. It is called *The First Seven Days: A Parent's Guide to Surviving Your Child's Sexual Abuse.*

Eighteen years after his daughter's sexual abuse, fortunately his daughter is doing well. She is now 26, a police officer, and she has completed her master's degree in criminal justice.

DNA Evidence

There is an amazing case that is just one of countless examples of how DNA evidence can help victims of a crime, even 32 years after the crime occurred. According to the MSN.com article, "A Chinese couple whose son was abducted in a hotel in 1988 have been reunited with him after 32 years," in 1988, a 2 year old boy, Mao Yin, was on the way back home with his father from the nursery when his father stopped at a hotel to get some water for his son. Within seconds, the boy was snatched.

His mother quit her job and devoted herself to trying to find her son. She even started a volunteer group called "Baby Come Back Home" which was responsible for reuniting 29 children with their families.

In April 2020, police received a tip about a man who had adopted a baby 1,000 miles away from where Mao Yin's family had lived in China. A DNA match proved that the boy was indeed the missing child. It turned out he had been sold for the equivalent of $840.

The importance of DNA evidence, even though the hit television program *CSI* went off the air after a decade, is still a significant development in the field of victimology and any work related to crime and victims. Certainly, the work of The Innocence Project, which uses DNA to exonerate those who are wrongfully convicted, is a prime example of DNA and its significance. The success of The Innocence Project affirms that not only does DNA help to solve crimes, but it can aid in getting a wrongfully convicted person released from prison after five, ten, twenty, or even more decades. Founded in 1992 by Peter Neufeld and Barry Scheck at the Cardozo School of Law, The Innocence

Project, to date, has exonerated 367, although of course that number will keep growing.

Considering the Families of Offenders as Victims

A category of victims related to crime that I did not address in either the original *Victims* or the 2015 Introduction that followed are the family and friends of the incarcerated or, if it was a murder-suicide, if the perpetrator was killed, of the deceased. Who are the family members of offenders who are also victims of crime? One example is Tosha Smith Mills, author of *Momma I Should Have Listened,* as well as her three other sons, her incarcerated son's brothers. Tosha shares how hard her son's incarceration is on her and her family in her memoir, with contributions by her son, BJ Smith. Her son was 17 at the time he committed the two robberies. He is currently doing a 40-year sentence in a Texas state prison since he received two sentences of 20 years for each of robbery conviction, to be served consecutively. Her son will not be eligible for parole until he has served 20 years, in 10 more years.

I have met Tosha several times when she was a guest speaker for several of my courses at John Jay College of Criminal Justice. Her presentations always leave a strong impression on me and my students because it is rare that they have considered, let along heard from, the family member of a convicted offender. Tosha and her family live in New Orleans where her son was raised. He had moved to Texas, to spend time with his biological father, whom he had not seen for many years, a few months before he was arrested. Visiting her son BJ in prison means traveling from New Orleans to the state prison in Amarillo, Texas, an expensive plane trip of almost $1,000 or an exceedingly long 12-1/2 hour drive.

Here is a segment from Tosha's powerful memoir about what the parent of an incarcerated adult child goes through and how she makes sure she is there for him:

> *"It has taken a huge amount of courage and
> determination to remain strong throughout this whole*

ordeal. No doubt, it is one of the most challenging battles for parents who are going through this to remain their child's keeper. There is an overbearing number of factors involved creating turmoil with each passing moment. The financial aspect alone can send the strongest to their knees begging for mercy. Sometimes all you have left to give is the time you can invest in making sure your incarcerated child has at least one visitor to know all hope is not lost. The visits alone will put you on an emotional rollercoaster that you find yourself riding along after each visit. It is all enough to break down anyone."

Daughter of a Serial Killer

I interviewed Kerri Rawson, daughter of the BTK serial killer, and she also did a Zoom interview with three of my John Jay College classes. Kerri and her husband and their two children are trying to live as normal a life as possible, now residing in Orlando, Florida. To recap for those who do not know her story, on Friday, February 25, 2005, when she was 26 years old, there was a knock on the door of her apartment in Detroit, Michigan where she was working as a substitute teacher. It was the FBI. The agent was there to inform her that Kerri's father had been arrested for being the BTK serial killer. He also had to collect a DNA sample.

As she shares in her memoir, *A Serial Killer's Daughter,* published in 2019 by Thomas Nelson, Kerri, who was unaware of her father's crimes beginning thirty-one years before, explains that she sees herself as a victim. In our interviews, she said she sees her husband, brother, and mother as victims of her father as well. As Kerri writes in her memoir:

"I'm now able to say—without shame or fear—I'm a trauma, crime, and abuse victim. I live with anxiety, depression, and PTSD.

30

"What's in my past is what it is; it can't be changed—Dad murdered ten people and devastated countless lives. Yet on the days when I'm not wrestling with hard, terrible truths, I will tell you. I love my dad—the one I mainly knew. I miss him."

It is hard to comprehend what Kerri Rawson lives with on a daily basis because of her father's murderous actions.

Mother of a Columbine Shooter

Sue Klebold wrote a memoir several years ago, *A Mother's Reckoning,* sharing about what it had been like for her, opening up for the first time since the Columbine High School massacre seventeen years before, when her son Dylan and his friend Eric killed 12 students and one teacher, wounding 20 others. I have not yet had a chance to read her memoir, but I have several times watched the BBC interview with Sue Klebold that is posted on YouTube and viewed her TED Talk. The BBC interview is a powerful one, as is the TED Talk. But what I especially remember from the BBC interview is the anecdote where Klebold describes what happened when she was paying by check in the supermarket after the tragedy had occurred. A woman nearby noticed her name on the check, and she asked if she was related to one of the Columbine killers. I do not recall the exact words that ensued after she confirmed that she was his mother, but it was a distressing confrontation that left enough of an impression on Klebold that she highlighted it in this interview.

Klebold's emotional TED talk further documents what she deals with as the parent of a mass murderer but also as a mother who has lost her child. Klebold concludes her TED talk, which has been seen by more than 8 million people, with these words:

"I know that I will live with this tragedy, with these multiple tragedies, for the rest of my life. I know that in the minds of many, what I lost can't compare to what the other families lost. I know my struggle doesn't make theirs any easier. I know there are even some who think I don't have the right to any pain, but only to a life of permanent penance.

"In the end what I know comes down to this: the tragic fact that even the most vigilant and responsible of us may not be able to help, but for love's sake, we must never stop trying to know the unknowable.

"Thank you."

Victimology

The subdiscipline of criminology, victimology, is considered to have started in the late 1940s when Benjamin Mendelsohn, a European-Israeli lawyer, is credited with coining the term *victimology* in 1948, and by Hans von Hentig, a German criminologist who emigrated to the United States in 1935, who published the groundbreaking book, *The Criminal and His Victim*. It has continued to grow in popularity as an area of study for college and university students majoring in criminology, criminal justice, and sociology, as well as with law enforcement, crime victim service providers, and law students.

Initially founded in 2012, the Division of Victimology, which is part of the ASC (American Society of Criminology), has over 200 members from around the world. The ACJS (Academy of Criminal Justice Sciences) has a section on Victimology. Two leading peer-reviewed journals, published by SAGE, are the *International Review of Victimology* and the *Journal of Victimology and Victim Justice*.

A subdivision of victimology is forensic victimology. In his textbook, *Forensic Victimology*, Brent E. Turvey describes this relatively new field as "the scientific study of victims for the purpose of addressing investigative and forensic issues....It [the textbook] gives readers the means and rationale for examining victims with a scientific mindset, as opposed to the mindset of a police officer, victim's advocate, or treatment professional."

From victim to survivor to thriver

According to the dictionary, the word *victim* originated in the late 15th century from the Latin *victima* meaning a creature killed as a religious sacrifice. In his textbook, *Crime Victims*, John Jay College of Criminal Justice professor Andrew Karmen makes a case for using the term "survivorology" instead of "victimology." Writes Karmen:

> "These days, many people who have been seriously harmed by criminals prefer to be called survivors rather than victims because of the term's positive connotations —that they are rebounding, exercising "agency" to regain control over their lives, and demonstrating their resilience to adversity. They see the term victim as carrying a lot of unwanted baggage, such as being a 'loser' who was 'bested' or 'vanquished.'"

But Karmen wonders if this term, *survivorology*, should replace *victimology* or if it should only be used selectively, "reserved for those whose recovery and resilience is unusually impressive?"

What about the word *thriver* instead of *victim* or *survivor*? There is no actual word *thriver* yet, but there is certainly the word *thrive* meaning to develop well or vigorously. So, let's keep the subdiscipline of victimology although I definitely see a case for survivorology. In the interviews I have conducted with victims over the last few years, I have seen a trend to ask to be viewed as a survivor, and not a victim, even emphatically rejecting the victim term or label.

How Not to Be a Victim

Is it possible to advocate teaching victims or potential victims' behaviors that will make them less likely victims without buying into the victim blame perspective?

I took the Active Shooter one-hour training provided by Diego Redondo, Director of Public Safety at John Jay College of Criminal Justice. He is retired from the FBI and his training was fascinating and useful. The information that you learn during this active shooter training gives the participant the tools to have a better chance of surviving if an active shooter situation might occur. Yes, everyone has the right to never find himself or herself in such a situation. But if someone would be in that situation, there are behaviors you can learn that will make you a less likely victim.

However, there is a fine line in all this because that does not mean that if someone tragically is a victim, whether that leads to an injury or a fatality, or emotional distress, that he or she is to blame. That is not to deny the well-respected findings of Dr. Marvin Wolfgang's 1957 journal article, "Victim Precipitated Homicide," that reported on his examination of 588 homicides in the city of Philadelphia over a four-year period. He concluded that 26 percent of those cases were deemed victim precipitated homicides because the victim struck the first blow, or the victim initiated the confrontation. These are unresolved controversies about victims and victimology.

Updated Statistics on Crime Victims

For 2018, the Federal Bureau of Investigation (FBI) has released the following statistics, based on the information provided by approximately 18,000 local police departments throughout the United States. Remember this is only *reported* crimes and that the departments, until the new system starts in 2021, apply what is known as the hierarchy rule. That hierarchy rule means if a crime is reported and someone was robbed, the offender was in possession of an illegal weapon, and the victim was killed during the course of that robbery, it will only be included in the information provided to the FBI as a murder. The robbery and possession of an illegal firearm will not be recorded and sent to the FBI for compiling in their annual national statistical report.

In 2018, according to the FBI Uniform Crime Report, there were 16,214 murder and non-negligent manslaughter victims in the United States. That is a rate of 5 per 100,000.

Compare that to the murder rate in other countries. The United States has a lower murder rate than the Latin American countries with excessively high murder rates, such as 61.80 in El Salvador, or 33.97 in South Africa, but certainly not as low as countries with low murder rates like 1.68 in Canada and 0.2 in Japan.

In 2018, according to the Federal Bureau of Investigation report, there were 807,410 reported victims of aggravated assault, at a rate of 246.8 per 100,000, making it the most frequent violent crime in the United States. These assaults can be considered felonies or misdemeanors, depending upon whether a weapon was used and if there was an intent to commit serious bodily harm or not. What are typical aggravated assaults? An example would be if Jill is on her way home from the supermarket and George approaches her, tells her to move aside, pulls out a gun, and says he will use it if she does not move.

When I was getting my master's in criminal justice, I took a course with the late Dr. Martin Symonds in "The Psychology of the Victim." Dr. Symonds was a New York City police officer for 8 years before going to medical school and becoming a psychiatrist specializing in crime victims. One of the many insights he shared with us during the semester was that the difference between an aggravated assault and a murder could be infinitesimal —did the knife miss major organs? Did the bullet miss the heart?

Look at the statistics for 2018 for weapons used in aggravated assaults and murders.

In murder, firearms were used in 72.7 percent of the reported murders. But in aggravated assaults, firearms were used just 26.1 percent of the time.

Personal weapons, defined as hands, fists, and feet, were used 25.2 percent of the time in aggravated assaults. Knives and other cutting instruments were used 17.3 percent.

By contrast, in murder cases, personal weapons were used only 4.8 percent and knives and cutting instruments 10.7 percent. As noted previously, firearms were used in 72.7 percent of those crimes.

Additional 2018 crime statistics in the U.S. – reported crimes are as follows:

Robbery   282,061   victims   or   86.2   rate   per   100,000

All property crimes 7,196,045 victims 2,199.5 rate per 100,000

Burglary, 1,230,149 victims 376.0 rate per 100,000

Larceny/theft 5,217,055, victims 1,594.6 rate per 100,000

Motor vehicle theft 748,841 victims 228.9 rate per 100,000

Clearance Rates

Having an idea about the number of violent and property crime victims for the most recent year that data is available is useful information. But there is another statistic that is also useful: clearance rates. The clearance rate is the number of reported crimes that are cleared by an arrest. Here is a chart showing the clearance rates in the United States from 2018:

Clearance Figure

Percent of Crimes Cleared by Arrest or Exceptional Means, 2018

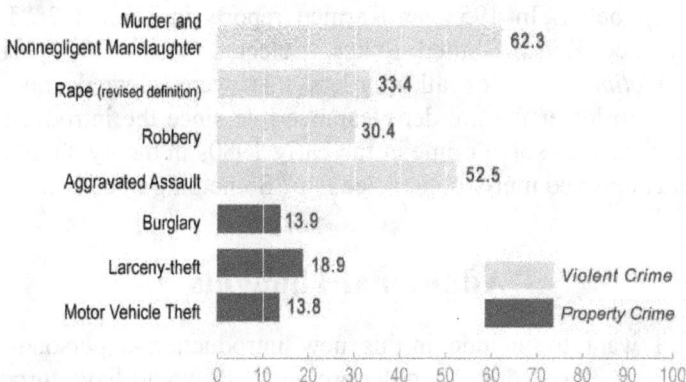

Crime	Value
Murder and Nonnegligent Manslaughter	62.3
Rape (revised definition)	33.4
Robbery	30.4
Aggravated Assault	52.5
Burglary	13.9
Larceny-theft	18.9
Motor Vehicle Theft	13.8

Violent Crime

Property Crime

0 10 20 30 40 50 60 70 80 90 100

Source: Federal Bureau of Investigation (FBI), *Crime in the United States, 2018*, Criminal Justice Information Services Division, FBI UCR (Uniform Crime Reporting) Program.

If we want to see declines in crime rates and the number of crime victims, it will help to see an improvement in these clearance rates for reported crimes. Only 13.9 percent of reported burglaries are cleared by an arrest and only 13.8 percent of motor vehicle thefts. Is the likelihood of getting away with these crimes as a factor in the decision to commit these crimes?

Returning to the most common reason for not reporting a crime to the police based on my survey of 225 men and women —the belief that the police would not doing anything about the crime anyway — could that be reflected in the low clearance rates? Or is it a Catch-22 — failure to report a crime makes it harder to solve crimes leading to the low clearance rates which reinforces the public's reluctance to report crimes in the first place. Some considerations to ponder.

Murder clearance rates are the highest clearance rates at 62.3 percent. That rate has remained consistent within a few percentage points since 1993. But prior to that year, the murder clearance rate was much better. In 1953, as Karmen reports in Table 6.2 "Trends in Clearance Rates, United States, Selected Years, 1953-2016, in *Crime Victims*, 93% of all murders that were cleared. So, what happened to lower the murder clearance rate since the introduction of DNA evidence to solve crime in the early 1980s in theory should have led to an improved murder clearance rate? Something to consider.

Additional Thoughts

I want to include in this new introduction a personal note. In 2020, on May 26th, my older brother Seth would have turned 75. His murder may have ended his life at just 23, but his memory lives on and fortunately he has two sons, now grown, Ariel and Sky, and they have children, also now grown., and one of his grandchildren had a daughter in 2022 so he would have been a great grandfather. I was able to compile and publish my brother's one act plays in an anthology entitled *In the Great Together* so his talent as a playwright lives on. Hopefully, some day one or all his plays will be performed. So glad Seth had children, grandchildren,and even great grandchildren, and that some of his creative writing is available, but that does not minimize the sad reality that I still miss my brother, gone much too soon.

In 1969, the year my brother was killed, there were 14,760 murder victims with a U.S. population. of 202.7 million. In 2018, there were 16,214 murder victims on a population of 327.2 million. The murder rate was going down but that positive trend got reversed. The CDC (Centers for Disease Control and Prevention) lists the number of homicides in 2021 as 26,031 and the number of firearm homicides as 20,958 with a rate of 6.3 deaths per 100,000 population.

Compare that to these 2018 global homicide rates: Finland, 85 murders with 5.5 million population and 726 homicides in Great Britain with a population of 66.27 million.

There is a debate about why the murder rate at least for a few years improved in the U.S. Certainly improved medical care with more aggravated assault and attempted murder victims surviving instead of dying at the scene is one factor.

We should all dedicate ourselves to finding solutions to the high homicide rate — 5 murders per 100,000 people versus just 1.82 homicides per 100,000 in Canada, or .08 in Australia. The U.S. is doing much better than El Salvador with a pre-pandemic murder rate of 61.8 per 100,000 but there is still so much room for improvement to create a much safer America where the Sandy Hook Elementary School massacre of 2012 is not followed up by the February 14, 2018 massacre at Stoneman Douglas High School in Florida, or Detroit, Michigan could once again be known as a vibrant midwestern American city rather than having the dubious distinction in 2020 of being named by escapehere.com as the most dangerous city in America.

Although I am focusing on homicide in this conclusion to this new introduction, lowering or eliminating the high crime rate for so many other crimes, from aggravated assault and burglary to motor vehicle theft, rape, and cybercrime, is also important.

Sociologist Emile Durkheim boldly declared in the late 1800s that crime is inevitable in all societies. He, and other sociologists, criminologists, and victimologists, have also noted that crime rates can vary for a range of reasons including how connected or disconnected individuals feel to their community. He referred to it as *anomie* when there is a disconnect. It is outside the objectives of this new introduction to enter a debate about how we can lower the crime rate in America or elsewhere, but it is a debate that America and so many other countries need to engage in.

Some of the many organizations working to end violence and crime victimization in America include the National Network for Safe Communities at John Jay College https://nnscommunities.org/ and Smart on Crime, based in Washington, D.C., which has been holding an annual conference at John Jay College for the last few years https://www.smartoncrime.us/. What organizations are working toward this goal in your community that you could become an active participant in?

Every homicide victim, every crime victim, is an individual who has gone through a trauma or, in the case of homicide, who has family and friends and even co-workers and neighbors who love and miss those victims. Whether it was a murder that happened because of an argument, during the commission of a robbery, a carjacking gone bad, or a mass shooting, murder is the ultimate crime with the greatest loss. Those who are left physically or mentally disabled from crime-related injuries are a close second. That does not even begin to mention the emotional and financial toll that crime can take on its primary and secondary victims.

I want to share in this introduction with a poem that I wrote the day after the mass shooting on April 16th, 2007 that occurred at Virginia Tech University in Virginia when a 23-year-old senior randomly shot and killed 27 students and five members of the faculty:

The Victims of Virginia Tech
by Jan Yager

Never to walk through the door again
Never to speak or dance or cry.
Thirty-two victims and a killer are no more.
And we mourn the dead
And we are numb with grief.

Lives cut down in their prime
Men and women with so much to give.
Daughters, sisters, friends with so many reasons to live.
Professors, mentors, fathers, and sons,
No more, no more.

Trying to make sense of such a tragedy
Words fail as we struggle to understand.
A demented, tortured soul
Who took others with him

On his suicidal rampage.

They would have been known for their deeds
Their achievements
Their contributions to the world.
Instead, it will be hard not to disassociate them
With the biggest gun massacre to date in U.S. history.

Rest in peace, unwitting victims.
We will all try to focus on your life
Not on your deaths.
We owe it to you all,
To your loved ones,
To your memories.

It *is* fortunately possible to lower crime rates. The National Network for Safe Communities at John Jay College of Criminal Justice at their annual conference shared that finding, and working with, the few individuals in a community who were responsible for most of the violent crimes in a particular neighborhood led to dramatic crime rate reductions.

In El Salvador, the murder capital of the world, during February and March 2020, murders went down by nearly half. Sadly, the reason was tied to the global COVID19 pandemic that was killing more than 300,000 around the world by the latest count, but the behavior changes the virus required had the unintended positive consequence of lowering murder rates.

As Kirk Semple and Azam Ahmed point out in their *New York Times* article, "Murder Rates Were Staggering. The Virus Has Brought Some Quiet, for Now," getting people off the streets because of strict lockdowns was credited with the murder decline. Besides murder, in Argentina, since mid-March 2020 when stay at home orders were issued, robberies declined in Buenos Aires, the capital, by nearly 90 percent, from 225 per day, on average, to 30. These declines show it is possible to lower crime rates, and have fewer victims, but we certainly do not want to require a global pandemic as the only way to lower crime rates or number of victims.

Follow-up

If you would like to participate in my ongoing research into primary and secondary victims of crime, I invite you to complete my confidential survey. I also welcome those who provide services or help to crime victims —crime victim advocates, lawyers, assistant district attorneys, trauma specialists or therapists, police officers — to complete my confidential survey as well. Here is the link to the survey posted online through my professional surveymonkey account:

https://www.surveymonkey.com/r/YMH8Q9P

Please note that you must be 18 years of age or older to complete the survey.

Although personal responses cannot be guaranteed, you could also write to me directly at: jyager@aol.com. Please visit my website and sign up for my mailing list or newsletter: https://www.drjanyager.com

Next are the Acknowledgments to this new introduction, followed by the 2015 introduction, and then by the original *Victims* book, published by Scribner's.

Jan Yager, Ph.D.
https://www.drjanyager.com

Acknowledgments to New Introduction

Every semester for the last seven years, as well as during the winter and summer breaks, I have been teaching Victimology at John Jay College of Criminal Justice, a senior college in The City University of New York (CUNY). I have also taught related courses including Criminology, International Criminology, Penology, Crime and Delinquency, and Sociology of Deviance. For the Victimology and other courses as well, I always invite several victims as well as representatives of the criminal justice system to be guest speakers. Over the years, those guest speakers once or multiple times have included: Kaitlin Roig-DeBellis, who saved her first grade class at Sandy Hook Elementary School during the mass shooting by hiding her students in the minuscule classroom bathroom, co-author of *Choosing Hope*; Nicole Hockley, whose 6 year old son Dylan was one of the 20 children who were murdered that day; Dorri Olds, who was gang raped at the age of 13 and whose first-person essay, "Defriending My Rapist," was published decades later in *The New York Times* in 2012; Val Rodriguez, whose first cousin, Diana, was killed and dismembered by her estranged husband; Nance Schick, a lawyer and expert in dispute resolution, who had been victimized several times beginning in her childhood up through an attempted robbery and assault five years ago; Kerri Rawson, daughter of the BTK serial killer; Janine Latus, survivor of intimate partner violence (IPV), sister of a homicide victim, and author of *If I Am Missing Or Dead*; Marty Tantleff, who was accused of killing his parents when he was 17, was convicted two years later, spent 18 years in prison, was exonerated after 18 years, in 2008, and went on to get his law degree; and directors and counselors for crime victim centers including the Crime Victims Treatment Center (CVTC) in Manhattan and The Rowan Center in Stamford, Connecticut.

Other guest speakers have included David Friedrichs, retired criminology professor at the University of Scranton and crime victim expert; Richard B. Hoffman, attorney and crime victim expert; the director of a domestic violence shelter; Barry Campbell, an ex-offender who works at The Fortune Society; David Rothenberg, who founded The Fortune Society; Bernard Kirk, former police commissioner of New York City and author of *From Jailer to Jailed*;

43

Vanee S., who served three years in a federal prison and now is running a home for women who have just been released from prison; Tosha Smith Mills, whose son, Blake, when he was seventeen, was sentenced to forty years for two robberies; Blake Smith; Mike Capra, Superintendent at Sing Sing Correctional Facility; Scott Ebanks; police officers and detectives; among others.

I also want to thank everyone who responded to my two queries in HARO (Help a Reporter Out) asking victims or those who offer victims help to contact me. I followed-up with more than a dozen of those responses and thank everyone, named or unmated, in this

Thanks also to my current and previous colleagues at John Jay College of Criminal Justice, William Paterson University, Kean University, and around the world for their input including giants in criminology and victimology who are no longer with us who I interviewed and who championed my work early on: Morton Bard, Ph.D., .; the late Marvin E. Wolfgang, Ph.D.; the late Marshall Clinard, Ph.D.; the late Frank Carrington; the late Martin Symonds, M.D. and the late Arthur Niederhoffer, Ph.D. Thanks to current colleagues and professionals around the world including Andrew Karmen, Ph.D., who maintains a website (http://www.crimevictimsupdates.com/) in support of his textbook, *Crime Victims*; Maria Volpe, M.D.; Brent E. Turvey, partner with Forensic Solutions, LLC and author of *Forensic Victimology*; Henry Pontell, Ph.D.; Robert Garot, Ph.D.; Amy Adamczyk, Ph.D.; Jana Arsovska; Jacob Felson, Ph.D., William Paterson University; Eileen Clancy; Joyce Nova, Ph.D.; Esther Kreider-Verhalle, Ph.D.; Eileen B. Hoffman; Bosco Villavicencio; Ruth Tekle; Greg Snyder, Ph.D.; Museum of Jewish Heritage; Robyn Goldstein, Ph. D.; John P. J. Dussich, Ph.D., Professor Emeritus, Fresno State; Julia Nevarez, Ph.D.; Vicky Cannon, Ph.D.; David Green, Ph.D.; Richard Ocejo, Ph.D.; Susan Opotow, Ph.D.; Alisa Thomas; Theresa Rockett; Richard Quinney, Ph.D; Stacie Goosman; and many others.

I also belong to various associations that address crime victims from an academic approach or from a victim services perspective including the ASC (American Society of Criminology), Division of Victimology, established in 2012; American Sociology Association

(ASA), Crime, Law, and Deviance section; Academy of Criminal Justice Sciences (ACJS), Section on Victimology, and NOVA (National Organization of Victim Assistance).

Finally, I want to thank my thousands of students in my Victimology, Criminology, Penology, and Sociology classes over the years. In addition to attending class and sharing in discussions, they have provided confidential interviews with primary or secondary victims of crime, or those who help victims, such as police officers, as part of their fieldwork assignment requirement. A verbatim transcript is required as part of the assignment which has allowed me to read hundreds of first-hand accounts of victimization with everyone from the friend of a murder victim, who watched her friend die from the gunshot wounds he received as he went outside a fast food restaurant to meet with someone only to be gunned down because he was trying to get out of a gang to an unemployed woman who fell victim to a clever mystery shopper cybercrime, who shared her embarrassment that she allowed herself to be deceived as she lost thousands of dollars before she detected the scam, to the robber of the same convenience store three times within the same week, leading to a five year prison term, or the 18-year-old who was robbed at gunpoint on a street in Brooklyn, New York of his $400 sports designer running shoes.

Updated Bibliography

Acker, James R. and David R. Karp, editors. *Wounds That Do Not Bind: Victim-Based Perspectives on the Death Penalty.* Durham, North Carolina: Carolina Academic Press, 2006.

AFL-CIO. *Death on the job: The toll of neglect.* Washington, DC: AFL-CIO, 2007. (Twentieth edition, 2011)

Agnich, Laura E. "A Cross-National Study of School Violence." Ph.D. Dissertation, Doctor of Philosophy in Sociology, Virginia Polytechnic Institute and State University (Virginia Tech), May 11, 2011, Blacksburg, Virginia.

Barkan, Steve. "Sociology: Understanding and Changing the Social World." Chapter 7, Section C, "Crime and Criminals." Modified 10-06-2013. Posted at http://www.peoi.org/Courses/Coursesen/socfwk/contents/frame7c.html

Barkas, J.L. *See also* Jan Yager

Barkas, J.L. "Let's Give Crime's Victims their Due." *Newsday*, September 10, 1978, pages 1, 10.

_____. "Reflections on Murder, Criminals, Handguns…" *Newsday*, December 12, 1980.

BBC. "China Abductions: Parents Find Son Snatched in Hotel 32 Years Ago." May 19, 2020. Posted one.

_____. "Harvey Weinstein timeline: How the scandal unfolded." February 24, 2020. Posted at bbc.com

_____. "Pakistan Taliban: Peshawar School Attack Leaves 132 Dead." December 16, 2014. Posted at http://www.bbc.com/news/world-asia-30491435

BBC Newsnight. Sue Klebold: My life as the mother of a Columbine killer. Interviewed by Kristy Wark.
Posted at https://www.youtube.com/watch?v=6fSKsPwP2JI
14:23 minutes.
Benbenishty, Rami and Ron Avi Astor. "School Violence in An International Context." *International Journal of Violence and School,* Dec
Bowley, G. and J. Jacobs. "Bill Cosby, Free But Not Exonerated, faces and Uncertain Future." New York Times. July 1. 2021.

Burgess, Ann Wolbert "Counseling the Rape Victim." Paper presented at the New York City Conference on Health Care for Rape Victims, New York Academy of Medicine, October 23, 1975, 12 pages.

_____. *Victimology: Theories and Applications.* 3rd edition. Burlington, MA: Jones & Bartlett Learning, 2019.

Burgess, Ann Wolbert and LL Holmstrom. "Rape Trauma Syndrome" in the *Encyclopedia of Trauma: An Interdisciplinary Guide.* Thousand Oaks, CA: SAGE Publications, Inc., 2012,

Burstein, Patricia. "Her Brother's Murder Drove Janet Barkas to Investigate the Sorry Plight of Crime Victims." (In Her Own Words) *People* magazine, pages 60-62, April 30, 1979, Vol. 11, No. 17.

Chapman, Ben. "Motor Vehicle Thefts Rise in New York City Amid Measures to Stop Coronavirus." Posted on April 14, 2020 at the website for the *Wall Street Journal.*

CNN Library. "September 11 Fast Facts." Posted on August 28, 2014, updated November 13, 2019, and posted at http://www.cnn.com/2013/07/27/us/september-11-anniversary-fast-facts/

Cook, Philip J. "Robbery Violence." *Journal of Criminal Law and Criminology*, Vol. 78, Issue 2, Summer 1987, pages 357-376.

Dixon, Lloyd, and Rachel Kaganoff Stern. RAND Corporation. "Compensating the Victims of 9/11." Research report. 2004. Posted at http://www.rand.org/pubs/research_briefs/RB9087/index1.html

Doerner, William J. and Steven P. Lab. *Victimology*.8th edition. New York: Routledge, Taylor & Francis Group 2017.

Dussich, John O. J. "Victimology—Past, Present, and Future." 129 pages.   n.d.   Posted   at https://www.unafei.or.jp/publications/pdf/RS_No70/No70_12VE_Dussich.pdf

Federal Bureau of Investigation (FBI). "30 Questions and Answers About UCR NIBRS Transition." Uniform Crime Reporting Program, National Incident-Based Reporting System. Washington, D.C.: U.S. Department of Justice, October 2018. (15 pages)

_____. Uniform Crime Report, "Murder" *Crime in the United States, 2018*. Washington, D.C.: U.S. Department of Justice, Released Fall 2019.

_____. "Property Crime." *Crime in the United States, 2018*. Washington, D.C.: U.S. Department of Justice, Released Fall 2019.

_____. "Violent Crime." *Crime in the United States, 2018*. Washington, D.C.: U.S. Department of Justice, Released Fall 2019.

Field, Peter. "Remembering September 11—the Day I'll Never Forget."
Posted at
https://www.risk.net/people/1506589/remembering-september-11-the-day-ill-never-forget (September 18, 2001. Revised and edited, August 2002.)

Fisher, Bonnie S., Bradford W. Reyns, and John J. Sloan III.
Introduction to Victimology: Contemporary Theory, Research, and Practice. New York: Oxford University Press, 2016.

Frosch, Dan and Kirk Jonson. "Gunman Kills 12 in Colorado, Reviving Gun Debate." Published at the *New York Times*, July 20, 2012. Posted at:
http://www.nytimes.com/2012/07/21/us/shooting-at-colorado-theater-showing-batman-movie.html?pagewanted=all&_r=0

Ganzini, Linda, M.D.; Bentson McFarland, M.D., Ph.D.; and Joseph Bloom, M.D. "Victims of Fraud: Comparing Victims of White Collar and Violent Crime." *The Bulletin of the American Academy of Psychiatry and the Law*. Volume 18, No. 1, 1990, pages 55-63.

Grabosky, Peter. *Cybercrime*. New York: Oxford University Press, 2016.

Greer, Desmond S. "A Transatlantic Perspective on the Compensation of Crime Victims in the United States." *Journal of Criminal Law and Criminology*. Volume 85, Issue 2, Article 2, 1994-1995, pages 333-401.

Guelden, Marlane (Marin Rape Crisis Center) and John Kim, Tiburton Police Department. "How to Interview a Rape Victim and Survive." 5-page handout/paper. Marin Rape Crisis Center, California. (n.d.)

Howard, Russell D., and James J.F. Forest. *Weapons of Mass Destruction and Terrorism.* New York: McGraw-Hill/Contemporary Learning Series, 2008.

Infoplease. "Timeline of Worldwide School and Mass Shootings: Gun-related tragedies in the U.S. and around the world." Updated February 28, 2017. Posted at http://www.infoplease.com/ipa/A0777958.html

Karmen, Andrew. *Crime Victims: An Introduction to Victimology.* 10th edition. Boston, MA: Cengage, 1984, 2020.
_____. Table 6.2 "Trends in Clearance Rates, United States, Selected Years, 1953-2016, *Crime Victims.* 10th edition. Boston, MA: Cengage, 2020, page 220.

Klebold, Sue. *A Mother's Reckoning: Living in the Aftermath of Tragedy.* New York: Broadway Books, 2017.

_____. "My son was a Columbine Killer. This is My Story." TED MED Talk. 2016. 15:10 minutes. Posted at https://www.ted.com/talks/sue_klebold_my_son_was_a_columbine_s hooter_this_is_my_story?language=en

Latus, Janine. *If I Am Missing or Dead: A Sister's Story of Love, Murder, and Liberation.* New York: Simon & Schuster, 2007.

Maguire, Mike; Rod Morgan; and Robert Reiner, editors. *The Oxford Handbook of Criminology.* Third edition. Oxford, UK: Oxford University Press, 2002.

McCoy, Kevin. "Estimate of Madoff Victims Grows." Posted at 4:16 PM EDT on May 14, 2014 at http://www.usatoday.com/story/money/business/2014/05/13/more-madoff-victims-estimated/9042383/

Miller, Chantal. *Know My Name*. New York: Viking Press, 2019.
Mills, Tosha Smith, Contributions by BJ Smith. *Momma I Should Have Listened*. New Orleans, LA, 2017.

Minutaglio, Rose. "When I Found Out My Father Was the BTK Killer, I Suddenly Saw the Clues Everywhere." *Esquire*, February 2, 2019. Posted online at https://www.esquire.com/entertainment/books/a25346777/kerri-rawson-btk-killer-dennis-rader-daughter-interview/

Morgan, Mannette. *Finding Your Voice: A Path to Recovery for Survivors of Abuse*. Issaquah, WA: Made for Success Publishing, Inc., 2019.

_____. *Finding Your Voice Workbook: A Path to Recovery for Survivors of Abuse*. Issaquah, WA: Made for Success Publishing, Inc., 2020.

Moriarty, Lauren. *Controversies in Victimology*. 2nd edition. Anderson, 2008.

Nadler, Eric. "among the Survivors…are the angry families of murder victims no longer suffering in silence." *New York Sunday News*, June 5, 1983, pages 8-9, 3032, 39,

National Crime Victims Rights Week (NCVRW). "Section 5: Landmarks in Victims' Rights & Services: An Historical Overview." Posted at: http://ovc.ncjrs.gov/ncvrw2014/pdf/Landmarks.pdf

National Crime Victims Survey (NCVS). "CAPI Interviewing Manual for Field Representatives." U.S. Census Bureau, 2008.

Olds, Dorri. "Defriending My Rapist." *New York Times,* January 13, 2012.

OVC (Office of Victims of Crime). "Good Samaritans: Volunteers Helping Victims Program Handbook and Training Guide." Publication date: April 2009. Posted at
http://www.ovc.gov/publications/infores/Good_Samaritans/crime.html

_____. "Victim Impact: Listen and Learn." Posted at youtube.com May 10, 2010. 57 minutes.

Palmer, Kim. "Victim's father attacks serial killer in court." June 3, 2016, posted at aol.com

Quinney, Richard. *Criminology.* Second edition. Boston, MA: Little, Brown and Company, 1979.

Rantala, Ramona R. with technical support from Thomas J. Edwards. "Effects of NIBRS on Crime Statistics." Bureau of Justice Statistics, Special Report. Washington, D.C.: U.S. Department of Justice, July 2000.

Rape and Sexual Abuse Crisis Center, Inc. "Volunteer Training Manual." February 8 through March 15, 1995. Stamford, Connecticut.

Rawson, Kerri. *A Serial Killer's Daughter: My Story of Faith, Love, and Overcoming.* Nashville, TN: Nelson Books, an imprint of Harper Collins Christian Publishing, Inc., 2019.

Ripley, Amanda. "WTC Victims: What's a Life Worth?" Posted at Time.com on February 6, 2002 at http://content.time.com/time/nation/article/0,8599,198866,00.html

Rothe, Dawn L. and David O. Friedrichs. *Crimes of Globalization: New Directions in Critical Criminology.* New York: Routledge, 2015.

Sharp, Debra Puglisi. *Shattered: Reclaiming a Life Torn Apart by Violence.* New York: Simon & Schuster/Atria, 2004.

Schwartz, Emma. "Giving Crime Victims More of Their Say." *U.S. News & World Report.* December 13, 2007. Posted at http://www.usnews.com/news/national/articles/2007/12/13/giving-crime-victims-more-of-their-say

Semple, Kirk and Azam Ahmed. "Murder Rates Were Staggering. The Virus Has Brought Some Quiet, for Now. *The New York Times*, April 11, 2020, posted online.

Silverstein, Jason. "There Were More Mass Shootings Than Days in 2019." January 2, 2020. Posted at cbsnews.com

Smiley, Stephen, and Angela Lavoipierre. "The Murders We Don't Hear About—and Why." July 9, 2018. Posted at www.abc.net.au.

Steinberg, Nick. "25 Most Dangerous Cities in the US in 2020." n.d. Posted at escape.com
Storm, Jennifer. *Awakening Blackout Girl.* Center City, MN: Hazelden Publishing, 2020.

_____. *Blackout Girl.* Second edition, Center City, MN: Hazelden Publishing, 2019, 2009.

Steiner, Leslie Morgan. "Why Domestic Violence Victims Don't Leave." TEDxRainier talk. January 25, 2013. 15:59 minutes. Posted at youtube.com

Surmon-Bohr, F., Alison L. Christiansen, P & Alison, E. "The Rights to Silence and the permission to Talk: Motivational Interviewing and High-Value Detainees." *American Psychologist*, January 16, 2020. Posted online.

Symonds, Martin. "Criminal Minds." John Jay College of Criminal Justice, CUNY, Fall 1975.

_____. "Psychology of the Victim." PSY 705. John Jay College of Criminal Justice, CUNY, Spring 1976.

Tonry, Michael. "Why Crime Rates Are Falling throughout the Western World." *Crime and Justice*, Vol. 43, No. 1, September 2014, pages 1-63.

Treen, Joe, senior editor. "Shattered Lives." *38-56.* magazine issue with reports by 16 correspondents of survivors of homicide including Ellen

Levin, Jennifer Levin's mother, Diana Wood, whose husband was shot 13 years before by muggers, and others. April 3, 1995. Pages 6,

Turvey, Brent E. *Forensic Victimology: Examining Violent Crimes in Investigative and Legal Contexts.* Second edition. Additional contributors: Stan Crowder, Jodi Freeman, Charla M. Jamerson, Michael McGrath, Shawn Mikulay, John O. Savino, Angela N. Torres. Waltham, MA: Academic Press, an imprint of Elsevier, 2014, 2009.

Von Hentig, Hans. *The Criminal and His Victim.* New Haven, CT: Yale University Press, 1948.

Walklate, Professor Sandra. "Who is the Victim of Crime? Paying Homage to the Work of Richard Quinney." 22-page paper.

Walklate, Sandra; Gabe Mythen; and Ross McGarry. "Trauma, Visual Victimology, and the Poetics of Justice." Unpublished manuscript. To be published in M. Haviid-Jacobsen (ed). *The Poetics of Crime.* Surrey, UK (2014).

_____. "Witnessing Wootton Bassett: An Exploration in Cultural Victimology." *Crime Media Culture,* volume 7, 2011, pages 149-165.

Wolfgang, Marvin E., and Simon I. Singer. "Victim Categories of Crime." *Journal of Criminal Law and Criminology.* Vol. 69, Issue 3, Fall 1978, pages 379-394.

World Population Review. "Murder Rate By Country 2020" Posted at https://worldpopulationreview.com/countries/murder-rate-by-country/

Yager, Jan. *Essentials of Victimology.* Boston: Aspen Publishing, 2022.

_____. *Help Yourself Now*. New York: Allworth Press, an Imprint of Skyhorse Publishing, 2021.

_____. "How to Avoid Ponzi Schemes" Posted at consumeraffairs.com, 7/11/2010 http://www.consumeraffairs.com/boomerific/2010/018_avoiding_ponzi_schemes.html

_____. *Productive Relationships: 57 Strategies for Building Stronger Business Connections*. Stamford, CT: Hannacroix Creek Books, Inc., 2011. (See especially: Strategy #49: Becoming More Aware of Workplace Violence.")

_____. "What Secondary Victims of Homicide Have to Deal with." February 11, 2023. Published at https://www.drjanyager.com/ what-secondary-victims-of-homicide-have-to-deal-with (Originally published on Americanthinker.com on January 22, 2023.

Getting Help*

Childhelp National Child Abuse Hotline
1-800-4-A-CHILD (800-422-4453)
Childhelp
Scottsdale, Arizona
https://www.childhelp.org/
Helpline available 24/7 offering support and information related to child abuse and neglect and at-risk children. The hotline was started in 1982 by children advocates Sara O'Meara and Yvonne Fedderson who co-founded the predecessor of Childhelp, children's Village USA. Their activities on behalf of children include

Elder Abuse
U.S. Department of Justice
https://www.justice.gov/elderjustice/find-support-elder-abuse
Information about reporting elder abuse with links to related help by state.

Help for Crime Victims
Helplines: Toll-free and Online Hotlines
Office for Victims of Crime
https://www.ovc.gov/help/tollfree.html
List of toll-free numbers for direct services for crime victims, online help, as well as information/referral sources with either phone numbers or links to online help.

The Innocence Project
New York, NY

https://www.innocenceproject.org/

Founded in 1992 by Peter Neufeld and Barry Scheck at the Cardozo School of Law, The Innocence Project uses DNA evidence to work toward the exoneration of wrongly convicted offenders. It also maintains a speaker bureau if you want to hire an exoneree to address your group.

Office for Victims of Crime
Office of Justice Programs
U.S. Department of Justice
Washington, D.C.
http://www.crimevictims.gov
From the website:
"As part of an integrated campaign to increase awareness about victims' rights, educate the public about the impact of crime, and promote crime victim resources, the Office for Victims of Crime (OVC) launched crimevictims.gov in 2005. At the time of its launch, the site was tied directly to the release of seven public service announcements (PSAs) that began to air nationally during National Crime Victims' Rights Week, an annual commemoration that promotes victims' rights and services in all sectors of society.

"Designed for three audiences—crime victims, volunteers, and victim service providers—crimevictims.gov provides a wealth of resources for each, including links to Web sites, publications, databases, and hotlines. The site intentionally mirrors the look and feel of the PSAs, "giving a face" to crime victims, volunteers, and providers through photos and brief testimonials."

Directory of Crime Victim Services
An OVC Online Service
Office for Victims of Crime
http://ovc.ncjrs.gov/findvictimservices/
Launched in 2003, you can search for crime victim services by location, type of victimization, services that are needed, and type of agency.

National Association of Crime Victims Compensation Boards
Alexandria, Virginia
http://www.NACVCB.org
From the website:
"The mission of the National Association of Crime Victim Compensation Boards is to provide leadership, professional development, and collaborative opportunities to our members to strengthen their capacity to improve services to crime victims and survivors. We share a vision of working together so that every victim compensation program is fully funded, optimally staffed, and functioning effectively to help victims cope with the costs of crime."
At this page you can find information about each state's crime victim compensation program:
http://nacvcb.org/index.asp?sid=5

National Center for Missing and Exploited Children
Alexandria, Virginia
http://www.missingkids.com
Founded in 1984 as a private non-profit organization, working in partnership with the U.S. Department of Justice, to find missing children as well as to stop the sexual exploitation of minors.

National Domestic Violence Hotline
Austin, Texas
http://www.thehotline.org/
1-800-799-7233 (SAFE)

This website offering help 24/7 is funded through government grants including the Office for Victims of Crime. (If you or a family member or friend are in imminent danger, call 911.)

National Center for Victims of Crime
Washington, D.C.
https://victimsofcrime.org/
Founded in 1985 by Ala Isham and Alexander Auersperg after their mother's crime victimization. The center offers many programs to help various crime victims including the Financial Crime Resource Center and the D.C. Victim Hotline.

National Organization of Victim Assistance (NOVA)
Alexandria, Virginia
http://www.trynova.org/
Founded in 1975, information and advocacy non-profit organization with an annual conference related to rights and services for victims. Also offers a training program and certification for those going through a crisis.

National Association of Parents of Murdered Children, Inc.®
Cincinnati, Ohio
http://www.pomc.org/
This is a national membership information association, offering information and support, founded in 1978 by Robert and Charlotte Hullinger after the murder of their 19-year-old daughter, Lisa, by her ex-boyfriend. POMC has one or more chapters in many states, for those who

have lost a family member because of violence as well as for professionals who help crime victims.

National Institute of Justice (NIJ)
Washington, D.C.
https://nij.ojp.gov/
From the website:
"NIJ was created in 1969 and has been in the forefront of nearly every innovation in criminal justice research and policy ever since. Understanding the nature of criminal careers, the effects of sanctions, the ways technology can improve practice, and the operations of the criminal justice system have all been deeply influenced by NIJ research findings."

National Sexual Violence Resource Center NSVRC)
Harrisburg, Pennsylvania
https://www.nsvrc.org/
Nonprofit organization founded by the Pennsylvania Coalition to End Rape. NSVRC opened in July 2000 and is funded through a cooperative agreement from the Center for Disease Control and Prevention's Division of Violence Prevention. Maintains a directory of victim services: https://www.nsvrc.org/organizations

Rape, Abuse & Incest National Network (RAINN)
Helpline: 800-656-HOPE (800-656-4673)
A non-profit anti-sexual assault organization founded in 1994 offering help 24/7 through its helpline.
(Remember: if this is an immediate crisis, call 911.)

Safe Horizons
(Locations in all five boroughs of New York City. Click on the borough you are in at the website to see the Safe Horizon resources located there.)
https://www.safehorizon.org/
Founded in 1978, and based in New York City, offers hotline help nationally through its three helplines:
For domestic violence victims 1-800-621-HOPE
For all crime victims 1-800-689-HELP
For victims of rape and sexual assault 1-212-227-3000
Safe Horizons helps domestic violence victims to find a shelter. In addition to crisis counseling they offer safety planning for those who want to leave an abusive situation as well as acting as an information clearinghouse.

StrongHearts Native Helpline
1-844-7NATIVE (844-762-8483)
Helpline for American Indians and Alaska Natives who are dealing with domestic violence or dating violence. This anonymous and confidential source of support is available daily 7 a.m. to 10 p.m. CT. (A project of the National Domestic Violence Hotline and the National Indigenous Women's Resource Center. After hours, you will be connected to the National Domestic Violence Hotline.)

Victim Support Services
(Formerly Families and Friends of Violent Crime Victims)
State of Washington
https://victimsupportservices.org/
Founded in 1975 by Lola Linstad and Linda Barker after the abduction and consequent murder of Lola's 19-year old daughter, Vonnie Stuth. This is one of the oldest local advocacy groups for violent crime victims and their families and friends.

DrJanYager.com
https://www.drjanyager.com/resources/
"Getting Help"
Excerpted information from my book, *Help Yourself Now* (Allworth Press, an imprint of Skyhorse Publishing, 2021), including several crime victim-related resources. Here is the link included in that section for those who want to share about an organization or resource that could be added to the "Getting Help" entries, or if you are seeking help and want to share, confidentially, about your crime victim-related experience. https://www.surveymonkey.com/r/D7S6F6H.

I invite you to join my mailing list https://www.drjanyager.com/join-my-mailing-list-2/
Check out my blog, https://www.drjanyager.com/jans-blog/, where I plan to post one or more blogs related to crime victimization.

Suggestions to Law Enforcement About Interviewing Crime Victims

Courtesy of Shutterstock, Photo contributor Tommy stock project

Daniel King, who was a police officer for 23.5 years with the Henderson PD in Nevada, shares these insights about interviewing, based on his training and practical experiences.

Be human: Newer officers, especially while in training, often speak like government robots, very square and to the point. While there is a time and a place for that, it's not when you are trying to connect with a person who has just been a crime victim, a witness, or a potential suspect and to elicit information from them.

Most people have never had contact with police officers as a victim before they personally experience it. They are usually anxious and expect something like an interrogation. Speaking to someone like a human allows them to relax, connect with you and carry on a conversation about what occurred. You'll get more information from them that way, and it will be of a better quality for your investigation.

No matter how an officer feels at the moment, you have the ability and the skill to flip the switch and to connect with people on demand.

Ask a question and be quiet: Let people talk. If you interrupt them every time you don't understand something, you'll cut off their thought process and they'll probably never return to it, losing potentially valuable information.

Frequently interrupted victims (and suspects) will begin to speak in shorter sentences and become more self-conscious of what they are saying. They may begin to worry if what they are saying makes sense to you. They will

also begin to speak directly to what they think you want to know. This is not good for the interview process.

As police officers, we're not looking for what we want to hear. We want facts, details, beliefs, and their perceptions, without our influence. Within their recounting of events, the important information will begin to surface. When you don't understand, ask clarifying questions after someone is done speaking.

Interviewing is a skill that takes practice: Like most other skills, interviewing can be improved upon with practice. The best police officers I know, the ones that seem to solve the most crimes, and get the most confessions, are those who have taken the time to develop the interview skills of connecting and communicating.

How do you get that practice? Daniel has these suggestions:

Attend classes, read books, review old interviews, and interview people specifically for the purpose of learning and practicing. Yes, you will make mistakes, and not do as well as you hoped, and you may fail to get critical information. But if you make these mistakes early in your career and on the relatively less important, or more forgiving cases, you will be improving your all-important interview skills.

Every police officer will have cases that you absolutely cannot fail on or you'll fail the victim. Intentionally practice and develop your interview skills for that day.

Since his recent retirement, Daniel King is doing Use of Force Investigations and Training (https://forceinvestigator.com) where he of course is constantly using and bettering his own interview skills.

Part 2
OVERVIEW (2015)

There have been quite a few changes for the victim since I first wrote *Victims* in the late 1970s and fortunately most of those changes are positive ones. Back then there were just 18 states that had a crime victim compensation program. But by 2002, all 50 states, as well as the District of Columbia, Guam, Puerto Rico, and the U.S. Virgin Islands, provided such a program - although what the program offers, in terms of financial compensation and other services, varies from state to state.

Crime victim support groups have continued to become more widespread following the examples of such crusaders like Edith Surgan, the mother of a homicide victim who relocated from New York City, where she used to live and where her daughter was murdered, to New Mexico. There, Edith founded the New Mexico Crime Victim Assistance Organization.

Although founded back in 1975, NOVA (National Organization of Victim Assistance), a non-profit crime victim's education and advocacy organization, has strengthened the training part of its mission. It now offers crisis response training as well as victims relations training and a National Crisis Responder Credentialing Program (NCRCP).

President Ronald Reagan declared one week in April the first "Crime Victims Rights Week" in 1981. Then, in 1984, the National Center for Missing and Exploited Children was founded to help coordinate local, state, and national efforts to find missing children and teens.

A major step occurred in 1984 with the passage of the Victims of Crime Act (VOCA) which founded the Crime Victims Fund as a way of using federal criminal fines and penalties to provide funding for state crime victim compensation and service programs.

The National Center for Victims of Crime (initially founded as the National Victim Center) was started in 1985 by the adult children of Sunny von Bulow. (Von Bulow was left in an irreversible coma for almost 28 years under questionable circumstances. Her husband's guilty verdict for her attempted murder from an insulin overdose was reversed on appeal.)

Victims committees were started by both the American Correctional Association, in 1987, and the American Probation and Parole Association, in 1991, to make the rights and concerns of crime victims more of a consideration in the criminal justice system.

Revisiting the white-collar crimes as "victimless" debate

In the original edition of *Victims*, I explored the crime victimization experience of victims of major property or violent crimes including robbery, burglary, aggravated assault including sexual assault and rape as well as the victims of homicide and the family members of homicide victims, known as survivors. I didn't give white-collar crime victims the consideration they deserved in the original book, probably because, at that time, those property crimes were informally known as "victimless crimes." But anyone who has been the victim of a white-collar crime, or knows someone who has experienced it, understands that is not the case. It took the Bernie Madoff case to sensitize experts and the general public to just how much of a "victim" white-collar crime victims are and how devastating such an experience could be. Having your life's savings wiped out by convicted white collar criminal Bernie Madoff through a Ponzi scheme that he perpetrated is of course not the same kind of victimization as being robbed at gun point, face to face with the offender, or having your home burglarized.

But the Madoff case, beginning with his arrest on December 11th 2008, forever changed the way white-collar crime and its victims will be viewed. The emotional as well as the financial toll on Madoff's victims helped the media, the public, and the criminal justice system to stop seeing white-collar crimes as "victimless." Just how many victims did Madoff have? According to a *USA Today* article, more than 51,700 claims from 119 countries were filed with an estimate of $41 billion net losses.

In addition to the loss of money to individuals or institutions, white-collar crimes can also refer to more severe business-related victimization. For example, in the 2011, 20th edition, of the AFL-CIO report, "Death on the Job: The Toll of Neglect," it is noted that more than 4,000 Americans were killed on the job, and an estimated 50,000 workers died from occupational diseases. How many of those deaths directly resulted from the failure of companies to make the repairs, or to keep their equipment up-to-date so it met the required standards?

Unfortunately, even today, despite all we have learned about getting away from the "blaming the victim" mentality, there are some who are still blaming the victim. For example, in the Madoff case, there are some who say the victims were at fault, accusing them of losing some or all of their savings because they were "greedy." Didn't they *know* that getting such a high rate of return on their investment must have meant something was wrong, that Madoff was doing something illegal to get them those huge profits?

But Madoff managed to gain the cooperation of his victims because they were all part of the same social or business networks. Friends introduced him to their friends and, until the Ponzi scheme collapsed, so many were vouching for Madoff over the 20+ years that he had been defrauding his clients they had no reason to believe his high rate of return was due to anything other than his brilliance as a money manager.

Cybercrime victimization

In addition to a change in the attitude toward white-collar crimes and white-collar criminals, there is the growth of perpetrators and victims of a particular type of white-collar crime: cybercrime. The 2013 United Nations Office on Drugs and Crime (UNODC) report, "Comprehensive Study on Cybercrime," estimated that victimization rates of cybercrime ranged from 1 to 17% of the online population in 21 countries in comparison with rates of under 5% for car theft, robbery, or burglary for the same countries.

Chris Strom's article at Bloomberg.com, "Cybercrime Remains Growth Industry With $445 Billion Lost," estimated that there are an estimated 40 million cybercrime victims in the U.S. alone with $445 billion in estimated losses.

Just how many people are online today? The UNODC report cited above claims in 2011 more than 1/3 of the estimated 7 billion people in the world were online in some way.

Who are the victims of cybercrime? One group are the musicians, authors, filmmakers, music companies, publishers, or movie studios or production companies whose copyrighted intellectual property is illegally downloaded for free so those creative individuals and the companies making their works available for a fee are denied those sources of income.

Another group is a much larger group, namely just about anyone who goes online. These are the good-intentioned Internet users who respond to what looks like a legitimate request to validate their information by a company that they know and trust only to become the victim of a phishing scam which opens their personal information to identity theft or credit card fraud. Unfortunately it turns out that the e-mail they responded to was from a bogus company, cleverly crafted by cybercriminals who then steal their identity and make charges in someone else's name. It takes time and effort to sort out the negative impact on someone's credit profile if not on their finances.

These cybercriminals are often faceless and nameless from around the world, hard to track down and to stop in their widespread illegal operations. But there are gains in this area, as educating the public about how to be more self-protective when conducting business online, or even responding to e-mails, is making it harder to commit cybercrime. Publicizing the apprehension and prosecution of cybercriminals is also helping to give a face to these perpetrators. In 2013, for example, the New York County District Attorney's Office issued a press release that announced the conviction of 15 defendants who trafficked almost 100,000 stolen credit card numbers that led to a theft of $5 million in a global cyber credit card fraud scheme. Four of the defendants were found guilty after a 3-1/2 week trial leading to significant jail time of 13 to 47 years, to be served in a state prison.

The Globalization of Crime and Victimization

Another change since *Victims* was originally published is that it has become necessary to include victims of domestic or international terrorism along with victims of so-called street crime or crimes committed by acquaintances or others known to the victim. Back in the 1970s, I, like so many other Americans, thought those issues were not something that had to be considered on our own land. But that myth was forever shattered on February 26th, 1993, when a truck bomb exploded in the parking lot of the North Tower of the World Trade Center buildings, killing six people. Then, on April 19th, 1995, Timothy McVeigh, a disgruntled American, committed an act of domestic terror when he masterminded the bombing of the Alfred P. Murrah Federal Building in Oklahoma City, which killed 168 men, women, and children, and injured more than 680.

Of course, the event that made international terrorism even more of a domestic threat occurred on September 11th, 2001. That day planes taken over by terrorists flew into the Pentagon and both towers of the World Trade Center. A fourth plane probably headed for another Washington D.C. target was diverted by passengers and crashed into a field in Pennsylvania, killing the 40 passengers and four hijackers on board. The total loss of life on September 11th, 2001 was estimated at 2,977.

Victims of School Violence

Although there have certainly been school shootings or violence here and there throughout history, another trend that was an anomaly in the late 1970s but has, sadly, become a dramatic trend in the last decade or two is the growth of violence on a massive scale, and its victims, in schools in the U.S. — elementary, high school, and college — as well as internationally. As recently as December 16th , 2014, 132 school children between the ages of eight and eighteen, as well as nine staff members, were killed by nine gunmen in a terrorist attack on the Army Public School in the city of Peshawar in Pakistan. Across the globe, in Rio de Janeiro, Brazil, on April 7th, 2011, a 23-year-old went back to the elementary school where he had been a student and shot and killed 12 children before committing suicide.

In the United States, the focus on school violence can be dated to the April 20th, 1999 Columbine high school tragedy, although there were certainly incidents here and there such as the infamous August 1st , 1966 shooting by Charles Whitman, an engineering student at the University of Texas at Austin, that left 16 dead and 21 wounded. That day in 1999 throughout America and the world so many of us, this author included, were glued to our TV sets or computer screens as the Columbine tragedy unfolded — as two high school seniors shot and killed 12 students and one teacher at Columbine High School in Colorado before committing suicide. That school shooting is sometimes cited as the beginning of the increase in school violence in America. But there were a growing number of school shootings before Columbine.

Sadly, that would not remain the worst school shooting in U.S. history for, eight years later, on August 16th, 2007, at Virginia Polytechnic Institute and State University, known as Virginia Tech, in Blacksburg, Virginia, a senior, in two separate attacks, shot and killed 32 students and faculty, and wounded 17 others; the shooter then committed suicide. It was dubiously labeled the worst mass shooting by one gunman in American history and certainly the worst school shooting.

Five years later, the media and our attention was again gripped by school-related violence. In this case, the shootings took place at a movie theatre in Aurora, Colorado on July 20th 2012. But the alleged shooter, who claimed the lives of 12 men and women, injuring more than 70, was a former graduate student who had just recently dropped out of the University of Colorado, Denver campus, neuroscience program he was enrolled in.

Then, just five months after the Aurora Colorado tragedy, on December 14th 2012, the Sandy Hook Elementary School massacre occurred in Newtown, Connecticut that took the lives of twenty children and six teachers and staff. The 20-year-old killer, who had shot and killed his mother before the mass killings at the elementary school took place, committed suicide. The Sandy Hook tragedy claimed the most victims of any elementary or high school shooting in the U.S. as it gripped the hearts and minds of Americans and throughout the world. The majority of the victims were in the first grade, so most were just six or seven years old.

Crime statistics trends

What I have also learned in researching crime victims and the criminal justice system over all these decades is that numbers and statistics may help us to pinpoint the prevalence of crime, and whether it is increasing or decreasing. Take, for instance, how crime is down in Manhattan now, in 2014, compared to in the late 1960s or even in the late 1980s. At the same time, crime in the city of Chicago continues to be rampant although it is actually ranked 16th in murder rate for cities with a population of 100,000 or greater, behind Newark, New Orleans, and Detroit, which had a murder rate of 53 murders per 100,000 residents in 2012 compared to 18.5 murder victims per 100,000 in Chicago.

But the numbers, although it might show trends up or down, fail to convey the experience of being a crime victim for that victim or, in the case of homicide, for that victim's family and friends. Whether a murder victim is the 18th, 53rd, or the one and only crime victim that year in a town, or city, that is one murder too many.

A crime victim bravely shares her story

I decided to include in this new introduction to *Victims* excerpts from an interview I conducted with a brave woman who survived being raped, kidnapped, tortured, and held hostage for five days, as well as the loss of her husband who was murdered by her assailant. You will notice that I use the complete name of this victim: Debra Puglisi Sharp. That is with her complete permission. Victims that I interviewed who are included in the rest of *Victims* asked to be anonymous. The reason I am able to use Debbie's real name is that she is the author of a memoir about her victimization: *Shattered: Reclaiming a Life Torn Apart by Violence.* Debbie courageously shared in her memoir what happened to her, as well as the aftermath, because she is committed to helping other victims, through her book but also through her speeches and her victim advocacy.

It was in the course of conducting research for this new introduction that I discovered *Shattered* by Debra Puglisi Sharp. I found the online description of her book at an online bookstore riveting. I immediately wrote to the author, told her I had just bought the e-book version of her book, and shared with her that my brother had been a homicide victim so she would know that beyond my formal training in criminology and sociology—M.A. in criminal justice and Ph.D. in sociology—I too had lost someone to violence. In that e-mail, I requested a phone interview.

Much to my pleasant surprise, I heard back almost instantly with an enthusiastic "yes." With her permission, I am sharing an edited version of Debbie's interview with me as well as information from our additional e-mails exchanges before and after our interview. Debbie provides a powerful and detailed account of both her victimization as well as what she went through after her rescue, especially how she has had to deal with the resultant PTSD (Post Traumatic Stress Disorder).

During the years I spent researching the original edition of *Victims*, which included two years studying for my master's degree in criminal justice and writing my master's thesis on crime victims, the notion that crime victims might be suffering from PTSD, much like soldiers of war, was not as widely acknowledged as it is today. The more common way of looking at what crime victims went through during and after the crime was through a comparison to the stages of grief as outlined by Dr. Kubler-Ross, the psychiatrist and author of the 1969 bestseller, *On Death and Dying*, based on what she learned caring for the terminally ill. It is somewhat ironic that the interview of a hospice nurse, Debra Puglisi Sharp, has led me to rethink the impact of being a crime victim as something closer to suffering from PTSD than to the stages of grief described by Dr. Kubler-Ross, who had been at the forefront of the hospice movement.

In her own words, here is Debra Puglisi Sharp's summary of the rape, kidnapping, torture, and release from captivity that she went through, and its aftermath, including the murder of her husband by her rapist:

> I was just an ordinary woman—wife, mother, and Hospice nurse—who never believed I would become a crime victim on a beautiful spring day, in an upscale neighborhood in Newark, Delaware.
>
> But on April 20ᵗʰ, 1998, my life changed forever.
>
> My husband, Anthony Puglisi (better known as Nino), and I had moved into our Cape Cod-style home just ten months prior. We were one month shy of our twenty-fifth wedding anniversary. Our 19-year-old twins were sophomores in college. Our son lived on campus nearby at the University of Delaware and our daughter had chosen to go to East Carolina University in Greenville, North Carolina.
>
> Here's how the day started out for me. A good friend and neighbor gave me four rose bushes so I was in the front yard planting those rose bushes in our garden. At around 3:15 PM, my husband Nino arrived home. He was a planner at his friend's funeral home only about five miles away. He came up to me as I continued planting the rose bushes and told me how happy he was that I decided to plant the rose bushes. Little did he know what waited for him inside our home.
>
> I would later find out that an assembly line worker at a nearby car factory with a crack cocaine habit was driving in the area and he would later confess to the police that he was looking for a woman to kidnap and rape. So, on this day, instead of reporting for work, this man —I would learn that his name was Donald Flagg—drove down our street and parked his car two houses away. I would later learn that he then walked behind our home and entered it through a French door that I thought was locked. High on crack cocaine, standing near a closed window, he waited for me to enter the house. He also helped himself to two beers in our fridge.

I can only speculate about how and why Nino walked through the dining room where Flagg was hiding. I later found out that Nino had been brutally shot and the killer had dragged his body to our first floor master bedroom, which was on the same floor, to hide it there.

I never heard the gun shot that killed Nino. Then, at approximately 3:45 P.M., I entered our home through the open garage door. I walked through the laundry room and upon entering the kitchen, I was suddenly attacked, bludgeoned on the left side of my head. My glasses were thrown from my face and I noticed blood spattering on the floor. I am very near-sighted so I only saw the outline of a dark-skinned male hovering over me, asking "Where is your purse?" Numb, and wondering where Nino was, I told him that my purse was on the counter near the sink.

At that point, I thought we were being robbed. Before I knew it, I was dragged down the hallway, down our basement steps, and thrown on to the cold basement floor. There, on the basement floor, I was raped. Stunned and frightened, I silently prayed for this nightmare to end. I kept wondering, where was Nino?

The rapist then tied me up and placed me on the floor near the kitchen sink. Then, he left.

Within a few minutes, I heard footsteps. But these were not the footsteps of my husband. It was the rapist. He had come back for me. He gathered me up in the quilt he had thrown over me and carried me to the foyer. I could see a car that had been backed up to our front door.

At this point, he was holding a knife to my throat as he told me, "Shut up!" I kept thinking that I had always been told that once you are taken from the scene of a crime, your chances of survival diminish. But with a knife to my throat, I thought that my best chance was to go along with his plan and get away later.

The rapist then threw me into the trunk of his hatchback car as if I was a sack of potatoes. Little did I know that he was planning on taking me to his home.

I tried to loosen my ties while I was struggling in the trunk. My plan was to loosen my ties so that when he opened the trunk, I would kick him and then run for my life. But no such luck. When he arrived at his home, Flagg opened his garage door, drove in, and the door closed behind us.

When he saw that I had started to loosen my ties in an attempt to escape from the trunk, he quickly punished me by carrying me into a back bedroom where he threw me face down onto a bed and sodomized me.

As I screamed in agony, he laughed as he continued to torture me. He then turned me over and raped me again.

When he re-bound my ties, he made sure they were taut. He placed a washcloth in my mouth and a blindfold, all secured with duct tape.

That first night I spent wrapped around the base of a toilet, adjacent to the bed where he slept. At one time during the night, I heard a clicking sound. I later found out that he had been doing more crack cocaine.

On the morning of the second day of captivity, I was taken to a second room. Again, I laid on the floor, still bound and gagged. Flagg put the television on and I heard the words "Anthony Puglisi was shot and killed, and his wife is missing."

I never allowed myself to think that my husband might also have been a victim. Now I was alone with my grief. My rapist opened the door, and he said, simply, "I am sorry, but I had to kill your husband."

The guilt overwhelmed me as I thought, poor Nino. This man wanted to kidnap and rape me, and because of that, my husband is now gone.

Within a couple of hours, the rapist returned to the room and raped me again.

That evening, Flagg decided to go into work late. He made sure my ropes were secure and he blasted the radio so no one would hear me if I tried to scream.

It was not until after midnight that he returned. Then there was somewhat of a turning point. He removed the ropes, the washcloth, and blindfold. I was ordered to sit in a chair. My rapist told me "I am thinking of letting you go." It was at that time that I went into survival mode. I immediately addressed him as "Sir." I told him that

I would do anything he wanted and promised not to describe him to the police. I offered to be retied and placed back in his trunk. I told him he could take me far into the woods and just let me go. However, he was concerned that I could describe his house.

At that point, it became obvious that he was not going to let me go. I was offered a bite of scrambled eggs and a sip of coffee. I had had nothing to eat since lunch on the Monday when Nino died. He also told me that he had gotten rid of all the drugs in the house. He felt that he would "only get ten years in prison" if the police found me and there were no drugs. I knew from that ridiculous comment that I was smarter than him and had to use my mind to overpower him.

Early that Wednesday morning, I was told to bathe. I had to disrobe in front of him. He watched me as I cleaned my beaten body. When he asked if I was going to wash my hair, I told him that my wrists were raw and it was too painful to do so. All I can say is now I wish I had tried. It was dehumanizing to have my husband's murderer wash my hair. Then I had to put on his tee shirt and sweat pants. Now wearing my rapist's clothes, I felt further betrayal to my deceased husband.

Afterwards, I was taken to a third bedroom where I was bound and gagged. (Later, during the trial, I would learn that at that time, he went out into his yard to cut the grass and that he was waving to the neighbors.)

Before going into work for a full shift that evening, I was raped yet again.

When he returned from work, he crawled into bed next to me. Yes, I had to sleep next to my husband's murderer.

On the fourth day of my kidnapping, my rapist told me that he wanted to feed me. By this time, I was on my best behavior and continued to befriend him. Rape is all about power and control. I made him think that I did not mind the rapes and refused to fight him. After all, I knew he had weapons and I was helpless. I knew I had done a pretty good job when he asked me for sex. Of course, I was sure he was testing me. However, I told him "sure." Another guilt to deal with later. I was fighting for my life and trying desperately to do anything I had to do so I could get back to my children.

For some reason, he decided not to go into work on that day. We had something to eat and he let me walk about the house, under his supervision. He even let me pick something on television to watch. When the news came on, my father and brother were being interviewed by the news media. It was chilling to hear my brother speak of me in the past tense. "My sister was a nurse....she would never have done this." Yes, I had been considered a suspect in my husband's murder. The plans for Nino's viewing burial were announced. It was then that I knew I had to make every attempt to get out of that house. I needed to say goodbye to my husband and be there to support our children.

Thursday night was a very long, sleepless night for me. It was painful for me to have another night of sleeping next to Nino's murderer. He had his arm across my chest to make sure I did not move. I may have drifted off for short intervals, but for the most part, I stared at the ceiling and grieved for my husband. The one time I did make a move, Flagg became irate. I coughed and tried to sit up. He sensed that it was an attempt to escape. It would then take me hours to regain his trust. I was so afraid that I had "undone" everything I had done when I had so carefully planned to befriend this man. But once I reassured him that it was an involuntary movement, his arm went back across my chest and I laid still....afraid to move.

I told Flagg that my wrists were getting infected and that there must be another way to confine me. He made several phone calls in an attempt to purchase handcuffs. But unless you work in law enforcement or security, it is not possible to buy a sturdy pair.

Luck was on my side. Later that morning, he decided to go to downtown Wilmington. In a pawn shop, he purchased two pairs of handcuffs.

When he returned in the early afternoon, he removed the ties on my infected wrists and ankles, replacing them with the handcuffs. What Flagg did not realize was that with the cuffs on my wrists and ankles, I had greater flexibility and was able to move my hands more freely. He then told me that I was becoming expensive. A definite red flag. He had spent less than $20 on food and the cuffs. I knew time was running out.

On the fifth day, my rapist told me that he was leaving for work. My gut told me that he would once again test me. I laid quietly in the same position for what seemed to be an hour. Indeed, the door opened and shut. I waited a while longer. When I felt the coast might be clear, I feverishly worked at loosening the hogtie that was connected to the cuffs on my wrists and ankles. It took about 15 to 20 minutes, but I loosened the knot and was able to sit on the side of the bed. I then stood and shuffled forward, first walking into a closet.

Starting to become emotional, I calmed myself down and shuffled towards the door. With my hands behind my back, I opened the door, not knowing if he was on the other side.

Another miracle was that Flagg had left a landline phone on his dining room table. I reached for the phone and dialed 911. A call taker answered asking me "What do you need?"

I remember having to spell my last name. The call was then transferred to Steven Conrad who dispatched the police to the address that had appeared on the 911 Enhancement Board of the Emergency Center. If this had been a cell phone, I would not be here to share my story. That's because back in 1998, Delaware did not have the capability to accurately trace a call from a cellular phone.

When the police got here, it was so quiet they didn't think anyone was there. But the police questioned the dispatcher, who assured them that I was there.

After a few minutes, a flashlight shone through the front window and I started to scream, "Help me!" It was when I started to scream that an officer kicked the door in, asking me to back away. All of the emotions of the past five days started to overwhelm me. I had not allowed myself to believe that this day would ever come.

I was taken to our local hospital where I was severely dehydrated and found to have forty-two physical wounds, not to mention the emotional and mental anguish.

The initial examination took several hours. Meanwhile, my family and friends gathered in a large conference room near the Emergency Room. I desperately wanted to see them, especially my children. However, it would be about two hours before immediate family were allowed to see me. I was a crime scene, and the police were being careful not to disturb the evidence. But it was bittersweet. Everyone was so happy to see me, but Nino was gone.

Meanwhile, the police were on their way to the car manufacturing plant to arrest Flagg as he worked on the assembly line.

When they approached him, he said two things: "I know why you are here," and "How is Debbie?" His chilling confession followed and he was taken directly to a prison in Wilmington, Delaware.

At approximately 1 A.M. two wonderful Sexual Assault Forensic Nurses (SANE) arrived to do the internal forensic examination to collect DNA for the rape kit. A volunteer from our local rape crisis center sat next to me, offering information and support. I did not arrive to my private room until about 4 A.M.

I spent Saturday and part of Sunday in the hospital receiving IV antibiotics and wound care. There were county police officers standing guard outside my room, a gesture that I will never forget. My rapist and Nino's murderer was in prison, but the police wanted to assure my safety and privacy.

I was discharged on oral antibiotics and my family did my dressing changes. I did seek treatment with a hand surgeon as well as a plastic surgeon for the deep cuts on both of my wrists soon after my discharge from the hospital. I now call my residual scars my "badges of courage," making the decision not to have them surgically removed. It also became necessary for me to visit a pain clinic for nerve pain in my left wrist.

My emotional healing period began a month later, after my children returned to college to take their final exams. A psychologist, Dr. Constance Dancu, who specialized in Post-Traumatic Stress Disorder agreed to treat me. She saved my life. Her mode of treatment was Cognitive Behavior Therapy (CBT). I had intense mental health counseling to deal with the survivor's guilt I was feeling as well as my abduction and rapes, and to prepare for the upcoming criminal trial.

During the trial, my beautiful daughter told the jury through tear-filled eyes that her father would not see her and her brother graduate from college. He would not get to walk her down the aisle when she married. I was so very proud of her.

The jury convicted Flagg on 18 counts to include first-degree felony murder, first-degree burglary, first-degree kidnapping, and first-degree unlawful sexual penetration. He was sentenced to eight life sentences plus 166 years. The Judge then handed down a unique sentencing. He ordered that every year for the first ten years of his incarceration, Flagg would spend five days in solitary confinement, from April 20th through April 24th, the anniversary of days of my imprisonment.

At a separate hearing a month later, the Judge heard another case against Flagg. There was DNA evidence that he had raped a young woman just three days prior to my attack. The judge handed down two additional life sentences plus forty-three years---an extraordinary penalty for rape and one that assures that Flagg will never be released from prison.

The dates April 20th through April 24th are still difficult for me, even 16 years later. My second husband Bill and I try to schedule a vacation during those dates as I enjoy getting out of the States. Over those days, I tend to do "daily reviews" of the events. But now that Flagg no longer goes into solitary confinement, I find it more difficult to deal with those April dates. At least when he was taken into solitary, I knew he would have to think about what he had done to me.

I asked Debbie to share with me what she had learned from her crime victim experience that she wants to share with other victims. Debbie replied:

A crime victim has two choices—either to remain in that victim mindset and refuse to deal with the pain, anger, despair, and grief of the victimization or to seek mental health counseling, refusing to let the offender to remain in control. Fortunately, I had a great support system and chose to heal. I have always referred to the ensuing years as my "journey of healing." I was diagnosed with Post Traumatic Stress Disorder (PTSD) and now speak across the country, sharing my story of tragedy to triumph and how I came to live as a survivor. In fact, I like to think of myself as a thriver.

I started speaking even before my book, Shattered, was published, so I really cannot say that promotion of the book was my initial goal in speaking. In fact, I continue to speak because I do have an important message to share. I firmly believe that victims do feel comfortable approaching me. Many have said "I feel like I can talk to you because you get it."

By the time Shattered was published in 2003, I had already appeared on several television shows (Oprah and 20/20 in 1999, also Montel and The John Walsh Show.)

My first invitation to speak was for the 13th Victims Rights Conference in Atlantic City, New Jersey in April of 2000. There were 450 in the audience: health professionals, law enforcement, victim service providers, etcetera. My brother Robert, who was a detective for a police department in a town in New Jersey, sat by my side as I spoke about my victimization. Afterwards, I was approached by so many and was told to continue sharing as my story would help others.

Law enforcement then invited me to speak so I continued my lectures for a group called MAGLOCLEN (MidAtlantic Great Lakes Organized Crimes Law Enforcement Network). I spoke for their Sex Crimes conferences. Many detectives tell me that they have become more "victim sensitive" because of my story. Listening to a victim's perspective of a horrific crime seems to create more empathy.

Back again to writing the book. Writing Shattered was a big piece of putting my life back together. I did collaborative writing with Marjorie Preston, a journalist. It made me really think about every detail of my victimization. Marjorie was great in making me feel. We wrote together, cried together. I actually remembered bits and pieces that I had buried, not wanting to deal with the pain. It was difficult to express my feelings to my family, as they were also victims and unable to deal with their own pain and grief. My psychologist warned me about the men in my life. It was true!! My father and brothers had a lot of trouble hearing me talk about the crime. Robert, who works in law enforcement, had his own guilt. At the time of my disappearance, he had been trying to convince my family that "Debbie is not coming home." I told him that this was to be expected because of his training. Most victims who have gone missing over two or three days are found dead. I am a miracle.

I am also proud that Shattered is required reading in many universities including for a criminal justice course, Victimology. I have been told that my book is hard to put down. I am truly proud of it. I also lecture to the criminal justice students after they have read my book. They need to hear a victim's perspective of surviving a violent crime.

I asked Debbie if she has seen any improvements in the criminal justice system since 1998 when she was raped and kidnapped and her husband was murdered.

The criminal justice system has progressed, however, we have a long way to go. I have met hundreds of victims as I lecture. Many approach me after my presentation, some disclosing for the first time. My goal continues to be to empower victims to become survivors. The best gift you can give a victim is yourself. Listen.

Most victims need to tell their story. A pertinent point I make during my lectures is that the first responder sets the tone for a victim's healing process. If you judge or disbelieve a victim, he or he will shut down.

I hope that my story of survival inspires others to become more passionate about victims who continue to suffer, especially those who have PTSD with constant triggers. PTSD never goes away. It is an illness that may rear its ugly head at any time. Time does not always heal all wounds. I actually do not like the phrase "Time heals all wounds." I've been a very big advocate of time doesn't always heal the wounds, and there are triggers, there are days when I've gone back to my time of my victimization.

I thank Dr. Dancu for the tools she gave me to survive. Whenever I find myself in crisis, I stop and think "What would Dr. Dancu say?" Unfortunately, she died in 2001. I hope to be able to inspire the many many victims who suffer from PTSD, letting them know that they're not alone. I know I care and I invite people to write to me. I try to be the kind of person who will listen because I know that's a gift that was given to me.

Counseling takes courage. I never hesitate to seek help when necessary. I have remarried. My husband Bill loves me unconditionally and he is always there when I have a bad day….and they do come.

I hope that I can continue my work in victim advocacy for a very long time. Turning my pain into purpose is rewarding, both for myself and for those whose lives I have touched.

Since my escape, I appreciate every day and see life as a gift. My work is my therapy. I enjoy speaking about the victimization because it's healing. By telling my story, it helps me, especially when I have people ask me questions. I have met interesting people or people simply coming up to me and saying, "I remember your case. I prayed for you."

But the most rewarding aspect of it all is when someone approaches me and says, "You have inspired me. This is what happened to me." And then they tell me their story. The ones who touch my heart the most are when they disclose that I'm the first one they're telling their story to. And I always ask permission first but then I give them a hug. I know that this person has been suffering for years. How long has it been since the crime occurred? I've been told as many as thirty, forty years back.

We still need to stop the hush and talk more about victimization. And we need to stop the victim blaming. Although we are making progress to some degree, I have found that victim blaming continues to be one of the largest obstacles in obtaining disclosure and justice. Too many women I have spoken to have failed to report the crime for various reasons, mostly because they fear they will not be believed and they do not want to go through the painful process of a criminal trial.

After what happened to me, there were actually some who said that if I had not gone into the yard in the middle of the day to plant those rose brushes, the crime would not have happened. Because of my friend Gene's guilt over giving me the rose bushes, I decided to use roses when I speak. In fact, in the last line in Shattered's acknowledgements, I write, "Yes, Gene, I will always love roses."

I also carried a rose into the court room when I testified, for my friend Gene. When Bill and I were dating, he brought me roses every week. I did not want my rapist to take away something else I love—roses. Even the 911 dispatcher, Steven Conrad, presented me with roses when he surprised me when we met each other for the first time on the John Walsh Show. For me, roses still signify peace, joy, and love.

When Time Doesn't Heal the Wounds

I also want to include in this new introduction the reprinting of my own essay, "When Time Doesn't Heal the Wound," that I wrote almost twenty years after my brother's homicide. It was reprinted in an expanded version, a decade later, in a sociology text, a collection of essays entitled *A Private Sociology*, edited by Dr. Art Shostak (General Hall, Inc., 1997).

I hadn't thought about this essay for a long time. As you'll see when you hear or read the original book *Victims* that follows this introduction, the book begins with a Preface entitled, "Why Study the Victim?" That was the hardest part of Victims for me to write because it was one of the rare instances in the book where I discuss what happened to my brother. I decided to share this essay because Debbie Puglisi Sharp mentioned in our interview that she didn't like the notion that time heals all wounds. And, as you will see from the title and theme of the essay that follows, as the sister of a homicide victim, I agree, up to a point. (You have to read the whole essay to know what that point is.)

There are very few thoughts that consistently bring tears to my eyes. Thinking of how much I miss my brother is one such thought. It's a loss that makes those silly slogans -"Time heals all wounds" and "Everything happens for the best" -- infuriating to me. Time hasn't healed the wound. His death didn't happen because it was "best". It just happened. Seth was a struggling freelance writer when he died, the victim of one of those senseless street muggings you might read about somewhere in just a few lines in the city newspaper. (A couple of teenage gang members tried to rob him, overpowering him as they thrust a knife into his back and side, then mercilessly twisting it, causing fatal damage to his liver.) I never had a chance to talk to Seth after the attack; by the time I got to the hospital, he had lost consciousness. After three days of operations, blood transfusions, and valiant efforts by the doctors and nurses, Seth died from his wounds.

*My brother was twenty-three when he died, and I was twenty.
Soon my brother will be gone as many years as we shared. I am
indeed fortunate to still have a sister, since I shudder to think about
what life would be like without any sibling at all. But one relationship does not replace another. One gain does not cancel out one loss.*

*I thought of my brother more in the last year than I had allowed
myself to think of him for quite a while because my nephew Sky, the
son born two months after my brother's death, the son Seth never lived
to see, graduated from high school. My family was there to share the
event. But it would be hard for my nephew, who physically resembles
my brother, but who never knew his father, to have his mannerisms,
personality, or even any concrete thoughts of him. Once I visited my
nephew Sky on a school day during his last year of junior high school.
My nephew had arranged a marriage of two dolls as a fundraiser for
a needy family who took in foster children. I attended that ceremony,
and saw how much affection and respect my nephew had from his
peers, one of my rare glimpses into Sky's character that so reminded me
of my late brother.*

*My sister-in-law has done a fine job raising my two nephews, and,
as much as possible, includes my family in holidays and even sponta-
neous get-togethers. I sincerely consider her more like a friend than
a "former" in-law. But it's difficult on her current life and relationships when the parental blood tie with nephews has officially ended
or changed, whether by death or by divorce, for I often feel like an
intruder on her family, and awkward about what role I should play.*

*My sister and I occasionally wonder what our older brother Seth
would have been like if he had lived. Would Seth have continued
writing, and made it big, or would he have gone into teaching, as he
had talked about doing right before he died? Or perhaps he would
have become a filmmaker or a politician? But alas, death has frozen
him at that earlier point in his life and I am unable to fill in his
looks "as if" the way they do each year on the anniversary of John F.
Kennedy's death. (This is the way Kennedy might have looked if he
were still alive ... or Marilyn Monroe, etc.)*

*I have found, for me, the best way to keep my brother's life
meaningful in the present is to try to focus on those extraordinary*

qualities that he had, and, if I can, to incorporate them into my own personality. For example, although I am somewhat shy, my brother was a networker before the word was even popular, since he loved people, and parties, and going to lots of extraordinary events and happenings. I remember when I was in my late teens and he invited me along to a poetry reading in New York's Greenwich Village given by a man to celebrate his 100th birthday. How did Seth find out about that party? How did he feel comfortable walking into that room of strangers, greeting the old man and his wife of 70 years, as if he had known them for decades? Where did Seth find out about all the wonderful happenings in New York that he shared with others, informally or through Slightseeing, the column he wrote in the New York University student newspaper?

My brother spent most of his time communicating with others— which is how he learned about all that was going on. Of course he read magazines and newspapers, but he involved himself with others, and they repaid him by letting him know about their celebrations, openings, screenings, and happenings. I have become more like that over these years, learning to pick up the phone, or go talk to someone in person, rather than remaining aloof, hiding behind a paint brush or a pen.

Seth also had a way of letting you know how much he approved of you. His verbal and written praise inspired even more efforts. If he liked one of my paintings, he expressed himself in a way that made me feel as if I just had a major retrospective of my work reviewed in The New York Times. I try to emulate his positive example, and to articulate my praise of the work of those I care about, even if my initial impulse is to be either a little envious, or somewhat blasé.

Certainly my brother, like all of us, had his faults, but his special wonderful qualities were dominant. As one of his professors said to me, "A lot of students say they're going to change the world. But I knew your brother was going to." Another aspect of the death of a family member that I rarely hear expressed is the loss of the network they developed, and that you shared, the end of those friendships and relationships.

True, for a while there may be ripples of those intimate or pro-fessional relationships. My cousin tells me that there was a catered party organized by the friend of her friend--my acquaintance--who recently died of breast cancer at the age of thirty-seven.

That was a nice tribute, but all those separate lives were once linked together by the young woman who is gone. The chain is bro-ken, and her family is separated from those associations. Thus you lose on so many levels when someone so close to you dies.

I think of how rich my siblings (?) made my life… what would my childhood have been like without my brother or my sister to share it with?

The emptiness that followed the tragic death of my brother is important to feel and not deny. The pain I feel makes my life richer, not poorer, for it reminds me every day how sacred are the moments we are blessed to spend with those we love and who love us. How irreplaceable we all are--not to our casual contacts, but to those few who truly know, appreciate, and love us. No, time has not healed my wound. It is remembering that helps…. a little.

In Conclusion

Thank you for reading this New Introduction and reading my original book Victims which follows. Although some of the statistics in Victims may be out of date, all the issues discussed are still timely, all the quotes from the extensive interviews I conducted with crime victims, their families and friends, police officers, lawyers, assistant district attorneys, crime victim advocates, offenders, ex-offenders, the media, and others related to the criminal justice system are just as powerful and worth reading today as when I first wrote this book. You will also find an updated bibliography, resource section, and author bio at the end of this edition of the book.

Back in 1979, in the Q&A that People magazine did with me back about my book Victims, I said, "Crime victims are a forgotten minority to which one in every 19 Americans belongs."

Sadly, that estimate is now "one in every seven Americans is a victim of violent or property crime" according to the International Association of Chiefs of Police, as reported by the Office of Victims of Crime (OVC) in its "Good Samaritans: Volunteers Helping Victims Program and Training Guide."

Could it be that crime victims, because they are no longer such a minority in America, are finally getting the attention, and the help, that they have long deserved? Just think of your own circle of friends, colleagues, family, or neighbors. Has someone you know been directly or indirectly impacted by rape, homicide, domestic violence, burglary, robbery, domestic or international terrorism, or white collar crime?

Understanding, and dealing more effectively, with crime victims is also not just an American concern. Just consider other countries, such as Norway, which has had to deal with the tragedy of the mass killing at a summer camp on the island of Utoya on July 22nd, 2011 which left 69 dead and 110 injured. Or Tokyo, which had sarin attacks in their subway on March 20th, 1995, killing 13 and injuring 50. Sadly, the list could go on and on, from country to country.

Eliminating crime is, of course, the ideal, whether it is a crime committed by a total stranger or by someone known to the victim, so there would then be no more crime victims. But till that ideal is accomplished, avoiding the attitude of blaming a victim for becoming a victim or glorifying or romanticizing the criminal, and providing crime victims with mental, medical, legal, or financial help, are steps in the right direction.

J.L. Barkas, Ph.D.
(a.k.a Jan Yager, Ph.D.)
www.drjanyager.com
February 2015
(Revised July 2015)

Image courtesy Shutterstock

Part 3

VICTIMS by J.L. Barkas (a/k/a Jan Yager)

Original VICTIMS published in hardcover in 1978 by Scribner follows, with updated statistics and selected revisions

The original text from the Scribner hardcover edition of *Victims* follows, through to page 241 (in the printed version). Please note that in February 2023, whenever possible, outdated statistics from the 70s have been replaced with more recent statistics.

Excerpted interviews, conducted by this author, and quoted secondary source materials, in the pages that follow have stood the test of time and are from the original *Victims*.

Please note: The Preface has not been edited or updated since that was written at one point in time, when I was completing the first edition of *Victims*. It remains in tact. But there are extensive updates, especially to statistics, beginning with Chapter 1. For example, the 1974 murder statistics compiled by the Chicago Police Department have been replaced with the statistics for 2021 from their Annual Report. Or in Chapter 4, "Victims of Rape" you will read that the FBI changed the definition of rape in 2013, eliminating the word "forcible" and making other revisions that made it possible for males and spouses to be considered victims of rape. (See that chapter for the exact wording of the new definition.)

PREFACE

Why Study the Victim?

One cold February evening, as a young man walked toward his car, two teenagers appeared out of the shadows. They asked the man for a dime. Before he could either comply or resist, one youth plunged and twisted a knife into the victim's back and side, lacerating his liver. During the next three days the victim fought to stay alive, but at six o'clock on a Friday he died—and became another crime statistic.

Whether the victim was an aspiring writer or a truck driver, whether he was single or married with a young son and a pregnant wife, whether he was a foreigner on vacation or my own brother does not matter. *Every* human being has the right to live. No one should be subject to unprovoked attack; no one should be harmed by senseless violence.

I had always been concerned about crime, but that evening, when I whispered the last good-bye to my older brother Seth, it became a source of outrage.

I was twenty at the time, and I was not prepared for the shock of Seth's stabbing or his death. No one in my family was. We had read about such crimes, or heard about them on the evening news, but we never thought it would happen in our own family. I had believed that one had to *do* something to become a victim—one had to provoke a burglary by carelessness, an assault by an innuendo that was unconsciously suggestive.

When I came home from classes that Wednesday and received the phone call from my mother explaining that my brother was in the hospital, my first reaction was shock. Seth was in his prime. His wife was seven months pregnant and his writing career was just beginning. I was sure the "mugging" would turn out to be only a nightmarish incident that Seth and I and the rest of our family would soon be talking about. I did not believe that my brother, the guy who I thought knew all the answers, could be so vulnerable as to die.

Yet once the seriousness of Seth's stab wounds was undeniable, my family automatically did what is necessary in an emergency. We needed blood for the numerous operations performed to try to save him, so we busied ourselves calling people to donate. Hundreds throughout the city responded to our telephone, radio, and newspaper appeals. Still certain that Seth would pull through, my parents postponed asking my older sister to return home from college. But Thursday morning I telephoned her myself, and she arrived as soon as she could.

The next evening, my sister held my hand and together we went in to see Seth. He was covered with a white sheet, his head turned toward the far wall, revealing only his profile. His brain and heart had given out at about noon and the machines would soon be removed, but still I spoke a few words to him.

When we went back to the house the first person I saw was my next-door neighbor. She was already in black and she just embraced me. Then I saw Margie. Margie who had raised us. It was hard to tell whether she had been crying. Silent, she looked at me with eyes that all my life had given me strength because they held truth. Then she hugged me.

I ran upstairs to the room that my sister and I used to share and slammed the door. My sister was already there. We held each other and then we locked the door and we cried. She said, "Maybe it will help if you remember Seth for how he lived, not how he died. Think of Seth up in heaven, typing away." I know it may sound corny, but somehow it helped me to think that my brother, a man who was so dedicated to improving the world and to admitting his fallibility, would keep on writing.

Soon after that, my emotions went numb; mechanically I experienced the ritualistic viewing, funeral, and week of mourning.

Seth was a victim, but my family and I learned that the violation committed by the criminal is only the *first* victimization. There are others, almost as devastating, perpetrated by society and the criminal justice system.

If I spoke about my brother's murder, people recoiled. They didn't empathize, they didn't sympathize, they didn't get angry. They said, "Well, why was he walking down that street?" "What time of night was it?" They acted as if Seth had done something wrong, as if I were now doing something wrong to mourn him, to be angry, to be devastated. The relatives or friends who looked for an explanation for my brother's murder in *his* behavior victimized our family. The anger that should have been directed at the criminals was mysteriously missing, as though the stabbing were an inconvenient detail to distinguish Seth's death from one caused by an accident or illness. It was as though Seth had done something shameful—and, in a way, he had. His murder had proved that crime might touch anyone. If my brother was not somehow to blame for his death, then no one was safe.

Another unanticipated victimization resulted from the inability of everyone I met, including those close to my family, to cope with our grief. Perhaps because they did not understand our anguish, and therefore could not deal with it, they acted as if we were contaminated. Acquaintances could not comprehend our need to discuss our loss, or to reminisce about Seth's life; instead, they changed the subject whenever Seth's name was mentioned. It was easier for them to avoid the shocking episode, and the tragedy of a promising life cut short, than to face the implications of his murder.

My family was also victimized because of our ignorance of the criminal justice system. Certain basic legal actions, such as obtaining crime compensation for Seth's widow, became crises. I naively thought the state would be as concerned about Seth's murder as I was, and I wondered whether the police would ask for my assistance in the capture and trial of the criminals. But they never called. Finally, almost five years after my brother's murder, I called the district attorney's office, told them I was a sister of the victim, and asked what had happened in his case. Not only was the D.A.'s office suspicious about why the sister of a victim would be calling, but I wasn't even treated civilly. I wasn't given any information or any help, and that baffled me. I also began speaking to those professors who had admired Seth and to his high school and college friends, but no one seemed to care enough about who had stabbed Seth or what had happened to his killers to have pursued the case. Then I realized that whenever the question was asked of me, I also could only say, "I don't know." Those three words began to gnaw at me. What was wrong with all of us that we let this life be torn from us for no reason? Seth's killing violated the expectation that life is an inalienable right, a tenet I thought everyone believed in.

The Supreme Court had reaffirmed "the rights of suspected offenders and incarcerated criminals, but what about victims? The only consolation for any victim is to say, "You will not become a victim again," That is the only justice. Everything else is only a band-aid on the wounds that infect every part of this country's economy, morality, culture, education, and philosophy. Seth's murder only strengthened my growing anger that the United States has one of the highest crime rates in the Western world. In the 1970s the number of crime victims was undoubtedly a more accurate barometer of our "progress" than how many cars or computers we could build.

Yet I was as blameworthy as everyone else, as I had done nothing to change either the conditions that caused my brother's death or the judicial system that affected his case. I could not even shout about my rights as a victim because I was uninformed of what they were.

Without knowledge, I was defenseless. In February 1974 I set about a self-structured program that led to years of travel, interviewing, reading, a master of arts in criminal justice, teaching and lecturing on crime and violence at colleges and universities around the country, and this book. That summer I went to London, Paris, and Amsterdam; I met with police officials, criminologists, and journalists. The "visible" students of crime and violence, they were more accessible and willing, even eager, to share their knowledge and insights with me. Upon my return I attended trials in the criminal courthouses of New York. I met judges, lawyers, assistant district attorneys, and police officers. I went through the training program given by OAR (Offender Aid and Restoration) and began meeting with incarcerated juveniles. I spent Christmas Eve on Rikers Island at a party for the adolescent inmates. I also continued my active participation in Women-to-Women, a volunteer program at Bedford Hills women's prison aimed at easing ex-offenders' reentry into "civilian" life. I published a query in an inmate newspaper and corresponded with almost two hundred offenders imprisoned for violent property and personal crimes.

During the summer of 1975 I traveled throughout Ireland, England, Northern Ireland, and Italy interviewing, observing, and researching wherever I went. But it was not until I visited Belfast, Northern Ireland, that I began to think more about *victims*. In the Irish press, in daily conversations, in the fears of the people, the focus was the innocent children, mothers, and workers killed by anonymous bombs. Rarely was the criminal mentioned. Without my knowing it, my education so far had "favored" the offender.

I returned to New York confused. On a Saturday afternoon about a week later, my father called to tell me about a television program on crime victims he had just seen. He asked whether I had thought of writing a book about the victims of crime. I reflected on the academic volumes on victimology, a subdiscipline of criminology, that were starting to appear. I knew that no one had yet published a study of crime victims for the nonprofessional. About the same time, I had read an article on crime victims by psychiatrist Martin Symonds, a former police officer. I wrote to Dr. Symonds, and he suggested I sit in on his graduate class at John Jay College of Criminal Justice on the psychopathology of the criminal; in the spring he would be teaching the psychology of the victim.

In September I was hired by the New School for Social Research to teach "The Roots of Violence," and my application to graduate school in criminal justice was accepted by Goddard College. Dr. Arthur Niederhoffer, a retired policeman with a Ph.D. in sociology and a law degree, agreed to sponsor me and to structure my academic readings. A student in my class at John Jay told me about a Crime Victim Hotline that the Vera Institute of Justice was going to be starting in Brooklyn. By January 1976 I had begun working part time as a hotline interviewer on Saturdays and Sundays.

In addition to lectures, guest speakers, papers, essays, and book reports, I arranged field trips for my class at the New School. Together my students and I sat in on night court, rode eight-hour tours with police officers in vari-ous parts of the city, went to hospital emergency wards and the city morgue, talked to inmates, and listened to judges, detectives, and former criminals.

I placed ads in local and national newspapers and, promising anonymity, asked victims to come forward with their stories. One rape victim I met had seen my notice in our university alumni news. I also selected names and sto-ries at random from the newspapers: if the victim had a phone, I would call. If there was an address and only an unpublished number, I would write. In almost all cases I was granted an interview, perhaps because I knew only too well the double victimization that most crime victims endure. I once drove to upstate New York to talk with a couple whose daughter had been murdered a year before. A sweet, warm, lovely girl, whose former high school boyfriend had shot her to death. When the father pointed to her high school graduation photograph and said, "That's our daughter," I shared their sense of anger and loss. We cried together. I entrusted them with my own grief about my brother, and we spoke with emotions that most others could not comprehend.

Almost four years after my research began, I felt ready to pull together all I had seen, heard, and learned into a book. At first, wanting to spare readers the pain, the suffering, the immobilizing confusion I had lived with all these years,

I stressed the academic descriptions of victimization. But I realized it is wrong to minimize the experiences of those I spoke with, for what we have been through is not unique. Millions of people are terrorized; millions' will not go out after a certain time at night, even though so many robberies, burglaries, and assaults are committed inside the home or outside in broad daylight.

Once in class we discussed the random murders of the Texas watch-tower killer of the late 1960s. I mentioned that the murderer had killed thirteen other persons before he killed himself. "Only thirteen?" a student responded. My body became like a brick, and I realized how much had happened since that time to make thirteen deaths seem insignificant.

I wanted *Victims* to reflect my training and education in criminal justice, my interviews with victims, criminals, judges, police officers, and lawyers. I wanted it to be a book by someone with academic and professional credits. I did not intend a personal statement. I was afraid to mention my brother, even though his death was the initial reason I became involved with victims and the criminal justice system. But my publisher questioned my omission. I exploded. "It's not fair to my family, I couldn't do that to them. I won't bring more pain onto them."

Reluctantly, I agreed to ask my family how they would feel if I now shared the fact that Seth was murdered. To my astonishment, they said, "If it will help, then tell it." I realized that I was not protecting my mother or my father or my brother's widow. They had survived the tragedy and the years of remembering the sad, undeniable facts; they had lived with it every day. It was I who would now have to face it, privately and publicly.

I went to my father's sixty-second birthday party last July. Eight years had passed since Seth's murder. The immediate family was there, and we all sat around as my dad opened his presents and read the poem I had written for him. At happy moments like that, the tragedy of crime comes back because someone is missing.

For a brief moment I saw my brother. He had big white teeth and thick, dark hair. I saw him walking toward us in his cutoff jeans, dirty T-shirt, and gray sweatshirt. And it was as though he'd just come back from California, like that summer he had taken a theater course at Berkeley. It was as if the years hadn't passed and he had just been away on another vacation. He joined us, and everything was the way it used to be.

1

Who Are the Victims of Crime?

1. For clarity I added this note: What follows is the transcript from the interview I conducted with Wendy, a student in my Roots of Violence course that I taught at The New School . She asked me if she could share with me what happened to her 17-year-old boyfriend Alan when they were both at the movies..

IT was December twenty-third. I remember the exact date because my boyfriend Alan and I were going to attend midnight mass the next night. Alan was the oldest of four children; the other three were girls. He was my first real boyfriend, and at that time we had been going together for about a year. We were a well-known couple both in my junior high school and in his senior high school since we lived in a very small community outside Los Angeles. Alan was a very warm and gentle boy, about my height, and very attractive. He was a good writer, but didn't yet know what he wanted to do with his life.

We sat in the back of the movie theater during the midnight show of two typically bad horror movies. (I don't have any recollection of what they were.) As Alan didn't yet have a driver's license, he had gone to phone my parents to ask them to pick us up since the movie was just ending. As Alan was returning, walking through the door that separated the lobby from the seats, a fifteen-year-old boy stuck a knife in his side and pointed it up. Alan managed to return to our seats, which were only two rows from the back. He lifted up his shirt and said, "He stabbed me."

The blood was running down. The person sitting behind us took him to the manager's office. Alan was lying inside; I was standing right outside the door, hysterical. But that kid was still! loose in the lobby, running loose, stabbing people at random. Several young children were also stabbed. It was like a grade B horror movie.

A girl that I knew from school saw me outside the office and called Alan's parents. As I stood there, several people who had also been stabbed fell down next to me. It was unreal. Another boy, a friend of Alan's, was also stabbed many times, but he kept getting up to fight the kid. Finally he fell down next to me. Each time he got up to fight the kid, his blood squirted out—like when you release the pressure on a water hose—leaving a puddle of blood when he fell down.

It stands out in my mind that this kid had a knife that was about eight inches long and double bladed. People didn't respond quickly because they just didn't believe what was happening, Finally, some people got hold of him. They were banging his head and his arms against the candy counter to get him to release the knife. I'll never forget how I kept hearing, "Help me. Someone help me." I didn't know what was going on, but I soon realized that the one asking for mercy was the murderer!

I would assume the police were called as soon as my boyfriend was taken to the manager's office, but all during that time, no one showed up. Finally, the ambulance arrived, but it was about half an hour after Alan was stabbed. You can gauge the time because my parents arrived shortly afterwards, and it would have taken them about that long to drive from my home to the theater after receiving Alan's call. They arrived just as the ambulance was leaving.

We went to the hospital, but Alan died either on the way or that night; I don't remember. The real trauma began the next day. It was two days before Christmas; his presents were still under my tree. It was awful. My parents were very concerned because I didn't get out of bed for several days after the murder. They were worried that I might do something harmful, so they stayed very close for quite a while. I did have some time to recuperate since I still had another week of Christmas vacation, but I had nightmares.

It was very difficult when I returned to school because it was a big news event. In a small town like that, everyone knew me and Alan; we were both popular. I was a little bit of a "freak" for a while, the girlfriend of the murdered boy. Quite a big drama. At first, people were stand-offish as I walked down the hall, and they would whisper. I felt very much alone. It was also a difficult adjustment since his three sisters all attended my school; running into them was a constant and shocking reminder.

But the most upsetting part was that every Monday for months, I had to go to juvenile court, since they didn't know exactly when I would be called. The assistant principal of my school actually suspected me of using the trial as a means of getting out of school. On frequent occasions she asked me if it really was necessary for me to miss school so often. The last place I wanted to be was in that courtroom!

Many times I would just sit in the courtroom or wait outside. The mur-derer's mother, who didn't speak English, was very broken up and very crushed. I saw her every week. She was really a broken woman. But his older brother—who was very Americanized, very much of a trickster, fairly well spoken, clever and really trying to make excuses—tried to get him out of it. His sister didn't leave much of an impression on me. The murderer didn't look upset; he just stared ahead. Sitting in the courtroom next to the murderer was awful. Every week I would go there and see him sitting there, staring ahead, chained to his chair.

The upshot of the whole thing was that he was committed to something like a mental institution for ten years, so he probably is out by now. What they finally concluded as a motive was mistaken identity. It seems that he was intoxicated when he entered the theater and that when he was in the bathroom, some boys had made fun of him. They claimed that my boyfriend looked like one of those boys, so he stabbed him when he passed him in the hallway. But they were also trying to prove that as a child, the murderer had fallen down a flight of stairs and had brain damage, and that he was emotionally upset.

Alan's murder was a turning point in my life. It was my first experi-ence with death; a realization that life is cheap, that it can be taken so eas-ily. I think I placed more value on life after that. In my relationships with people, I no longer could take things so lightly. I feel more insecure in that I don't like to leave people angry with me, or leave things unsaid or undone, because you never know what can happen. I like to let people know how I feel about them.

I suppressed a lot of emotion, although outwardly I seemed to get over the murder rather rapidly. I was back in school in a few days, but I felt a little bit removed and different—perhaps more mature because of the experience.

I really didn't put Alan's death out of my mind for some time. Every week, for months afterwards, I would bring flowers to the cemetery. Although my family moved away from the community the next year, I would still go back to the cemetery whenever I visited my old friends.

But it has had, I'm afraid, negative long-range effects on me. I just started therapy recently, so I'm beginning to get more in touch with my feelings. But at times, even with my husband, I am anxious when he is away for a long time. If he is coming home from the office, I have visions of him *being run over by a car. I always prepare myself for his death. Although I went into the relationship with my husband very much in love, I think at times I've tried to keep a psychological distance from him so that if some-thing were to happen, it wouldn't be that crushing. In other words, I won't allow myself to let my husband be my whole life—to avoid having my life completely broken a second time.*

2.

Sixteen-year-old Alan is a member of America's most forgotten minority. A minority that in 2019 was officially 8,129,485 --1,203,808 violent crime victims and 6,925,677 property crime victims, according to the *2019 Crime in the United States* FBI report.   Those numbers, however, are less than half of the number of actual direct victims that year since only 40.9% of violent crimes and 32.5% of property crimes are estimated to be reported. (Source: John Gramlich, "What the data says (and doesn't say) about crime in the United States," Pew Research Report, November 20, 2020) One person who was robbed or whose home was burglarized, who was raped, assaulted, or murdered. A minority that does not officially include such persons as Wendy, Alan's girlfriend, a secondary victim, in those statistics. A "minority" that swells when you consider that everyone must pay higher prices because of theft, or more taxes because of the billions of state and federal dollars spent trying to control crime.

Wendy and Alan are part of a minority whose victimization costs billions in lost wages, medical expenses, and property losses; a minority that receives as compensation a minuscule amount of the federal or state money spent on criminals; a minority that seldom gets justice—arrest rates have fallen dramatically and out of those arrests, fewer still will be tried, convicted, or imprisoned.

The year Alan was murdered, there were about 10,000 homicide victims in the United States; fifty-five years later, in 2020, the number had more than doubled to 21,570. Yes, the population increased from 194,770,000 to 329,500,000 over that time period. Few will disagree that the U.S. has far too many murder victims. (As you will see in Chapter 2, the U.S. murder rate is dramatically higher than other westernized countries.) Yet most crime victims are not murdered. They survive robbery, larceny, auto theft, burglary, rape, and serious assault—and they continue to suffer.

Crime victims are, however, unlike other minorities. They are not a cohesive group, unified by religion, race, habitat, or language. Crime victims usually are randomly chosen targets, unified only by fate. Too often they are blamed for their misfortunes—accused of provoking the criminal, of not resisting strongly enough, or of resisting too strongly.

Like other victims of prejudice, crime victims may blame themselves. For example, Wendy, whose story began this chapter, shares her self-blame for her boyfriend's murder:

> *I didn't really want to go to the movies that night. I felt we'd be too tired since the next evening we were going to midnight mass—if we stayed up late two nights in a row. Alan usually did what I wanted, but that evening he just insisted on going. I might have felt guilty if it had been reversed.*
>
> *But I didn't want to go and I pleaded with him not to go to the movies. It was one of the very few times that he insisted on anything, so I went along with him. For that reason, I've never felt I contributed to what happened.*

Like other victims of prejudice, some crime victims inflict on others what they themselves have suffered, so that the next time, the *criminal*, not the victim, is the unfortunate one. Homemade, but fatal, booby traps, guns, or immobilizing karate chops may aid the victim-turned-aggressor. Other victims, so petrified of the seemingly all-powerful criminal, may do just the opposite: they may become overconcerned about the care, treatment, and rehabilitation of the offender. But the majority of crime victims, until only recently, reacted to their violations and losses in the same way that their society had—by trying to ignore or forget about them.

Who is the victim? Some political scientists, psychologists, and criminologists say that the crime victim is the obvious result of the criminal's victimization by society or "the establishment." indeed, criminology evolved in the late nineteenth century primarily to reform harsh criminal laws. Later it broadened to include the study of the reasons for crime, suggestions for its prevention, and the treatment of criminals. In the more than eighty international criminology conferences from 1846 until the 1970s, the victim was rarely mentioned.

In some way everyone involved in a crime is a victim—victim, victim's family, criminal, criminal's family. The radical authors Frantz Fanon and Eldridge Cleaver are just two proponents of the "everyone is a victim" philosophy, but the strongest advocates are the criminals themselves. A man who has been convicted on four separate occasions for atrocious assault and battery writes from an eastern prison:

> I am the Ghetto's Child! Born and raised in the slums in a city in New Jersey, From what I can recall of my adolescent years, the Ghetto section where I was born was "fairly clean," considering. . . . My father died when I was four years old and shortly after him, a sister, just under me died. I was placed in the second grade but, at ten years of age, it was seen that I could not read or write. I am not and never have been a "criminal," in that particular sense of the word! I say that I have been the "Vic-tim of Circumstances" and the "Play Toy" of many people who took all my "gentleness and kindness" for weakness (especially Women!), I eventually found myself being a "number" and no longer a "name!"

Another theory is offered in part of a letter from a forty-two-year-old white male who writes that he has been "incarcerated for a period of twenty-five years in numerous penal facilities . . . for a dull repetition of sociopathic offenses (mostly petty)" that included strong-arm robbery ("purse snatching"), grand larceny, parole violation, prison escapes, bombing a gas station, possession of stolen property, and others. From his experiences sharing his cell at different times with three mass murderers, he came to believe that "each one was the victim of homosexual rape [in reformatories] while at a very young age. My theory is that the *forced* attacks on these individuals has twisted them to the point that they are striking back."

Why persons become criminals and their actual or imagined victimizations clearly are important subjects, but ones beyond the scope of this book. Countless studies already exist on the causes of criminal behavior and the treatment of incarcerated felons, and a dual offender-victim emphasis would result in an enormous and cumbersome volume. What little literature on the victim of crime exists too often dwells on the crime itself rather than the consequences of that unexpected encounter with violence or property loss for the victim. A more specific definition of crime *victim* had to be found. As used in the following chapters the term *crime victims* means those who have directly or indirectly suffered as the result of a specific illegal act considered to be a crime. By this definition, Alan is the direct, or primary, crime victim in the introductory story, and Wendy, Alan's family, friends, and teachers are all indirect, or secondary, victims of that crime. They suffer psychological trauma and social discrimination similar to the suffering experienced by surviving primary victims.

3.

VIOLENT, and even nonviolent, crimes usually provoke four types of reactions; physical, financial, social, and psychological. These shock waves are felt immediately as well as over a long time; sometimes they are indefinite. The first two—physical injuries and tangible material losses—are described in newspapers, in everyday conversations, or on TV; they also are recorded by police and in other official reports. The second two—social and psychological aftermaths—are not identified so easily, yet they may paralyze the victim more. Since these reactions are more easily obscured, society and the victims themselves may ignore their need for help or their need to reverse deep-seated anti-victim prejudices.

The physical residuals of violent crimes are the ones with which non-victims are apt to be the most familiar, and the most sympathetic. Injuries suffered by crime victims are usually dramatic, visible, and painful. Victims are shot, stabbed, stomped, bruised, burned, slashed, beaten, or run over. They may be blinded so that they cannot identify the criminal; they may be tortured until they reveal the hiding places for their valuables or submit to sexual demands against their will. They lose arms, legs, toes, fingers; faces are mutilated; organs are permanently damaged. Even the slightest blow to the head may cause temporary loss of memory, judgment, and orientation; a more serious head wound may cause permanent brain damage and subsequent physical paralysis or mental retardation.

Often these serious physical injuries lead to a psychological wound that may be as severe or as permanent. Unlike victims of diseases or natural disasters—hurricanes, tornadoes, or floods— who can rationalize their sufferings, crime victims know that their injuries were willfully inflicted by another human being. They were acts of man, not acts of God. In many cases, the victim sees his attacker—in effect the crime victim engages in face-to-face combat (or surrender) in a time of supposed national peace.

Knowing, firsthand, how violent and defiant another person can be may instill in the victim a persistent and unshakable fear of strangers. Being a crime victim can also permanently alter one's morals, philosophy, and religious beliefs. A murder victim's sister has said, "It's not the same thing as a car accident. It's not the same thing as even cancer. It's the idea that another human is capable of inflicting violence on another. And that's a realization that destroys your whole equilibrium. You're vulnerable. You realize that there are people who are just not nice." Another woman, a primary victim who was robbed at knifepoint but physically unharmed, also has scars that affect her everyday behavior and view of the world: "I got a letter from a very good friend of mine who is living in Rhode Island. She wrote, saying, 'Don't let this throw you. There's still beauty in the world.' She's right; but it's very hard to all of a sudden turn it off. Now I'm very aware when I walk alone. It was horrible and what followed was horrible. I didn't sleep well for a few nights. I would just lie there and try to go back to sleep, and the whole thing just went through my mind. I don't know how long it will take me to shake it."

One of the most overlooked categories of crime-related injuries is psychosomatic injury, although there is much information about psychosomatic conditions triggered by wars or natural disasters. In London during the German blitz, for example, there was a marked increase in the incidence of peptic ulcers. A 1970 study found that those residents of Bristol, England, who had lived through the serious floods two years before had a 50 percent increase in the number of deaths and twice as many hospital admissions and referrals as those residents who had been away during the floods.

So far only some informal research compiling case studies has been done on the psychosomatic effects of stress and fright on the victims of violent crimes. One man who was studied developed colitis about a year after his daughter's murder. Very often victims describe less severe reactions, such as nervousness, insomnia, and "edginess."

Victims who are physically handicapped because of a crime will have more difficulty resolving their fears and anger about the crime only because they must first deal with the handicaps before dealing with their causes. For example, when Walter retired he did not want to be idle, so he got a job as a security guard in a St. Louis bank. On his first day of work, Walter and the bank manager were shot during an attempted robbery. Both victims were left permanently paralyzed; two years later, the bank manager died. Walter remains institutionalized, unable to feed himself, in constant pain from chronic bed sores. He may never be well enough to deal with the initial crime.

> *"Alan's murder was a turning point in my life."*
> *"I feel more insecure."*
> *"I suppressed a lot of emotion."*
> *"I really didn't put Alan's death out of my mind for some time."*
> *"But it has had, I'm afraid, negative long-range effects on me."*

These statements show just a few of the long-term psychological shocks experienced by primary and secondary crime victims. On the basis of hundreds of interviews with crime victims, psychiatrist Martin Symonds and others have established four post-victimization stages, all similar to the experiences of terminally ill patients first described by psychiatrist Elisabeth Kübler-Ross. Any sudden, unexpected, and potentially fatal calamity, whether an attack by a mugger or a diagnosis of cancer, causes predictable psychological reactions. Crime victims experience shock, denial, and disbelief during and immediately after a crime; then fright and fear that the crime will happen again, often accompanied by clinging behavior such as uncontrolled talking or needing to be taken care of; next, apathy alternating with anger; and, finally, resolution of the suffering. The time spent in each of these four stages varies for each person. For some crime victims, and for the families of murder victims, the final resolution may never be achieved.

"I was in shock. I couldn't believe that this was happening," says a victim of purse snatching. "Something's happening, but I didn't know what was happening." Over and over again, crime victims use different words to echo the same first stage—shock, denial, and disbelief.

The victim's disbelief *during* the crime often leads to a post-victimization denial of its occurrence or, more commonly, of its horror. Wendy, who rarely shared the story of Alan's murder, was startled when she first read a transcript of her interview: "No question that it's accurate. If you said, 'Tell me the story today,' those are the facts that I would say. But I never thought about it as a savage crime. Isn't it funny that reading it, it seemed very dramatic and almost sensationalized. I guess to make things easier, I had downplayed it. When I first read it, I was a little angry. But it's only my way of coming to terms with what happened,"

The second psychological stage, fright and fear, may occur during the crime, or afterward, as part of a delayed reaction. Often criminals purposely try to elicit fear in their victims so the victims will follow orders; by rendering a victim helpless, the criminal may ensure his successful escape. Some victims become so paralyzed with fear that they are unable to speak or move; others laugh uncontrollably.

This paralyzing fear does not vanish after the crime. It can persist close to the victim's consciousness, or it can smolder below the surface, to be reignited years later by either obvious provocative incidents and situations or completely unconscious associations. A man who was mugged while laden with grocery bags may thereafter have to have his purchases delivered. A burglary victim may give up her low-cost apartment for a luxury doorman building that she can ill afford. An elderly woman who is assaulted on the subway may never again venture out of her immediate neighborhood. Two women, threatened at knifepoint in the park near their home, may never feel comfortable walking through there again:

MARILYN: Since both of us own dogs, we spend a lot of time in the park walking them. What happened was, I see one of my dogs coming toward me carrying a box of Kentucky fried chicken in his mouth, I yelled, "Stop it. Drop it," and he dropped the chicken and ran under the bench. So I bent under the bench to really smack him, and this woman took her satchel and smashed me on the head. It was so unexpected. I just turned. I really got scared. Then she pulled out a knife and I said, "We'll pay for the chicken. We'll pay for the chicken." Then the man said, "Well, give me the knife, woman." And

I thought that would end it, but he says, "That's my woman." And he started after us and the dogs, slashing at us with the knife.

PHYLLIS: I had the baby strapped into his carriage and Marilyn was screaming, "Phyllis, take the baby and run." I was paralyzed. I attached my key ring to the dog's leash and ran out of the park, running down Second Avenue with the carriage, trying to find a policeman.

MARILYN: I was stunned. All you can keep saying to yourself is, "f don't believe this is happening." Thereafter I was just terribly paranoid about going into the park.

PHYLLIS: I find myself straining to tolerate hostile comments now, whereas before if someone said something to me, I'd scream, "Go away." But after this incident, I was much too frightened. I never really had anything happen to me before.

The fear that victims experience either during or after a crime may also be accompanied by a feeling of utter helplessness. Dr. Robert Flint, a psychologist who has counseled crime victims, studied the problem of helplessness and concluded:

> We compartmentalize conflicting thoughts to maintain our safety. One is, "I can't control and predict the future." The other is, "I know how to maintain my safety." Victimization destroys this separation, and anxiety rushes in. Helplessness, as I see it, is not only a reaction to what has happened but the fearful antici-pation of its happening again. Therefore, unequivocal support and sympathy must be given to the victim to reestablish the feel-ing of an alliance with society and resources which can be called on to prevent future victimization.

During or after such crimes as rape, robbery, or abduction— when there is an opportunity for prolonged contact between the victim and the criminal—the second stage of fear and fright is more pronounced. The clinging or submissive behavior that often accompanies this stage may later embarrass the victim; it may also provoke self-blame. One robbery victim was surprised that she reacted to the fearful situation with aggressive behavior:

> *I was so indignant after having spent a hundred dollars at the supermarket, and only having seven dollars left in my pocket, that I was just damned if I was going to give it to him. You just don't know how you're going to react. I always thought it was just, "Here. Just take it and go." But then he said, "Lady, I mean it." So I said, "I mean it too. I just spent all my money at the supermarket and I don't have any." He looked at me sort of funny, and said, "Do you really mean it?" And I said, "I really do." At that point the elevator door opened and he just casually turned around, like he had just been talking to me, and walked to the front door and took off.*
>
> *And that's when I fell apart. Being so strong and talking back to him and all—I shook for the rest of the day, literally. I couldn't stop my body. ... I was nauseous. Then, later that day when I had to go to the police station to identify him, I had to vomit. After that, I just shook all day long.*

That crime victim was as stupefied by her brazenness as other victims are humiliated by their compliance. Fear can render a victim irrational so that after the criminal leaves—or the victim escapes—he or she may do things that seem senseless or silly to others, like calling the police for help but giving them the wrong address or dialing his or her own phone number instead of the police number.

The crime victim's last two psychological reactions— apathy/anger and resolution of the victimization—both usually occur after the crime. However, if both fear and anger surface during the attack, anger will be submerged and fright will take over. Becoming angry at the criminal while still in a dangerous position may be fatal to the victim. The criminal is less likely to do harm if fear (not anger) is present. If it appears to the victim, however, that he will be killed regardless of his reaction, anger often over-rules fear.

After the attack, the victim may experience a delayed response of increased anger, leading to increased fear, which in turn leads to increased self-blame or punishment as the victim further restricts his or her activities out of fear.

A nineteen-year-old girl was grabbed from behind by a man near her apartment elevator. He held a knife to her throat and threatened to cut out her eyes if she didn't do what he asked. He forced her to her knees and made her perform fellatio. When the attacker left, the victim remained on the floor for some time, then got up and calmly went to her apartment, walked past her mother's room, and went to sleep. The next day, she called a girl-friend whose father was a detective. The victim did not want to tell her own mother because the mother had told her never to come home alone at night; the victim felt guilty about what had happened and feared that her mother would blame her. The victim's apathy immediately after the sexual assault was caused by her fear of the criminal (who had forced her to comply) and of her mother.

Whether fear or anger determines the victim's behavior during the attack may affect when, or if, the victim resolves the experience. Psychiatrist Martin Symonds has found that victims, and society in general, are less accepting of the frightened (and therefore compliant) victim than of the one who fights back. Yet Symonds quickly notes that how a victim behaves during a crime is dependent upon three basic factors outside his or her control: the mental health of the criminal, circumstances surrounding the crime, and the victim's early life experiences. Although there are numerous exceptions, Symonds suggests that, in general, working-class male victims fight back whereas victims from the middle class and women of all classes tend to freeze and therefore comply with the criminal.

The period of apathy after the crime may be a long one. It is usually accompanied by rage that is directed at society as well as at the victim's own behavior. Symonds notes that he often heard expressions of that rage in such statements as, "The hell with people, who needs them? You got to look out for yourself. People are animals. The world is a jungle. No one gives a damn." Others have said, "There is no justice." "How can you explain the frustrated rage and the hurt?" A victim's rage is often directed toward the self and is exemplified in the numerous "If only . . ." comments a victim or a victim's family may make.

All crime victims express their anger. It may be directed at the police, the examining physicians, the district attorney, or newspaper reporters. Until recently, that anger was generally considered justified since the victim was usually treated poorly. But when a victim's anger is directed toward the criminal—the person toward whom the victim legitimately should be hostile—it is termed revenge. A preoccupation with revenge, or "revenge fantasies," in time may intensify, particularly if the criminal is not apprehended. Although criminologists and the criminal justice system seem to ignore a victim's wish for revenge, people who work closely with victims have described how prevalent it is.

Criminologist Gilbert Geis reports that a California woman, when asked to describe just punishment for the man who had raped and beaten her, said, "Just give him to me. I shouldn't feel this way, but I could kill him. He's really sick. If he can be helped, he should be. But if he can't be helped, why waste taxes on him? He should not be in society." Geis also recorded the anger toward the criminal expressed by the daughter of an attempted-rape victim. Her mother, a psychiatric nurse, suffocated during the assault because the would-be rapist placed a pillow-case over her head; the daughter did not think the murder was intentional, however. The assailant was caught, but escaped from jail, and two years later was shot in the spine during an attempted burglary. He was left permanently paralyzed. The daughter felt "he got what's coming to him" and expressed relief that a lifetime of paralysis would be "worse than life imprisonment."

When the murderer of his girlfriend was finally apprehended, a young man was quoted as saying, " I wish he would have come looking for me. I wanted to get my hands on the guy ... I just want to take him apart and show him what he is without a gun. I wish they could put me in the cage with the guy tonight.' " Yet a week before the alleged murderer was caught, an editorial in the *New York Times* decried a wish for personal vengeance: "The street chorus calling for the ultimate public revenge on 'Son of Sam' . . . does the city a disservice. . . ."The mother of one victim said, "I want him to be tortured and his eyes gouged out." A neighbor of a victim said, "You know what I'd do with him? I'd cut both his legs off and say to the police, 'When you give me the reward, I'll bring the rest of the body.' "

How, when, or whether a person resolves victimization depends on many factors. Experiences early in a victim's life and his or her ability to overcome sudden trauma affect resolution of less severe crimes, such as thefts without violence. Whether the criminal is someone known and trusted by the victim or a complete stranger may also be significant. ("Confidence" attacks may have more severe long-range consequences since the victim, who was probably already leery of strangers, now is afraid of acquaintances and friends as well.) It might take months or years for another episode to demonstrate that instead of being resolved, the victimization was simply repressed. Without the outside intervention of a therapist, the cause-and-effect relationship between the crime and certain subsequent behavior may also go undetected by the victim. For example, a rape victim may ascribe her inability to have sexual relations to "not finding the right person" rather than to her two-year-old trauma. A burglary victim may explain that her move to another neighborhood was because her "lease was going to be up soon anyway" rather than admit her fear of walking into her former home.

The ability of the survivors of a homicide victim to resolve their victimization depends upon the same factors that determine the intensity and duration of bereavement in general. Those two dimensions, studied by Professor Larry A. Bugen, are the closeness of the victim to the mourner and the survivor's belief that the death was preventable. Interviews with families of homicide victims conducted by this author substantiated Bugen's theory: their inability to resolve the victimization is based upon a consistent belief that the death was pre-ventable. Rather than decide that nothing could have been done to avoid the attack, homicide-families tend to deny the cause of death. They may resolve the loss temporarily and function, but reopening the discussion of the crime brings renewed guilt, loneliness, depression, and strong emotions. Similarly, a victim may apparently resolve one victimization—a burglary—but a later unrelated victimization—an obscene phone call—may trigger an exaggerated response that is in fact a delayed reaction to the first trauma. For victims of violent crime, it is more realistic to say they achieve the ability to carry on with healthy, everyday work and personal relationships but do not effect a complete resolution of their victimization.

4.

MUCH of the social discrimination and psychological suffering that crime victims feel could be minimized, and perhaps avoided, if anti-victim preju-dices were eliminated. The victim's family, friends, and acquaintances, the media, and the criminal justice system should be pro-victim. Instead, their ambivalent and sometimes negative reactions devastate the victim almost as much as the crime. To begin erasing those attitudes, we must understand why so many people need to believe that, in some way, the victim is responsible for the crime.

There are some instances in which victims *do* provoke crimes and therefore *should* carry part of the blame. But the guilt of the victim, as well as the guilt of the offender, must be carefully weighed against the type, degree, and severity of any precipitating act. If a woman cocks a gun, aims it at her husband's head, and tells him she is going to kill him, but is herself killed when her husband struggles to save his life by grabbing the gun, the victim is guilty of provoking her own death. By contrast, if she had merely insulted her husband, stepped on his toe, or thrown a book at him, there would not have been sufficient provocation to kill her.

A defense attorney is often expected to convince a jury that the victim precipitated the crime as one way to prove his client innocent. It is less understandable when police officers or state prosecutors also blame the victim. In a judicial system characterized more and more by unsolved crimes or known criminals being freed on "technicalities," blaming the traumatized becomes easier than faulting other parts of the system.

This need for a victim scapegoat may arise from conscious motives as well. For instance, John and his friend Laurie were both about twenty years old at the time of the crime that involved them. They were completing college at eastern schools and had each earned enough money during their junior year to have ample funds for a summer vacation in California. But when it was time to return, they found themselves broke, and rather than borrowing their air fares from their parents, they decided to hitchhike back. The last ride they accepted was in Nevada; two teenage boys offered them a lift. After driving a short while, one of the youths interjected a racist remark into their conversation, for which John criticized him. The youth replied, "That's not the way we feel about it out here." Seconds later, he pulled out a revolver and shot John in the chest. The driver stopped the car and threw the unharmed but panicked Laurie by the side of the road. John's body was tossed after her.

The youths were soon apprehended by the local police; a few months later, John's parents flew to Nevada to oversee the prosecution of their son's murderers. They were shocked to find that the police and the public prosecutor were trying to ignore the murder since the victim was an outsider and the alleged murderers were "nice local boys." Not only was John's comment being trumped up as a serious provocation, but the police and defense attorneys had spread around a rumor that John was a drug addict.

Furious, John's parents hired a private prosecutor who eventually was successful at clearing all drug accusations and in compelling the court to proceed with the murder trial. One of the youths died in an automobile accident before he could come to trial; the other one was convicted of sec-ond-degree murder and served only four years of a fifteen-year sentence. Although nothing could undo the tragedy, the parents had some sense of resolution in clearing their son's name and in the active way they pressed for the murderers' trial. Laurie never returned to college and since that time has never been close to another man.

5.

IT was clearly for vested interests that the defense attorney, law enforcement officials, and townspeople blamed John, the murder victim, for the crime. So, too, can a defense attorney try to free his client by trying to convince a jury that a rape victim provoked the attack, in effect "wanted to be raped."

But what about the majority of unpublicized or unsolved crimes whose victims are also blamed? Why would Wendy, besides blaming herself, need to blame Alan for insist-ing that they go to the movies despite her wish that they stay home? Crime, particularly violent crime, threatens the ingrained belief that the world is just. Blaming the victim is the quickest and least expensive way of overcom-ing that threat to the "just-world hypothesis," a theory proposed and devel-oped by social psychologist Melvin J. Lerner. In essence, if victims somehow get "what they deserve," then the world is still a just one.

This theory explains why victims of ongoing, involved, and provoca-tive situations—such as the battered wife or the Good Samaritan who gets involved in a crime by aiding another—may be the victims who receive the *most* sympathy from the media and from friends. "How could you have put up with him as long as you did?" or "How did you find the courage to take on those menacing teenagers?" are questions frequently asked of those victims in contrast to the insinuating inquiries, such as, "*Why* did you even resist>" or "Didn't you know he didn't live in your building?" that the totally random victim has to cope with.

Psychologist Dr. Melvin Lerner's research into victim blaming began in the 1960s. In one of his early articles, "Observer's reaction to the Innocent Victim'" Compassion or Rejection?", co-authored with C. H. Simmons and published in the *Journal of Personality and Social Psychology* in 1966, the co-authors studied the responses of 72 undergraduates in an experiment. The victim in the study was supposed to be receiving electric shocks. The researchers' findings supported their hypothesis that "rejection and devaluation of a suffering victim are primarily based on the O's [Observer's] need to believe in a just world."

In 1971, the phrase, "blaming the victim," was popularized by the title of the book, *Blaming the Victim* (Vintage, 1971, 2nd edition, 1976) by psychologist William Ryan. Ryan was actually referring to the way that a "blaming the victim" mindset was used to justify racism and social injustice against African Americans. But the phrase "stuck" and got applied to other victim groups, like crime victims.

Psychologist Albert Ellis explains this unreasonable tendency to fault the victim as a universal need to find logical explanations for all happenings:

> *One of the most irrational beliefs of humans consists of the idea that special reasons for human conduct must exist—and that, for example, we can always find a "rational" or "pay-off" reason for the irrational attack by a mugger or a rapist. They consequently find—or, rather invent—such "reasons" in many instances.*
>
> *Actually, criminals often commit crimes, or commit them in a particularly senseless way, because they have powerful irra-tional tendencies, largely innate rather than acquired, to think and behave foolishly and impulsively. Why do they have such tendencies? Mainly, because they simply have them (just as many productive and creative people simply have such "good" tendencies and would require unusual environmental condi-tions not to actualize them). Also, what almost amounts to sheer accident plays a part in a considerable amount of social and antisocial behavior. A*

mugging victim may make a little move which the mugger may falsely "see" as "dangerous," and the mugger may therefore kill that victim. We all find it easy, after the fact, to make up "good" explanations for a criminal's actions. The cleverer this "good" explanation seems, the more we feel sure that it rings true. More frequently than not, it prob-ably has little truth to it. Our nutty need for certainty influ-ences us, in this respect, much more than the seeming "reasons" for the criminal's behavior.

Oftentimes, either during a crime or immediately afterward, victims' actions unwittingly encourage others to blame them. Yet certain basic reactions are physiological mechanisms that occur naturally in the face of danger. Likewise, psychological responses to a first victimization may be as unconscious—and as uncontrollable— as the physical ones.

There are marked physiological changes that humans undergo when faced with a menacing situation: secretion of adrenaline, deepened respiration, more rapid heartbeats, higher blood pressure, freed sugar reserves for use by the muscles, suspension of digestive activity, and dilated pupils for better vision. These body changes occur when fear and rage necessitate self-protective behavior, typically running from danger or fighting and overcoming it. But others are too paralyzed with fear either to flee or to fight. They comply. (Conventional wisdom has it that compliance is the best strategy when facing an armed criminal.) Still, there are always those who blame a victim for failing to resist.

Some victims identify, and even sympathize, with their attackers. This loyalty (indeed, warmth) toward a tormentor is parallel to psychoanalyst Anna Freud's concept of "identification with the aggressor." Hostages, in particular, identify with the robber or kidnapper. After their release, hostages often express their "gratitude" to the criminal for "saving" (sparing) their lives. One victim who was tied up and robbed by knife-wielding men spoke of them as "nice guys" because "they let me keep my wedding band when I told them it was a gift from my wife and that we were not living together anymore." In Sweden, a man held hostage by a robber shouted, "I won't let you hurt him," at the police entering the bank to subdue his captor. An American woman, taken hostage during the robbery of a suburban bank, later described a similar reaction:

> I sit at the front desk, and I was taken by the fact that he was a nice, tall, good-looking boy. He didn't look like the type who was going to come in and hold up the bank.
>
> It just seemed to me that he was good to us in that he didn't really treat us mean. He didn't push us with the gun. He didn't curse at us, although he swore at the policemen. In fact, he kept reassuring us that he wasn't going to harm us, and that we weren't going to be hurt. I guess I believed him.
>
> Actually, when I was in the vault, L was more concerned if the others were ali right. I kept asking them if they were okay. One girl that he held hostage till the very end when he surrendered has trouble with her feet; he kept sending her back and forth. I kept saying, "Oh gee, couldn't I go in her place?"
>
> I developed a warm feeling toward him in the sense that the whole time this was going on, I almost believed what he was saying. I was starting to feel sorry for him.

6.

POPULAR entertainment—movies, television, and novels—are frequently, and correctly, accused of glorifying the criminal, making his violence appear acceptable and encouraging imitation of criminal acts. In *Dog Day Afternoon,* a movie said to be based on a bank robbery and hostage-taking situation in New York, the viewers are made to empathize with the criminal. In fact, the bank employees did "side" with the criminal while they were his prisoners, but the movie accurately demonstrates how even those who had to "identify with the aggressor" gave up their temporary loyalty when they were released and out of danger. *Real* hostages do not romanticize their experiences as the cinema is prone to do:

> Since this all happened, I haven't been able to read one newspaper report on it. I can talk about it and

people that were involved here [at the bank] speak about it and it doesn't bother me. I've saved the papers and brought in copies, but the minute I pick it up and try to read it—even talking about it right now or about the newspaper reports—I get a feeling in my stomach. Maybe not really wanting to believe it actually happened. Talking about it and having others talk about it is one thing, but maybe just seeing it in print, that's the finality of it. It really did happen and here's what happened going over it ali again.

In Boston, teenagers doused a young woman with kerosene and tossed a lighted match at her for no apparent reason. A week earlier, a movie had been televised that portrayed a band of delinquents who set Boston derelicts on fire for "kicks."

In San Francisco, a mother charged that a boy and three girls, aged ten to fourteen, "raped" her nine-year-old daughter with a broomstick. Just before the assault the youths had seen a similar broomstick attack on a made-for-television movie about juvenile detention homes.

In Ottawa, a Canadian boy saw a movie about a sniper; soon afterward, he shot eleven women.

In Indore, India, two young men saw a movie about a clan of thieves; a few days later they were caught trying to rob a commission agent.

Shortly before Arthur Bremer shot Governor George Wallace in an assassination attempt, Bremer recorded the following activities and thoughts in his diary:

> *I had to get away from my thoughts for a while. I went to the zoo, the lake front, saw "Clockwork Orange" & thought about getting Wallace all thru the picture—fantasing myself as the Alek on the screen come to real life—but without "my brothers" & without any "in and out." Just "a little of the old ultra violence."*
>
> *I've decided Wallace will have the honor of—what would you call it?*
>
> *Like a novelist who knows not how his book will end—I have written this journal—what a shocking surprise that my*

inner character shall steal the climax and destroy the author
and save the anti-hero from assasination!!

It may sound exciting & fascinating to readers 100
years from now—as the Booth conspricy seems to us today;
but to this man it seems only another failure. And I stopped
tolerating failure weeks ago.

The critics of television violence are quick to cite horror stories such as these as an argument for banning or reducing the number of violent television programs. Whether violent films and TV shows mirror the gruesomeness of everyday crimes or whether they help "cause" them is an ongoing debate, but only the most naive persons will doubt whether far worse atrocities existed before the introduction of celluloid or television depictions. Numerous articles have been written about contrasts or similarities between fictitious police officers, judges, and lawyers and real ones. But while police experts are assessing whether TV dramas are factual or why "TV's Cop Shows Are Crazy about Psychotics," others are concerned with the long-range impact of television's distorted view of the criminal justice system.

Dr. George Gerbner of the University of Pennsylvania and other social scientists have estimated that by the age of fifteen most Americans have seen over 13,000 persons murdered on their TV screens. The American Medical Association, Parents and Teach-ers Association, the National Citizens' Committee for Broadcasting, and Action for Children's Television have taken up the anti-violence fight, and by 1977 there was considerably less raw aggression on television. Motion picture films appeared that were almost the antithesis of *The Godfather* and *In Cold Blood*. Whereas in earlier movies such as *Straw Dogs* and *Death Wish* the victims used violent means to accomplish their "righting of wrongs," in more recent films, such as *One on One*, the vic-tim uses a nonviolent means to win.

But are long-term consequences of those TV or cinematic interpretations of life any less dangerous simply because graphic violence was removed? Far worse social consequences arise from the prejudiced and stereotyped view of the victim they present. Those effects are more subtle, and for that reason interpretations of victims and victim behavior must be monitored as closely as the degree of violence in the media.

Most movies and novels about crime are told from the perspective of criminals or from that of the police officers, detectives, or private citizens who are trying to apprehend them. The victims are seen either as bodies carried away by ambulance attendants or ill-defined and little-noticed characters whom the audience or reader can rarely sympathize with or know. For example, in Bertrand Tavernier's French film *The Clockmaker,* based on a Georges Simenon novel, the victim is a licentious womanizer described as a "deserving" victim by the murderer and his girlfriend. In *The Laughing Policeman,* an American movie, the victims are murdered at the outset of the film and are seen again only as bodies laid out in a morgue; the focus throughout the movie is on the murderer. Countless other examples of the anonymous or, worse, deserving, victim can be culled from television series such as "Kojak," "Starsky and Hutch," "Perry Mason," "Police Woman," and movies such as *Taxi Driver, The Godfather,* and *Helter Skelter.*

When victims are given a larger role, they are usually unpleasant or colorless characters—a nagging wife, an "unsavory" woman, a greedy husband—or others who are similarly blamed for their fate or at least are considered no loss to the community when dead. A short radio advertisement for a 1976-77 Broadway hit musical replayed these lines from one of its songs: "He had it coming. He had it coming. He only had himself to blame." The song continues with one of the leading characters justifying the murder she committed: "Nobody walks out on me." Another prophecy is included: "You would have done it too." Could the negative subliminal effect of repetitious exposure to that theme song ever be measured?

Current novelists and screenwriters are not solely reflecting the anti-victim social prejudices that are ingrained in our culture. They also write out of a literary tradition of victim blame that has been carried on over the past one hundred years by some of the world's greatest and most widely read novelists, for example, Stendhal, Theodore Dreiser, Agatha Christie, and Truman Capote. (Those who have seen the victim as innocent are fewer in number and include short story writers Katherine Anne Porter and Edgar Allan Poe.) Sometimes subtly, sometimes openly, their stories have influenced public opinion and the social scientists who created an academic specialty of studying the victim. The following are just a few examples chosen from the many novels, poems, and plays that are responsible for nurturing the myth of the blameworthy victim.

In Dostoevsky's *Crime and Punishment,* the principal character, Raskolnikov, an impoverished and bitter student, axes to death his pawnbroker, Alyona Ivanovna, and her sister. Just before the murders, Raskolnikov overhears a conversation at a small restaurant that foreshadows the murders he is about to commit by providing him with his justification: "Kill her and take her money, with the aim of devoting yourself later, with its aid, to the service of humanity and the common good. , . . For one life, a thousand lives saved from decay and disintegration. . . .She preys on the life of others; she's vicious."

Dostoevsky implies that Ivanovna has been selected because she is a "perfect murder victim." Implicitly, in the episodes preceding her brutal slaying, she is described as a greedy, vulturous pawnbroker feeding off the financial hardships of serious students. She is a "diminutive, dried up old crone of about sixty, with sharp, malevolent little eyes, a small, sharp nose and bare head" whose graying hair was smeared with oil. Her long, thin neck "looked like a chicken's leg," and she constantly coughed and groaned.

Despite his theme that murderers need to confess and be punished, Dostoevsky unfortunately glamorized murderers through the romantic characterization of Raskolnikov and his devoted girlfriend, Sonya. Few will deny the contemporary fictional glorification of the powerful central character in *The Godfather*—in spite of his murdering, stealing, and illegal underworld activities. That the "average" murderer does not resemble Dostoevsky's or Puzo's conception is rarely depicted to the general public.

In the summer of 1906, Grace Brown was drowned by her boyfriend, Chester Gillette, in a lake in New York's Adirondack Mountains. Theodore Dreiser, a newspaper reporter turned novelist, used the Brown murder as the basis for his 1925 best-selling novel, *An American Tragedy.* Dreiser saw the Brown murder as a prototype of numerous other murders occurring at that time in American history: status-seeking young men provoked to murder the women who thwarted their ambitions.

In *An American Tragedy,* Chester Gillette becomes the fictional Clyde Griffiths, a lonely youth born in the Midwest to parents consumed by a missionary zeal. Clyde, however, aspires to the material and social success of his uncle Samuel, who owns a factory in New York State. Clyde is given a job there. He has an affair with lower-class Roberta Alden, but Roberta's pregnancy complicates Clyde's plans to many a rich girl, who can guarantee him financial and social success.

Throughout the novel Dreiser's sympathies are with Clyde, not with the murder victim. Roberta is depicted as someone whose "entrapment" of Clyde is inexcusable since the dream of rising above one's low origins is one that Dreiser believed all Americans shared,

In a 1935 article written for *The Mystery Magazine*, Dreiser gave his opinion on what was a recent and factual "American tragedy"—the murder of Freda McKechie at a lake near Wilkes-Barre, Pennsylvania, by her boyfriend, Robert Edwards. The following quotation from that article reflects the anti-victim and pro-murderer prejudices that motivated the characters in *An American Tragedy:*

> I think that if this is carefully and honestly considered, you will realize that Robert Edwards cannot be judged as a murderer in the common sense of the word. Actually, man when motivated by violent love is more to be pitied than otherwise. He is the vic-tim of a frenzy. Robert Edwards was the victim of a frenzy, just as the girl he murdered, and just as was the girl he desired. And yet, of these three, the key victim, the one who is most violently involved, is judged to be a sane, coldly reasoning person who deliberately proceeded to murder.
>
> The assumption is false, The law is false. The notions of society in regard to a situation of this kind are unsound. . . .
>
> I ask for the legal modification of our present crude Ameri-can way of dealing with at least this one phase of American tragedy.

In *The Prophet,* Lebanese-born Kahlil Gibran expressed similar sentiments more openly:

> The murdered is not unaccountable for his own murder,
> And the robbed is not blameless in being robbed.
> The righteous is not innocent of the deeds of the wicked,
> And the white-handed is not clean in the doings of the felon.
> Yea, the guilty is oftentimes the victim of the injured,

And still more often the condemned is the burden bearer for the guiltless and unblamed.

You cannot separate the just from the unjust and the good from the wicked;

For they stand together before the face of the sun even as the black thread and the white are woven together.

And when the black thread breaks, the weaver shall look into the whole cloth, and he shall examine the loom also.

Agatha Christie has been one of the most influential proponents of the theory of the "deserving victim," the victim whose actions precipitate his or her own murder. In *Evil under the Sun* (which by 1975 had been reprinted twenty times in paperback alone), Arlena Marshall is the archetype of the predestined victim because of her beauty and the way she attracts men who believe her to be "wanton." Detective Hercule Poirot considers her "predestined prey for an unscrupulous man of a certain type."

Arlena's role as the "eternal victim" is compounded by negative descriptions of her by the novel's other characters as a person without brains, an "eternal seductress," and a "scandalous woman." Her only positive trait seems to be that she dresses well. Poirot sums up Christie's view of the victim by saying:

> "There is no such thing as a plain fact of murder. Murder springs, nine times out of ten, out of the character and circum-stances of the murdered person. Because the victim was the kind of person he or she was, therefore was he or she murdered! Until we can understand fully and completely exactly what kind of per-son Arlena Marshall was, we shall not be able to see dearly exactly the kind of person who murdered her. From that springs the necessity of our questions."

In his "nonfiction novel" *In Cold Blood*, Truman Capote expresses his anti-victim prejudices with more subtlety. Susan Kress, an English professor at Skidmore College, has written a paper pointing out that Capote does not give the Clutter family (the murder victims) the .same kind of sympathetic description that he accords the murderers. According to her, Capote's description of the Clutters' house at the beginning of the book shows one of the "obvious moments when we are alienated from the Clutter world; take the description of the tasteless, plastic interior of the Clutters' house: 'As for the interior, there were spongy displays of liver-colored carpet, intermittently abolishing the glare of varnished, resounding floors; an immense modernistic living-room couch covered in nubby fabric interwoven with glittery strands of silver metal; a breakfast alcove featuring a banquette upholstered in blue-arid-white plastic. This sort of furnishing was what Mr. and Mrs. Clutter liked, as did the majority of their acquaintances, whose homes, by and large, were similarly furnished.' "

Even more revealing is what Kress notes as a student's response to one of the victims, Nancy Clutter:

"I remember once teaching this novel in a class on contemporary American fiction and one of my students remarking (to a chorus of approval) that she really *disliked* Nancy Clutter. That student's response is necessary to the plan of the novel; it is linked with Capote's need to draw us away from engagement with the Clutters and involve us in the complexity he establishes for the killers."

Like Dreiser, Judith Rossner fictionalized a sensational murder case in her novel *Looking for Mr. Goodbar*. Rossner's victim, Theresa, is a Bronx-born schoolteacher whose childhood illness leaves her with a limp and a back deformity that affect her self-esteem and appearance. Rossner describes Theresa's affairs and the loneliness and isolation that lead her to pick up men in bars. It is implied that Theresa had an unconscious death wish,

Rather than emphasizing how unfortunate and unlucky Theresa was to bring a psychotic man back to her apartment, Rossner's novel seems to indict Theresa for bringing on her own death. Women who read *Goodbar* may be comforted, albeit unjustifiably, in knowing that if their habits and self-image differ from Theresa's, their chances of being murdered as she was are lessened.

The interest and controversy over the movie version of *Good-bar* are evidenced by the fact that even before the film was completed, two major features on it appeared in the Sunday drama section of the *New York Times*. According to Aljean Harmetz's article "Will 'Mr. Goodbar' Make Voyeurs of Us All?" Richard Brooks agreed to direct the film after Mike Nichols, Paddy

Chayefsky, Sydney Pollack, Bob Fosse, and Roman Polanski had turned the property down. Brooks, who also wrote the filmscript, supposedly did not base *his* Terry Dunn on either the "real" Terry or Rossner's fictitious version. Brooks hoped to portray a woman whose victimization is affected by everything in her life—TV violence, her friends, every person she meets. Rossner's character, on the other hand, seems a woman predestined to become a victim. In the last line of the novel— *"Help Mommy Daddy Dear God, help me—do it do it do it and get it over w"* —Terry evokes persons and forces outside herself, asking that her killer just get it over with. Despite the sympathy viewers may have for Terry, few women would want to identify with someone who seems to have brought on her own death.

7.

NOVELS, movies, and the popular prejudice that victims are responsible for their fate have influenced the criminologists, lawyers, and psychiatrists who have recently founded an academic discipline known as victimology, or the study of the victim.

Many victimologists have accepted and perpetuated the anti-victim prejudices of most novelists. In strict etymological terms, victimology should mean "the study of the victim," Instead, the subdiscipline began with narrower goals: the contribution of the victim to the criminal act. Over the years this relationship has been described variously as "the penal couple," "the duet frame of crime," and "victim-precipitated criminal homicide." The initial "victim-blame" school of victimology has had a great impact on the theories of popular writers and scholars in other disciplines. It was not until the 1970s, when psychiatrists, sociologists, and other social scientists joined the criminologists, that victimology was stretched to its broader and more neutral definition.

The credit for "founding" the study of the victim is usually given to Beniamin Mendelsohn, a Romanian attorney who now lives in Israel, or to the late Hans von Hentig, who fled to the United States from his native Germany during the 1940s. Mendelsohn's first study on victimology was published in a Belgian criminology journal in 1937; von Hentig's appeared in an American journal four years later.

The Mendelsohn article was based on the results of a survey that he made among criminals, their families, and their victims. The results convinced him that the personality of the victim was crucial in attracting the criminal. In an article published three years later, "Rape in Criminology," Mendelsohn stressed such factors as the "extent to which the woman is able to resist rape." He argued that the victim's behavior and her relationship to the accused rapist should be studied seriously and critically since this relationship might be more significant than material evidence in determining the guilt or innocence of the defendant.

Hans von Hentig took a similar approach in his 1941 article, "Remarks on the Interaction of Perpetrator and Victim," in which he wrote, "Possession of money has certainly to do with robbery and prettiness or youth are contributing factors in criminal assaults. ... If there are born criminals, it is evident that there are born victims, self-harming and self-destroying through the medium of a pliable outsider."

Von Hentig also developed victim typologies. One set was for "four perfect murder victims": the depressive, the greedy for gain, the wanton, and the tormentor. The depressive was described as a perfect murder victim because his depressed state made him someone who "lacks ordinary prudence and discretion." As an example, von Hentig cited the case of Guillaume Bemays, a Belgian lawyer who had been lured to an ambush in a deserted house and then slain by the brother of his wife's lover. To support his contention that Bemays was the perfect depressive murder type, von Hentig quoted from a letter the victim had written just before his death in which he "confessed 'his secret longing to withdraw from the world, and ... to live, forgotten by everybody, as a missionary in a far cut-off country where he might be devoured by cannibals or carried away by the yellow fever.' "

Later von Hentig expanded these original four victim categories to thirteen. Among these new "perfect victims" were the young, the old, females, immigrants, minorities, normal people who are "dull," the acquisitive, fighters, and the lonely and the heartbroken. In his classic book on victimology, *The Criminal and His Victim*, von Hentig introduced his influential concept of the "duet frame of crime"—the criminal and his victim. Given the all-encompassing and therefore vague nature of von Hentig's "perfect victim," almost any person could be part of this duet.

The political discrimination in Europe in the 1940s may have had a far greater impact on the formation of victimology than any sociological concepts. The mass victimization of Jews, Catholics, "subversive" academics, and minorities such as Gypsies was soon thrust on all peoples when the world went to war. Unable to stop or control the aggressor—Hitler and his henchmen—people began placing blame on the defenseless victims. In that way the just-world hypothesis was preserved—"I was not a victim because I did not want to be, therefore I do not have to fear being a victim in the future."

An indication of this orientation can be found in a criminology textbook by Professor Walter Reckless:

> *The person, unconsciously forgetful or not, who leaves the keys in the automobile when he parks on the street is inviting automobile theft. The female shopper in the crowded store who absentmindedly leaves her large purse open and dangling on her arm beckons the pickpocket or purse snatcher or tempts an ordi-narily honest person into theft. The scatterbrained person, man or woman, who gives the store clerk a $10 bill in payment, while talking to a friend or being diverted in other ways from the trans-action, tempts the clerk to shortchange him.*

Another casual application of victim precipitation can be found in Morton Hunt's popular book, *The Mugging*. In a section called "The Victimal Behavior of A. Helmer" Hunt argues that Helmer, a murdered mugging victim, was guilty of provoking his death because he bragged about his finances with casual acquaintances and lived in an area "where predators were coming to abound, and . . . where his personal traits marked him out as potential prey."

In 1957 criminologist Marvin E. Wolfgang published an article, "Victim-Precipitated Criminal Homicide," in which he examined 588 consecutive homicides recorded in the files of the Homicide Squad of the Philadelphia Police Department. Of these 588 cases, 150, or 26 percent, were designated *victim-precipitated,* a term Wolfgang was very careful to define as "those criminal homicides in which the victim is a direct, positive precipitator in the crime. . . . The victim is characterized by his having been the first in the homicide drama to use physical force directed against his subsequent slayer . . . the first to commence the interplay or resort to physical violence."

Here are four of the eleven anecdotes that Wolfgang gives as examples of victim-precipitated criminal homicide:

> *A husband accused his wife of giving money to another man, and while she was making breakfast, he attacked her with a milk bottle, then a brick, and finally a piece of concrete block. Having had a butcher knife in hand, she stabbed him during the fight.*

> *During a lover's quarrel, the male (victim) hit his mistress and threw a can of kerosene at her. She retaliated by throwing the liquid on him, and then tossed a lighted match in his direction. He died from the burns.*

> *A drunken husband, beating his wife in their kitchen, gave her a butcher knife and dared her to use it on him. She claimed that if he should strike her once more, she would use the knife, whereupon he slapped her in the face and she fatally stabbed him.*

> *A victim became incensed when his eventual slayer asked for money which the victim owed him. The victim grabbed a hatchet and started in the direction of his creditor, who pulled out a knife and stabbed him.*

In spite of how specific Wolfgang was in showing that the victim had to be the first to employ *physical* force if the homicide were to be considered victim-precipitated, later criminologists, journalists, and police officials loosely applied the term, as in this excerpt from Barbara Gelb's 1975 book *On the Track of Murder:* "The extent of her [the victim's] complicity in her own murder consisted of the kind of harmless vanity anyone might indulge; she went about her daily business somewhat overdressed. Had she refrained from wearing jewelry and driven a less noticeable car on the day she went shopping at Alexander's, Eugene O'Toole probably would have passed her up and waited for a more promising victim." Ostentatious jewelry or a flashy car might be reflections of the victim's taste, but they are hardly suitable provocations for her murder.

Even Wolfgang's finding that one-fourth of the 588 homicides studied were victim-precipitated has been misrepresented. In an article published in August 1976 in the *Washington Post,* the police chief of a large American city wrote that "two-thirds of all murder victims in some manner precipitate their demise and thus are not average, typical citizens."

As the interviews and facts in the next chapter demonstrate, homicide is horrific enough without unnecessarily burdening the families of its victims with half-truths and misplaced blame.

2

The Silenced Victims
(Homicide and Murder)

1.

HIS voice quivered. "My father-in-law died at twelve-thirty today. I just left the morgue."

The caller worked as a security guard in Staten Island. Early the night before, his father-in-law had been walking home from the hospital where he worked and was apparently attacked by muggers. Now his son-in-law was calling a crime victim hot line to ask about crime compensation for his mother-in-law, who still had three children to raise. *I was working on the hot line, and I took the call.* But the caller first need to share about the way his relative had looked in the morgue before we could discuss the crime compensation plan. He said, 'They really did a job on him. Broken collarbone. Cuts on every part of his body. I hardly recognized him."

The death of a homicide victim is never dignified and is almost always unexpected. From the moment they are notified of the tragedy and sum-moned to the morgue to identify the corpse, a victim's family and friends begin to suffer a grief unique to this kind of violent death. They may see the wounds and they may begin imagining the pain.

The visit to the morgue is so traumatic that the Los Angeles coroner's office uses a closed-circuit television system for a victim's family to view the body. But in most other towns and cities, the body is still pulled out of a drawer or rests on a sturdy metal operating table or on a cart that is wheeled over to the family for identification.

As families glimpse the remains of a father, mother, brother, sister, or child, they can see that his or her pain is over. But their pain is just begin-ning. This morgue visit—which may in itself be a haunting vision for years to come—is just the start of months, perhaps a lifetime, of extended grief and suffering.

The families of homicide victims experience a torment that is differ-ent in intensity and kind from that known by people whose relatives have died from natural causes. Studies of the families of terminal cancer patients, families who have usually been able to anticipate their loss, show that their responses to the death are divided into seven stages: (1) rage, anger, and despair immediately after the death; (2) denial of the death; (3) a temporary postponement of feelings because of practical considerations, like funeral arrangements, or by visits from relatives or friends; (4) after the funeral, a sudden return of feelings of emptiness, abandonment, and isolation with an accompanying need to share anecdotes about the deceased as a way of overcoming shock and grief and building a gradual acceptance of the death; (5) resolution of grief; (6) a long period of mourning; (7) an acceptance of the death.

The family of a homicide victim usually experiences the first three stages of grief as do the survivors of terminal cancer patients. The length of time each family member spends at a particular stage will differ, depending on his or her relationship to the victim as well as each survivor's own emotional makeup, including how separation and loss are handled in general. But for the homicide-family, each of those three stages is intensified because of the violence that accompanied the death.

It is in the fourth stage—after the funeral—that victim families begin to differ radically from other mourners. The feelings of abandonment and aloneness are the same, but the shock of murder may perpetuate a denial of the death. Furthermore, the family may feel guilty for having failed to protect the victim from being murdered, and that guilt, however unfounded, may cause them to avoid sharing anecdotes about the life of the victim, reminiscences that may offer strength and comfort. Outsiders may discourage talk about the victim to avoid facing the possibility that they, too, might be as vulnerable or unlucky. Since some of the ways to overcome after-funeral emptiness are closed to the homicide-family, they often take much longer to reach the final stages of mourning—resolution of grief and the acceptance of death.

Sadly, some never reach these stages. Instead, years later, they are still disturbed by the crime. Their worst fears about the possibility of becoming a victim have been fulfilled, and their own vulnerability to violence and even murder have been reinforced:

After Hope, my nineteen-year-old sister, was killed, my parents became more protective of my younger sister, brother, and me. I was sixteen when it happened. Whenever I go off on a long trip, my father will say, half-jokingly, "Don't get yourself killed."

For the first few years, I just suppressed Hope's death. But when I was in Israel about a year and a half ago—I don't know if you'd call this dealing with it—I said, "She's dead. It's finished business. Life goes on." I wasn't going to worry about it anymore. But still, I might feel better if I cleared up some of the loose ends about the events.

One thing that sort of lingers is an increased sense of your own mortality. That you could die anytime. It probably makes me more cautious than I would be, but it's hard to say if that's bad or not.

In the months and years after the death, families of homicide victims must cope with a conflict between their desire for revenge against the murderer and a concerted effort to understand the possible social and economic conditions that are deemed responsible for the slaying. Often they mentally replay the killing over and over, substituting themselves for the victim as a way of shar-ing his or her final moments. They may also fantasize a different outcome of the crime, one in which their loved one escapes.

Too often the funeral is the only organized memorial service for murder victims; even in death, many are denied their due. Yet most families of homicide victims are in such shock, and have still not accepted the death at the funeral, that even the most supportive comments are forgotten. When a second post-funeral tribute is arranged by the family or friends of the victim, the family of the homicide victim, what we now refer to as secondary victims of homicide, or as homicide survivors, may find the grieving period is aided by this tribute which reaffirms that their loved one, who has died in such a violent way, is not forgotten. The funeral marked the victim's death; a later requiem applauds and celebrates that victim's life.

For the secondary victims of homicide, the funeral service may be the least distasteful of the numerous legal public procedures that unintentionally keep the focus on the victim's death. Even if the family wishes to ignore that a relative was murdered, the coroner, police, district attorney's office, and perhaps the newspapers will not. If the crime is never solved, the autopsy and legal work may still be upsetting to the family. If a suspect is apprehended, and there is a trial, the member of the family who identified the body may have to testify to that fact in court. If the mourner was also an eyewitness to the crime, the grisly details may need to be retold for the jury. The stoicism with which many survivors brave these post-murder formalities may be misinterpreted by friends and employers as a sign that they are past mourning. Instead, their suspended disbelief may dissolve a month or a year later into belated grieving.

Gloria knew her killer. She had opened her apartment door to him because he was the son of her best friend, who was also her upstairs neighbor. But the twenty-one-year-old youth, a married man with a one-year-old child, wanted more than just a friendly visit. He wanted Gloria to make love to the male companion that he had brought along that afternoon. He would watch them.

According to the murderer's taped confession, Gloria refused his request. "I'm not even going to call the police," Gloria said. "I'm just going to tell your mother."

Immediately upon hearing the word *mother*, the youth flew into a rage, pulled out a knife, and proceeded to stab Gloria again and again in cadence with his rantings: "Don't tell my mother! Don't tell my mother!" Gloria's' youngest daughter, who was then six years old and was in the bedroom, became frightened and ran into the corner. The murderer and his friend followed her and callously proceeded to eliminate the only witness. When Gloria and her child were found by the police, their bodies had been pierced by over two hundred stab wounds. Even their eyelids had been cut off.

The murderer and his accomplice were arrested. They both confessed, and although the friend said he had only held the victims, the murderer stated he had also joined in the stabbings.

Two years later Gloria's mother was unable to talk about the killings. Gloria's brother Paul and her sister Lorraine could; they were both still enraged and preoccupied with the murders. The murders had altered Lorraine's daily routine. Unable to walk home from the subway alone, every night she went directly from the train to the nearby police station and requested that an officer escort her to her apartment door. If Lorraine was expecting a visitor, even if the guest had called from the lobby of her building and she had identified him or her through the peephole of her front door, she was cautious and fearful upon opening it.

Lorraine knew that although these precautions might help *her*, they would not have saved her sister since her sister's murder showed that avoiding strangers could not prevent the unpredictable attack by an acquaintance. Now Lorraine was wary of her friends as well and seldom visited them:

LORRAINE: I kept hoping I would wake up and find out it was all a bad dream. But when I got to the project where she lived and I saw all the police cars and emergency vehicles, I knew it was the real thing.

I'll never forget that odor. I still have problems today, after two years, over that blood-soaked apartment.

My [estranged] father called that night—I didn't even know he had my number—and he said he thought they probably killed the little girl so she couldn't identify them.

What gets me is that the guy that killed Gloria had the nerve to pretend that he discovered the body, and then to ask me to diaper his baby because he was too upset about Gloria's murder. But they had his voice on 911, and they got the confession on tape. At five o'clock that next morning, when I heard that he had confessed, I thought, "He's got his damn nerve. He walked around this house saying how sorry he was, and how this, and how that."

Luckily, I didn't go to the morgue to view the body. My mother wanted to go, so we let her, but she broke down when she saw her. Gloria was so mutilated around the face and you could see where they had stitched up her neck. When we went to clear out her apartment, there was still blood all over the place. That is cruel. It's like staring you in the face.

You kill one person, that's one thing. But if you kill two people, that's another. I mean, where do you go from up? His sentence is twenty-five years, but he'll probably be out in seven. Yes, I believe in capital punishment when there is not a shadow of a doubt whether that person has committed the crime, particularly the crime of taking a person's life, and if the criminal's asocial. The way it is now, you put them in jail, and you can't kill them; then they come out, do it again, and you still can't kill them.

PAUL: Go to any other country and you find that violent crimes are *not* socially acceptable. But we're geared from youth, all the way up the line, that violence *is* socially acceptable, I know guys who are from the West Indies, and they say that if you commit murder there, you *know* that your ass is grass—you know that you're going to be killed. No ifs, ands, or buts. In return, there aren't as many murders in the West Indies.

But there are different kinds of murders. If you rob someone and the guy dies of a heart attack while you're robbing him, that's one thing. But if you break into somebody's house just to rob and kill them, that's a whole different thing.

LORRAINE: There's always been a lot of murder, it's just that there's better reporting now. That very summer day in 1974 [when Gloria was murdered], there was another murder. But that was a white woman who was found on the roof of a downtown apartment house. They gave full coverage to *her* life, *her* murder, *her* funeral; they just gave one line to my sister. I must have heard about that other murder every three minutes on the radio station.

PAUL: Just to show you how the media works—a black man had quintuplets in Chicago a few weeks ago and *his* wife had them naturally, but he didn't get anything. A white guy had them down in Florida, and *he* got a house. I bet you didn't even hear about the Chicago births. Likewise, murder on a poor level is one thing, murder on a rich level is something else again.

The society is geared so that it's all okay; he's still my son, no matter what he does. Whereas in other cultures, there's no way that certain crimes are tolerated. Maybe [he shouldn't be] in the society, even if he *is* your child.

LORRAINE: It's a good thing my other niece was away at camp or they probably would have killed her too. She's ten years old and she's just coming out of shock now. But she's been behaving with the classic symptoms of the grieving child—poor attention span, fearful if my mother leaves her alone in the house. She's a very frail child and small for her age; I'm afraid she may also be emotionally fixated at this particular age because of the shock. I've even tried to talk my mother into getting her into therapy so she can scream and shout about it if she likes, She asks my mother, "Who killed my mother?" My mother says, "I'll tell you when you're older." Or she'll say to Paul, "Your mommy's alive and mine is dead. That's not fair." She remembers different times; so you talk to her, and let her remember.

As a footnote to this, I had to go into therapy. I just didn't know how you could take a life. So I asked the shrink, "How long does it take to cut somebody that many times?" He said, "Oh, about twenty minutes. Maybe a half-hour." So I said, "Twenty minutes to a half-hour! Your rage should have left you by then!" Then he said, "If he were in my country in South America, the trial would have been the week after the murder and he would have been executed the next week."

The part of Gloria's death that is hardest to take is that we were getting closer; now I'll never know what's it's like to have a close sister. I'm also more afraid, that's for sure. I won't even get into the elevator with a man. It's made me more distrustful of men; after all, Gloria knew him. I used to trust few men; now I trust even fewer.

The murder's affected my son, too. He's afraid that I might not come home some day. "Mommy, is Aunt Gloria a dead old piece of meat?" he asked me one day. I told him that we shouldn't think of Gloria like that. My daughter started talking about having dreams that there was blood in the hallway.

PAUL: How did Gloria's murder affect me? I reevaluated my life for the second time; the first time was when was in Vietnam. Vietnam taught me about killing, but it wasn't so much that I was killing them, but that they were shooting at me. I was up near the DM2, flying air missions, so I had my taste of the "funs." I didn't really want to shoot at them and I didn't fire until I *took* fire, regardless of what they instructed us to do. But before this happened, I thought "that" was over there and "this" was back here. Now I realize there is no difference.

There's no way I can justify what he did. I've seen people die, and I've seen different ways of killing, and the method he chose was unjustifiable.

> That's why I don't think he has the right to live.
> When you take a life, you violate the victim's rights.
> No one cares about the person who is killed in this
> country, or about their rights.
>
> But now I don't take life too seriously. Instead I
> escape by reading science fiction. I'm not too quick
> to open my door now, and when I do, I'm expect-
> ing something.

LORRAINE: They say time heals all wounds, but I doubt it.

Paul and Lorraine, like so many other secondary victims of homicide, have not resolved their guilt, fear, grief, and anger. Lorraine is still fixated on the image and memory of Gloria's mutilated body. She finds it incomprehensible how long the killer took to stab Gloria and her daughter. Paul is still angry about the leniency of the murderer's punishment, and that America seems as filled with killing as Vietnam had been. Two years has not been long enough for Gloria's surviving daughter, sister, brother, mother, nephews, and nieces to come to terms with the murder. But these victims are never tabulated. As Lorraine said, time may never heal her family's wounds. The absence of personal vengeance or suitable compensation to their family has made it that much more improbable that their anger and grief will ever be resolved. Death by homicide seems to be one death a family can *never* accept.

Despite these insurmountable difficulties, most survivors force them-selves to live in the present. They may try to "right the wrong" as a way of coping with the psychological effects of the murder. Homicide-family mem-bers may campaign for gun control legislation, join groups trying to reform the criminal justice system, or petition for the rights of crime victims. Peter Schneider, a Manhattan attorney, did just that when he and two other homi-cide-family members started Citizens Crusade Against Crime. The organi-zation is "an elitist group," explains Schneider. "You have to be a victim to become a member." Unfortunately, in September 1971, his family became eligible when his brother Seymour, an auto dealer in the Bronx, was robbed and then shot to death in his office. "You're aware of crime all the time but [it's] only when it hits home that you're likely to try to do something about it. I'd been familiar with criminal law and criminal procedure—although

I don't engage in a criminal practice—for many, many years, but it took something like this to get me to think of the obligations we all have, and that we neglect until it's too late. The victim's survivors are very lonely people. There isn't anybody to pay attention to them."

Other victims find strength in taking karate courses, buying and carrying a gun, moving to a different city or country from that where the crime occurred. A man whose friend was murdered in Manhattan says, "I made up my mind the very day I got the news that I could live in New York no longer." But many homicide-families are unable to direct their grief and rage into positive activities. They slip into fantasy, planning revenge if they were to find the killer or inventing confrontations in which they "save" the criminal by showing him what he did wrong. Often they obsessively recriminate themselves with "if only." "If only he had told me he was going out alone that night, I would have joined him and together we would have fought off those bastards." A homicide victim's survivors may have regrets unrelated to the actual murder, but about the suddenly ended close relationship. A friend of homicide-parents writes, "If only they [his parents] could talk to him just once more and tell him how unreasonable they had been. Even though they have two other children and two grandsons, nothing, they say, will ever compensate for the loss of their son." She notes that the slain boy's mother said, "Though it doesn't surface as often as it did at first, there are times when we still ask 'why?' and then the tears come."

Whether or not the murderer has been apprehended, a victim's survivors may revisit the scene of the crime in hope of the criminal's return or to imagine what actually happened. Others may have the opposite reaction: they may never be able to go near the scene of the murder. One woman who moved to another state a few months after her husband's murder cannot feel comfortable visiting the city where the crime took place. After six years, when she finally did visit a friend about half a mile from the killing, it precipitated an irrational burst of hysteria necessitating sedation and her prompt return home. Years after the crime, some survivors may continue offering rewards for any pertinent information about the case. If they can afford to, some families hire private investigators with the hope of finding out who committed the crime and why. Many victim families believe it is impossible to overcome their grief until the killer is caught. One out of every four homicide families will never know *who* did it; none of the survivors will ever really know *why*.

Susan Fisher was a twenty-seven-year-old psychologist employed at a New York State psychiatric institution for offenders who were undergoing evaluation before being tried or "doing their time" in the hospital in place of jail. One Saturday, Susan was beaten to death in her Westchester County apartment. Sal, her suspected killer, vanished, but soon turned up in a Texas prison on another charge. Before the two sets of fingerprints were matched, he fled to Mexico.

The suspect had been one of Susan's patients, a young man in his mid-twenties who had confessed to murdering his fiancée three years before. Although committed by the court, Sal often left the hospital, unnoticed. He also frequently called Susan at her home. Allegedly, Sal beat Susan to death because she refused to see him that weekend since she already had plans to go boating. Her parents relate what they have been able to reconstruct:

MRS. FISHER: We were the ones that found her in her apartment. When she didn't call Saturday, I figured that she was away on that boat trip. But Sunday she didn't call either. Susan usually called Sunday evening, even if she was away. So I called again and there was no answer. I called later and there was still no answer. I felt apprehensive. Monday morning we got up early, and called again, and there was no answer. I knew then that something was very wrong. I waited until she should have been at work; I called there and she hadn't shown up. I just knew then that she was dead.

The superintendent opened the door and we went right in. We called the police. They came and they were very nice and very, very sympathetic and cooperative. I can't say enough for the local police.

The place had been wiped clean. They couldn't even find Susan's fingerprints, but I believe they have two of his—one on the mirror and one on the coffee table. The last person who saw her was a young man [in her apartment house] on Friday night. . . . He said that Sal was in the elevator with her. I believe that he was the last person who saw her. And her car was gone.

MR. FISHER: They found her car a week later and they found his fingerprints in the car. They're sure Sal was there [in her apartment], but he could always say that when he left the apartment, she was fine. The problem now is finding him. He has relatives in this country; he has a brother down south. According to some information from a friend of his, his brother wanted him to get out of the country.

MRS. FISHER: This is what's so frustrating. I was certain of one thing— that Sal was not in Westchester. I would have staked my life on that. But all the local police could do was to try to contact whatever contacts they had in New York City. . . . And they did, but it seems so asinine to me to think that they had been stationed in the town where she lived when that was the last place on earth this man was going to be. Sal had no connection [there] except Susan, and he certainly was not going to be sitting around.

MR. FISHER: The next Tuesday, the Daily News published Susan's picture. They should have published his picture; they knew where Susan was. We did go into Manhattan ourselves and ride around. But everyone looked alike. Suppose we did see him. What would we do? Would Sal recognize us? He probably would, since Susan had brought him to our house one weekend. The next thing, we'd be dead, You know, it's a fear-type thing. But we thought, "Well, maybe well see this Argentine restaurant that he once worked in somewhere over on Eighth Avenue." We also tried the YMCA.

MRS. FISHER: As soon as it happened, we had asked about offering a reward. But the police said, "Wait a little while," Finally they said, "Well, yes, if you want to." We thought, "Well, certainly a lot of people will tell for a price. They'll do just about anything for money," but this brought nothing. Not a single thing. And we hoped this would be the clincher to get the FBI in on this. We said, "Isn't there anyone in New York City who wants this five thousand dollars?" Your first thought is, "Get him, oh, get him."

We called the police every day. They were down here a few times each week. They told us every single thing that happened as it happened—different leads they had called, and what happened when they went to New York. In fact, soon after Susan, the uncle of one of the detectives was killed by someone robbing his apartment. He also had a niece killed shortly after that. So he knew what it is to be personally involved from the other side.

MR. FISHER: When you start thinking it through you realize Sal *is* insane. You just don't kill two young girls who may have told you "I don't want you as a boyfriend" or something. You don't kill them unless you are insane. So I am convinced that Sal is a charming young man who usually acts very rational, and a terrific conversationalist who speaks five languages, but at some point you would have to call him a psychotic killer or something.

MRS. FISHER: Sal may have committed the act, but he is insane. The person who was responsible for it happening was the head of the psychiatric hospital [whose job it was to make sure none of the violent patients left], and to my knowledge he was never relieved of his position.

Eighteen-year-old Leslie was bicycling in New York's Central Park when a teenage youth struck her on the side of the head with a golf club and stole her ten-speed bicycle. Two days later, she died from the head wounds.

Leslie's murder received extensive press and television coverage. She was the kind of victim who generally receives attention; a white, upper-middle-class, young, single woman. Her mother, Tracy, was a high-powered administrator for a cultural organization. There were four other children in Leslie's family, an older sister, Karen, and three stepchildren from Tracy's husband's previous marriage.

The following interviews with Tracy and Karen show how victim families try to cope with murder and how they are often haunted by guilt and fear.

TRACY: I was out of the office having lunch with one of my oldest and dearest friends when I got a call from one of my staff members at the restaurant that said Leslie had had an accident, but she didn't think it was serious. I jumped in a cab and went right up to the hospital. At that point Leslie was still conscious. The doctor told me what had happened, and that they would have to operate, which they did later that evening. The doctor said she was fine now. Leslie said she was in pain. She was still conscious, but unaware of what had happened to her.

The next day Leslie was okay, but the following morning she had a seizure; that was the end. As a matter of fact, I went to see the doctor recently because after many months I still haven't been given a satisfactory explanation of what really happened. He doesn't really know either. He said that as a side effect of the brain concussion caused by the golf club, the hypothalamus was malfunctioning, so she absorbed water to the point where the pressure may have destroyed the cells. Whether or not this is a logical explanation, I don't know. We sent the records to a friend of ours who is a diagnostician; he said there was nothing that could have been done that was not done.

Those were days of real terror, but the one thing that drives me bats is that I went back to the office and sat there thinking that she was going to be fine, but she wasn't. Why didn't I call in a consulting doctor! I said to the doctor, "She's going to be all right, isn't she?" "She'll be out of here in ten days," he said. "She'll be able to go to Europe by the end of the summer. She'll have to get a wig, but she'll be a big shot when she starts college in the fall." He was making jokes, so I guess even he was taken completely by surprise by what happened. But now I realize that you're at their mercy. You really have to expect the worst and bring in every big gun you can think of.

I think if Leslie had been killed instantly, I would not have felt I had any control of the situation. But once I became involved, I can't help but feel that there may be something I left undone, or something that could have been done. I guess to some extent that will always bother me.

My husband says, "You're sitting here, blaming yourself. Why don't you blame the kid who did it?" That's an interesting thing because when the fifteen-year-old was sentenced, a newspaper reporter called me at ten-thirty at night to ask what my reaction was to his [sentence of] eighteen months in a treatment center, with weekends at home. I said I would see the district attorney the next day before I made any comments. The prosecuting attorney was very surprised that I seemed able to accept the sentence, as if I should have wanted him strung up. But I just can't think in those terms. Then I experienced the same reaction when another reporter called; little by little I began to feel that maybe the sentence *is* insane.

We were brought up as liberals, but maybe there is a time when it just doesn't work anymore. My feelings have changed considerably over the past few months; I've begun to feel that there comes a point when you realize there *is* no excuse.

Leslie and I had an idyllic relationship. She was a very independent person and we just had a good, secure, respectful rapport with each other. She was a very private person with a great many friends and interests. She had so much going on; she was a potter as well as a musician. She kept remarkable journals. There was little she did not do beautifully. Leslie was expert on the bicycle; since the age of fourteen she had taken bike trips throughout Canada and Vermont. Even though she was only five feet tall, she was very strong and capable.

At night, when I take the subway home, I look at the people in the car and I think, "All these people are alive and she's dead." Where I live, downtown, the worst possible dregs of humanity are walking the streets and I wonder if it's not a matter of justice, [then] why does this happen? But that doesn't resolve anything either, and I just get more frustrated.

Are there any solutions? The judge and the police said that the murderer seemed to be remorseful after the crime and that was why they gave him the sentence that they did. Whether he was conning them or not, I don't know. I've thought of trying to meet him, but I don't think I'm ready for that yet. This particular boy did not come from the ghetto; he had a relatively secure situation and we were told his home environment is more middle class than impoverished. It's a very difficult and frustrating question [about capital punishment], because you don't want to advocate cruel and inhumane treatment of anyone, and yet they're committing cruel and inhumane treatment on others.

I guess I used to always feel very sorry for anyone that had to go to prison. I thought that was just terrible. I also thought a criminal did something because there was reason for it— usually poverty or deprivation. But now I look at people differently. No matter what, there is no excuse for them behaving the way they do. Deprivation is no reason for them to murder or harm other people and they should be punished for it. What I wrote in my letter to the editor is that a fifteen-year-old is more protected than the victim. He or she has the security of knowing only a sentence up to three years can be given. But I don't know if it would be more effective if we chop off their hands, put them in jail for twenty-five years, or publicly whip them.

How did people react to the tragedy? One of the most interesting things I found was that many, many people, particularly men, couldn't talk about it. I came back to work almost immediately; I have a very close staff and they practically sat shivah* with me. But those in the other parts of the building found it very hard to talk to me. I sort of had to help them over the bridge and to provide them with a sense of what they could say. I soon realized that many of my acquaintances were avoiding me. It made me uncomfortable. I had the feeling that people looked, and still look, at me very differently.

---

* *Shiva* is the mourning period observed by Jews after the death of a close relative. The family spends the first week after the funeral at home, receiving relatives and friends.

Perhaps I'm paranoid, but I think people I don't know very well are always conscious of Leslie's murder. People don't want to associate themselves with tragedy. Also, I think part of it is just not knowing how to deal with it and being afraid of saying the wrong thing.

At the time of Leslie's murder her sister Karen was attending a prestigious women's college in the New York metropolitan area. She had transferred from a midwestern school because she missed the city, her family, and her friends. She still lives in New York, but she shares her tiny apartment with a huge guard dog; she is also surrounded with her sister's photographs and personal possessions. As with Gloria's brother Paul, Karen's life and her philosophy have been changed by the murder. A year and a half later she is still enraged at her sister's killer and, aware now of her own vulnerability, is taking self-defense classes:

KAREN: Most of my time is taken up studying karate. I started it about five months ago, and it takes more time than school. But I commute back and forth around ten o'clock at night, so it seemed a sensible skill to have. Just last night I saw a purse snatching across the street. It happened too quickly for me to get there to help, but I looked out the window and several neighbors were there assisting in a flash. I had never witnessed anything like that before and it was a good experience.

              I grew up in the city. I never experienced any fear or un-settledness about it. We moved here when I was twelve from a suburb in New Jersey. I found the city kids much sharper and more aware of what was going on. I knew my way around the neighborhood and I was always out alone, it used to worry Mom a lot, but I could never understand why she worried. Now I do. It's scary.

Right before Leslie was killed, I had been planning to get my own apartment, but afterwards I stayed home for a few months. I just moved in recently; it's working out okay. My older stepbrother lives right upstairs, and that helps.

Leslie and I were close, even though our interests were pretty far apart. She had her music and ceramics and I had my papers and books. But we were always intertwined, whether we wanted to be or not, since there was little or no privacy. We got along well even though we beat each other up every now and then, the way sisters do.

Do I find I think about it less as time goes on? *No! I* mean, her picture's over there. I think about her all the time, I don't want to think of her any Sess. I don't. I'm not as weepy as I was before, though when she was killed I felt I had to hold it in because everyone else was crying and screaming. But that passed. I cracked up a bit but it's getting better. When people say, "Remember when you and Leslie and I got together?" I don't get upset now. They're good memories, I do think about what Leslie would be doing now. My brother's girlfriend goes to the college where Leslie was to go and I ran into an old classmate of hers from school and she's going there, too, and I say, "Oh my God, they would have had so much fun together." But it's evening out now and normalizing. In a few months it will be a year since she died. . . . The one thing I keep thinking is that Leslie will always be eighteen. And she'll always look like that picture over there.

I was at camp when I first got the news, but she seemed to be okay, so I took the train down a few days later. When I saw her in the hospital, it looked like a scene from one of those television shows with all the tubes coming out of her head. That shook me up more than anything else because it was all so surreal. But when I saw Leslie, I knew it was really so and that it was bad. At the same time, I knew I had to go back to work because I just couldn't sit around. Mom was making arrangements for organ transplanta, and she didn't need me at that point. So that day I went back to work in the country. They unplugged her as I was on my way back to camp, The whole summer was basically a void after that.

I didn't go to the cremation, but afterwards we had a party. All her friends were there and they played the kind of music that she would have liked to have heard. It was great; almost like an Irish wake because Irish music was *her* music. Everyone got drunk and cried and did whatever they wanted to do. It wasn't strained or formal; it was just a letting go. I got to meet some of Leslie's friends I hadn't met before. It was just a general getting together and rejoicing at what Leslie liked to do. Then we took her ashes to some property that we own in upstate New York and we buried them and planted a tree in that spot. I go and visit it whenever I can. I was up there in January, but it's pretty far away and I don't have a car.

The worst part of the whole thing was that they wouldn't give me her bicycle. I had to go down to the prosecutor's office and the receptionist said it was Sidney's [her murderer's] bicycle. I screamed, "Give me that bicycle. It's my sister's bicycle. He stole it from her." I had to go out to a warehouse in Queens to finally get it. I keep it at a friend's in the country; Mom doesn't want to ever see it again. But I feel Leslie would have wanted me to ride it.

I found myself more prejudiced against blacks since Leslie's murder, especially blacks on ten-speed bicycles. It bothers me, but I can't help it. I don't know what to do about it, and I hope in time the situation changes. I haven't been in Central Park since this happened either. I don't think it's worth it. It's really not worth the pain. I don't think you can ever really understand unless you've lost someone, and losing someone like that is something I hope no one else has to understand. It's a terrible revelation that things happen like that.

I'd just like to see the boy [who did it] to see what he looked like physically. I don't even know if I could say anything to him. He certainly didn't have any feelings toward me and he probably didn't even see Leslie's face. I don't know what I'd say to him. . . . There was a point when I would have said that I would kill him, but the grief is stronger than the anger. I will probably always feel frustration. I will never understand why someone did such a stupid, needless, pointless thing.

Homicide-families often feel responsible for the murder. In particular, the parents of a homicide victim believe that there must have been something they could have done to protect their children. As Leslie's mother said, "I can't help feeling that there may be something I left undone or something that could have been done." Again and again one hears phrases such as, "I don't care if he said he was my son's friend, she shouldn't have opened the door," "I told her Central Park was dangerous," "I should have taught her to defend herself so she could have killed him before he got her."

Brothers and sisters of the victim echo their parents' guilt, particularly if they believed that the murdered sibling was more favored or talented. Many ask, "Why wasn't it me instead?" They also feel responsible if the victim faced the murderer alone. "If I'd been there she would be alive today" is a frequent lament. Practically all siblings and parents are troubled by the certainty that the death was avoidable. But most siblings do not have the chance to share their feelings, especially if they are still in their formative years, since the parents are also grieving and unable to provide much-needed support.

The mother of a homicide victim recounts: "Our son is eleven. He doesn't talk about it. Our other daughter, Sally, will be seventeen. Kathy [the murder victim] and Sally were very close and I think it was extremely difficult for Sally." The victim's father added: "I don't think we realized in the beginning because Sally seemed to take it so well. She seemed to be pretty together about it. We realized after a while she probably was putting on a lot of it because she didn't want to upset us."

A spouse may feel the guilt most acutely. Spouses who later remarry report that they reflect upon the past or speculate about what their lives would have been like had the victim lived more than those who remarry after the natural death of a partner. Untimely, unforeseen, unprepared. The spouse does not just have the occasional companionship of a friend cut off, but the routine of an everyday partner and integral family member. As with countless primary burglary and rape victims, the secondary homicide victim, the spouse, may immediately move—to another apartment, to another city. Therapy may sometimes be necessary to resolve the deep, often incapacitating guilt stemming from the murder.

One widow was upset by newspaper reports that followed her husband's murder, as her fight to get financial reimbursement for the $6,000 in funeral and legal costs looked as though she was "getting money out of his death. But I make less than five hundred dollars a month and needed Bill's salary to cover our basic expenses. Bill always wanted to be famous and it's weird that it all came about on his death. Two hours after the funeral, the TV reporters came over." Her guilt over her husband's death becomes apparent in her constant apologies for trying to go on with her own life. A year after the murder, she said, "Why should I keep suffering from all this? I believe in life and creativity, not the other way around. *I* didn't kill anyone. *Death Wish* was a fantastic movie. Sometimes when *you* take the law into your own hands, that's when people respect you. I still sometimes think I see Bill coming across the street...."

2.

A prison inmate writes:

> *The Death Row of today is not the dark, dingy, dungeon type of place that one might imagine. There are televisions provided, radios built into the individual cells and all areas are brightly lit.*
>
> *The food is not what you would expect either. Milk is served with all meals. The meals are arranged so that they fill most of a person's basic needs. What is not served at meal time can be purchased through the commissary, including soft drinks, snacks, canned food, candy and all writing material imaginable.*

Throughout history, capital punishment has been debated. Opinions are sharply divided: "We can't invest in society a respect for human life by taking life," said former California Governor Edmund G. Brown. "Society has a right to protect itself against cruel and unusual crimes. Especially crimes like murder and rape. The alternative is life imprisonment. But isn't it cruel to lock up a social animal for life?" asks North Carolina Deputy Attorney General Jean Benoy.

Since 1960 over 200,000 Americans have been murdered. During the same time 192 persons were executed.

What positions on capital punishment do families of homicide victims generally take? Quantitative studies have not yet been done, as they have for the general population. (Of two hundred adults in an eastern city interviewed in 1976 by political scientist Austin Sarat and psychologist Neil Vidmar, 54 percent favored capital punishment, 33 percent were opposed, and 13 percent were undecided.) But interviews with families of homicide victims reveal three general positions: (1) they want the death penalty as a consistent punishment for all murderers; (2) they want the death penalty solely as punishment for the killer of *their* relative; or (3) they cannot endorse the death penalty as punishment for murder under any circumstances. It is this third group that is usually the most troubled. They are torn between ideological and moral condemnation of capital punishment and their personal wish for revenge.

The mother of a twenty-three-year-old "old-fashioned girl who didn't smoke or drink," who was murdered in 1974 and whose killer has never been found, said: "The death penalty is the only fair sentence. Probably it is the only deterrent. But it seems so hopeless. So many cases go unsolved. What can we do? What can we do? My daughter was the most unlikely victim."

A professional man who considered himself to be politically liberal became vehement in his endorsement of capital punishment after his only son was killed:

> I'm only talking about murders that are committed in the course of a robbery or premeditated murder, not self-defense killings. But we've got to get a deterrent so that people know they won't get away with murder. If it deters just one other person from killing someone, I'm in favor of it. Look at these sixteen-year-old creeps that just killed that elderly couple in Brooklyn. What do you think they'll get? The biggest rise in crime is amongst your juveniles. You can't treat a thirteen-year-old like a child if her or she commits an adult crime. If the so-called capital crimes are on the rise, they have to be punished in a capital way.

The father of another homicide victim expressed an opposing view:

> I don't think capital punishment changes anything. If I thought it would change anything, I would believe in it, but I don't think it changes anything. It's almost like a revenge. What I would rather see is society head for something—we're far from civilization. We have all the amenities—sewing and washing machines and all those magic things—but as far as improving humanity is concerned, we're not doing it that well. I would rather see our facilities and our resources headed toward solving this many-faceted problem. You've got to have speedier trials, more judges; just everything is antiquated. And I think this is what has to be changed.

His wife disagreed:

> I wouldn't mind if they killed him [their daughter's murderer], I don't think he's going to be any good to society anyway. There's no rehabilitation.

The mother of a homicide victim expressed another justification for the death penalty:

> Instead of spending money on supposedly rehabilitating these criminals, let's take that money to help the victims and aid the victims in restoring their lives. If you have that disease in a body, you don't let the cancer grow rampant so it kills the good tissue. Those killers are killing society.

If you don't want to kill them, expel them. Throw them out of the United States. Send them to a place like Devil's Island.

3.

IN just ten years homicide has become the twelfth leading cause of death for white Americans; the fifth leading cause of death for nonwhite males; and the eighth for nonwhite females. After accidents and suicide, murder is now America's third leading cause of unnatural deaths. In 1975 it was estimated that one out of every two hundred persons—"over the course of a normal life span"— would die at the hands of a murderer.

The chances of getting killed in Houston or Los Angeles are greater than in other cities around the world with the same populations. The following 2021 statistics indicate the number of homicide victims in comparably populated cities. Sources: Josiah Bates, "These Major Cities Reported the Highest Homicide Rates in 2021", Time, October 19, 2022 and "Homicide in Canada, 2021" by Jean-Denis Davis and Brianna Jaffray, Canadian Centre for Justice and Community Safety Statistics, 11/21/22; "Crosstown" Jon Regardie, 1/10/22, "Statista;"

Population: 6.5 to 7 million or more

Los Angeles	Tokyo*	London
397	260	124

Population: 1-2 million

Houston   Stockholm

464   41

Perhaps the extent of violence in the United States, which has been called "as American as apple pie," is best seen by contrasting the U.S. homicide rate with Canada's. In the United States in 2021 the rate for murder was 6.9 murder victims for every 100,000 persons; in the same year, the murder rate in Canada was 2.06 murder victims for every 100,000 Canadians.

A person is almost as likely to be a homicide victim in an American city with a population of over 250,000 than in Belfast or any other city in Northern Ireland—even during the peak years of fighting there, 1968 to 1974. During that bloody six-year period an average of 8.8 out of every 100,000 residents of Northern Ireland were killed. In 2021 in Atlanta, 20.2 of every 100,000 residents were murdered; in San Antonio, Texas, 11.15; Chicago, 29.6; and in Jackson, Mississippi, a shocking 100. It would have been safer to be in London during the blitz—between 1940 and 1945 when 21.7 of every 100,000 Britons were killed in German air raids— than in Jackson, Mississippi or Chicago, Illinois in 2021.

Murder touches the poor and the rich, the anonymous and the famous. The list of celebrities murdered in recent years reads like a *Who's Who*: tele-vision actress Barbara Colby, shot by two robbers in a Hollywood parking lot; the former managing editor of *Holiday* Magazine, beaten to death near San Diego; movie star Sharon Tate, knifed; newspaper heir John Knight III, beaten and stabbed in his Philadelphia apartment. But if most homicide victims are less glamorous than those recognizable names, the contributions they might have made are just as noteworthy. The largest concentration of homicide victims is in the sixteen- to thirty-year-old range—the prime years.

Homicide is a crime dominated by men killing other men, although women are victims too. In 2018, there were 10,914 male murder victims and 3,180 who were female. That year, more Blacks were murdered (7,407) compared to Whites (6,088). Remember that Blacks only make up 12.1% of the population in the U.S. In 2018, firearms were used in 72.7% of the murders. There were

2,819 victims under the age of 18 that year; 12,855 were 18 and over.

In 2018, you were more likely to get killed by an acquaintance (2,592), followed by a family member (1,859), but close behind was the likelihood that the perpetrator was a stranger (1,392). Remember, however, that there are an astonishing 6,808 murders that year where the victim-offender relationship was unknown. So those victim-offender relationships could look quite different if we learn what those relationships were. (J Yager, *Essentials of Victimology*, Aspen, 2022, pages 252-253)

We have learned that homicide happens to all social classes. The poor may be targets if they live in neighborhoods with a higher crime rate or someone in their household is engaged in questionable activities that expose them to violence, such as drug dealing. The rich might be victimized more frequently but they can take taxicabs or an Uber late at night, instead of walking home alone from work or a party from the bus stop or subway, hire bodyguards, or live in more secure dwellings with a doorman in safer neighborhoods. The middle-class victims, especially the young and college-educated population, may have liberal beliefs and a blind trust that may cause potential victims to give everyone "the benefit of the doubt" as they ignore the warning signs. Some people may fear appearing prejudiced; rather than fleeing someone who "looks" dangerous, they dismiss their apprehensions as negative stereotyping which unfortunately might lead them to get robbed, shot, assaulted, or stabbed. The *2021 Annual Report* of the Chicago Police Department, which they publish online, shares these statistics for that year:

- There were 800 murder victims in Chicago in 2021, a 3.53% increase over 2020.
- Of those murder victims, 81.13% were African American including 549 males and 72 females.
- There were 26 White murder victims (21 male and 5 female) or 2.63% of the total.
- There were 119 White/Hispanic murder victims (109 males and 10 females) or 14.75% of the total number of victims.
- The most common relationship or murder victim to offender was stranger (60% or 138) followed by "unknown relationship" (570).
- Acquaintance was the next most frequent relationship (23% or 53)

- Victims were a romantic partner (8.3%), family member (4.3%), or friend (1.7%) for a total of 33 out of the 800 murder victims.
- Ninety-three percent or 745 of the murder victims were shot.
- Next is stab wounds (3.8% or 30 victims) followed by blunt force injury (1.1% or 9 victims).
- Age range of murder victims was from 0-17 years (56 or 7% victims) to 50+ (74 or 9.3%), with largest age group 22-to-30 (295 victims or 36.9%). Others include 18-21, 103 victims or 12.9%; 31-40, 189 victims or 23.6%; and 41-50 age group, 83 or 10.4%)
- 77.5% of victims and 85.6% of offenders had a "criminal background"
- Gang-related most frequent motive (49.1%); next was dispute (28.9%)

Another worrisome phenomenon is the increasing frequency of mass murders. Not only are there more murder victims from a broader range of social and economic classes living in rural, suburban, and urban communities, there are more victims per murderer. In 1958 Charles Starkweather killed ten people and the entire country was shocked. By 1 977 the Manson murders, twenty-five migrant-worker victims in California, and the twenty-six boys killed by a Houston candy maker had accustomed Americans to mass murder. Yet the 1976 trial and conviction of an ex-convict who murdered nine Manhattan women who lived in West Side hotels attracted much less attention. Alternatively, consider the media and public focus in 1976-77 when "Son of Sam" targeted and killed six young adult New Yorkers.

An increase in mass murder in the last few years is everyone's concern, especially Americans. As *USA Today* notes in "Mass Killing Database," published on August 18, 2022, and updated on January 28, 2023, "2022 saw the second most mass killings in a single year since tracking began. The number of victims was the third highest total, only surpassed in 2017 and 2019." It is a horrific trend spotlighted by the media, part of an exceedingly high murder rate overall.

The rise in mass murders is also tied to a phenomenon known as murder followed by suicide, or murder-suicide. Cambridge University criminologist and psychiatrist D. J. West, in his classic study of this problem, *Murder Followed by Suicide,* showed that in England, where he was based, one out of every three murders was followed by the murderer's suicide. In his analysis of about

150 cases, West placed these murderers into three categories: the insane, the sane killing under stress, and a small number of criminally motivated persons. An early study of murder-suicides States was Dr. Wolfgang's Philadelphia study of reported criminal homicides in 1948 to 1952. Wolfgang found that there were only 24 murder-suicides out of a total of 588 vic-tims (and 621 offenders).

The Violence Policy Center reported on its "Murder-Suicide" fact sheet at their site that 1,200 die in the U.S. annually from these crimes.

In 2020 the FBI estimated that just 54% of homicides were cleared (or solved) nationwide by police but that rate can fluctuate greatly. In the 4th quarter of 2019 in New York City, 86.3% of murders were cleared; in 4th quarter of 2020, just 46%. In the 1960s, it has been estimated that 90% of murders were cleared.

As these varying clearance rates indicate, the likelihood that the the killer may "get away with murder" is also greater. One reason is the growth of "stranger-murders." No longer do most killers know their victims. Nor is it still true that a person is safer on the street than in his own living room. A 1976 Rand Institute study indicates that in the new murder pattern that evolved in New York City between 1965 and 1975, the 60 percent increase in homicides that occurred between 1968 and 1974 over-whelmingly involved strangers. Headlines such as the following are more and more common: "Widow, 84, Is Slain in Co-op City; Brooklyn Youth, 16, Is Charged"; "An Old Man Stabbed in His Home—for a Lousy $40 or $50?"; "Elderly Couple Slain in Apartment in Luxury Building on East 66th St." All classes, not just the poor, are represented in the police blotter reports. Some names may not appear as homicide victims; an unknown number of assault victims, who subsequently die from crime-related injuries months or years after the attack, may not be disclosed to the police who provide the data for official statistics) unless a relative needs substantiation for filing for crime victim compensation.

In 1953, 10 percent of murders in the United States involved strangers. In 2019, although the FBI reported that 9.9% of murders committed by strangers, there were 48.9% where a relationship between the victim and the offender was unknown. It is possible a large number of those cases were committed by strangers. As noted previously, in Chicago in 2021, 60% of the murders were by strangers.

In Canada, according to "Homicide in Canada, 2020"by Amelia Armstrong and Brianna Jaffray, Canadian Centre for Justice and Community Safety Statistics, 18% of the murder victims were killed by a stranger. (November 25, 2021)

Stranger murders a/may also be a felony murder because the vic-tims are usually killed during or after a felonious crime like robbery, burglary, rape, or assault. Some criminologists and police detectives theorize these murders enable the criminal to eliminate a potential witness and, often, the only witness. On a December evening in 1966, two men in their thirties swallowed pep pills, drank beer, and then held up a gas station in Salt Lake City. They drove the station's eighteen-year-old attendant to the desert and flipped a coin for who would kill him:

MURDERER 1:   Yeah, I lost, so I did it. Simple . . . easy . . . 'cause all's it is is just when you put it in. I don't know if you ever cut foam rubber or cut your skin with a razor blade. Once you get through the little skin and the little layer that's there as a protective shield there's nothin' but just a bunch of blood and intestines—they're soft. It's just like you take your veins and that. It's just like boiled spaghetti. ... He says, "Oh my God, I got a wife." That was his dying words.

MURDERER 2:   At the time we thought it was kind of funny, really, because, well, everything we was doin' at the time we thought was funny. And I think one of us even commented on "Did you see the way he squirmed? Wasn't that funny?"

These two murderers went on to kill five other robbery victims who were potential eyewitnesses. Eventually tried and convicted, their death sentences were commuted to life imprisonment following the United States Supreme Court *Furman* v. *Georgia* 1972 decision against capital punishment. (In 1976 in *Gregg v. Georgia*, the death penalty was reinstated.)

Previously, that similar punishments for murder and theft might have encouraged the murder, and elimination, of witnesses to a theft was noted in the sixteenth century by Sir Thomas More when he wrote in his book *Utopia*: "If a thief knows that a conviction for murder will get him into no more trouble than a conviction for theft, he's naturally impelled to kill the person that he'd otherwise merely have robbed. It's no worse for him if he's caught, and it gives him a better chance of not being caught, and of concealing the crime altogether by eliminating the only witness. So in our efforts to terrorize thieves we're actually encouraging them to mur-der innocent people."

The situation More referred to in sixteenth-century England has not really changed; the stakes are simply different. Then robbery was punished with the same severe sentence as was murder —hanging. Today murder is punished similarly to robbery—with imprisonment up to life.

Another disparity in our judicial system in regard to sentences given convicted murderers reflects social attitudes; people convicted of the classic "crime of passion" murder may receive more lenient treatment than those who kill during the commission of a felony—stranger-murders. Sentences may differ as greatly as zero to fifteen years in the former instance and twenty years to life in the latter. The public and the courts seem more willing to "forgive" the murderer who kills a "friend" or a member of his family. Yet most classic crimes of passion are as vicious—and as unacceptable—as stranger-murders.

The grisly details of the following three-person tragedy are still vivid to the responding police officers, years after the crime occurred:

> When we got to the apartment, there was a tail black man who was over six feet; he had wounds from a fight. He told us that his girlfriend was hurt. It seemed her husband had walked in and found them; now he was beating her up. I wondered, "How big is the husband going to be if this guy's over six feet?"
>
> We walked into the apartment and there was this little guy. His wife was lying on the floor with a huge hole in her neck. He had hit her with the television and a chain and then he picked up a four-legged chair and hit her with that—that's what made the hole in her neck. She had been cooking sweet potatoes, and he poured the hot water over her; her collarbone was broken too.

> We told her that she was going to die and asked her, "Who did this to you?" And she pointed to her husband.

Although that story might be considered a description of a crime of passion, from the way the police officer described it his condemnation was clear. He, like many other law enforcement officials, is disturbed by the growing public sympathy with crimes of passion. Robert J. diGrazia, former police commissioner of Boston, believes that the term *crime of passion* should be eliminated from the legal vocabulary. He says:

> The phrase "crime of passion" is misunderstood by a wide segment of the public. It has come down to us with sexual overtones and undertones and, in the strict historical sense, concerned the murder of a wife by a husband who had caught her *flagrante delicto* [in the very act of committing a misdeed]. This gave rise to the no-jury-will-ever-convict-him type of thinking, and the "unwritten law" thinking. Realistically, a crime of passion is one in which the perpetrator is in a state of extreme rage; therefore, a barroom-brawl killing is a crime of passion. A crime of passion is one committed with circumstances of mitigation which, while not justifying the felonious act, tempers the judgments of those considering it. I do not believe the term should be used at all, even if it is almost acceptable.

4.

WHETHER killed by friend or stranger, wife or lover, member of the same or opposite sex or the same or another race, there is a constant that runs through most murders: guns. According to the February 3, 2022 Rew Resaerch Report by Josh Gramlich, "What the Data say About gun Deaths in the U.S.,"Nearly eight-in-ten (79%) U.S. murders in 2020 – 19,384 out of 24,576 – involved a firearm." In 2020, the report goes on to note that 59% of the guns used in murders and non-negligent manslaughter in the U.S. were handguns.

In most states, handguns may be bought over a counter; only eight states demand that the guns be licensed. The 1968 Federal Gun Control Law requires that a person complete a form before purchasing a gun and provide the reasons for buying the handgun. But names, addresses, and legitimate reasons may easily be invented. The ineffectiveness of the law is demonstrated by the fact that ex-convicts are able to buy handguns and that the number of privately owned handguns has increased from ten million in 1965 (before the law) to forty million in 1975. A 2022 CNN article by Harmeet Kaur, "What Studies Reveal About Gun Ownership in the U.S.," references a 2017 report by researchers at Harvard and Northeastern University that there are 265 million privately-owns guns in the U.S. "about half are owned by 3% of the US adult population," Kaur writes.

Kathy was shot and killed with a Saturday Night Special fired by her former boyfriend, Billy. Five months before her murder, after he had seriously injured Kathy, Billy was indicted for attempted murder but released on bail. The weekend before he was to appear in court, somehow he got a handgun and murdered Kathy on the campus of her rural upstate New York college campus. Kathy's mother and father offer the details:

LUCILLE: Kathy was a bright girl, and she was always looked upon as a brain, but she was very unseeming about it. She was quiet. She really liked Billy when she first went with him. He would write her poetry and she felt that there was something there. It was her first real romance, and she just didn't listen to us.

SAM: Billy was a moody person, but I think Kathy, like a lot of girls, felt, well, she could change him. One of her favorite books was *Jane Eyre* and I think she thought she was Jane and he was Edward Rochester.

We never cared for him, but instead of trying to break it off—we did try a couple of times—we talked it over and decided that the way to go was to let Kathy decide when she wanted to break off the relationship herself. She had tried to break away

LUCILLE: slowly that summer even before she went to college, but he was a very possessive type of person. It wasn't like she left him for another guy or anything. She just changed, She had a new life up there. When she broke up with him, he just got upset. "It's either me or nobody else."

SAM: She just outgrew him. Then, it was on the anniversary of their first date, Billy went up to her college. They were talking. Later she told us that she felt that as she said, "Let's go back to the campus," he sort of edged nearer the water and Kathy was concerned that he might jump in. So she reached for his hand and turned and when she did so, he picked up a rock or a brick and he beat her over the head. Twenty-three stitches. In protecting herself, she broke her hand.

LUCILLE: Billy took her to a hospital. Kathy talked him into it. "What are you doing to me?" she asked. And he said, "I don't know. What am I doing?" Kathy said, "Are you going to take me to the hospital? Pick me right up and take me to the hospital." Billy then said, "But they'll put me in jail." And she said, "Oh, I won't tell," you know, just so he wouldn't do anything worse. When they got there, Billy tried to say that he found Kathy like that. But when she was safe, with other people, Kathy told them about what had happened.

SAM: Then he immediately confessed.

LUCILLE: The next day he was out.

SAM: Out on ten thousand dollars bail.

LUCILLE: Out and on his own.

SAM: It finally was charged as first-degree assault and attempted murder. . . . After that, Kathy wouldn't see Billy or have anything at all to do with him.

LUCILLE: Except that he kept calling. Billy's stepmother—he was estranged from his mother—was very upset. She explained that Billy's father was like that—attempted to be violent at times. She called one time and asked me if I would drop the charges. I said, "There's no charges to drop. This is the state's case. I have no control over it. The state is charging him with attempted murder." She told me that she felt she finally realized what Billy did.

SAM: We discussed removing Kathy from the area and sending her to a different college. But she was very happy. She loved it there.

LUCILLE: She said, "Why should I move? I didn't do anything. Let them take care of him." Who would have thought that in a matter of a few weeks, they [the judicial system] wouldn't be doing something with him. All these calls of "I'm sorry," and Billy crying. I begged his mother to do something with him. "It's not just the state, you could see that he's not normal," I told her. "Don't you see?" "Well, yes I do, I do." His brother was the one who bailed him out. His brother was going to school and working in a mental hospital. Well, he should have been on the inside.

Two months before the murder, Billy stopped calling Kathy altogether.

It was early evening. Kathy was with her girlfriend when she saw Billy at a distance. Then she started to run and Billy chased after her. So she ran into the cafeteria to get to a phone.

SAM: That was the instruction from security—if she ever saw him on campus, go to the nearest phone—and that's what she did.

LUCILLE: So she went in there and he just followed her. She went into the office to call security, but it was there that Billy pulled the gun. He actually shot past one of the cafeteria workers. Stili the manager tried and said, "Leave her alone."

SAM: Kathy said, "Oh, don't worry. I'll take care of it."

LUCILLE: He got everybody out of there. It was just him and her.

SAM: They had no choice [but to leave]. He had a gun. There's nothing to argue. That's the thing. See, if you had a knife, if you had a club, but if you have a gun, you can't argue.

LUCILLE: Knowing her, she would be very worried about anyone else getting hurt on her account. I think maybe she thought she could talk him out of it. Maybe in a bigger room she would have been able to get out somehow. But she wanted to get to that phone in there and that was her downfall There's a lot of maybes. But then, someone else might have been shot. I don't think Billy wanted her to talk him out of it because I think he felt she might. I think Billy just said, "I'm here to kill you."

SAM: They say about a minute after the people got out of the office, there were three shots. And there was a scream. Her wounds were fatal—she died in a matter of minutes—but, you know, nobody knew that at the time. The police called, but Billy wouldn't answer the phone. I think he answered it once and just put it on the desk. The police were talking to him through the door, and he wouldn't answer.

LUCILLE: They didn't know whether Kathy was dead or not and they were afraid to just break in.

SAM: The police climbed the trees, looked in through the window, and they could see the blood. Finally, an hour later, they said, "Well, we have to break in." So a couple of police went in with bulletproof vests on. During that whole hour, Billy had been sitting there at the desk, rocking back and forth, going through pictures of when Kathy and he were dating.

LUCILLE: There are people who say they should have done something sooner. I don't feel that these local police really know enough. They don't know what to do in a case like this. They're used to giving parking tickets.

SAM: Just about everywhere I've spoken [favoring gun control], someone has said, "Well, he would have killed her some way or another." Maybe he would have. But the gun makes it that much easier. Now I can stand over here [in the living room] and I can shoot you out there [in the driveway]. But I can't throw a rock and kill you and I can't, probably couldn't, hit you with a knife. Guns are important, very important. But that's not all of it. It's the whole system, the whole judicial system has to be changed.

Last February, on the anniversary of Kathy's death, I spoke with the district attorney. Nothing has been done because Billy was found to be in a catatonic state immediately after the murder and was in a mental institution for eight months.

LUCILLE: There's still a question of sanity. This is what's going on now. One psychiatrist claims, "Yeah, he understands what's going on," and another says, "Uh-uh, he's still incompetent to stand trial." Billy's been in jail since November. We feel that if he's truly mental, he should be in a hospital, but if he's not, then he should stand trial. They should get it over with.

SAM: How many people do you know who get killed with a gun? Not very many. But it is many. But I understand, and I think it goes throughout the society, that "I'm not going to get killed in an automobile accident. Nothing'll happen to me." I think it's the same way with guns.

Before Kathy's death, sure I was aware of all these social problems, but not the way I have been since. Because then you realize that all our societal systems that are supposed to protect us just don't work.

I think it's a great country, but it can get a lot better. A lot better.

3

"It Might Have Been Murder" Victims (Aggravated Assault and Family Violence)

1.

A TWENTY-SEVEN-YEAR-OLD woman living in Pittsburgh with her two children describes how her common-law husband used to treat her:

> He hit me on the head with a telephone receiver and I needed eleven stitches in the top of my head. The last time I needed ten stitches on the inside of my mouth. He cracked my nose and my cheekbone and had my right ear bleeding. The whole right side of my head was black and blue.
>
> The only thing that the police could do was to put him in jail overnight—in the drunk tank—and release him in the morning. The only way they could do anything about it was if I would file charges against him.
>
> I didn't talk to anyone about what was happening because I was embarrassed that it was happening and that I was letting it happen. I was also afraid that it would get back to him, and I would get beaten again.
>
> This went on for about three years. We're not living together anymore.

The weapons used to commit homicides and assaults are the same—guns, knives, household objects (such as a telephone), hands, and feet. But in assault, guns or similar weapons are less frequently used than in homicides. In 1975, 66 percent of all American homicide victims were killed with a gun, but only 25 percent of all assault victims died from bullets. Conversely, 9 percent of all murders were committed with hands and feet, but 26 percent of all assaults were accomplished with these "personal weapons."

Quite simply, a telephone is not as lethal as a gun. Many assault victims survive only because their attacker, lacking a gun, used whatever was handy—a stone, a chair, a knife, or his own fist.

Homicides and assaults basically manifest the same kind of aggressive criminal behavior and crime profiles; they are most likely to occur between 5:00 P.M. and 2:00 A.M.; the victims and offenders in both crimes are usually males between the ages of eighteen and twenty-five. A little more than half of the assaults occur outside; the rest inside. And as in homicide, more assaults are now committed by strangers than ever before.

The more serious type of assault, aggravated assault, is also becoming more common. It is technically defined as "assault with the intent to kill or for the purpose of inflicting severe bodily injury, whether or not a dangerous weapon is used." In this chapter *assault* denotes an attack resulting in serious injury to a victim, whether the weapon is part of the body, such as a foot, or an extension of the body, such as a knife or a gun, as long as the attacker's intent was to cause serious bodily harm.

Aggravated assaults—stabbings, scaldings, beatings, stampings—are divided into the categories of aggravated assault, simple assault, and intimidation. Most of the attention is on aggravated assault which may also be termed attempted murder, assault with intent to kill, or assault with intent to do great bodily harm. (Yager, *Essentials of Victimology*, pages 488-489) the most common violent crime, in the United States in 2019, there were 821,182 reported. (FBI, *2019 Crime in the U.S.*)

Aggravated assaults can be divided into four broad categories determined by the relationship between the victim and his or her attacker: (1) between strangers; (2) between peers and nonrelatives, such as dating couples, neigh-bors, and co-workers; (3) between family members; and (4) between author-ity figures and the persons they regulate, such as prison guards and inmates, police and criminals and citizens, and teachers and students.

Assault victims are represented by all races, classes, and ages. They range from an innocent youth mistaken for a "hippie troublemaker" who was unjustly beaten by the police to a lower-class woman's fifteen-year-old daughter who was shot by her infuriated landlord to a suburban mother beaten at a party. A composite picture of the "typical" assault, assembled from numerous surveys, is that the average victim is attacked with a knife, and a verbal disagreement is the most common provocation, although the victim is seldom responsible for the first act of violence.

Unlike homicide, assault is rarely committed for profit. And unlike rape, few assaults are premeditated; they result from arguments, longstanding but volatile feuds, and minor disagreements. Two types of assault, child abuse and wife battering, have received great attention in the past few years, but assaults by strangers are also indicative of a society whose members seem to use physical means too quickly and too often to "settle" differences.

2.

COMPARED with the violence and physical pain that they cause, the supposed "provocations" of assaults by strangers can be incredibly petty. A misinterpreted stare, a misconstrued gesture, or a misunderstood comment have all been grounds for attacks that leave their victims physically or mentally crippled. An offhand remark may be answered with a kick in the face; an accidental brushing against someone in a crowded bus may be avenged by a knife in the thigh.

In *The Zoo Story*, playwright Edward Albee presents an example of how a disagreement between two strangers might prompt physical blows or even death. The play revolves around the casual park-bench meeting between Jerry, a drifter in his late thirties who lives alone, and Peter, a married man in his early forties who works for a publishing company.

The fatal disagreement that climaxes the drama is sparked by Jerry's obsession that he must claim Peter's place on the park bench as his own. Peter refuses to relinquish "his" bench, and as the argument intensifies, so does the degree of violence in their menacing gestures—from an insult to a poke and then to a punch, a push, and finally a belabored indictment of Peter's manliness:

> PETER [*quivering*]. I've come here for years; I have hours of great
>   pleasure, great satisfaction, right here. And that's important
>   to a man. I'm a responsible person, and I'm a GROWNUP.
>   This is my bench, and you have no right to take it away
>   from me.

JERRY. Fight for it, then. Defend yourself; defend your bench.

PETER. You've *pushed* me to it. Get up and fight.

JERRY, Like a man?

PETER *[still angry]*. Yes, like a man, if you insist on mocking me even further.

JERRY. I'll have to give you credit for one thing: yon *are* a vegetable, and a slightly nearsighted one, I think . . .

PETER. THAT'S ENOUGH, . , .

JERRY. . . . but, you know, as they say on TV all the time—you know—and I mean this, Peter, you have a certain dignity; it surprises me. . . .

PETER. STOP!

JERRY *[rises lazily]*. Very well, Peter, we'll battle for the bench, but we're not evenly matched. *[He takes out and clicks open an ugly-looking knife.]*

PETER *[suddenly awakening to the reality of the situation]*. You *are* mad! You're stark raving mad! YOU'RE GOING TO KILL ME!

Another example of the kind of mild provocation that can stimulate a vicious stranger-assault is demonstrated in the following story retold by a woman in her early twenties:

One day my boyfriend and his three male companions took me into downtown Philadelphia to shop. They were all strong, attractive young men about twenty-three years of age and dressed in blue jeans with moderately long hair. As we were walking through the street, a car, driven by an impersonal-looking man, brushed my skirt, almost hitting me. The car did not stop. My boyfriend was outraged, and in his anger and protection of me made an obscene gesture at the driver, who was looking at us through his rear-view mirror. But the driver did not seem to care and just drove away. However, we were all very aggravated and spoke about the incident for a few minutes as we continued walking down the street.

In a little while our conversation changed and we were no longer thinking about the careless driver. We were all happily walking in a group when we began to hear the faint sound of running footsteps. These footsteps approached until we turned to see a man running up the sidewalk towards us. We moved against the building to give him room to pass. However, he ran right up to my boyfriend and grabbed him by the coat collar, calling him a "young punk" and saying that he couldn't get away with such "disrespectful behavior." The man, being large in stature and about thirty-five years old, was capable of a brisk, solid punch in the jaw, which sent my boyfriend flying. Meanwhile, I had pancaked myself against the building to avoid getting hurt by this maniac, and I was screaming to the three other boys to stop the violent action. They stood frozen and silent. The attacker simply walked away, muttering angrily and leaving his victim in dazed surprise.

That story is typical of the stranger-assaults that have become commonplace in the 1970s. Fifteen years ago, the average assault, like most homicides, occurred within a family or among friends. Official statistics, however, fail to reflect accurately the growth in stranger-assaults since it is one of the crimes that victims are least likely to report to the police.

A survey based on interviews with 5,500 households and more than 1,000 store owners in the Dayton, Ohio, and San Jose, California, metropolitan areas showed that 75 percent of all violent-crime victims had been assaulted; 51 percent of the Dayton assault victims and 59 percent of the San Jose victims had been attacked by strangers. In larger American cities, such as New York, Philadelphia, Detroit, and Chicago, the incidence of stranger-assaults in about 10,000 households and 3,480 commercial establishments was even higher and ranged from 66 percent in Los Angeles to 86 percent in New York. The following stories give a sampling of the violence which characterizes stranger-assaults:

1. During the 1975 Christmas holidays, a nineteen-year-old boy on vacation from the Texas university he was attending stood on the lawn of his parents' home in suburban Philadelphia. As the boy talked to his girlfriend, a car drove by, and one of its occupants threw a bottle. The boy shouted something, and within moments the car' returned, two men got out, knocked him to the ground, and as one held him by the hair the other methodically kicked his face. For a while, doctors feared the victim would lose his eyesight, The episode traumatized his family, even though the victim's eyesight was regained, and over a year later they were still unable to discuss the incident.

2. A young man saw four teenagers starting to fondle a young girl. "Why don't you just leave this girl alone?" the man said. "That's all I said to them," the victim continued, "and the next thing I know, they're all over me with the knives." Stab wounds in his diaphragm, stomach, kidney, liver, lower intestines, and colon necessitated eight operations. He still moves with difficulty and is unable to work. Poor reward indeed for attempting to he a good samaritan.

3. With no apparent motive, a sixteen-year-old boy was attacked by a fifteen-year-old delinquent. The victim's injuries included a blackened eye, bruised face and ribs, and cracked fingers. Later, the victim's father learned that the attacker had had three prior arrests in the five months preceding his son's assault. Charges from the first two arrests had been dropped; it was while the attacker was awaiting trial on the third charge that the fourth assault occurred.

4. A black newspaper reporter was physically assaulted by a stranger in a bar. The victim defended himself and called the police for help. However, since the victim had a black belt in karate, the attacker hired a lawyer and successfully sued the genuine victim, winning $20,000 for damages.

It is impossible to know whether many stranger-assaults, categorized by their victims as attempted rapes, robberies, or thefts, might have gone on to become those crimes as well if the assailant had not been stopped. In the story that follows, Veronica believes that the attacker's motive might have been rape:

On St. Patrick's Day about two years ago, I was coming home from work at about six-thirty. I got off before my usual stop and went shopping along the way. I was down about something and wasn't in too good a mood.

I went to my building and went inside and started to unlock the door. There was this man there. I don't know if he followed me or anything; he was just there. He was dressed rather nicely in a camel's-hair coat—a white man about thirty years old—and he was carrying an attaché case. He seemed pleasant enough, but a bit tacky. I thought, "Gee, I wonder if he lives in my building. Maybe he's a new neighbor." I remember that for a moment I thought of asking him who he was, but he looked like he belonged there, so I let him in.

I walked to the elevator and when it opened—it was a very tiny elevator—he let me go first. You know, a gentleman. I knew he was looking at me, but I didn't get any bad vibes.

I went to press the button for my floor. This is hindsight, but he didn't press a button. "Oh, you live on the top floor," he said. I really was not in the mood to talk to anyone so I said, "Yeah." I was annoyed that I was being spoken to. Then he said, "Do you have a studio apartment?" *Then* I realized something was wrong and started to get a little nervous. I looked at him and I could see that he was starting to get a little nervous— cold-sweat nervousness—and he was trying to keep smiling. I said something like, "Oh, there are all kinds of apartments in this building."

Then he said, "Do you have a roommate?" I don't. I live alone. But I said, "Yes." He said, "Would she mind if I came in for a drink?" Now I was getting angry, and I said, "I'm not inviting you in for any kind of drink." He said, "Oh yeah? Look what I've got for you." Then he pulled out a knife.

When I saw that, I went crazy and started to scream. I remember I wasn't planning anything, but all I know is I wanted that knife away from me. I kicked him, and pushed against him, and pulled up his hand with the knife. I was actually able to lift his hand up. It was a very peculiar thing; I never thought I could be that strong. I was screaming, "Help! Help! Help!" He said, "Shut up, or I'll kill you."

He was panicked now. I had caught the blade on my fingers, which I couldn't feel. I just wanted to keep that knife away from my body, because I thought that then he would have control on me. So I just kept pushing against his hand and pushing against him, when the elevator opened. I pulled out of the elevator and I never stopped screaming. I never screamed so loud in my life. I figured maybe he was behind me. The groceries went flying and I slammed into the first apartment, banged on it, and no one came out. I went to another apartment and then I was in a corner. I felt trapped, whereas before maybe I could fight with him, yet now I saw no help was coming.

I saw how cut up my fingers were, very bad in fact. It was very quiet. I could hear someone saying, "Where are you? Where are you?" I didn't want to move. I thought maybe it was him.

I saw one of my neighbors come out with a baseball bat, but the guy had gone. He had been gone a long time. I was hysterical. My neighbor screamed out the window for the police. [This happened at a time when the telephone lines were down.] A friend of mine lived in the neighborhood and she came with me to the hospital, I was still screaming my head off; I was hysterical about my fingers.

The attendants came over and they were very nice. They said, "Let me see your hand." When I showed it to them, they said, "Don't worry. You won't lose your fingers unless you bite your nails off too much." Which immediately relaxed me because I thought, "They wouldn't joke about a thing like that."

It was very painful. Nerves and tendons were cut right through. I didn't ever feel the knife, though. I don't know how I could have held it, but I didn't know I was cutting myself when I held the knife.

By then, because of the drugs, I was almost high. I had to call my parents, which was not very easy. But afterwards, when my friend left and they took me up for the operation, I crashed and it was terrible. Lonesome. I can't tell you how lonesome I was at that moment.

They wheeled me in front of the operating theater and I was lying there until the surgeon was ready. And that was really the worst. I started to feel like a victim. "Why is it happening to me?" All the rage from before. So much energy.

I was frightened of the operation and I got scared. I went back to what had happened and got scared for the first time, really terrorized. My knees were jumping up and down involuntarily. The doctor put his hand on my legs and said, "Look, you've been through a terrible experience, I know. But that's over and you're in safe hands and I can assure you that the outcome of this operation will be a complete success. We're going to put everything back together."

I couldn't go back to that house. I mean, I couldn't even walk in the neighborhood. The thought of going in the house drove me crazy. I got so scared. I thought this guy was going to come back after me. Everybody assured me—the police, my psychiatrist, everyone—that that's not what happens. They don't come after you. They want to get away from you as much as you want to get away from them.

One night I tried to sleep there. I took my friend with me. Her father's a policeman. I was encouraged to try; someone said, why should I be driven from my home? This is weird. I got a phone call and the person hung up. It drove me bananas and I said, "We're getting out of here." I would never go back. I don't know what that phone call meant. I don't know how he would have known my name. He didn't know my apartment, only my floor.

I still watch everyone I see on the street. I won't take the subway. I moved into a doorman building. My left hand is permanently bent and is numb.

3.

ASSAULTS involving persons who are acquainted—co-workers, distant relatives, and neighbors—can be as brutal as Veronica's attack. They are usually as senseless. Often they occur because the victims are unaware of "how
far they may go" in what they consider harmless kidding or mild criticism.
Sometimes they fail to recognize the danger signals that precede an assault;
sometimes there are no obvious signs.

When Yvonne was assaulted at a party given by one of her co-workers,
she was in her early twenties and living in a Maryland suburb:

This happened at the party of a guy I saw every day when
we worked at the same office for about a year. I arrived about
eleven o'clock, and I had a couple of drinks, but I was very sober
because I'm not a drinking person anyway.

I was probably dancing with the host, since he was the only
person I really knew at the party, but I don't remember exactly.
I said something to him about this other guy's wife being a cold
person. It was a private remark. But I guess he passed it on to the
husband, who told his wife, who said, "Did you say that?" I said,
"Yeah, I did, but I'm sorry. It wasn't meant to be an insult, and it
wasn't meant to be overheard, either."

The next thing I knew, these dudes were beating me up, and
I mean hitting me in the face and smacking me. Nobody was
doing anything about it! Everybody was leaving. I know I was
knocked unconscious a couple of times. My clothes were ripped.
The people who were beating me didn't even know me, and I'm
not the kind of person that comes off as being rough. I mean, I
can take care of myself, but I'm only four foot ten and I weighed
then what I weigh now—one hundred pounds. But no one called
the police. No one interceded.

I remember being on the kitchen floor, and this guy that I
never saw before in my life standing over me, hitting me, and
about five other guys just standing there, looking and not doing
anything. I mean they all looked like Joe College. I was hysterical.
I didn't know what was happening.

Eventually I woke up in the bed of the guy that was giving the party and I realized I hadn't been raped or anything like that, so I just went home.

The next morning I realized I had in fact taken quite a beating, so I went to the hospital and went through the whole routine of an investigation. I had a hemorrhage in my eye, multiple bruises, and lacerations on my face. I had two black eyes and scratches on my arms and breasts. The doctors couldn't believe that nothing was broken. It took about one month before my face went back to normal.

By failing to deal seriously with assaults—whether by strangers, acquaintances, or relatives of the victims—the courts and police are contributing to the increase in homicide victims. For many criminals, an aggravated assault is a preliminary to murder. Many convicted killers have histories of charges, indictments, and convictions for aggravated assaults. Again and again, the records of convicted murderers reveal assault charges that never came to trial.

Sometimes an assault offender fails to murder his intended victim, and the courts unwittingly give him a second chance. If an assault defendant on bail fails to reappear in court, a bench warrant is customarily issued for his arrest. Especially in larger cities, the police rarely find these offenders, who may then kill the complainant in the assault case or an unrelated victim.

The police and the courts are not always at fault. Sometimes the victim fails to report the assault to the police, fearing reprisals from the criminal. A forty-one-year-old woman decided to terminate a relationship with her eighteen-year-old lover. The youth, angered by her decision, beat her so badly that hospitalization was necessary. Embarrassed by the disparity in ages between herself and her lover, she failed to notify the law enforcement authorities. Instead, she moved to another apartment and obtained a new, unlisted phone number. He discovered where she lived, however, and began to harass her. About two years later, the ex-lover attacked her again and this time stabbed her.

She moved again, and when interviewed she explained that the man had been arrested just the night before after he had climbed through the window of her new residence and tried to choke her. (This last time, even renting the apartment under an assumed name had failed to conceal her whereabouts.) She was fearful because even if he were imprisoned for a few months, upon his release she believed he would continue in his obsession to kill her. It seemed there was little, short of life imprisonment, that the courts could do to keep him away from her.

4.

EACH year in the United States, 10 million couples experience physical abuse, according to the National Coalition Against Domestic Violence (NCADV). American Society for the Positive Care of Children (ASPCC) estimates that in 2020 there were 3.1 million reports of child maltreatment. The most horrific statistic is that 90.6% of the mistreatment is by one or both of the parents and that, even more tragically, in 2020, 1,750 children died from neglect and abuse in the U.S.

The petitions charging family violence filed in New York City's family court indicate how family violence has grown and how it has been treated. In 1974, 4,800 of these petitions were filed; in 1975, more than 7,200 were filed. In only 34 of those 7,200 cases was the offender sent to a workhouse or prison, where the maximum sentence did not exceed six months. Otherwise, the court handed down suspended sentences and warnings. Consequently, most offenders returned home and usually continued attacking their wives, husbands, children, or siblings.

There is nothing exceptional about New York's family court. Throughout the United States, a spouse can do almost whatever he or she pleases as long as the attacks are confined to someone in the household. Sociologist Murray A. Straus and others helped to motivate change in the lenient way family violence used to be treated by pointing out that husband-wife violence is legitimized by the courts and the police because the husband was immune from being sued by his wife for assault and battery; because police too often failed to make arrests; because prosecutors failed to bring these cases to trial; because in too many states a victim was denied crime compensation for injuries if he or she was related to the offender; and because of the seeming legal and cultural approval of violence within the family violence as evidenced by the immunity of husbands from being prosecuted for raping their wives. (As you probably know, that changed in 2013 when the FBI definition of rape changed so that spouses could be arrested for raping their partner.)

Officers are often reluctant to intervene in family disputes since these domestic entanglements account for more police deaths and injuries than any other type of call for police help—in 1975, 22 percent of all police deaths and 28 percent of all police injuries occurred while officers were trying to resolve family arguments. (The second highest incidence of assaults on police officers occurred in attempted arrests for charges other than burglary or robbery.) Police officers are also confused by family disputes because frequently the same feuding couples request "emergency" help every week for years. Not only has the fighting usually stopped by the time the officer arrives, but the arrival of the "do-gooder" may inspire a reverse aggression against the officer, now seen as a meddler. Civilian good Samaritans run the same risk if they attempt to interfere in domestic squabbles.

Even when outside intervention is successful, the laws limit the help that can be given the wife in most states. For example, when police were summoned to the parking lot of a shopping center in Pittsburgh, they found the mother of the children who called them inside her car with the estranged father. They restrained the husband from further assaulting his wife, but they then asked the women, "Whose name is the car registered in?" When she replied that it was registered in her husband's name, the police answered, "Lady, there's nothing we can do. You and your husband are having a domestic quarrel within your community property."

Until the laws change, some judges are finding imaginative ways to prevent a recurrence of domestic violence without imprisoning the offender. In Hammond, Indiana, for example, City Court Judge Jack F. Crawford has made some wives court-appointed probation officers. Their probationers are their violent husbands. In that way, hitting a wife would also constitute hitting an officer of the court. Only used in a select number of cases so far, and only where the parties do not want to divorce, Judge Crawford said that in the first few months of the program no new incidences of physical abuse were reported. (If there had been, immediate revocation of probation would have been ordered and the police could have arrested the offender without the legal rigmarole that used to take three to six weeks.)

Some women continue to endure attacks by their husbands because they never give up hope that the abusive behavior will change. Others stay because they are still emotionally, if not financially, dependent on their husbands or to preserve the marriage for the presumed welfare of the children.

There are few legal moves that a wife can make without irreparably damaging her husband's earning capacity and thereby impoverishing herself and her children. Even after years of beatings, women who have no earning power of their own and nowhere else to live will stay with their husbands, hoping that the beatings will stop and their marriages will be saved. The beatings do sometimes suddenly stop—after the wife or husband has been murdered.

A twenty-two-year-old woman who has repeatedly taken beatings by her husband believes it will never get that far and so she continues returning to him. She has had all her fingers broken and her eyes perpetually blackened from her husband's blows, but still she says:

> I love him, but he knows that there's a part of my love gone. You get hit so many times that every time they do it, they beat the love out of you . . . and it's happened about six or seven times to me over the seventeen months that we've been married. But this time he says he wants to make it up to me, and that's the first time he's ever said that.
>
> As long as he doesn't drink, nothing will happen. He's going to be seeing a counselor, he's going to AA, and he's got a good job now. I think he was taking out his frustrations on me because he had been unemployed for a while. He gets mad and . . .

An older battered wife, who finally decided to file for divorce, is more realistic:

> I'll tell you this—if you take one beating, you're going to take more, if a man beats up a woman and she's still there, she must really love him. I waited eighteen years for this man to change and I finally gave up hope. There's no way this man is going to change.

A woman's traditional position as her husband's property, the leniency of the criminal justice system, and alcoholic intoxication are three key factors in wife-beating cases. Many women who many men who are physically abusive to them do so for unconscious reasons they never come to understand. Such women may have been raised by alcoholic mothers or fathers and are duplicating the pattern. Often the abusive qualities of assaultive husbands are "matched" by superlatives in all other circumstances. Dolores, a twenty-two-year-old Michigan woman, finally went to a women's shelter for advice. In her case, she feels her husband's beatings and drinking are related:

Believe it or not, he did it before we got married, I lived with him a total of three years; I've only been married to him the last year.

I blamed it all on his drinking, and before we got married he quit drinking for about four months. That's the only reason I married him. In fact, at the wedding reception he got drunk and it all started up again.

He drank whisky, beer, anything he could get his hands on. He drank day and night. He worked many jobs, mainly at the auto plants. He worked as a janitor. He tried to go to school, but that didn't work out. Even his dad was a very bad alcoholic.

It started out that he'd just slap me around. It got to the point where he was beating me up with his fists. He'd kick me; I've had stitches in the head where he's kicked me. At the same time, I've had two black eyes, my jaw swollen twice its size. The whole inner side of my ear has been purple. My face would just go back to normal and he'd do it all over again.

I went for a long time trying to convince myself that it didn't happen and making excuses for him. Then I realized what was happening wasn't right, but I was too scared to do anything. I thought if I were to leave him he'd follow me and kill me. Plus I didn't have money to leave him. I felt like I was stuck with him the rest of my life.

The real thing that happened was that when my son was two weeks old he accidentally hit him when he was beating me up. That kind of snapped something in my mind. I don't know what. I realized it couldn't go on anymore. My parents had a bad marriage and finally divorced. All I can remember is unhappiness, but my father never touched my mother physically. So I was brought up in a house with yelling and screaming and it drove me crazy and there was no way my son was going to go through that, or I'm not going to. It's like you get into a rut. You're so scared and you live like that for so long that you think like that's the way it is.

Dolores's divorce was going to be finalized a month after she shared her story and eight months after she got the courage to walk out on her husband. With the assistance of a women's shelter and counseling program, her progress is just one of many examples of how women change their status as abused wives and fault the myth that these victims are masochistic and "like" the beatings:

I've started school and I'm doing really well now. My husband still comes over and wants me to take him back, but there's no way.

Perhaps if Dolores's husband had not accidentally hit their child she would have continued to live with him, in the hope that he would change. But whether repeated physical assaults push a spouse past that individual's tolerance for brute force, the psychological damage may be as severe as the physical pain and disfigurements. Because so many beatings are unexpected, unwarranted, and unpredictable, the wife lives in a continuous state of helplessness and fear. She is both powerless to halt the attacks and ashamed to admit to others that they occur. The only person in whom she is supposed to confide is instead her victimizer. Frightened, abused, and alone, she lives from moment to moment. Her physical well-being, her financial existence, her children's welfare, and even her life are at the mercy of the uncontrollable moods of someone she may still, in spite of all this, continue to love.

The daily routine of the battered spouse fluctuates between anger after an assault has occurred, fear that without warning her partner will beat her again, and guilt. The wife often searches for the cause of her husband's violent behavior in her own actions. Like other victims, the battered wife blames herself, asking, "How am I responsible for these attacks?" For the majority of battered wives, their denial of the problem is probably their gravest mistake. Help for the battered wife means help for the batterer and, if he is unwilling, an alternate course of action for the victimized family. Sometimes temporary separation is necessary, and the growth of shelters in

England and the United States has been a major advance; these shelters offer an opportunity for financially dependent women to reevaluate their circumstances and to decide whether they wish to return to them or not. Shelters usually provide a twenty-four-hour telephone crisis counseling hotline as well as emergency food, clothing, and lodging. One such shelter, Women's Advocates of St. Paul, Minnesota, the first shelter to open in the U.S. in 1972, provided its services to more than 1,100 women and children in 2019-2020. Emergency shelter was provided to 276 victims/ survivors and their children and another 824 people called and were helped through their 24/7 crisis line.

The interview that follows is with a woman in her forties who withstood ten severe beatings over the eighteen years of her marriage. It demonstrates how wife-battering counseling centers are helping victims to break the cycle of physical abuse. The victim's injuries included two black eyes, a twisted arm, and a back out of place from being pushed against the wall. During one attack, she was beaten to unconsciousness.

The center helped me with everything because I didn't know what to do. I didn't know what my rights were and I didn't know how to go about things. They helped me to get the legal help that I needed. Of course, because of my husband's income, I had to get a lawyer, who by the way hasn't been paid a dime.... I had to go to court to force him to pay a hundred dollars a week child support for me and the four kids.

Kathleen Fojtik, who has counseled hundreds of battered wives at an Ann Arbor, Michigan, center, describes the obstacles:

It seems everyday we come back full circle to how difficult it is in many of these cases to help the woman when she, num-ber one, is financially dependent, number two, has children and wants them to have a father, number three, does not understand her legal rights or know anything about the law, and, number four, has the women in her family or her religion telling her she's got to stay married.

In a year and a half we've had over three hundred women ask for help—almost half of the seven hundred cases reported in police records. That old myth that these women are masochistic and enjoy it and want to be beaten just isn't true.

Women's Aid in Chiswick, England, one of the first refuges for battered wives, is an excellent example of the comprehensive services available to the women. The house has several floors with bunk beds crowded into the sleeping rooms. The women, eager to keep busy, paint the rooms, clean, share kitchen duty, and have rap sessions in the tiny living room. Down the street is a temporary schoolhouse so the children will not fall behind while their mothers recover and decide on a plan of action; the major—and most difficult—decision they must make is whether to return to their husbands. Erin Pizzey writes about founding her shelter in 1971 in *Scream Quietly or the Neighbors will Hear (Penguin)*.

5.

PARENTS kick, punch, and bite over one million children each year; they beat them up, attack them with guns or knives, or neglect their health. In 2018, New York City's Administration for Children's Services (ACS) looked into more than 58,000 child mistreatment reports regarding more than 80,000 children. For the death of 110 children in New York in that year, parental abuse and neglect was given as the cause. In its less severe forms, physically abusing a child is known as discipline; in its more lethal forms, it is aggravated assault and a crime. Yet the growing consensus in the United States that husbands do not have the "right" to beat their wives is not yet matched by a corresponding agreement that parents should not hit, or beat, their children.

A child's age or innocence does not protect it from brutal assaults. The fact that a child is too weak to fight back may even encourage harsh and frequent assaults, so horrible that they resemble torture. Babies in America have had scalding water poured on their faces and down their throats. They have been stomped, strangled, and burned with cigarettes, matches, and hot irons; shut in closets for weeks and then freed, only to be beaten again by intoxicated, drugged, or just plain assaultive parents. In 1976 a young girl who was dying of malnutrition came to the attention of the police. Her parents had locked her in a room for two years and given her a diet of only bread and water. Her older sister had tried to get help but she, too, was confined and severely beaten to ensure her obedience and silence. Finally, the older sister escaped and led police to her home.

Child abuse seems to have reached epidemic proportions in the United States. The little girl locked in the room and her frequently beaten sister are only two of the more than one million children who are beaten by their par-ents every year. Child abuse and neglect includes physical abuse, sexual abuse, emotional abuse, and neglect. Based on research known as Adverse Childhood Experiences (ACES), add witnessing parental or other family violence in the home as a fifth form of child abuse and neglect because of its negative immediate and long-term impact.

As in the case of most victim statistics, these, too, are probably under-stated. All fifty states have passed laws requiring that doctors, social workers, and teachers report any known or suspected cases of child abuse to law enforcement officials. Some states, like Texas, go even further and require mandatory reporters like counselors, physicians, or teachers to also report any suspected cases of neglect or abuse of the elderly or disabled, those who are physically or mentally dependent on others.

The first comprehensive study of baby battering was conducted by C. Henry Kempe, a doctor who has set up the National Center for Prevention of Child Abuse and Neglect in Denver. Kempe surveyed seventy-one hospitals and found a reported 130 cases of battered babies, of which 33 had died and 85 sustained permanent brain damage. In one-third of these cases proper diagnosis was followed by some legal action. Kempe stated that the type and degree of child abuse varied from cases with no overt harm, to the extreme of murder, where the offending par-ent was seriously disturbed. In the former cases the offending mothers and fathers usually visited a psychiatrist to discuss feelings of guilt and anxiety related to fantasies about harming their children.

John D. Madden, when he was clinical director of pediatrics at Weiler Children's Hospital in Chicago, attributed child abuse to three factors: emotional immaturity of the parents, a family crisis, and parents who advocate corporal punishment as a proper childrearing method. David Gil of Brandeis University analyzed 13,000 child abuse reports and found that "much abuse takes place because the use of physical force in dealing with children is so widely accepted in our culture."

Dr. Kempe and others see abuse as a treatable disease and have set up treatment programs for adults, such as the one operating at the Denver center. Parents Anonymous, started in California by a former abusing mother, now has hundreds of local chapters throughout the United States. Indeed, child abuse and baby battering are crimes in which treatment of the offenders is urgently needed to avoid the possibility that bruised children will eventually become murder statistics or that there might also go on to mistreat their own children because that is how they were socialized.

In an investigation by British researchers Smith, Hanson, and Noble pub-lished in the *British Medical Journal,* 214 parents of battered babies and children under five were studied over a two-year period. They were compared with 76 "control" parents. Of the battering mothers, 76 percent had abnormal personalities, close to 50 percent were of borderline or subnormal intelligence, 48 percent were neurotic, and 11 percent had criminal records. Of the battering fathers, 64 percent had abnormal personalities, more than 50 percent were psychopaths, and 29 percent had criminal records. The battering mothers studied were, on average, 19.7 years of age at the birth of their first child, much younger than the national average of 23.3 years. Twenty percent were displeased with pregnancy, compared with only 6 percent in the control group; 12 percent had considered abortion, compared with only 2 percent in the control group. Although the findings of that study indicated that the battering mothers came pmostly from the lower social classes, we know that higher economic status does not preclude a woman from being an offending abusive mother.

A New York City policeman described an incident of baby battering that demonstrates the critical nature of the problem: a mother killed her six-month-old infant by pouring scalding water over it. The policeman believed the death intentional; but the grand jury did not return an indictment; the mother went free. The policeman expressed his anger at about that and wished the mother would one day be crossing the street so he might "accidentally" hit her with his car. "My partner and I were going to pay for a funeral together because she was just going to have the baby placed in the unclaimed cemetery." In another incident, a 29-year-old mother dropped her 8-month-old child out the window during an argument with her boyfriend the girl's custody. The infant died. "Take the child with you," the mother reportedly said to her boyfriend, "or I'm throwing her out the window." Even if a battered child escapes the grave and becomes an adult, the psychological damage are serious and potentially everlasting. A 31-year-old bachelor ,beaten as a child, said: I can still remember what it was like when I was ten years old. At least once a month my father would go wild. As a kid, I was scared. Always expecting it and never understanding why he flew into a rage and became violent. I'm still scared of it, even though my father's been dead for seven years and I don't see my mother very often. But I'm afraid that if I lived with a woman all the time I might have those same blinding impulses. I just couldn't live through that again; I'd rather be alone.

Many child-abuse victims later exact revenge by ignoring their parents in their old age—"I don't see my mother very often." Others become criminals and revenge themselves on society with still more violence. Like the man who wrote the following account, adult felons were often beaten during their childhood:

I first remember being in a children's shelter with a lot of other parentless children. Next I remember living with a German family. They were very pro-German and this was at the height of Hitler. I was constantly called Jewish scam. Right next to my room there was a bathroom, but I was not allowed to use it, nor were my sisters. We had to use the outhouse, even in the winter. For years afterwards, I associated taking a crap with being cold. If I had to piss during the night, I would sometimes sneak into the bathroom and piss in the sink, and slowly run the water to rinse out the piss, Other times, I would just piss out the window.

One morning I awoke and my room smelled of shit. I searched around and found where someone had taken a crap in a corner between the dresser and the window. She (my foster-mother) came up and seeing the shit on the floor, she went berserk hitting me and cursing and calling me Jewish filth.

Another convicted felon recorded his similar memories.

From the ages of 6 to 11, I was beaten by my older brother. I was hit with wire hangers, chains, and electric wiring and the thing is that those experiences didn't make me afraid of punishment. Years later, when I was in Unit 14 in Dannemora [state prison] it seemed to be a continuation of what I knew as a child. The guards seemed to have the same problem and masculinity complex my brother had.

6.

ASSAULTS by authority figures on those whom they regulate are some of the most unpopular abuses in free societies. Both power and weaponry seem to weigh the odds unfairly on the side of the stronger—police, prison guards, schoolteachers. Yet rarely are statistics compiled on how many civilians are abused by those in authority; the emphasis is on how many leaders are harmed by their followers. Assaults by the powerful or by the seemingly powerless are both undesirable. However, the details of each interaction must be analyzed before concluding who is the victim and who is the criminal.

The interview that follows is with an actor who, when he was twenty-three and bearded, was mistaken for a terrorist. The incident occurred during a period of extreme anti-police sentiment among America's young people.

In February 1970, when a judge's house was bombed in New York, my girlfriend and I left a dinner at about nine-thirty. We had been smoking so we were high. We had a disagreement and we started walking toward the Hudson River. We were talking and then we realized where we were—that it was a dangerous neighborhood—so we started walking back. Betty heard something that sounded like a shot and we got scared and started running the other way. We heard someone running after us, so I went down some stairs of a basement apartment and ducked under the overhang in front. I thought we could hide there. The next thing we knew there was a light shining in our faces. A man's voice said, "Come on out." The police started questioning us. We didn't know what was going on. A paddy wagon pulled up and they said they were going to take us to the station. I said, "Are we going in that?" They said, "No. We'll walk you over there. It's right around the block. Charles Street Station."

We started walking. There were two cops. It was cold and Betty put her hands in her pockets, This one cop was pissed off and grabbed her hand as if she were going for a gun or something. I overreacted and I pulled my arm away from them and said, "Don't do that."

The next thing I knew I was on the ground. Cops came out of everywhere. Later Betty said there were about eleven of them. They shoved Betty against the wall of the side of a building. They beat me up. Broke my glasses. Knocked me unconscious and hand-cuffed my hands behind my back and carried me to the station,

I don't know how long we were there but no one would listen to her. Finally a detective came in and realized that we had noth-ing to do with what had happened—someone had blown up a car in front of the police precinct. I really don't know how long I was unconscious; I was kind of swimming in and out of it. It was soon after I woke up that we left. Some medical guy came in and wanted to do some work on my eye but I wouldn't let him and we were allowed to leave.

We called up friends and they drove in from Mount Vernon and took us out to their place. We couldn't stop the bleeding [from the cut under my eye] so they took me to the hospital. They stitched my eye up and I stayed there for twenty-four hours. I still have a little scar. I was sore on my body and had bruises where they had hit me.

I found out the police had taken my telephone book and my Social Security card, I went back about two weeks later and they said it never happened, and I wasn't able to get my things back. Betty and I went to a lawyer who told us that we had a legitimate complaint but that if we wanted to take it to trial, we'd have to be prepared to spend three years of our lives on call. Also it would probably be very difficult to win because the jury would be more or less sympathetic to the police because of the jury's background.

The lawyer said that I could probably expect some police harassment since they had my telephone book. Then he asked, "Do any of your friends smoke pot?" I said, "Yes." They said I could expect some harassment there.

About a week later, my apartment was broken into. I thought it was the police because the circumstances were too hazy to be true—it was a daytime break-in and someone supposedly saw someone come in my window and the police came over and were let in by the superintendent. But I never found out who it was that saw it. It just sounded fishy.

I had a watch on the table and the watch was still there. It looked like they were looking for drugs. They looked in the refrigerator. There was a hole in the wall that was patched up by a piece of plywood and they took the plywood off. I could be wrong, but it seemed kind of fishy—so soon afterwards.

We were discouraged by the lawyer from doing anything. He did write a letter to the police review board and when we called up they said to come by in about three weeks to look at mug shots. But why it was in three weeks, I don't know. Again that sounds fishy because the more time that elapsed, the harder it would be. Also the lawyers said that the TPF [Tactical Patrol Force], the ones that had beaten me up, move around a lot between precincts.

I think it might have affected Betty even more than it did me because she's the one that had to watch it and was helpless to do anything. We stayed together for a while after that. If anything, it brought us closer together because she was so supportive. It didn't have anything to do with our splitting up six or seven months later.

The victim's anti-police sentiments are not without reciprocal feelings on the part of the police. In a 1967 survey of police attitudes toward their clientele conducted by sociologist Arthur Nie-derhoffer, police officers identified sixteen "types" of persons they disliked confronting.* In the order the officers disliked the "types," the sixteen were:

1. Cop-fighter	9. Known criminal
2. Homosexual	10. Motorcycle group
3. Drug addict	11. "Psycho"

---

* Arthur Nicderholfer, *Behind the Shield,* Table V, p. 130 (Garden City, New York: Dou-bleday Anchor Books, 1969, 1967).

4. Chronic letter-writer	12. Motorist who doubleparks
5. Annoying drunk	13. Peddler
6. Bookie	14. Woman complainant
7/8. Gang of juveniles	15. Bohemian
7/8. Prostitute	16. Minority group member

An experiment conducted in 1967 by Dr. Charlotte Lackner Doyle and the students in her social psychology class at Sarah Lawrence College might provide further evidence of authority figures' hostility. In her lecture "On Being a Woman and Becoming a Psychologist," delivered at East Stroudsburg State College on May 2, 1975, Professor Doyle explained that several students had returned from participating in a Washington, D.C., anti-Vietnam War demonstration, expressing anger and bewilderment at the police brutality that most of them deemed unwarranted. Professor Doyle had her students improvise the demonstration scene and role-play the opposing sides. Five students were "police officers" whose job it was to guard the "Pentagon," the corner of the room where the television was; the other six were cast as demonstrators.

The first confrontation the students reenacted was tame; the demonstrators sang and displayed peace posters; the police merely observed good-naturedly, and the TV set "was touched" after minor resistance. The police were more resolute the second time, armed with brooms for guns and a vow not to smile or look in the faces of the demonstrators. Despite warnings that the brooms were "lethal," once again the demonstrators reached the "Pentagon" easily. In the third battle the police used the brooms as actual weapons, and the defending warriors had elected a leader for strategy decisions. Police used water in the fourth reenactment and, for the last trial, they were also armed with cleanser containers for an imaginary tear-gas-bomb assault so sincere that Professor Doyle began to fear that a real injury might occur.

The following week, after discussing their encounters, the students analyzed their reactions and described them in essays labeled by Professor Doyle, "the most moving set of papers I have ever read." "Police" conceded fear of the demonstrators as well as a need to depersonalize the "victims" in order to perform their assigned duty. "Demonstrators" and "police" also agreed how "we" and "they" intensified and rigidified as the improvisations continued.*

Our society, it seems, offers no alternatives to violent confrontation. "Show-downs," such as the Symbionese Liberation Army (SLA) shootout in Los Angeles, or inmate insurrections in prisons, where prisoners abduct hostages, are the ways that are used to resolve any impasse—ways requiring violence and often death. "Waiting it out" is alien to action-oriented authority figures.

Whether police officers have authoritarian personalities or not, however, is a controversial question. A negative view is provided by Christopher Wren in "Two Policemen Talk: Letting Rizzo Do the Thinking," an article that appeared in the December 1973 *Washington Monthly*. Wren suggests that the basic assumption of police authoritarianism might be incorrect; to support that view, he quotes Gerald Leinwand, who edited an anthology entitled *The Police*:

> There is a common feeling that it is the authoritarian personality that thrives on police work and is lured to the police department. Here, so it is said, the authoritarian personality can find an outlet for his tendency to enjoy both giving and taking orders. Yet, [a study of the Denver police force] found that this was not true at all. "On all personality scales the data show that policemen are absolutely average people and when they do differ from the community norm it is in the direction of better or more nobly disposed than their fellowmen."

Seven years after his beating, the actor whose experience was described earlier reflected upon how he felt at that time and how his opinions about the police have altered in the interim:

> It was hard to connect, I went back and they said it didn't happen. I talked about it to friends and people seemed to be

---

* Another academic reinterpretation of police behavior is provided by criminologist George L. Kirkham's firsthand experiences playing cop, "Doc Cop," in the May 1975 *Human Behavior*.

sympathetic because of the times. That's when the cops were the pigs and all that. It colored my opinion of the police. I thought they were pigs. I thought they were garbage men,

But my opinion's changed. I've seen the other side of the coin through listening to people who have seen the police more closely than I have and reading about them more. And the times have changed. I still feel that how the police react is an individual thing. Overall it's a very difficult job, but somebody has to do it.

I know I would handle the same situation differently now. I probably wouldn't be there in the first place. But even before that incident happened, my attitudes were different than they are now, I saw the police as part of the establishment and they were against what I stood for in terms of the Vietnam War , . . justice. And my attitudes have changed there. I wouldn't be as hostile or defensive to them either.

4

Victims of Rape and Child Sexual Abuse

1.

VIOLENT crimes are all invasions of privacy and self. Except for murder, the crime of rape is the ultimate invasion, the one with the most severe physical and psychological consequences for its victim. Burglary is the violation of a home—an extension of the victim's identity, A robbery victim loses his independence; not only must he surrender money and possessions, but he must also follow the orders of the thief. The rape victim undergoes all of these invasions as well as a biological one—the penetration of the physical and psychological self.

Rape is a crime of violence; only incidentally is it a crime of sex. Rape perverts an act that is usually a tender and loving one, turning it into one characterized by coercion and fear. Some men mistakenly consider rape to be a sexual, even a passionate, act simply because it involves the use of the penis instead of an assault weapon such as a knife, a gun, or the hands. But rape is a hostile act in which the penis is used as an assault weapon to invade, control, and humiliate the victim, not as an instrument of pleasure.

Today we know that men as well as women* are rape victims. However, ninety percent of rape victims are women; ten percent are male.

"Although I would certainly agree that rape is a hostile act," says

---

* The original FBI definition of the crime of rape, followed since 1927, was "the carnal knowledge of a female, forcibly and against her will." Then, in 2013, the FBI Uniform Crime Reporting system issued a revised definition of rape, removing the term "forcible." Here is that definition: "Penetration, no matter how slight, of the vagina or anus with any body part or object, or oral penetration by a sex organ of another person, without the consent of the victim. Attempts or assaults to commit rape are also included; however, statutory rape and incest are excluded."

Malkah Notnan, a Harvard psychiatrist, "the sex of the victim is as important as—if not more important than—her weak-ness. There are varying motivations for rape, but hostility to women *is* an important one. That doesn't mean it's primarily sexual [a sexual crime] but the use of sex for aggression." Former Manhattan Assistant District Attor-ney Jeffrey Rovins, who has tried 20 rape cases and handled another 250, expressed it another way: "The crime of rape is not love. It's not even lust. It's hatred and the desire to hurt and humiliate another human being."

A twenty-five-year-old addict who broke into a building and raped an eighty-year-old woman was later asked by the police why he had raped such an old woman. He answered, "Because she was there." No woman is safe from rape. A rape victim advocate center in Florida found that their young-est rape victim was two months old and the oldest eighty-five. No age group, social class, choice of companions, style of dress, or way of walking and talk-ing can guarantee a woman that she will not be raped.

Nevertheless, many women believe they will never be raped. Typical comments are: "I'm too streetwise to get raped." "I live in a nice neighbor-hood." "I'm careful about delivery men." "I never go out alone at night anymore." "I would never put myself in a compromising situation." But recent rape statistics show that these women are denying the facts. According to the "Criminal Victimization 2019" report, released in September 2020 by the Bureau of Justice Statistics, there wee 459,310 reported rapes in the U.S., which is a rate of 1.7 per 1,000 persons.

The actual number of rapes is even greater than the statistics show. The FBI and local police departments agree that rape is probably the most underreported of all crimes for reasons ranging from denial about what has happened to fear of retaliation, shame, or victim self-blame.

---

* What some persons refer to as rape may be redefined in the criminal statutes including sexual misconduct. rape in the third degree, sodomy in the third degree, aggravated sexual contact, abusive sexual contact, and sexual abuse in the third, second, and first degrees.

In her book *Against Our Will,* Susan Brown-miller argues that a figure of 255,000 rapes and attempted rapes in 1973 (when the FBI reported 51,000 cases) is an "unemotional, rock-bottom minimum." Some victims try to forget about their rape as quickly as possible; others are ashamed that they didn't fend off their attackers; and still others deny that the rape occurred. Rapes are most commonly not reported because the victim wants to keep it a secret from family, neighbors, or relatives; fears press or media disclosure of her identity and residence; believes that hospitals, police, and courts will be abusive; fears that court testimony will expose her personal life; fears that she will be blamed for the crime; believes no one will accept her version of the story; and fears that the rapist will return to seek revenge.

Even if the rape is reported to the police and the rapist is apprehended, he is rarely convicted and imprisoned.

RAINN (Rape, Abuse, and Incest National Network) has a chart at its website (rainn.org) that "Out of 1,000 Sexual Assaults, 975 Perpetrators Will Walk Free." The chart visually shows how of the 310 that are reported to the police, 50 will lead to an arrest, 28 cases will lead to a felony conviction, and 25 offenders will be incarcerated.

2.

THE statistics of *reported* rapes show that there is roughly an equal number of rapes by strangers and rapes committed by family, friends, and acquain-tances of the victim. The psychological damage of a rape committed by someone *known* to the victim, and with whom she may have, or have had, an intimate relationship, is severe and long-lasting. Robert Flint, a Minneapolis psychologist who has counseled rape victims, notes: "My clinical experiences suggest that rape by someone whom the victim knows and trusts can have a more powerful effect on her confidence in her ability to judge men, to feel safe, et cetera, than being attacked by a stranger. Similarly, a street rape is less devastating than being raped in one's own home."

Nevertheless, it is rape by strangers that women seem to fear the most. The basis for this fear is in part its unpredictability— stranger-rape can happen to anyone and at any time. According to the police arrest reports for seventeen of the largest American cities, a little more than 50 percent of all rapes were committed by strangers; almost 30 percent were committed by acquaintances; and about 10 percent were committed by family members, close friends, or lovers (in the remaining rapes, the rapist's relationship to the victim was unknown). Another fear, being assaulted during the rape, is dramatized by statistics. In a survey of fifty-six victims treated at the rape center at Jackson Memorial Hospital in Miami, Florida, weapons were present in 50 percent of the sexual assaults, and almost half the women reported physical injury in addition to the rape.

There is probably a higher percentage of unreported rapes by someone known to the victim than of unreported stranger-rapes' Victims who know their assailants are often hesitant to approach the police because they fear retaliation or blame for having encouraged the rapist. Children, who may fear the authority figure who raped them, or homosexuals, who fear they may be ridiculed by helping personnel, may be particularly reluctant to report their rapes. Married women, because of prevailing social mores, may also withhold information about their rapes even when the attacker is not their husband. One Manhattan assistant district attorney noted that of the numerous rape cases to which he had been assigned, less than 5 percent of the women were married. In the Jackson Memorial Hospital study, most respondents were single: out of forty-four who indicated their marital status, thirty-four were single, eight were divorced, separated, or widowed, and only two were married.

BRENDA: In August 1973 I was staying at a friend's apartment in Chicago, taking care of her plants and her turtles. I had gone to dinner that night with an old girlfriend of mine and her mother, who were visiting Chicago from California. I didn't get out of the restaurant until about eleven-thirty at night and I was sitting there trying to decide whether to take the el home or to take a cab. So her mother said, "Take a cab. Tomorrow morning in the paper, I don't want to read about you being raped and robbed." We all laughed and I hailed a cab.

I went home, took my bath, got into bed, watched a little bit of Johnny Carson, and fell asleep.

I woke up at about four o'clock in the morning. It was a hot August night but I woke up freezing to death. I was very, very cold. So I got up and went to the bathroom. Then I came back, looked at the time, and went to the air-conditioner, which is under the window, to see if I'd left it on because I usually don't like to sleep with an air-conditioner on. J looked at the air-conditioner, saw it was off, and I went back to bed. I was still cold so I put on a blanket.

Right after that, I saw a flash of light at the window, it was like a kitchen match that gives a nice big flame; maybe it was a lighter. I thought, Something is on fire. So I went to the window again, and I looked out. I couldn't figure out what it was. All I could see was a flame. I thought maybe the leaves out around the fire escape were on fire or something, I was very confused and kept trying to figure out what to do. Then I saw a hand attached to the light, and I saw feet and shoes.

I started screaming. I don't remember seeing him come in, but I remember my screams. I can also remember that I tried to fight him off, but I don't know for how long, I could tell afterwards that there'd been a fight because of the way the room looked.

The next thing I remember, I was on the bed and he had a knife at my throat. He told me to shut up or he was going to kill me. But I was so scared that I couldn't shut up, so he kept cutting me on the face and neck. Finally I was able to calm down and stop screaming and he stopped cutting me.

Then he pulled a bed sheet over my head and raped me. While he raped me, I was trying to bang on the wall so someone would know that something terrible was going on and connect it with the earlier sounds of the fight. I must have been able to do this because the guy next door called the police.

I thought that the rapist had stayed in my apartment for about forty-five minutes, but he was actually only there for about fifteen. When he had finished raping me, he started to look around the room for valuables. I told him that there weren't any real valuables and that it wasn't even my apartment. He asked me when my friend was coming back and I said that I didn't know. All this time I still had the sheet over my head.

At this point I thought he was going to kill me. He wasn't going to leave, so I figured I had a lunatic on my hands. I remember just lying there. I could hear him go into the kitchen and wash something—he turned the water on. And the other thing I could hear was my heart—it was just incredible. My heart was pumping. I was breathing really hard because I was scared. I finally remember thinking, Okay, I'm going to die. And my mind went into a different stage. It kind of started to float away.

Then all of a sudden I heard the door open and close. He had run away. I heard a knock on the door and I looked up. I was afraid that he was returning, but it was the police. After that, my mind goes blank, I can't remember anything. Afterwards, the police told me that they put me in the apartment next door and then chased the rapist and caught him out on the street.

When the cops ran after the guy, all of the other people in the building came out of their apartments. Only one person, the guy next door, had called the police, although everyone had heard me, As a matter of fact, a few days later a lady in the street came up to me and said that she lived two buildings away and she had heard the entire thing.

3.

BECAUSE her neighbor alerted the police, Brenda never had to decide whether or not she would call them herself. Other women who have had this choice and decided not to report their rape are often influenced by two destructive "rape myths." The first myth is that a woman is responsible for her own rape because she encouraged the rapist through her provocative actions, clothing, or comments. At the center of this myth is the belief that only women who really want to be raped are raped. This myth survives despite the fact that the Federal Crime Commission has concluded that only 4 percent of all reported rapes occur because of any precipitative victim behavior.

The second myth is that victims secretly enjoy being raped. The evidence for this myth is supposedly a woman's failure to fight off her attacker, accompanied by a calm and relaxed manner after the rape.

These pernicious myths encourage many women to conceal their rapes, even from their husbands, and also prevent victims who do report from receiving fair and compassionate treatment from doctors, police, courts, the press, the public, and even their own families.

The standard family reaction to rape is too often a reiteration of what this mother of an attempted-rape victim said: "When my daughter finally confessed to me that she had been sexually assaulted, I asked her if she had been hurt putting up a struggle. But she said, 'I didn't try to fight him off. I was afraid. I just knew I had to do what he told me to do.' After she said that, I began to reexamine her entire story and soon I became convinced that my daughter was as guilty as the man. That opinion hasn't changed all these years. I know I'm right—but to this day she hasn't forgiven me for mistrusting her and for failing to understand why she felt she had to comply."

The myth that prettiness or formfitting clothes will attract a rapist, and that *only* this kind of woman is raped, is accepted by many women. For example, in a review of television journalist Betty Rollin's book *First, You Cry,* Barbara Howar describes how Rollin's mastectomy made her unconcerned about the possibility of being raped because now—since Rollin no longer fit the presumed rape-victim type—she could not be raped: "The sense of self-detesting persists to the point where, as a New Yorker who once bolted her doors with chains, Rollin becomes careless with the locks, figuring, 'I was no longer afraid of being raped because, I thought, who'd want me now.' She ceases to pull her window shades at night because, of course, no self-respecting Peeping Tom would care to sneak a look at her."

Another indication that the public still accepts the myth that women are responsible for their own rapes is the reluctance of juries to convict rapists, Brenda, the rape victim whose experience was described earlier in this chapter, talks about the jury experience of a friend:

> She called me after jury duty was over. She was upset. She was the forewoman of the jury, and it was hung. She said, "You wouldn't have believed it. They didn't talk about the merits of the case. I kept going back to, 'Let's talk about the evidence.' But they just talked about the fact that she was stupid to fall for this guy's line and it [the rape] was just her fault. It was absolutely frightening what was discussed and voted on In there. It was not the evidence but whether this girl was stupid to fail for this guy's line that he owned a model agency and that she should come to his apartment for an audition.

Feminists explain these myths as further examples of how women are victimized and abused in a male-dominated society. Therefore, rape, a crime most often against women, is not considered serious by the male-dominated criminal justice system. To an extent, that is true, but it obscures the fact that these rape myths are part of a general social prejudice against all crime victims. In a society that emphasizes competition and achievement, just as "losers" are blamed for lacking initiative, so are crime victims blamed for their sufferings. The person who should be blamed for rape is the rapist.

Another popular rape myth is that most rapists are depraved black men who assault white women strangers. Some black revolutionaries have expounded on this myth, adding a political dimension. In *Soul on Ice,* Eldridge Cleaver wrote:

> *To refine my technique and modus operandi, I started out by*
> *practicing on black girls in the ghetto—in the black ghetto*

where dark and vicious deeds appear not as aberrations or devia-tions from the norm, but as part of the sufficiency of the Evil of a day—and when I considered myself smooth enough, I crossed the tracks and sought out white prey. I did this consciously, deliberately, willfully, methodically—though looking back I see that I was in a frantic, wild, and completely abandoned frame of mind.

Rape was an insurrectionary act. It delighted me that I was defying and trampling upon the white man's law, upon his sys-tem of values, and that I was defiling his women—and this point, I believe, was the most satisfying to me because I was very resent-ful over the historical fact of how the white man has used the black woman, I felt I was getting revenge.

FBI statistics, based on local police reports, dispute that myth. According to the FBI, rapists are equally divided between whites and blacks. In the majority of reported attacks, the rapist is under twenty-five years old. In family rapes, however—which are probably the least often reported—the offenders are predominately older white males. If all these offenders were reported, the FBI statistics for black rapists might conform more closely to the proportion of blacks in the general population.

The FBI does not include the racial breakdown of victims and offenders, but numerous studies of sample populations indicate that about 90 percent of the time, the rape victim and her attacker are of the same race. Statistics reported in a 1974 article on rape in New York City revealed that 55 percent of the rapists were black men whose victims lived in their own neighborhoods. The most recent national survey, conducted by the National Commission on the Causes and Prevention of Violence, found in 1967 that in seventeen major cities black men raped white women in 10.5 percent of the cases and white men raped black women in 3 percent. The remaining racial profiles were black men raping black women in 60 percent of the attacks, and white men raping white women in 30 percent.

A second misconception about rapists is that they are all mentally ill. But a California parole officer who worked with rapists does not agree. He was quoted in a classic article, "Rape: The All-American Crime," by Susan Griffin: " 'Those men [the rapists] were the most normal men there [in prison]. They had a lot of hang-ups, but they were the same hang-ups as men walking out on the street [had].' "

Psychiatrists have discovered that the common denominator between rapists is not that they are black or "sick" but that they have lower intelligence levels as a group and that they are likely to commit a variety of violent crimes in addition to rape.

Police officers divide rapists into categories based on techniques, such as (1) a rapist who also assaults his victims and is impotent; (2) a sexually inadequate rapist who tries developing a "love" relationship with the victim, asking her to act out his sexual fantasies; (3) a predatory, streetwise rapist who knows where, when, and whom to attack and is most likely to commit other crimes besides rape; (4) a sadistic rapist who is often witty and intelligent, and who is sexually aroused by his victim's struggle. He usually commits his rapes far from where he is known. This rapist is psychotic and unpredictable and is the most dangerous type, for he is the most likely to torture and kill his victims.

4.

THE suffering experienced by rape victims begins during the rape itself and continues most acutely during the first twenty-four hours after the rape, but it may persist for weeks, months, or for the remainder of the victim's life. Besides the trauma experienced during the rape itself, the extent of the victim's subsequent suffering depends largely on how much "blame" is placed on her for the rape by her family, friends, the police, doctors, the courts, and even by herself.

During the Rape

The compliance of many victims during their rape is usually caused by fear and a strong instinct for self-preservation. The male rapist usually has greater physical power than his female victim, and he uses the victim's predictable fear to commit the crime, knowing that if he produces a gun or knife or hits or verbally threatens the victim, she will usually comply with his demands rather than be killed.

The following interview with Marion shows how a victim's fright and desire to survive predetermined her cooperation with the rapist. Marion is a twenty-six-year-old single college graduate, the daughter of well-educated, professional parents. She immediately confided in them about her rape in September 1975 in her Manhattan loft apartment:

I had just come back to the city from my vacation in Nantucket. I had spent the first night at a friend's house. The next night I was out with some friends I hadn't seen for a while. We stayed out until after the bars closed. I came home at four, cooked some food, watched TV, turned out the lights at about a quarter to five, and thought how wonderful it was to be in my own bed again.

Then my cats began making a tremendous amount of noise, you know the way cats sound when they cry. I thought something might have been wrong with them, so I walked out of the bedroom and saw this thing coming into the room with a knife. He was a black man about twenty-six. I guess he must have weighed about a hundred and sixty pounds and was about five foot seven or eight.

When I saw him come in, I couldn't believe it. I kept saying, "I can't believe it. I can't believe it." I didn't have any clothes on but I ran to the door, even though I knew my neighbor wasn't home. He ran very quickly from the window, put the knife against me, and told me that if I didn't shut up, he was going to use the knife. I told him the only way I would stop screaming was if he put the knife down. When he easily put the knife down, t thought that there might be a chance for me. I knew I had to do what he wanted, but I hated the thought of having to go through with it.

He was at the end of the bed. I felt I had to talk to him, to try to make him relax, because he had so much adrenaline in his system that he could have reacted to the slightest little thing. I asked him his name and he said, "James." I said, "It doesn't matter if it's your real name or not, but at least I want to know if you're going to make me fuck you." He said, "it is. it is."

I asked him if I could put in my diaphragm, since I didn't want to get pregnant, and he said I couldn't. He mentioned that he thought I hated blacks, so my tone of voice switched to a street level and I said, "I've gone out with a lot of blacks," just to make him think that I wasn't going to do what I had to do only out of fear. I felt I had to make sure he believed that I might even enjoy it, so he would really be convinced that I wasn't going to turn him in to the police or anything.

He grabbed my arm and he took me to my purse. He wanted to watch as I put in my diaphragm, I said, "You can't do that. You have to turn around. This is a very private thing." My legs were shaking and he asked me to relax. I told him he could fuck himself if he thought I could be relaxed after his coming through the window with a knife. I just had to rely on my intuition and say what came to my mind.

While he was raping me, I was concentrating on the fact that it was *not* going to be pleasurable physically and so my body didn't react to it at all. There was a point where I thought I might be having an orgasm, but I refused, this time, to let my body rule my mind and I prevented it from happening. I kept thinking how disgusting it was. He wasn't a dirty person, but he wasn't someone I would have gone out with either—black or white—because he was just a turnoff. I knew when it was all over, I would have more worries about staying alive.

After it was over, I was sitting on the bed and he said that he felt very ashamed about what had happened. I kept talking so he felt that he was communicating with me, even if it was bullshit.

I told him to go out the front door because it was getting light and it wasn't safe to go out the fire escape. The whole incident took about two hours, but most of the time was spent talking.

After he left, I put on a pair of shorts and a T-shirt and went to the phone. I knew that my downstairs neighbors were sleeping and I didn't want to wake them up, so I thought of calling the guy that I had been with the night before. He had wanted to come home with me, but I said no, that I wanted to be alone, and it occurred to me that maybe if he had come . . . But the guy would have come anyway, not knowing that someone was there.

So I decided to call the last guy I had been dating. I woke him up. He was so sleepy he didn't know how to respond or deal with it. But I felt paranoid that the guy was going to come back. I felt as if I were hanging in space; as if there were no walls. So then I called someone else that I was dating—a Greek man, a very possessive type. But he didn't know how to react to it either; he felt I just wanted anybody to come down and be with me.

So then I called a fellow I had met in Queens—we had a platonic relationship; he wasn't even a boyfriend—and told him what had happened and he was there within fifteen minutes.

I had spent so much time convincing the guy that I wouldn't go to the police that I convinced myself as well, reinforcing the feeling that something terrible would happen if I picked up the phone to call them. So we [my male friend and I] tried to find an information service that I could call for help, because from everything I read I figured I was in for a terrible experience, but every number we tried only had an answering machine. At eight that morning I called my job and told them what happened. They're Italians and very conscious of our laws, so they said I should call the police. Finally, about three hours after it had happened, I did call them. I spoke to a policewoman and two police officers were sent over. Then I called my gynecologist, and he didn't make a big deal out of it since I had my diaphragm in. But the policemen took me to a hospital anyway; it was a city hospital so I wouldn't have to pay.

For the next five days my male friend was more or less my bodyguard. We stayed at my girlfriend's apartment because I couldn't stay there in my own apartment. If it had happened in the street, I could still go back to my own home and my own things, but now I couldn't.

At first I thought I was handling it pretty well, but about ten days later, when I was in bed with a man for the first time since the rape, I just burst into tears because it kept flashing through my mind. I stayed with different girlfriends for the next two weeks, Monday through Wednesday at this friend's house; Wednesday through Saturday at another friend's. The few times I did stay in my loft, it was with a man who spent the night with me.

About two months later I sold the loft. A week after that, I moved all my stuff into my new apartment uptown. I still haven't moved in physically; I think I'm a little uptight about the windows, although I put gates on them and a friend of mine who's a detective came over to check on the security and put the best locks on the front door so I would feel safe.

A rapist doesn't need a knife or a gun to persuade his defenseless victim to submit to his desires. The following interview with a woman who at the age of sixteen was forced to perform fellatio on a man from whom she had hitched a ride shows how effective verbal threats can be:

Even now, my face winces as I recall the nausea and disgust with which I was forced to perform fellatio on this middle-aged stranger. Forced? Did I say forced? True, he didn't have a knife or a gun. He didn't do anything more threatening than pull my hair with all his strength, pushing my face over his unzipped pants. But I was scared. So scared I couldn't move . . . couldn't run . . . couldn't even scream. I guess something inside me—would you call it instinct?—said that I'd better do what he asked if I wanted to come out of it alive. Or maybe part of it was that I kept hearing my mother's warning that something like this would happen if I ever took a ride from a stranger. I guess fellatio seemed a "light sentence" in comparison to the horrors she guaranteed were in store.

Some victims resist. They kick, scratch, bite, and use karate. They scream threats that he must leave or he will be caught by a neighbor or a husband who is soon due home. If these tactics are used early enough they may scare off the attacker. However, there is always a danger that resistance may provoke a rapist to even more violent assaults. Gloria, the victim whose brother and sister were interviewed in chapter 2, tried to avert a sexual proposition by threatening to "tell your mother." She was murdered.

One victim stopped fighting her attacker when she realized her resistance was pushing him toward other abusive violations:

It wasn't until early in the morning, when he heated up grease—hot oil—to throw in my face, to disfigure me, to ruin me, it wasn't until then that I changed my tune [and did what he asked]. Also he was getting ready to do something else—he wanted to go back to my house and put a gun to my boyfriend's head and have my boyfriend go down on him to prove to me that he was nothing but a pretty-boy jerk.

(The fact that she had stopped resisting, however, later made it difficult to convict her rapist.)

After the Rape

"I KEPT hearing my mother's warning that something like this would happen if I ever took a ride from a stranger."

As soon as the rape is over, many victims immediately begin to blame themselves, directing toward themselves the anger they should feel toward their rapists. At the other extreme, some victims initially deny that the rape was either serious or significant. This somewhat common reaction can confuse medical and law enforcement personnel who see the victim immediately after the crime. Sometimes this denial takes the form of joking about what happened or appearing composed and calm. These behaviors only reinforce the erroneous impression that the victim precipitated or enjoyed the rape. For example, one rape victim told a policeman, "I've had bum lays before, but this was the only time I thought he was going to kill me." The smile and flip manner that accompanied her words gave the officer the impression that she was a hard woman, too controlled in her emotions. Instead, she was trying to endure the trauma of the rape by denying the gravity of her experience and joking about it.

The most serious aftermath of this "denial technique" is that the victim may fail to report her rape. In view of this pattern, some states have lengthened the maximum time allowable for a victim to report a rape in order to be eligible for compensation. For example, New York extended the maximum period for filing after the occurrence from ninety days to one year.

There are other factors besides denial that determine whether or not a victim reports a rape in the twenty-four hours following the crime. An Illinois rape center found that "whether or not a victim reports the crime to the police is significantly affected by the degree of injury sustained, by the way in which the rape situation developed, and by the relationship between victim and assailant."

The more severe the injury, the center found, the greater the probability that a victim would report the crime. Fifty percent of the rape victims who were uninjured reported their attacks to the police; 64 percent of those slightly injured and 100 percent of those seriously injured made reports. If force was used to instigate the rape, 86 percent of the victims reported, but in the "social" class of rapes, only 45 percent reported. A victim would more likely report the rape attack if she was assaulted by a stranger (74 percent) than by someone known to her (47 percent). The center's conclusion was that "women are more willing to report rapes which fit the stereotype of a violent attack in which the woman is resisting."

In the twenty-four hours following a rape, the victim is extremely vulnerable. Among the people she is likely to see during this period of vulnerability are:

- The medical establishment, represented by either the emergency room personnel of a hospital, crisis intervention psychiatrists, her private physician, her own therapist, or paraprofessional counselors at a rape crisis center.
- Police officers, detectives, members of a sex crime squad, or, if a he detector test is administered, the person administering the test.
- Representatives of the criminal justice system, including the assistant district attorney, the lawyer for the defendant, the judge, the court clerk, the jury, and the court officers.
- Her immediate family—spouse, relatives, and parents—as well as boyfriends, co-workers, and neighbors.

The anguish and suffering of a victim in the months following her rape are either diminished or increased by the attitudes, comments, and actions of these people. Any behavior on their part that increases her anguish is usually caused by the recurring, destructive rape myths.

Within hours of a rape, a victim needs immediate medical care for her physical injuries and for the prevention of venereal disease and the termination of pregnancy if conception has occurred. Brenda, the young woman whose account began this chapter, had a typical medical experience. In the hours alter the rape she had become calm and detached, but an intern mis-read the reasons for her reaction:

Peggy [Brenda's friend] came and got me dressed because I was just standing there. Then the cops came back and they took me in a squad car and drove me over to the squad car that he [the rapist] was in. They asked me, "Is that the guy?" I said, "I don't know." Then they took me to the hospital. I was the only one in the emergency room except for some junkie who was complain-ing about something.

I sat for an hour or so. Then an intern came up to me and asked me questions—name, address, and so on. I remember I was very calm. That's my reaction when I'm very upset—I get extremely calm, very organized, and extremely rational. It's incredible. So I was just giving him the answers, one by one, and he looked at me and asked, "Has this ever happened to you before?" I said, "No." He said, "Oh, you're so calm, I thought it happened to you all the time." I was so mad. I didn't say any-thing. I was just really angry.

I'd been waiting for an hour or so and I'd had it with that intern. I got up to leave, but the nurses grabbed me and told me to sit down and that the doctor would be there in a second. Finally a doctor came and took me into the next room and put a little sheet around me, and he did the internal. It's the last one I'll ever have. I think I'd rather have cancer than have a Pap smear. I mean I will never have an internal again as long as I live. The doc-tor wasn't particularly nice, and it was making me very nervous with people walking in and out. I just wanted my privacy; there was just a little sheet. It was awful.

The medical examination of the rape victim is also an important part of the legal process. The presence of foreign pubic hair, sperm, and other evi-dence can be crucial for a rape prosecution to end in conviction. Yet many doctors are reluctant to treat rape victims or collect this evidence because they fear they spend days waiting to appear as a witness at the rapist's trial.

To overcome these obstacles some cities, such as Houston, designed special rape victim programs that include a standardized system of collection, transference, and analysis of medical evidence. Such programs led to increased rape convictions. In 1974, 48% of Houston's rape indictments were dismissed, 39% because of "insufficient evidence." In the first four months of 1976, after the introduction of the evidence kit, only 25% of the 34% dismissed indictments were because of insufficient evidence. SANE (Sexual Assault Nurse Examiner) programs that began in Memphis in 1976 and is now widespread to provide better care for rape victims in the emergency room.

The Months Following the Rape

Here is an excerpt from Sara Crichton's 1976 newspaper article, "The Most Misunderstood Crime:"

A friend of mine was raped four years ago. Like all of us who were raised in the city, she rarely walks these streets without constantly being on her guard—always wary of those about her, always checking storefront windows to see if she is being fol-lowed, always listening to footsteps to determine the distance of those close behind. But she let the protective barriers slip one tipsy Harvest Moon October night. When it was all over, when she was told she was free to go, she ran home, as she said, "faster than Halley's Comet."

Once home, she immediately called the police. "Well, honey," drawled the snide sergeant who answered the phone, "want us to come over and check you out?" She hung up.

The sergeant's response reported in this excerpt used to be the rule. Now, fortunately, it is more likely to be the exception. The denigration of rape victims is slowly disappearing, brought about by the introduction of female-staffed sex crime units who are usually available to interview the rape victims, as well as intensive special training, including films and lectures, of both male and female officers.

The police who responded to Brenda's neighbor's call and subsequently apprehended her assailant were professional and sympathetic. (Brenda was quoted earlier in the chapter) One policeman had his wife accompany Brenda to her first court hearing. Instead it was the legal profession—the prosecutors and the defenders—and the continual court delays that victimized Brenda by prolonging and exacerbating her suffering. Following her rape Brenda went without rest or sleep for one entire day while she submitted to tests and retold her story:

The cops came back to the hospital, picked me up, and took me down to the station. There they had me look through one of those two-way windows, but I couldn't identify him [the rapist]. I could have recognized him if they had put him in a lineup. I did identify his shirt and his shoes, I remember that.

But when I saw him at the police station, I didn't think that I could honestly say that I was positive that he was the one. If I had been told something like, "You don't have to say you are absolutely positive," then I would have felt better. Anyway, I figured that since the cops had caught him I was covered and he would still be prosecuted.

Next I went down to the D.A.'s office and told my story. I was very calm and precise. By the time I finished telling him my story, it was about one o'clock in the afternoon. They told me I would have to have someone take pictures of the knife wounds on my face and neck, so I spent the rest of the afternoon scrambling around getting a camera. And I remember that I asked for tranquilizers. I had a feeling that I was going to need them, it was the first time that I had ever taken them.

A few days later I returned to the courthouse for a preliminary hearing. I went to the police precinct first and one of the cops had brought his wife with him to go around with me that day. The preliminary hearing was held in a judge's chamber. It was a closed session. The people present were his [the rapist's] defense attorney, me, the [assistant] district attorney, and the people who take records. I took a tranquilizer just before I went in because I had no idea what was going to happen.

I told what happened, step by step, and then the defense attorney cross-examined me. He wasn't very hard on me. But it was still a little bit scary. It's just like a mini-trial. The judge, I recall, was very very nice. I just remember him saying to me, "Did he do that to you?" You know, my face. I wouldn't look at the guy.

They'd say, "Is that ... ?" I'd just look over like that... I could not look at him. I knew it would make me sick. So the cops took me home after that.

I guess about a week or so later they called me again. "Can you get down for the grand jury?" I didn't know what the grand jury was either— it sounds like the Spanish inquisition. So I was nervous about that one, too. But it was easy. I just went there with the D.A. and the defense attorney. The defendant wasn't there. The grand jury sounded like a big important thing, and the people on the grand jury were sitting bored out of their skulls, and I thought, Jesus Christ ... at least you could sit up straight. I was mad about that. I just told my story very quickly. So for a while, that was the last I heard about my case.

The preliminary hearing and the grand jury happened in August. By the end of October or November, I got a subpoena in the mail, telling me to come to the grand jury. I called the D.A. and told him I had already been to the grand jury. He wouldn't believe me. So I had to take off work and come down.

When I got there the D.A. wouldn't tell me anything and I kept insisting that I'd been to the grand jury and I described the room and I described what happened, and he just wouldn't believe me. I remember him asking me one thing that infuriated me, "What were you wearing at the time?" I said, "My nightgown." And he said, "Is that all?"

After that the D.A. checked some more and when I came back from lunch he said, "I apologize, you *have* been to the grand jury." But he wouldn't tell me if the guy had been indicted or not. He claimed that he couldn't tell me, which was a lie. When I left his office I told the two cops that the D.A, wouldn't tell me what the charges were. When they heard this the cops, both of whom were big guys—the D.A. was small—went into the D.A.'s office, picked up the indictment from his desk, read the charges, and then came outside and told me what they were. This is how I learned that the guy had been charged with eight counts of felony, rape one, assault with a deadly weapon, and breaking and entering. They had thrown everything in, even a misdemeanor because he took four dollars from me. But for months, that was the last I heard of the case.

I'd call the D.A. to ask him what was happening. He didn't tell me. He just kept saying, "I just can't tell you when it's going to happen." If he'd given me some reason behind it, I wouldn't have been so pissed off.

By December I called and told him I was going to the West Coast for Christmas. He wanted my phone number and address out there and I said, "You can't have it. I haven't told my parents and I'm not planning on telling my parents, and they're going to wonder why the Chicago D.A.'s office is calling me." But he thought it [the trial] was going to come up around December, but how do I tell my mother, "Excuse me, I'm going to fly home to Chicago for a few days, I'll be right back." So I said, "You told me this would be over by January," and we both ended up hanging up on each other. At that point I got a new D.A.

Brenda's victimization by the criminal legal system had scarcely begun. For Brenda, and for many other victims, the trial of the accused rapist, if and when it finally occurs, turns out to be more like a trial of the victim. Even if the judge and defense attorneys are humane and understanding, the victim may still have to recount the rape and also disclose details about her personal life and private habits. For example, in one rape case reported *in Juris Doctor,* the defense attorney asked the victim, "Why did you have a dildo in the drawer?" The defendant was burglarizing the victim's house when she walked in. He tied her to the bed, continued to rummage through her bureau drawers, and used the dildo that he found to rape the victim.

Because of unsympathetic defense tactics, many states have changed or are reevaluating their rape laws. In Maryland a special governor's commission has recommended that aside from a few exceptional situations, any evidence about a rape victim's sexual habits should be excluded as evidence. If revealing the victim's sex life were deemed necessary, it would first have to be discussed in the privacy of the judge's chambers. The judge would then determine whether the information was relevant and whether it should be presented before the jury and courtroom spectators.

Reforms such as this one might have made Brenda's "trial" less traumatic:

My trial did not come until eighteen months after I'd been raped. All this time the guy had been out on only twenty-five hundred dollars bail, and he had raped and shot a woman in Evanston and had immediately gotten out on bail again. In the meantime they kept using every delay tactic in the world. The defense attorney, who is now a civil court judge, was famous for his delaying tactics. Finally, one of the judges checked up on him and he said, "Oh, I'm on a case today, I can't go." So they called, and he wasn't on any case, he was just trying to post-pone the trial.

This kept going on and on. I must have been driving every-body there berserk. I certainly drove myself berserk. It was so nerve-wracking because I was really terrified of going to trial.

The awful thing was that when I was finally beginning to feel that I'd recovered, that my life was my own again, then the trial began.

When I got to the courthouse I remember there was a great deal of confusion. I remember someone saying, "Come on, hurry up. We've got to get over to the courtroom. The judge is pissed off." I said, "I waited eighteen months; he can wait fifteen min-utes for me." Then just as we got to the court, I said, "Where's the bathroom?" And I went in and threw up.

I must have been one of the most prepared persons to ever go into trial. First question, your name. Second question, your address. But I forgot my address. And I pooped out. So, I figured, oh, this is going to be awful. I mean, I was so scared that I was shaking.

The guy who raped me had a wife and twin babies. Well, I don't know if they were really his, or if he rented them. But, they were there anyway. He had a suit on, was cleaned up, and he really was a nice-looking guy. There were also D.A.'s from other offices to watch this one.

It was the ugliest experience I've ever had. It was equal to the rape, because it was humiliating to have the jurors and everybody else watching. They were all men, except one woman who was a social worker. I hate social workers now. There were two young guys on the jury, and one of them was giggling,

The prosecutor led me through the direct examination and I told what happened. And then it came to the cross-examination. It was terrifying. He more or less implied that I was a whore and I had gotten in a fight with my pimp or my John or something like that. It was implied that I was a whore because I hadn't worked when I had lived in Amsterdam, and I was unemployed in Chicago at the time it happened. I had to go through my whole finances and everything. And he just kept implying that I was a hooker.

I don't think the whore thing was going over too well. So then he tried to make it appear that I'd been raped by someone else, even the super of the apartment building. He asked me, "Do you know the super?" And I said yes. And he said, "And *he* certainly knows you." My answer should have been, "Yes, I spoke to him over the phone one day because the stove was broken." It's very frustrating. It's yes or no or I don't remember. You can't explain anything. You seem to always say it in a way that doesn't sound good for you. He even tried to imply that maybe the rapist was the guy next door who called the police. That guy was all of five foot three and he had a Prince Vallant blond hair-do and I do not think he was interested in women at all.

So the next thing he tried was "Okay, so maybe it happened, but she deserved it." The question was, "When he had you on the bed, you didn't scream?" "No," says I, "because . . ." "Judge," he says, "would you please direct the witness to answer yes or no." So it was, "No, I didn't scream." The reason I didn't scream was because I'd already been screaming and he had a knife at my throat. But you can't explain that. "Well," the defense attorney said, "why didn't you get out of the apartment? Were both of your legs broken or something?" So in the end, it was my fault that it happened to me anyway.

I was on the witness stand for two days and it was the most vicious attack I've ever been through. It was just so incredibly ugly, you wouldn't believe it.

The trial kept going on. The defendant never got on the stand. I was at work the next week and the D.A. called and told me that it was a hung jury. And I just started crying, I was so upset. Then two minutes later, the cop called and apologized and said they were going to go through it again. And I just said, "I don't know."

After the trial I felt really awful. The whole thing seemed to have nothing to do with me, It was just a game people were playing in a courtroom. I was just . . . disgusted.

It was after the trial that I went into one of the worst depressions I have ever been in in my whole life. I got very mean to people. I didn't want to be around them. I was destroyed by the fact that he got loose after what I'd had to go through. And that's when I put on weight. I just didn't want to see people.

Luckily he went to trial In Evanston for the rape and shooting of the woman he had assaulted while he was out on bail in my case. He was convicted and then he pleaded guilty to my rape charges. He got five years for the rape and ten for the attempted murder in Evanston. But I never found out what he got in my case. I'm still trying to find out. And I never got my property back from the court either and It's been three years. It was just a little money and my nightgown, but it's important to me as a symbol.

Lifetime Consequences

LONG after the actual rape, and long after the completion of any legal proceedings stemming from the rape, the victim continues to suffer and to fear that she will be raped again.

Because of this fear, many victims move or take precautions against future rapes. They enroll in self-defense courses, buy guns, and avoid men or being out late at night.

Sharon, a thirty-year-old divorcee, awoke in her suburban Miami home to find a young man holding a pair of scissors to her throat. "If you don't scream I won't kill you," he said. She obeyed him. He raped her and the next morning she packed and left her home:

I stayed away for a couple of months. They have motel rooms in this private club that I belong to and I stayed there, where there were a lot of people around. I didn't know if I should move or what. But the police told me—and this is true—that no matter where you move, how do you know who's going to be there or where?

But when I moved back to my house—down here there're pretty Cuban window bars—I barred up my entire house, which was very, very costly, I dead-bolted, chain-locked, and barred up the house—it cost a couple of thousand dollars.

I must tell you that to this day I do not stay alone in this house at night without waking up. Even when my kids are here, I use spotlights around the house. I tell you what I also do: I keep a gun in my car. No, I don't have a license. Someone had a twenty-two and, well, I keep it in the house when I'm here, but I don't like keeping it in the house when I'm not here. I've never gone to a range to practice, but if somebody ever tried to break into this house, I would not hesitate to shoot to kill. I keep it loaded. I wouldn't flamboyantly use it, but if the same situation came again—if I am aware of someone coming into my house and I am awake—then I would take that gun and kill.

Sharon is one of the many women who move, either temporarily or permanently, after a rape. Thirty percent of the questionnaires mailed by a Miami rape-victim center were returned because the victims were "unknown" or had moved without leaving forwarding addresses.

Moving can be prompted by more than a psychological need to avoid the scene of the crime; it can also result from a fear that the rapist will return. Sometimes, it is a justifiable fear. For example, a New York woman was killed by two men who broke into her apartment and bound her and her common-law husband; the police later announced that the men who slit her throat were apparently the same two who had raped her two months earlier.

The aftershocks of a rape are similar to those described by victims of other personal and property crimes: insomnia, nervousness, depression, lethargy, and changes in eating habits. Brenda experienced many of these physical and psychological torments:

I was twenty-six when the rape occurred. In the months following the rape, I aged so incredibly that my friends back home

were shocked when they saw me. I had put on thirty pounds and, for those first three months after the rape occurred, hardly slept. As soon as the lights went out, I was terrified. Any little sound would absolutely drive me crazy. I'd do my best sleeping from about seven in the morning till about nine, if I did any at all. it was incredible. Even tranquilizers didn't work.

My friends were really good, but I thought I was just burdening them, and I didn't want to talk to them about it anymore. I had no one . . . but I couldn't stop thinking about it.

Peggy is the friend I went out to dinner with that night. She's also from California. I started seeing her. I never could see her before, she's a nightowl and she was always going to have a party that would never start until eleven o'clock. I used to go to bed at ten or ten-thirty.

Now she was the only person who was awake at the same time I was, She was living with her boyfriend and I started seeing both of them a lot, but it was more like protection. I could stay up with anybody who stayed up late, so I'd go over to her house and they'd have all-night poker games. I hate cards, but I'd just sit there and watch.

During the first three months I had sex only once; it was not pleasant. Finally I called the rape center and I found out that not sleeping, and not eating, and throwing up constantly, and being a nervous wreck were all normal reactions.

After months of this kind of physical and mental suffering, some victims finally accept that they have been raped and begin realistically assessing their own responsibility, if any, for the crime. Self-accusing statements such as "I should have known better" are replaced with anger more appropriately directed at the rapist.

However, complete resolution of the experience is as rare as it is for the families of homicide victims. Usually fear, anger, and guilt remain at least partially unresolved as the psychological aftermath of the rape continues. For example: a thirty-three-year- old woman who was raped by a black man in her apartment house elevator when she was nineteen still has a fear of black men and finds it impossible to relax during sexual relations with her husband; a thirty-year-old actress who was raped in college continues to demand that her lovers "reenact" her rape; a twenty-nine-year-old secretary has not been able to date since she and her roommate were raped at knife-point two years before; a suburban Virginia woman, who has been unable to afford to move from the apartment in which she was raped eight months earlier, talks anxiously about the night a masked man entered her apartment through the kitchen window, raped her, and carved X's on her cheeks, neck, and breasts. This last woman lives with the fear that her assaulter will someday return:

I don't know whether the man who came in here knew me, had a plan, if I was picked at random, or what. It's a very spooky feeling to have to live with. I just never expected something like this to happen. I wanted to believe it would never hit home. I always had that kind of attitude. It's just unreal how the whole thing was handled [by the police].

But I'M be prepared—I won't let it happen the second time like it did the first. Now I carry a sharp scissors with me and a fingernail file. Sometimes I go so far as to carry a knife. I've even contemplated buying a handgun, but I don't know if I could bring myself to shoot somebody because in my heart I know that any-body who does something like this is sick. And I don't know if I could live with myself if I ever physically hurt anybody.

An intensive study in 1975 of fifty-six rape victims who were treated at a Miami hospital during the previous year further indicates their physical and mental sufferings: 70 percent of the women interviewed complained of "ongoing anxiety and emotional strain" since the rape; 25 percent had "lingering physical problems"; another 25 percent had altered "their love or marriage relationship."

Among the lingering physical effects of the rape were:

Asthma

Migraine headaches

Difficulty sleeping

Painful intercourse

Lesion on lip caused by scratch

Sore vagina

Difficulty with bowel movements (because of rectal injuries)

Sores on chin

Vaginal infection

Possibility of being unable to bear children

Venereal disease

Pelvic infection

Extreme pelvic discomfort and pain

Some of the mental aftereffects reported by the rape victims were:

Extremely afraid of being alone.

Fearful of people, strange men.

I am afraid and at times very nervous.

Confusion, temporary paranoia.

Noises in the middle of the night make me jump.

Made me more cautious.

More cautious with strangers.

As the mother of the victim, I'm very alert—young male teens are too friendly with young girls.

Not to be so trusting.

I don't trust men very much anymore.

Fear of being involved with men for a while afterward.

Fear of sex.

No one likes me.

Frigid emotionally.

My personality has become much harder towards the public and friends.

Bitter—I hate all [racial epithet].

Became withdrawn, isolated, frightened, bitter.

I wonder why someone would do this kind of thing.

Bad dreams. Child thought he was molested because he was bad. Reminders when having B.M.'s,

That the world is not as nice as I thought.

Some of the reported changes in the victims' personal and social lives were:

My boyfriend left me.

Fiancé reneged.

We have a great marriage until we get into bed.

I just have trouble having relations with my husband.

Dislike sex.

It wasn't the same afterwards. Guilt maybe.

Can't seem to fall in love.

I couldn't handle relationships with men for quite some time.

I've never told a man. I'd be afraid of his reaction. So many accuse a woman of really wanting it.

It's harder for me to trust or fully love.

Fray that child won't have sexual hangups.

I'm meaner in heart; and every man I meet, I turn away from.

I parted with the man I was dating—I didn't want to be touched for about two months.

Loved one reminds me of it.

A few rape victims are able to emerge from their experience with a positive attitude. One girl who was raped during her senior year in high school changed her career plans and decided to become a lawyer specializing in rape cases. In 1976, three years after her attack, she expressed the effect that the rape had had on her life:

I think an experience like this can affect you in two ways—you can dwell on it and not deal with it, or you can personally deal with it so that you come to terms with it. I should say the trial was harder to deal with than the actual incident. But I didn't have nightmares or guilt feelings.

It's not an experience I would recommend for people to go through to become strong; it depends on the psychological makeup of the victim at that time how she uses it.

Another rape victim who believed that she had "profited" from her experience said:

I'm probably farther ahead now than if it had never happened to me. When it happened, I was suddenly set back ten years emotionally and I acted like a child. Right afterwards, I started drinking heavily and almost became an alcoholic. Within eight months I was in the hospital; I had lost twenty pounds that I couldn't afford to lose. Finally I decided I had to confront myself. I had been stripped of all my defenses and realized how hard and mechanical I had become [before the attempted rape]. I think I'm in a better place now than I would have been.

These seemingly "happy endings" to a rape are encouraged by those closest to the victim since any changes, such as a new job or another apartment, are generally applauded as signs of recovery. But there are often unrecognized dangers: if these new directions happen too quickly, they may camouflage unresolved anger and fear. It may still take the victim months or years to resolve the rage or guilt that initially caused these "positive changes."

5.

Judith Becker's article in *Victimology*, "The effects of sexual assault on rape and attempted rape victims," published in volume 7 in 1982, concluded that "...attempted rape and completed rape victims have similar treatment needs and that counseling for their trauma should be available for both short- and long-term problems subsequent to a sexual assault." This was based on the researcher's interviews with 20 completed rape and 20 attempted rape victims between the ages of 15 and 64.

Sasha's attempted rape left her acutely aware of her vulnerability. She was angry at the bystanders who failed to come to her assistance, and at her husband for failing to empathize adequately with her:

About ten o'clock one night I walked out of the supermarket carrying a bag of groceries with some bananas, milk, and hot chocolate. I had about three cents left in my purse. A man came up from behind me and grabbed my collar. He was white and under twenty-five. He put his arms outside of my arms. I'm sure that he had been watching me, because he came right up to me; I never heard him. But he put his hand over my mouth so there was no time that I could make a lot of noise. He never said he wanted to rape me, but I kind of gathered that. I then tried to get into my car, but he got in with me. I put the groceries on the floor and put the key in my right hand. He said, "Drive somewhere." I said, "Okay, but let me put the groceries in the back seat." Then I hit the lock on the door and fell to the floor. He fell on top of me. Next I was somehow out of the car, and we rolled onto the parking lot.

The strange thing about it was that there were about eight men gathering and watching us. They just stood there and did nothing. Our wrestling match went on, and he said, "You're really trying to screw me up now. When I get you alone, that's it. That's the end. You're dead."

"No, you misunderstood me," I said. "I'm not trying to screw you up, I'm just scared."

That went back and forth for a while. Finally because there were so many people watching, he let me stand up. But I saw a car. There was a lady and a man in it and I just ran for the car. He followed me to the car. I was telling the people that I didn't know him. He stayed there for a few minutes, and then he just took off.

Finally one of the people who were watching the entire thing went into the supermarket, told one of the stock or check-out boys, and he called the police. They didn't come for fifteen minutes. The police tried to get some of the people who were standing around to give an identification, but they didn't. Their general attitude was that it was amusing, and I guess they assumed I was somehow connected with him—either his girl-friend or his wife.

I asked a policeman to come home with me, just to walk me to my house. Then I woke up my husband and told him I was just attacked by somebody. He told me to go to sleep—which I couldn't do because of the amount of adrenaline that was going through me.

The next day I was really frightened. I didn't want to go outside and I asked my husband if he'd stay home from work. I had to fight with him to get him to stay. I got no reaction at all from him. I don't even like to think about it because I get really angry. He was the first person I told about the incident. I didn't tell anyone else until about six months later at work. The girl I told had a little bit of horror, a little bit of fear. It was probably on my mind a lot during those six months, because it took almost one year before I started to go out alone at night again.

Sasha's isolation and fear of strangers continued for more than a year after her attack.; her anger lasted even longer. Unable to forgive her husband's indifference, two years after the attempted rape, their marriage had become strained and seemed to be heading toward divorce.

6.

MANY rape advisory services and rape experts now advise rape victims to use violence to repel their attackers. Among the techniques suggested are the "eye push" or the "testicle smash," suggested by Frederic Storaska in *How to Say No to a Rapist and Survive:*

> . . . *affectionately place your hands on the sides of your assaulter's face, gently putting them exactly where you would if you were going to tenderly pull his face toward yours for a kiss. Then you put both thumbs over his eyes and press, about as hard as if you were attempting to slip your thumbs into a jar of pre-serves. . . ,*
>
> *What you're doing, if you haven't guessed, is putting your assaulter's eyes out, actually pushing your thumbs into his eye-sockets. Press hard enough and the eyes will be shoved back against his cortex killing him. At the very least, he will go into shock and pass out. He may be temporarily blinded. He may be permanently blinded. Not nice, you say? I agree, but you have the right to defend yourself any way you can if you're in immediate danger of your life or severe bodily harm. It's you—or him. . . ,*
>
> *For the next best technique, the gentle approach is also the key. All you have to do is reach down slowly and carefully to your assaulter's testicles, tenderly place your hand on one of them, and, suddenly, without warning, squeeze. Hard. The testicles are about the same consistency and strength as a ripe plum—with-out the pit, Any woman can squeeze one flat in a single motion.*
>
> *One squeeze will send your assaulter into instant shock. If he is standing he will fall to the ground, If he is conscious he will be in excruciating pain, moaning, unable to rise. If he is lying down he will go limp.*

7.

According to the National Children's Alliance, two-thirds of all the cases handled by CACs (Child Advocacy Center) are for child sexual abuse. In 2021, 249,879 cases if sexual abuse allegations were investigated. A study of the records of the children admitted to the emergency room of a

Boston children's hospital for all injuries revealed that less than 10 percent of all possible sexual abuse cases had been reported.

In spite of disagreement about the *extent* of child rape and sexual abuse, its basic patterns are described more consistently: (1) For every ten girl victims, there is one boy victim. (2) The offender is known to the child in 80 percent of the cases. (3) Two-thirds of the child victims are emotionally damaged by the experience, and 14 percent are severely disturbed by it. (4) In 41 percent of the cases, the offense was repeated for periods ranging firom a few weeks to seven years. (5) In less than 5 percent of the cases was there actual penetration, attack, or any type of violence. (6) The offender was ten or more years older than the victim in 54 percent of the cases. (7) There was one assailant in 77 percent of the cases. (8) With girl victims, two-thirds of the offenses occurred in the girl's home; with boys, one-half of the offenses took place in the boy's home.

Child sexual abuse is not restricted to the poor or to minority groups, nor is it an interracial crime, for in almost 90 percent of all cases the victims and offenders are of the same race. The most frequent type of family rape is that of a father raping his daughter: the girl is usually about ten years old and the father continues molesting her for about two years.

Child sexual abuse is often broken down into two types: "incestuous abuse," in which a child is sexually assaulted by a parent or an older person in a similar position of trust, such as a babysitter, relative, sibling, or stepparent; and "sexual assault," in which the attacker is a stranger and the child is a randomly selected victim.

The popular image of a child molester is that of a stranger lurking near a playground and luring a child, with candy, into the bushes. Yet children are far more frequently raped in their own bedrooms by a family member. A word more comprehensive than *incestuous* is needed to describe these abuses since many are committed not by members of the child's nuclear family but by more distant relatives, neighbors, and older friends. Although child abuse by a stranger will often be reported and prosecution will follow if possible, incest is much less likely to be reported to the police. The family often chooses to resolve the problem privately because they view it as a private, not a criminal, matter; state penalties are indeed very harsh for this crime.

Sexual abuse by parents and acquaintances takes more subtle forms than child rape. It can include "loving parental gestures" that are too lingering, or that continue too long into adolescence, or that become centered on the sex organs; lewd behavior; indecent exposure; or attempted rape.

Even touching or looking at a child's private parts, although not attempted or actual rape, may have long-term effects on that child, especially if the offender is someone in a trusted position. Florence Bush, an experienced social worker who is completing a book on sexually abused children, knows from her own experience that all sexual activity with children will leave scars:

> I came from a very stable family which was both culturally and economically advantaged. At age six, my mother sent me alone to the friendly family dentist who did more feeling than drilling. When I told my mother of my experience, she did not believe me. At age ten, I was molested by the father of a boy I secretly loved and I somehow connected my secret love with the father's treatment of me and felt ashamed and guilty. At thirteen, my uncle, my mother's brother, came to visit from Chicago and wouldn't keep his hands off me. Again I told my mother and she scolded me for making up stories. Repeated lack of success taught me never to report such incidents again.
>
> At about that same time, I became obsessed with movies, I loved them and went every time I could, but found I could never get through a double feature without finding the hand of some gentleman up my skirt. My girlfriend Jane and I worked out a system. If a man would get "funny"; that is, if in the middle of a great Fred Astaire and Ginger Rodgers movie, one of us discov-ered a strange hand between our legs, it was time to get up and say in a loud voice, "I must go home now because my mother is expecting me." Jane and I would then change seats and hope we would be left alone long enough to see the end of the film. It never occurred to us to holler at the man, hit him, or report him to the management. It never occurred to us to hold the man responsible for what he had done. This was our problem, not his, and we handled it as best we could. In subsequent years, Jane and I reported regularly to each other on the number of exposed men we had seen, how we handled attempts to be touched and how we escaped from what might

develop into something violent and dangerous. After a while we became rather casual about our experiences, rarely became outraged, but simply tried to develop greater skills in avoiding and extricating ourselves from the sexual aggression of men without embarrassing the offender. This was excellent training and prepared me in later years for the breast grabbers, the bottom pinchers, and the body rubbers. The horror, the shame, and the humiliation never left me, but until recently I never knew I had the right to be outraged and fight back. I was, after all, trained to be a woman.

Unfortunately, the concept of victim precipitation is not applied to adult victims alone; even children are accused of "leading the assailant on." In this excerpt from an article by child psychiatrists Renée Brant and Veronica Tisza, that curious attitude is present:

> Frequently it is not possible to view the child as a passive victim in such cases; the child may in fact be an active participant. Father and daughter, for example, may be involved in physical games, such as the daughter's playing at riding a horse while being bounced upon her father's leg. At times such physical games generate more excitement and stimulation than a child is able to manage.

Both child and adult rape victims frequently suppress their anger. Later it may be released through the commission of violence, thereby concluding the cycle. This was the case of the woman whose reflections follow. Sexually abused as a child, she grew up to commit felonies for which she served time in prison:

> At the ripe old age of 11, I was sexually molested by my stepfather and this was to continue to happen to me periodically for the next eight years. My mother had been married to this man for about three months. I told him that I was going to tell my mother. He told me that my mother would not believe me and, if I did, he would see that I was sent to a home for bad girls.

Later that evening he proceeded to prove to me his influence over my mother. He told her that I had been disrespectful to him and needed a whipping. She obliged him by whipping me. Any childhood that I might have had was over. He had made his point. Of course, I didn't tell her.

A pattern emerged and the game of cat and mouse was continually being played. He seemed to enjoy trying to catch me alone while I desperately tried never to be alone with him, and to avoid him as much as possible.

I lived with guilt, hate and fear. Guilt because when he touched me it felt good. Fear because I didn't want to be rejected by my mother. She was all I had. Hate because I really hated this man. I didn't like him as a human being yet he generated all kinds of emotions that I wasn't ready to cope with or to understand.

As I grew older I believed I was amoral. I learned how to curse to keep him away from me and to sleep with a knife under my pillow. The fear was that I would one day kill him. I finally married to escape.

The marriage failed for I had become an alcoholic on top of everything else. I suppose when I look at it now it is not unusual that I would end up in prison. I lived full of contained violence for many years. My greatest difficulty has always been on a deeply personal level. Marriage has never been any great institution to me.

8.

IN Madison, Wisconsin, a judge refused to sentence a fifteen-year-old for rape, saying, "I've struck a raw nerve, but women are sex objects. God did that; I didn't."

In Los Angeles, California, a judge reversed a rape conviction, explaining that unless there is an emergency situation that necessitates hitching a ride, the female hitchhiker invites trouble since "it would not be unreasonable for a man in the position of defendant here to believe that the female would consent to sexual relations."

Certainly few crimes of violence have received more overnight exposure than rape. Within a few years in the 1970s during the decade of the woman's movement and, then again, during the #metoo movement in the 2000s, especially during the sexual assault trials of actor Bill Cosby and

Harvey Weinstein, have Americans reached a saturation point in books, TV movies or programs, articles, and films about rape? From the most unspeakable crime, has sexual violence become the most exploited and too often still misunderstood crime?

There have been many advances over the last decades for victims/survivors of rape and sexual assault. Almost every community now has a rape crisis center staffed by well-trained rape victim/survivor workers or therapists. Forty-hour training programs for their hot line volunteers help to provide additional free help. The VOCA Act of 1984 created by Congress provide funds to state and local programs to help victims, including victims of rape and other forms of sexual violence. There are federally funded rape victim units attached to local district attorneys' offices offer help to those victims who have reported their victimization and who may be witnesses in that rare trial.

Police have special sex crime units providing female officers and trained male officers offering sensitive approaches to the victims' problems, an unit popularized in the long-running hit TV show *Law & Order: Special Victims Unit (SVU)*. It has been on the air in the U.S. since 1999, starring Mariska Hargitay, who is also a fierce victim advocate through her nonprofit, the Joyful Heart Foundation. As mentioned before regarding the SANE program, hospital personnel are addressing the specific evidentiary needs of the crime.

But how to stop men or women from committing sexual violence has not yet been conquered. Perhaps the common knowledge that a rape conviction is rare and anxiety about how devastating a trial can contributes to the low (less than 30%) reporting rate for rape. Counseling and other assistance may be available to all rape victims, whether they report the crime or not, even if it is outside the criminal justice system. However, until the causes of rape are determined, and the crime is stopped, victims will continue to be traumatized by the predictable stages of post-victimization reactions. The damage done to the victim of either child. teen, or adult rape should never be minimized, and the crime should never be rationalized as a "natural" consequence of being a woman or a man.

5
"I Want What You've Got" Victims
(Robbery, Burglary, Larceny-Theft)

1.

I WAS coming home from school to babysit. It was about three in the afternoon. Three guys came toward me. I just said, "Oh well, they're just kids." All of a sudden, one guy grabbed me around the neck and the other two guys were holding my arms. One of them had a knife and said, "Give us all your money." They weren't very professional. When they left, instead of crying, I started to laugh. If someone had shown me a movie, I would have said, "That isn't me." The time went so fast when it happened—I'd say a minute or two—but it seemed very long, like about ten minutes. (From an interview with a robbery victim.)

Every year millions of Americans suffer violations similar to that one —or this one:

On July 23, I was mugged, robbed, and seriously injured. One moment I was a vital human being. The next moment I was a lump of flesh and broken bones on the ground, helpless, a hair's breadth away from death. (From an interview with a robbery, aggravated assault victim)

In 2019, 6,471,780 Americans reported being victims of a robbery, burglary, and larceny-theft (267, 988 robberies; 1,117,696 burglaries, and 5,086,096 larceny-thefts, according to the FBI's *2019 Crime in the United States*). However, that is only *reported* property crime victims. It is probable that those numbers are low since, according to the Bureau of Justice Statistics (BJS), only 32.5% of property crimes are reported to police. One reason might be the widespread belief that finding the criminals is slim—as noted in the New Introduction, only 13.9% of burglaries, 30.4% of robberies, 18.9% of larceny-thefts, and 13.8% of auto thefts led to an arrest. These offenses account for over 90 percent of all major offenses reported in the United States, and they are increasingly more violent and fatal.[*]

Robbery by definition implies the use of violence, for it is the taking of property in possession of its rightful owner by force or intimidation, with or without the use of a weapon. A robbery means that criminal and victim have confronted each other. Burglary is the "breaking and entering" into the premises of another and taking money or goods rightfully owned by these occupants. (If a homeowner suddenly appears while a burglary is in progress, it then becomes a robbery.) The term *larceny*, or theft, encompasses the crimes of shoplifting, purse snatching, pickpocketing, and auto theft, but excludes embezzlement, forgery, and fraud. Once again, if physical violence is used in the theft it becomes a robbery.

Today such strict definitions are blurred since property crimes, like purse snatching or burglary, are often as violent to their victims as robbery. Burglary is increasing—one is now committed every ten seconds—and its practitioners are becoming younger (in 1976, 84 percent of all arrested burglars were under twenty-five), more inexperienced, and more violent. While preparing a report, criminologist Marilyn Walsh explored the factors that distinguish younger burglars from older ones, as a possible explanation for the growing incidence of burglary violence:

> If you take the records of older thieves and then the records of juvenile thieves, the older thief appears to be a more stable offender. That is, his crimes and his police records are very consistent and read with monotony. It's all burglary, grand larceny, and so forth.
>
> It's really frightening, however, to look at the young thief's record because perhaps you'll see a larceny charge, then you'll frequently see a gun charge, like "carrying a concealed weapon." The next thing you're likely to see is an assault, which was probably plea-bargained down from a robbery; and then, as in the

---

[*] As you probably know, the police departments and the FBI switched completely to the NIBRS reporting system on January 1, 2021, with robbery now considered a property crime. Previously, under the UCR (Uniform Crime Reports), since it started in 1929, robbery was categorized as one of the four violent crimes (along with murder, rape, and aggravated assault).

case of one eighteen-year-old I studied, you'll see that the next thing is a double homicide.

An older, good thief—one in his forties—never has a gun charge or anything like that. In fact, a really professional thief in his mid-twenties who turned state's evidence in New York State said he made a point of letting everyone know, including the police, that he had never had a weapon on him and never would carry one.

Burglary is generally a crime of stealth, not violence. I think violence has become a substitute for the planning and skills necessary to the successful burglary. Burglary requires a certain amount of planning, and the younger thieves seem to have a lack of patience with this. The mean arrest rate for the [cases I studied] was six; for younger thieves, some violence popped in by the third or fourth arrest. It's hard to know why this is happening. Certainly it's a combination of the availability of weapons and a lack of fear or hesitation to use them.

When you read the theft reports on these kids, you have this awful feeling that here's a juvenile who takes a knife or gun along when he goes out to commit a crime and says to himself that if anything goes wrong, he's prepared. But he doesn't really think it through beyond that, so what we find are juveniles responding with the weapon in situations that really are not that threatening, where there is an avenue of escape and no need to resort to violence.

In addition, there aren't as many older, stable thieves in the environment to help them along. Older thieves are not generally sharing their skills because once they do, they become pretty useless. You have older safemen, who are still roaming around picking up younger partners who do the legwork or secrete themselves in buildings, but you don't find many younger safe-men actually cracking the safe because the older safe-men are not teaching the skills.

I would say, in general, that a different premium is placed on skills. It's just like everything else where there's been a real decline in craftsmanship. At one time, a good part of the theft population was skilled and had definable ways of operating. But skills and craftsmanship have been lost. Now, literally anybody can execute the skills demonstrated by the bulk of the theft population. They're not subtle. That's one reason why the clearance rate is so low on burglaries. If you walk into a place that's been burglarized, it could have been done by any member of the [theft] population. Even the least skilled of burglars is going to wear gloves. People watch television and take the minimal kinds of precautions.

Although the OJJDP (Office of Juvenile Justice and Delinquency Prevention) reports in its "Juvenile Arrests, 2019" that juvenile arrests for robbery and other property crimes have declined, there is another notable trend.   Since 1980, female juveniles getting arrested has increased from 18% of arrests in 1980 to 31% in 2919.

It is hard to estimate how much property crime committed by juvenile offenders is related to gang membership; the National Gang Center notes only 20% and 30% of law enforcement indicate gang membership in their arrests for offenses beyond homicide and graffiti.   In   Seattle,   Washington,   a   one-family   gang consisting of seven brothers from ages eleven to   twenty   were   arrested   192   times between   1968   and 1977.   One   convicted   accomplice   to   a felony-murder,   released at   twenty-two   after   serving   a   seven-year sentence,   admitted committing   more   than   thirty   increasingly   violent   muggings   before his arrest. Some of the "yellow sheets," or arrest records, on these youths may fail to note the degree of violence or force that was used.

OFFENSE	DEPOSITION
Burglary	Sent home with warning
Robbery (took bicycle at knifepoint)	Sent home with warning
Robbery (mugging)	Dismissed (no complainant)
Robbery (mugging)	Dismissed (no complainant)

* Source: Joseph B. Treaster, "Tale of 2 Young Muggers Who Prey on the Elderly," *New York Times,* April 11, 1976, pp. 1, 42.

Robbery (mugging)	Dismissed (no complainant)
Robbery (mugging)	Dismissed (no complainant)
Robbery (mugging)	Dismissed (no complainant)
Burglary, possession of stolen property	Pending; youth failed to appear in court; reminder mailed, but no warrant issued
Robbery (mugging)	Pending; youth failed to appear in court; warrant issued
Robbery (mugging), assault, burglary, possession of stolen property	Found guilty on all but burglary charge; awaiting sentence

As youths become older and more confident, their property crimes may also become more violent. Many graduate from "mugger"—a younger, less professional thief who tends to attack on impulse and in a close, one-to-one confrontation, such as on the street or in the park—to a robber, a seasoned thief acting alone (rather than in a band or group), going for "bigger stakes," such as stores or gas stations, and often planning the crimes far in advance and relying on guns, a well-planned escape, or a witness-elimination scheme.

Given the choice between their lives and their property, most victims would probably hand over whatever a robber demands. But victims can no longer be certain that they will escape a violent attack simply by surrendering their money and possessions, as explained by a mugging victim who survived:

From absolutely nowhere I was suddenly confronted by a very tall man. He had a huge butcher knife in both hands. He didn't say, "Stick 'em up" or "Give me your money." He was going to kill me first so he could rob me silently.

The minute I saw this knife coming toward me, I reached for his arm and caught it in time to divert the knife from my chest, so instead it went through my arm. As I started pulling the knife out, with his hands still on the knife, his partner came up from behind me, grabbed my two arms, and frisked me for my wallet. He took my watch off my wrist. Then, as though they had been trained in Vietnam, they calmly kicked my head with big boots. Then they took their hands and made sledge hammers out of their fists and started beating my chest.

Some robbers may stab and shoot first and then remove a wallet from the pocket of a dead victim; muggers may rape, and burglars may shoot if they are surprised during a theft; and purse snatchers and motor vehicle thieves may kill their victims.

The expression "Your money or your life" takes on more meaning when you consider the reported deaths in 2019 related to property crimes: robbery (509); burglary (84); larceny-theft (29); motor vehicle theft (38); arson (73). A total of 733 Americans were killed in 2019 as they were victimized during those crimes. (FBI, 2019 Crime in the U.S., Murder Circumstances, Table 10)

The headlines from American newspapers offer an indication of some of the violent "techniques" becoming more common with these young and inexperienced property criminals:

"Hunt 4 Burglars in Fatal Gunning at Queens Home"

"An Old Man Stabbed in His Home—for a Lousy $40 or $50?"

"Mugged Woman Dies Describing Attack"

"Two Grocers Slain by Holdup Men"

" 'Amateur' Kidnappers Slay Doc, 2 Sisters"

"Man Slain and Youth Wounded as Police Thwart IND Holdup"

"Tourist Slain Defending His Wife"

"5 Bind 3 in Family in $200,000 Theft on 9th Avenue"

"33% Slain in New York Don't Know Killer"

"Youth Held in Theft of Slain Girl's Pocketbook"

"Storekeeper Found Slain"

"One Killed, 3 Wounded by Uninvited Guest"

"Laborer Indicted in the Murders of 4 Brooklyn Robbery Victims"

"A Mugging Widow Slain"

2.

DESPITE his grisly crimes, the property criminal—particularly the robber—has traditionally been popularized and romanticized. Robin Hood, Jesse James, Billy the Kid, and Bonnie and Clyde have all been celebrated in ballads, stories, and, more recently, in movies and television programs.

The typical American arrested for robbery is quite different from the legendary one. About 7 of every 100 arrested are female, over half are less than twenty-five years old, and more than half are black. The typical robber may well be a drug addict; he is unemployed, unskilled, and poorly educated. Although there is little chance that he can be rehabilitated, he will be eligible for release within eighteen months of his incarceration. He has probably already been imprisoned for a previous felony and is likely to commit another soon after leaving prison.

The only common ground between this modern thief and the romanticized, fictional one is that they both use violence, and, as the following interview with a convicted thirty-four-year-old robber demonstrates, the modern thief identifies with the legendary myth:

I found there's the excitement of the kill. Like a John Dillinger. You're awake, alive, free, defying society. The eleven thousand, two hundred dollars I got for the first robbery lasted me three or four months. The forty-six thousand that I got for the second one—that's the robbery that led to prison—was half of the take. They never caught my partner, but they traced the merchandise to me through a sale, I got zero-to-twelve for robbing a store and holding two policemen as hostages; I'm getting paroled next month after doing seven years.

Nothing could have changed my committing the first or second rob- beries because I don't have any motivation. But man makes his own destiny, so I don't believe there's an excuse for anything. One time I come back from a job with money bulging out of my pockets. I showed it to my girl; but it was useless, because there was nothing legit we could funnel it into, so we stuffed it somewhere. What did I do with the money I stole? I spent it on wine and women.

We know about the violence of the "real" Dillinger. What is often over-looked is that other fabled thieves were also quick to use a gun or knife to get what they wanted. The Robin Hood legend is probably based upon the exploits of a band of outlaws, led by Eustace de Folville, who were pursued by a Nottingham sheriff. Although de Folville's band did perform some "good" deeds—robbing corrupt government officers and unpopular land-owners and abbots—they also frequently murdered their victims. In his book *The Outlaws of Medieval Legend*, Maurice Keen writes:

> At the pinch of necessity Robin's merry men spared neither man nor child. When Little John and Much the Miller's son sur-prised the monk who had betrayed Robin Hood to the sheriff, murder was the order of the day and they had no scruples about their manner of dealing with the boy who rode with him:
>
> > *John smote off the munkis head,*
> > *No longer wold he dwell;*
> > *So did Much the litull page,*
> > *Ffor ferd lest he should telle.*

So much for the innocent child; but even the dead had scant respect from the outlaw. When Robin slew Guy of Gisborne he cut off his head and put it on his bow's end. Not content with that:

> > *Robin pulled forth an Irish knife,*
> > *And nicked Sir Guy in the face;*
> > *That he was never on woman born*
> > *Could tell whose head it was.*

Robin Hood's life was a long struggle against the forces of tyr-anny and injustice, but his victory was only achieved in the blood of his enemies, and his admirers rejoiced to see it run.

Yet only the "heroic" Robin Hood is remembered. The public image of other, later, robbers, like Jesse James, was molded to fit the Robin Hood hero myth. In *Armed Robbery,* psychiatrist John Macdonald gives this analysis: "In 1866 or 1867 Jesse became the leader of a group of outlaws who held up banks, stagecoaches, and trains. Much has been written about Jesse James and his adherence to the code of Robin Hood. The names and locations change but the stories remain the same. Oppressive barons are replaced by autocratic railroads, grasping abbots by usurious bankers, and peasants by Southerners at the mercy of Yankee carpetbaggers. Helpless widows are featured as the recipients of kindness by both Robin Hood and Jesse James."

The hero worship of the modem robber has continued; in "The Sad Ballad of the Real Bonnie and Clyde," John Toland compares the real murderers and the characters in the film:

> But once the lights came on, I recalled again what Bonnie and Clyde were really like—that they were in the flesh about as lovable a pair as Use Koch and Martin Bormann. A contempo-rary reporter for The New York Herald Tribune wrote: "Clyde Barrow, a shifty-eyed young Texas thug who spoke with a whin-ing drawl, wrote taunting letters to the Rangers and struck only when he had the advantage, would have been an object of deri-sion to the old-time Texas 'bad man.' " The New York Times called him "a snake-eyed murderer who killed without giving his victims a chance to draw."

Besides an addiction to violence, current and legendary robbers both share an inability or unwillingness to consider the feelings of their victims. For example, one inmate writes:

> At present I am serving for three different crimes, all related to violence that society condemns me for, but in all reality, they don't understand. These crimes are: Assault with intent to mur-der—15 years, Assault—10 years, and Assault—1 year, all run-ning consecutive. Total of 26 years and to which I have served 6% years so far on this sentence to date and go up for parole again in June 77. I have done many violent things in my life, from fighting professionally to shooting people for money. After spending the past 23 years of my life in one prison or another,

I can't truthfully say that I'm sorry for what I've done or sorry that I hurt so many people. The only difference now is that I'm growing older and much wiser to the ways of life.

I got five years for that first burglary in 1952. I came from a broken home and was quite confused at an early age, Please allow me to explain. While living with my Mother in a very poor neighborhood, I had to steal buns and milk from the stoops early in the morning so that myself and my sisters and brothers could eat. Violence was just another part of life to me, even at such a young age, simply because we knew no other way. Our world was, and may I also add "Still Is," completely separate from what we know as society today. For instance, the neighborhood where I was first raised consisted of nothing but bookies, pimps, and thieves of every sort and the only Law and Order that we knew or understood was The Law. Therefore, no one ever went to the Police for Law and Order. If one was done wrong, You had to solve your own problems "Anyway you could."

A formerly incarcerated man writes:

I never thought about the victim at all. To a certain extent I never really saw him as a person but more as an obstacle that had to be overcome to get what I wanted. I do not see my crime [supermarket robbery] as a crime against any one person, but had it been such, I still would have thought in the same way.

Robbers are generally out for themselves, and their belief that "my needs are all that count" enables them to violate the rights of others. An assistant district attorney in Manhattan offered a man charged with the armed robbery of a food concession a sentence of four to seven years' imprisonment in exchange for a guilty plea (and the waiver of a court trial). "He wanted me to offer him two and a half to four years instead," the attorney says. "I explained to him that that was just too low. I also told him that it was pretty stupid of him to go back to the scene of the crime two weeks later. 'But times are bad,' he said. 'But times are also bad for the people you're ripping off,' I tried to explain to him."

According to one formerly incarcerated man, prison authorities and criminal rehabilitation programs seem to make little effort to encourage offenders to sympa-thize with their victims:

> When younger, I participated in armed robberies and mug-gings and sometimes employed force—often leaving a person injured physically. At the time, I gave no thought to the victim but as time went by I gave it thought as the question kept com-ing up.
>
> When I was in prison, I used to lay in a cell and think of the victim and what if it were somebody in my family. At that time, a sense of remorse set in. But at no point did the prison authorities attempt to deal with my feelings on this subject.

Lack of sympathy for the victim is a necessity for the property criminal's success. Further, these takers-by-force must have contempt for the victim's personal and property rights, as well as for such values as trustworthiness, friendliness, and concern. In the story that follows, the victim's concern for a neighbor's welfare "set him up" for the robbers:

It was early evening. I was home, talking on the phone to a friend, and there was a knock on my door. So I told my friend, "Just a minute. Somebody's at the door." I put down the phone for a moment, and I went to the door. I looked through the peep-hole in the door and there in the hall was a man. He was very excited, he was upset. I said, "Yes, what is it?" And he said very excitedly, almost hollering, "The lady down the hall." He pointed to the apartment where this lady lives. I've known her for years—she's an older woman. He said, "She fell on the stairs and she's unconscious, can you help?" I didn't even think about it, I said, "Yeah, just a minute." I went back and picked up the phone and told my friend that I'd call him back, then I hung up and went to the door. The man kicked it open and I backed up a little bit and before I knew it he had a switchblade out and was coming down my hall toward me. He grabbed my tie and I immediately turned away from him and he said, "Don't look at me, just give me your money," but I didn't have any money in my pocket or anything like that. I can't remember what I said if anything. Another man came in behind him immediately. I never saw this man. I never saw his face.

[The first man] had me up against the wall and just around the corner through the archway to my kitchen there's a cabinet and there within easy reach is a jar full of knives. Afterwards I fantasized that I could have reached around and grabbed a knife, but ... I was very frightened, extremely frightened, and I think something almost instinctively happened, like if you're in pain, your body goes into shock and you don't feel the pain. So I reacted in what I think of as the right way, which was to just become an object.

The other man had come in by this time and was beginning to look around the apartment. Very quickly they came back to me and proceeded to tie me up with neckties that were hanging in one of the closets. They tied my ankles together very tightly and then put my arms behind my back and tied my wrists together very tightly. Then they tied my ankles to my wrists, they tied a tie around my neck, and then they tied that tie to my ankles and wrists, so I was bent backwards kind of like a bow, I couldn't struggle because if I struggled or kicked I would tighten the tie around my neck and I would choke. They also gagged me somehow.

I thought, "This may be it," and the one thought, a sort of funny thought, that came to my mind was that I had considered about a month before giving up smoking and I was really pleased that I hadn't given up smoking because I thought if this is the end, I'm glad I didn't go through this month of agony without cigarettes.

They proceeded to collect everything in the apartment that was valuable. I had just cashed an unemployment check and so about seventy-five dollars in cash was right there on top of my dresser. They gathered together everything. I had thought about being burglarized and to protect myself from being burglarized where they might come in the back window, I had taken all the new items, the TV, the record player, the tape recorder, and I had taken cable locks, bicycle cable locks, and chained everything up to the heat pipe in the apartment so that if anybody did come in they couldn't get these items away. But in this instance, of course, my plan didn't work. I was lying there and they were talking and eventually one of the men came back with a knife and put it to my throat and said, "Where are the keys?" And I immediately said, "They are on the bookshelf, fourth shelf up from the bottom," so he went away and came back a couple of minutes later and put the knife to my throat again and said, "They aren't there," and I said, I couldn't say anything but, "Try the fifth shelf." I was cooperating with them in every possible way. I called them "sir" and I was really polite. So they got the keys, they unlocked all of the equipment from the heat pipe and just gathered it all in the center of the room.

After a while they came back into the room and pulled the sheet back [from over my head] and looked at the silver ring that í had on my finger. [One of them began] fingering this ring on my finger, this silver ring, and he said, "How much is that ring worth?" And I said, "Thirty dollars." And he said, "Is it a wedding ring?" And I said, "Yes," which it was. And he said, "Oh, well, we won't take that." So they didn't take that ring.

It was almost as if we had met at a party or something. Their attitude is what I think was remarkable. To get intimate in that way—you know, someone puts their hands on you, someone is close, someone is talking in a low voice, someone is ... I mean when someone has a knife or a gun they can do it or not. It's maybe the closest you ever come to—to death. It's like the ultimate power this person has and you seem absolutely powerless.

Robbery victims, like the Swedish bank hostage who yelled, "I won't let you hurt him," may often feel a closeness or gratitude to the criminal—for sparing their lives—that non victims find hard to understand.

A bank hostage describes her feelings with a similar sense of detachment from what she was experiencing:

Crazy things go through your mind. You know when you have someone pointing a gun, you don't ask them if it's real or not. it could have been made out of soap and dipped in silver paint for all I knew. But when I heard that thing go off in the vault, you have no idea the noise it made. When he was shooting it out the window, I remember looking to see the bullet holes. I knew it was a real gun.

I think I was most frightened of all when he recognized me [as someone who worked in another bank that he had also robbed]. I actually held my breath and I thought, "This is it," because I would be a witness against him for the other one as well. It wouldn't be an alleged holdup anymore. But as soon as [I realized] he didn't [recognize me], I took a deep breath and thought, "I guess it's going to be all right."

Statistics from the FBI, although incomplete, indicate that burglary is a crime committed by strangers 24% of the time, although the identity of the burglar is unknown in 46% of reported burglaries. (Reagan Homan, "Burglary Statistics 2022," Published by Bankrate.com, Almost 90 percent of all robberies and burglaries are committed by criminals unknown to their victims.

The psychological impact of a robbery or burglary, even if the victim is unharmed or the material losses are minimal, is stronger and more lasting than is popularly imagined. Victims of property crimes often lose their sense of security and their money, jewelry, or smartphones. They may feel violated and become wary of strangers. Yet too often they may receive too little sympathy from friends, family, or law enforcement officials, who, minimizing their trauma, may say, "Be happy you weren't killed." That is some comfort to someone traumatized from becoming the victims of a theft perpetrated on a crowded bus:

The bus was jam packed. Being the "good citizen," I moved to the back so the people up front would have more room. I fig-ure the way they grabbed my wallet was that one kid kept push-ing me and apologizing while the other one was unzipping my shoulder bag. Of course at the time I didn't realize it. I just felt a little annoyed.

About two stops after they had gotten off the bus, I sort of instinctively ran my hand over the top of my bag. It was open; I immediately felt around on the inside and then I started to cry uncontrollably.

"What's the matter?" my husband screamed.

"They took my wallet," I wailed. He gave me his seat, but I just couldn't stop crying. It wasn't the driver's license or the family photos or the measly five dollars that upset me. It was an awareness of my own vulnerability. If those fifteen-year-olds could look me in the eyes and *still* steal my wallet, would my life be next?

"I just couldn't stop crying. ... It was an awareness of my own vulnerability." Property crime victims usually describe the same reactions to unexpected violations as do victims of personal violence, namely, denial, shock, anger, and then guilt and isolation. The difference is the intensity and duration of those feelings. Robbery is not as devastating as rape, but it is a defilement. As in rape, the robbery victim has the feeling of being close to death. "I could have been killed," is a common response to a robbery experience.

But what if the woman on the bus had known she was being robbed? Is it better to fight or resist? A convicted robber writes from prison: "Unlike women, most men are hurt when they are mugged. The reason seems to be that they tend to resist and thus put their lives in jeopardy by so acting. Women tend to scream for help and often run from the scene. Men try to keep their mouth shut but to follow the criminal and apprehend him alone. Thus, the pattern."

Only one out of every ten robbery victims fights his attacker, and this resistance can be dangerous. In a study of 500 armed robberies in Denver, for example, one in four of the victims who used firearms against the criminal was injured; only one in twenty of the victims who complied was injured. Three ex-muggers said at a conference in New York City in 1975 that would-be victims should *give in* to muggers. One retired professional mugger was quoted as saying: "Most of the time, people get hurt when they resist because the mugger doesn't want to get caught. Don't fight. Don't fight."

Sometimes victims must fight back or be killed. That was the choice presented to a victim whose experience was related earlier in the chapter. If he had not diverted the butcher knife from his chest, he would have become a murder victim.

Sometimes a victim may not know whether the criminal has a weapon. This was the case with Nancy, a nurse who was mugged in a quiet residential neighborhood in Queens, New York. Although the robbery occurred seven years before her interview, Nancy recounted it with as much fear, animation, and emotion as if it had been a more recent attack:

It was about four-thirty on a rainy, dark afternoon. I remember walking down the street and this youngish guy was walking toward me. I was even thinking about what a good-looking black guy he was. The next thing I know is somehow he's on me and I don't know what's happening and I said, "What's going on?" Then I realized he was trying to grab my bag. I just remember trying to hit him with an open umbrella and finding out you couldn't get anywhere with an open umbrella.

He's pulling me and I'm still not thinking, I'm just reacting. The next thing I know, I'm being pulled behind the building. I was really afraid and I thought, "Shit, he can have *anything* he wants." So I let go and he ran up the street with the bag.

Then I remember some white guy running up to me and saying, "What happened, lady? What happened?" "He just took my bag!" Then he ran after the guy, so I ran after him. And I'm thinking, "Maybe I'll get it back." But the next thing I know, I see these two guys in a car taking off. They were working together. I said, "Holy shit!"

You don't even know what's happening. When I got home and I looked down, the whole front of my coat was ripped from knife slashes. The guy had a knife and I didn't even know it! I didn't have much money, only my papers and my driver's license.

I went out to the movies that night to keep occupied. I was still a little shaken, but what did I go see but that Audrey Hepburn movie, *Wait until Dark* [about a blind woman being terrorized].

I just sat there; the movie never really hit me because you still don't react.

Strangely enough, they found my pocketbook a few weeks later behind someone's garden. And everything was in it, except my cosmetic kit. It really surprised me because my gold nursing pin was in there and all my papers. I wonder what they were looking for.

Many robbery victims would like to fight back but they can't. They are among the growing number of elderly who are attacked by teenage muggers:

I was coming out of a health-food restaurant in Queens at six o'clock in the evening. It was sort of gray because it was drizzling and there were very few people on the streets. I later learned there is a drug clinic nearby. Walking along I saw two tall young men in their early twenties coming toward me. I said to myself, "They're not black, so I guess they won't have any hostility toward a white person." Somebody later said, "If you weren't prejudiced, this wouldn't have happened."

So I continued [walking] instead of stepping off into the gutter, as I would have done [if they were black]. I had a shoulder bag on my arm. As I passed them, I wondered why one of them looked at me out of the corner of his eye; without turning his head, the pupil moved. I thought about it, but that was the last thing I thought about because the next thing that happened, I saw stars. I seemed to go up in the air and I said to myself, "Well, this is death—I'm dying." When I came to, I was lying on the sidewalk with my feet across the gutter. There was traffic going by, but no one stopped. I turned to the side, and my pocketbook had been ripped, but nothing was taken. S don't know what scared them off, except they might have thought they had hit me too hard and killed me.

I spent a hundred twenty-five dollars for the hospital expenses. Every part of me ached. I had always been cautious before that since living alone. I had not even gone on a subway for three years. I was always very cautious, extremely cautious. It happened to me when I least expected it.

For months and months and months, walking in the street, I was afraid of my shadow. When I told residents of the neighborhood that it had happened there, they couldn't believe it. I no longer walk that street at all; I park right in front of the restaurant. I feel pain in that spot when I talk about it, but I guess it's just psychosomatic.

The elderly poor are extremely vulnerable to robbery and burglary. They often live in decayed, high-crime neighborhoods. Their apartments may lack basic security devices, since in most cities it costs between $100 and $200 to purchase and have installed the most rudimentary drop-bolt lock and chains.

If the elderly leave their apartments, they become an easy target for young street robbers. Many cannot run fast enough to escape muggers or fight hard enough to overcome them. Yet despite their defenselessness, the elderly are often brutally assaulted during a robbery. Because of these assaults, women over sixty-five account for 10 percent of all murder victims; in some cities the figure is as high as 16 percent.

The fear of crime keeps many old people from leaving their apartments. They remain inside under a self-imposed house arrest and arrange for food and other essentials to be delivered. Meanwhile, those who prey upon them walk the streets.

Most of the elderly people who are mugged each year are those who can least afford it, both psychologically and economically. A robbery multiplies the fear, loneliness, and sense of isolation that may have been already present for an elderly person because of abandonment by his or her children, the death of friends, and the decay of a neighborhood where the person may have lived most of his or her life.

Among teenagers and young adults, being mugged has become such a common urban experience that "Have you been mugged?" has become as casual a question at parties as "What do you do?" or "Where did you go to school?"

Younger robbery victims appear to be cooler and more rational about their experiences than older ones. They "know" that mugging is supposed to be such a normal part of urban life that they stifle their rage, deny the fear that they felt at the time, and are unreasonably detached from the violation they have endured.

Yet, when the scenarios of their muggings are retold, it becomes clear they they were harrowing experiences. A young woman in a department store finds a mugger pushing a gun into her stomach and hands over her pocketbook. An economics professor is forced into his apartment at knife-point by two youths; one searches for valuables while the other sits on the victim's chest and holds a knife to his throat. These are moments of terror that will haunt these victims for years.

Writers, too, have a tendency to camouflage their fear with a wit and insight that make their experiences as victims appear to be less terrifying. In an article, "Letter to a Robber," novelist Lois Gould describes how she and her two young sons were tied up by two "burglars" who then proceeded to ransack her house. Gould described the incident as a writer rather than a victim. Later she summarized the letters she had received in response to the article:

> Sure, some people pointed out some pretty horrible examples of how quiet passivity has not worked. And some feminists said I was reacting to old stereotypes in feeling guilty about it. But almost everybody reinforced my own instincts and observations that it's better to be cooperative with intruders. There's no way of knowing what will trigger the rage mechanism that is working in these people, Not long ago a woman was eating a sandwich in her store when a robber demanded all her money. She said to him, "Please leave me just $5"—and he shot her.

Everyone living in America today is a potential robbery victim; since "decreasing crime" is too vague and unrealistic a remedy, many citizens are finding more immediate ways of ensuring their safety. One way is exemplified by the "strike first" technique employed by a woman in her mid-thirties who owns a small shop in San Francisco:

If I hadn't been held up before, I wouldn't have been pre-pared. I never would have had a gun. I didn't open up a shop and buy a gun the same day. I mean, I had no intentions of ever own-ing a gun. I bought the gun because I had been a holdup victim once, and I didn't want to be a victim twice. The first time, I felt angry that somebody could come onto my property and threaten my life and get away with it. I was very angry. First I was scared, but then I was angry.

The guy I killed had been in jail. He'd killed somebody in 1969. He wasn't convicted, he was only arrested on the murder charge, but obviously he did it. The murder charge was dismissed on some technicality. He was a junkie. The gun he used was loaded, and it had been stolen in another robbery.

Well, it deterred *him* from going into another shop and hold-ing someone else up. He's not going to be holding anyone up again, and I'm sure if he would have gotten away with the money from me, he would have gone on to another [robbery]. My forty or fifty dollars would not have stopped him from a life of crime afterwards. It wasn't his big score.

Unless you realize that the police have their hands tied by the liberal court, who are more interested in the rights of the criminal than they are in the rights of the victim, you are going to continu-ally be a victim. You have to find out about *your* rights, and that's what I did after I was robbed the first time because I *had* cooper-ated with the police. I asked them to drive me around the neigh-borhood, looking for the guy, and I went to the files and sat there for about two hours looking at pictures. The police were practically laughing at me. They said, "Look, even if we catch him, he's going to be out on the street again because we have to almost catch him in the act. Your identifying him now doesn't mean anything." So I said, "What can I do? You know, what do I have to do? I have to sit in the store and be a victim?" And they said, "No. Get a gun and kill the next one that comes in. If he comes in with a gun and your life is threatened, you have every legal right to kill him."

So the police are the ones that are advocating this [tactic] because their hands are tied and they're just as helpless as we are. The only thing is to turn the law around, and let it benefit the victim. The police attitude about the whole thing was one of joy that I killed one of these fuckers. They're the ones that arrest them and have to see them out on the street the next day.

Some people didn't think I should have killed him. Some people were happy I killed him. It was split. The people who didn't think I should have killed him, I didn't consider my close friends. In other words, I didn't lose any friends over this. They were knee-jerk liberals who had never worked for a living or been a victim of anything. They could sit back in their easy chairs and talk about how oppressed these poor people are and we should give to them instead of killing them.

But a lot of little old ladies come over to me in my shop and thank me for what I did. I've had people come in who want to buy me dinner and presents and who've congratulated me. They've told me about their crime experience , . . little old ladies who've had their pocketbooks stolen and people in their thirties who've had their apartments ripped off three times.

There's been a lot of crime and violence on the street where my shop is. It wasn't an isolated incident. In other words, there's been a huge surge in burglary and robbery on the block and almost all of the shopkeepers can relate to what I did and are very happy about it. Most of them carry guns [now] too.

Although that kind of vigilantism is growing in America, the majority of citizens are still old-fashioned enough to believe that no form of violence can be condoned. Those citizens have to content themselves with wishful thoughts that they would "never" become victims or with such nonviolent techniques as analyzing victim-types and avoiding precipitative behavior.

Obviously there is no guarantee that a person will not become a victim, but one mugger offers as a warning the criteria he uses to select his victims:

> A potential victim is always self-inviting. That is, a person with unusual amounts of money tends to act different than a person without money or with the usual amount. For example, a female with plenty of money (more than usual) in her handbag will tend

to keep it closer to her body and often and perhaps unconsciously she will keep a tight grip. Not only that will give her away, [but] the fact that she keeps looking around for something that she is not aware of will be the real clue to what she is carrying. If you notice that is very contrasting to the free girl that walks very sure of herself and don't even have a hand around her bag.

There are several other clues that will give away a person, specially females. They are very particular due to the fact that a female is always very conscious and when she acts in a different than usual way she is in fact attracting attention to herself for some unknown reason. Of course this is dependent on the type of neighborhood or the class strata from where the woman comes. For example, a woman wearing very sophisticated clothes and a real tight grip on her bag in a poor neighborhood attracts mug-gers like honey attracts bees. Why, she will act different since she is in fact out of place. The same woman will not atract so much attention in a middle class area where she will feel at home and will be a lot more confident. Besides, the criminal that work the middle and upper middle class areas is a more sophisticated person. He will know how to talk these people's language and is most of the time interested in jewelry, coins collections, stamps collec-tions and the like. These criminal are not muggers.

Now, men. Men are the most stupid subjects as far as being potential victims is concerned. Men tend to trust their own force and their masculinity tells them that it does not matter what, they are capable of protecting themselves. As such they tend to brag when they have money. They exibit it, use big denomina-tion bills to pay for very inexpensive items. One example, pay a drink costing no more than two dollars with a twenty dollar bill. Also, buying drinks for everybody in a bar just to show that he has money. So, as you can see, men are not really spotted in the street but by looking at a bar and seeing who is buying the most is easy to tell who has the cash. Another bad habit that men have is to have the money folded twice and then it is kept in the front pocket. This bulges the front pocket, a very distinct clue to money thus a potential victim.

4.

BURGLARY victims are beginning to fight back too—one New York City man, tired of being repeatedly burglarized, electrified his apartment windows. A few weeks later a thirty-three-year-old drug addict was electrocuted when he broke through the "victim's" window.

The physical violence that occurs during a burglary that harms a victim is known as the "burglar surprise," such as when a victim unwittingly interrupts a burglar at work. Statistics are not available on how many of these confrontations occur, for such a "burglary" would be recorded as a "robbery" or a "larceny with personal contact." Such was the case of a New York woman in her forties who surprised a burglar as he was climbing through the window:

I said, "What are you doing here? You don't live here." The man quickly left.

The housing police took so long to get to the apartment that he was already out of sight. They looked over the situation, saw my girlfriend, and asked me in an insulting manner, "Do you always spend the night with her? Are you sure you sleep on the couch and not in the same bed?" The other policeman said, "Are you sure it was a man that you saw? Maybe it was another woman."

By the time they left, the New York City Police Department came. They said they would write up the incident and search the area.

The morning after the incident, it hit me. I had to go home to Staten Island and I was afraid to go into my own apartment. I got a terrible headache and butterflies in my stomach.

About two weekends later my friend told me the man was caught after burglarizing other people. He was a young guy about twenty years old. Still, I haven't been back to my girlfriend's house since the incident happened and that was on Memorial Day weekend over three years ago.

Even if victim and burglar do not meet, having one's home invaded is still usually traumatic. Distrustfulness is a common reaction, both immediate and long-term. For example, victims quite frequently accuse a neighbor or a friend, whether the suspicion is reasonable or not. After she was burglarized, an Evanston, Illinois, schoolteacher carefully interrogated both of her roommates. Even though the three women were close and long-standing friends, the victim still thought that they might have stolen her money. Finally she concluded that the culprits were probably the two men who had visited her apartment the day before on the pretext of buying a chair. But still, she blamed herself:

There were two reactions—one was humor because it happened in such a nice town as Evanston, Illinois, and the second was blame, because I hadn't locked the door.

After calling the police, I looked around and saw that the typewriters, clock radio, and television were also gone. The apartment was not messed up at all. I never really knew who did it. Thoughts at the time were disbelief, annoyance, and guilt because I thought a group of black guys who had looked at furniture for an apartment sale we were having, and had not bought anything, might have done it because they hadn't come back the next day to buy the chair that they had looked at. I didn't—and don't—like to think I have that prejudice.

The policeman who first came was very self-important and didn't seem too interested. His parting comment was, "Better lock your door because men like to come back after young girls like you." The detective that came the next day was nice and concerned. He told us to call him if we ever got into trouble.

A professional woman had an identical "first blame your friends" reaction:

You first accuse all your friends and anyone whom they might know. You start getting really paranoid and then you ask yourself, "Why am I doing this?" You know it wasn't your friends.

My burglary occurred on the day before Thanksgiving. My first impression was, "I'll really have to start making the bed in the morning. This place looks like hell." Then I noticed that all the pillow stuffing was on the floor, and that something had to be wrong. But it took me a good ten minutes to realize what had happened because you don't think it can happen to you.

It's a very very funny feeling, the feeling you've been raped. They went through *everything*, including my dirty laundry. It's just like you have no privacy anymore. Everything had been looked through, cased out. I had bills I was going to pay sitting on the table; they went through that. All my checkbooks were out.

I ran next door and called the police. The detectives arrived within fifteen minutes. Their attitude was blasé. But I tried to be honest and to say exactly what was stolen, to the penny. It amounted to thirty-five hundred dollars' worth of equipment. Still the detectives acted like, "Don't call us, we'll call you."

My apartment was built like a fortress. I had a Segal lock, a police lock, and an alarm system. I even had Operation Identification stickers on the windows and on the doors and all my things had my Social Security number. I had padlocks on the windows and grates on the padlocks. But they had walked in—right off the roof and onto the fire escape. They had taken these fantastic padlocks and grates off and walked right in. It was obvious they must have been there for the entire afternoon.

Sometimes they say it's not worth hiding things, but I had all my jewelry hidden in the kitchen, up on top, and at least they never found the hiding place. I heard from someone that you should never hide things in a candy box, in case the burglar is a drug addict.

My neighbors were very concerned. They decided that they would catch my burglar. Over the next two weeks they caught two burglars— but neither one was responsible for *my* robbery.

Do I feel any differently towards material possessions now? You bet! I'd like to get as many as I can. I want another typewriter and answering service. I realized how much these things meant to me.

Other burglary victims become *less* attached to possessions, almost as an unconscious technique to avoid the same feelings of violation and loss if a second burglary were to occur.

A dentist in his early thirties could withstand material losses from his burglary far more easily than Lhe emotional trauma it provoked:

I was really bummed out when I discovered the robbery in the morning, so I called in and took off the first day from work since I've been practicing dentistry. I knew I couldn't work on people. The rest of the day I was hostile and mad.

I guess I feel that maybe it's retribution for things that I've done in my life that have been bad. Something I've learned as a kid, like feeling shitty because I had to break up a relationship.

But then I began to feel the essence of the burglars in my apartment. I was cursing them. I began hating things and hating everybody. I began hating the girl that I was with the night these people were ripping me off. Hating society. Hating the people that robbed me.

The cops finally came over and they didn't help matters. They didn't really do anything but look and write out a report. Then they asked me how much rent I was paying and told me what a nice apartment I had. That didn't help either.

I went to see the girl I was with the night before and just left the apartment the way I found it for a day or two. I didn't look for the missing things because after I saw that my five hundred dollars was stolen—I had just cashed my paycheck—and my camera and my tape recorder, I knew they had gotten everything of value. They just lifted the door off the molding! I figured out they came through the window. They must have walked in from another building in the back. But I still can't figure out how they kept the dogs quiet. That's the room I keep them in. My downstairs neighbor said she heard voices and movement that day at about three o'clock, but she thought it was me. I haven't been home during the day in all the time I have lived here. Couldn't she have called the police just to check?

Another burglary victim, a woman in her thirties, was also distraught by the invasion:

> I opened the door, and there was all my stuff just thrown into the middle of the floor. You could see right through the door. They must have taken a crowbar and pushed it back. My checkbooks were gone. My TV was gone. My stereo was gone. I just looked around and promptly called my sister and started crying and carrying on.
>
> I felt violated. I felt people had been rummaging through things that were personal and very private. I consider my apartment personal and private. It's how I put things, how I do things, how I live; and somebody just came in and violated it. So I was really shaken up. I remember being very angry, upset, crying.
>
> I called the cops. I had to sleep in the apartment that night because I had nowhere else to go. I immediately made plans to move, but it's hard to find an apartment. And it cost me, because I didn't have any insurance.

A complaint common to burglary victims is that police are unsympathetic and unhelpful. Typical victim comments are: "The policeman who first came was very self-important and didn't seem too interested"; "The cops finally came and they didn't help matters"; "Their attitude was blasé."

A New Jersey detective says, "Most police believe that the victims themselves really don't care much about being robbed. Therefore, why should the police? I'd say most victims of property crimes take them as a consequence of urbanized social life. They report it for insurance purposes, and that's it. They don't ever expect to see their property again, nor do they feel they'll see the person apprehended. It's disheartening, but there's no real investigation for a burglary unless it's a major type and they're usually the ones covered by insurance."

Sometimes this police reaction is reinforced by victims themselves, who often deny the seriousness of burglary. For example, the professional woman who lost $3,500 worth of equipment said, "Burglary is just such a routine matter and it happens to so many people that nobody cares."

Yet most burglary victims, although willing to admit they know they will never recover the belongings stolen from them, frequently fantasize that the burglar is captured and the goods found intact. From the suburban woman whose pocketbook is snatched in the laundromat to the elderly man whose shoes and radio are stolen while he is hospitalized, to the vacationing family whose cash and jewelry are stolen from their hotel room, burglary and robbery victims are usually despondent over their loss and hopeful that their property can be restored.

The police determine which burglaries receive full precinct attention, yet their criterion is not the value of the stolen merchandise to the victim but the dollar value "on the street" as well as the status of the victim. In order to receive the "full departmental treatment" burglary losses must be above $5,000, except in Manhattan, where the base is $10,000. Unfortunately, the relationship of the amount of a theft to a victim's income, a more telling indication of the importance of the robbery to the victim, is ignored.

One midwesten woman was so determined that her aunt's valuables would be recovered, she became an expert in tracking down stolen goods. Few primary or secondary victims have the luxury of unlimited time for such pursuits, as this woman did, but the results were astonishing:

I went to about twenty places where the property might be— antique shops, pawnshops, They were family hand-me-downs, some nice antiques that she and my uncle spent time collecting. I asked questions wherever I went about who might be dealing in the property; sometimes my aunt went with me. We got some interesting answers, like "I was offered the property, but I knew it was hot. So I didn't take it." Or "I know what kind of property you're talking about." Like everybody knew what was going on except us. It was just like an inside circle and these people knew and wouldn't say anything. None of these legitimate antique dealers wanted to blow the whistle on the illegal operations. It was like a close-knit fraternity.

About three weeks after the burglary, I recovered some of the stolen property at a well-advertised and well-known auction place. I know that they knew they were dealing in stolen property. It even turned out that their son, who was a real estate agent, was selling stolen appliances to the clients that he placed in apartments. One of my friends bought an apartment from him; she also bought a refrigerator from him, which turned out to be stolen.

An incarcerated felony-murderer queried some of his fellow inmates who were confessed burglars and found that the criminals did not divide property crime into robbery or burglary but rather into commercial or residential burglaries. (They considered auto theft to be kid's work and therefore did not even classify it.)

Commercial burglaries are those crimes committed against commercial establishments, regardless of whether they are done at night or during the day. In residential burglaries, a person's possessions are stolen, as in the burglary of a home, breaking open of lockers in a bus station, and "airport picks." Some techniques used by residential specialists are described in detail by this inmate:

> *George X usually calls a home and ask[s] for the best time to see the owner for the purpose of selling something. He will ask for the best time to be there and upon being informed he will claim that he'll be busy at that time and will suggest another time. This will hopefully tell him when the owners will not be home and since people are very confidential [with] people over the phone it['s] easy to learn at what time there is going to be nobody at home. The rest is simple. (Another method is by find-ing if both persons work and how many children they have and the age of the children.)*
>
> *Frank X will call homes and ask the persons for data such as his and her birthdays, amount of children, ages of children, and so on. His pretext to get the person involved is by telling them that he is an employee of such and such a firm and is taking a survey. (Another method is informing the people that he is a col-lege student and needs the information for a class paper and his deadline is near thus can not come in person but "would there be any inconvenience in taking this data over the phone?" Surpris-ingly, most people will agree.)*

There is another breed of residential. The young and unex-perienced. They enter through windows or the door and they do so by just walking up to the home and knocking. If no answer is given the risk is taken. These kids commit a series of crimes and [it] is very fortunate [because] these kids take very little from the houses. Unlike the professionals who take everything, they clean up the place.

Unlike amateurs, the commercial criminal deals in cash, negotiable instruments, jewelry, paintings, and the like. He is not interested in clothes unless he is taking a clothes store.

5.

LIKE burglary, auto theft is treated lightly by most victims and officials—it is usually considered just another property theft. Most drivers have car insurance to cover at least some of the financial loss. But when Mrs. Lawson and her son surprised the thief trying to steal their car, the results were tragic—the thief stabbed Mrs. Lawson seven times and her nineteen-year-old son was stabbed to death. The car had been parked in front of their home in a quiet, middle-class, residential neighborhood in New York State. A year and a half later, Mrs. Lawson shared this advice:

Don't be overconfident. Where I live, there's always young boys hanging outside. The neighborhood boys even play basketball in front of my house. I was never afraid to go out of the house at night. I was always confident that everything was okay.

The car was parked right in front of the house. People say, "Just go right outside. What can happen?" That's what can happen. This happened right outside my front door.

It was completely unnecessary. My son was a boy who was never involved in any kind of fighting. He was an athlete and a college student. He went to college during the day and worked part-time in the evening. He wasn't one to stand on the corner with gangs. He had a motorcycle of his own, which he used to go back and forth to work, and he had his own car. Everything he bought by himself with money he earned by himself. He was really exceptionally smart.Good at everything he did.

It was just a complete waste. Something completely uncalled for. He was the last person in the world to deserve something like that to happen.

I really don't know where he [the murderer] is now. Nothing was said to me at all. I haven't heard one word from the police since the whole thing happened—what they did with him or anything else. Even the information about what prison he was in came from someone else.

Crime compensation? I did fill in an application, but they made it sound like I really had to be destitute to get anything back.

We [my husband and surviving son] really don't talk about it that much. It's just too painful.

Although it cannot be any consolation to Mrs. Lawson and her family, most of the 721,885 cars that were stolen in the United States in 2019 were stolen "nonviolently." (FBI, *2019 Crime in the U.S.*) Throughout the nation only 13.8% percent of those car thefts resulted in arrests. However, of all stolen property, the highest rate of recovered items is for cars (56.1% in 2019, according to the FBI) compared to just 3.5% of jewelry and precious medals.)

A disturbing new trend in 2020-2023 is the increase in auto theft and car jackings, up 29%, which may be more violent because the driver is present at the time of the theft. (Nicole Sganga, "Auto thefts, Car Jackings, in Major Cities Spike, New Report Finds." CBSNews.com, updated on January 26, 2023.)

6.

ANYONE who pays taxes or buys anything is a secondary victim of property criminals because of the hidden costs of crime passed on to consumers—expensive alarms, salaries of security guards, and losses due to shoplifting, employee theft, vandalism, burglary, and robbery. When pub-lic buildings are vandalized or more police are needed to ensure public safety, taxpayers pay.

For example, in 1965 the special police force responsible for patrolling New York's subways was tripled in response to a sudden increase in subway crime. Although the average theft from either a passenger or a token booth was about $50, the fear and violence associated with the crimes called for drastic measures. After the number of police patrolling the subways increased, there was a dramatic and sudden decrease in subway crime. In October 2022, facing rising subway crime in New York City, Governor Kathy Hochul announced a similar plan that included the payment by the state to the city for 1,200 overtime shifts for police to patrol the city's subways. (Emma G. Fitzsimmons, "New York City Will Increase Police Presence in Subways to Combat Crime," *The New York Times* online, October 22, 2022.)

The public are not only primary victims of property crimes, they may also find themselves unwitting criminals when they buy stolen merchandise from a "fence." Few property thieves steal for the sake of possession. Instead, they take items that they can quickly and easily convert into cash by selling those stolen goods to fences who then resell the goods to the public.

If the public asked questions about enterprises that appear to be illicit and refused to buy from unlicensed street corner "salesmen," property crimes, particularly burglary, might decrease. By not exercising good judgment, people may be contributing to their own future victimization. For example, a man in his early thirties bought a color TV off the street for a very low price. It was a new set but he ignored the fact that there was no sales receipt or warranty. For about a week, he enjoyed his new console. (He already had a working TV but planned to sell it or give it away in the near future.) When he returned from work one night, not only was the new TV missing but his stereo, his old television, and every appliance in his apartment were gone. Describing the burglary, he admitted that reporting the theft was out of the question. But he also realized that in telling the "merchant" where to deliver the (stolen) color TV, he also permitted the "delivery men" to case his apartment and probably unknowingly provided him with information about when he would not be home.

To combat the fencing operation so necessary to the disposal of stolen goods, many police departments have started special anti-fencing units. Millions of dollars' worth of goods have been reclaimed by impeding the operation of just one big-time fence. To accomplish this capture, however, thousands of work hours and months of careful observing and planning are necessary. To act too soon, and tip off the thieves, may inhibit any future measures as well. Citizens are becoming active in aiding the police in their anti-fencing operations by "spreading the word" about how to detect pos-sible stolen goods when going through flea markets or rummage sales. One way of deterring property crime is for people to engrave an identifying numbers on all valuables. (But be careful not to use a number, like a Social Security number, that would open someone up to potential identity theft.) These programs, that used to be known by a variety of names—Operation Ident, Operation Identification, Stop a Burglar with a Blue Hand— enable the police to prove possession of stolen property if they catch someone with a numbered article not his own. (Before, the criminal could claim that he just bought it up the street and lost his receipt.) It is extremely difficult to burn out the engraved number, and stolen goods can be traced across state lines with this system. A study conducted among inmates in a Missouri prison showed that the burglars engrave their own property with Operation Identification numbers since they know how difficult it is to dispose of such items. The laws are very strict about what happens to any pawnshop or retail store caught with marked goods for sale, so they too are on the lookout for such items. Although exact statistics are not available, one police officer active in developing the program among New York City residents estimated that the rate of recovering stolen but identified valuables is about 90 percent, compared with a recovery rate of about 10 percent for unmarked items.

Stealing has to become a more difficult way to earn a living for property crimes to decline. Yet far more urgent is the elimination of theft-related injuries and murders. Those who buy an appliance, jewelry, or other stolen goods with "no questions asked" may think they are getting a bargain. But one appliance store manager who had several acquaintances who were injured or killed during armed robberies knew that those indifferent buyers were also getting more than they bargained for. "Buy stolen goods and you're buying an orphan."

6

Considering the Victims
(Compensation, Restitution, and Civil Actions)

1.

FOR an overwhelming number of crimes today, the offender is never caught. For the victims, personal revenge is only fantasy. When the offender *is* found, justice rarely belongs to the victim:

In 1973, George needed money to take a trip to California with his friend. He got the funds by robbing, and then killing, Mr. Hecht, a lawyer. George sold the victim's television set to his mother; he was later arrested in Wyoming when he tried to buy a tire with the victim's credit card. He was returned to Boston. During the trial, George's friend testified that George had said to him: "I killed him. I strangled him with my bare hands. I strangled him until he was dead." George was convicted of murder in the sec-ond degree. But it was the Commonwealth of Massachusetts, not the victim's family, that was seeking to punish George.

Occasionally the fictitious revenge killings of movies such as *Death Wish* or *Lipstick* are replicated in real life:

In 1977, Mrs. Santiago was shot through the head and killed dur-ing the robbery of the family-owned grocery store. Within twenty-four hours, her widower, their teenage son, and a family friend engaged in a gun battle with one of the alleged felony murder-ers. A month later, a Brooklyn grand jury decided not to indict any of the victims-turned-killers. A spokesperson for the D.A.'s office declined to comment over whether that was an indication that the "revenge killings" were being sanctioned.

Revenge killings, however, are rare in contemporary civilized societies. The fact that the right to punish is vested in a public official *(public law)* distinguishes ours from a primitive society in which the right to punish is vested in the victim or the victim's kin *(private law)*. It is only among the world's surviving primitive societies that individual retaliation and collective responsibility survive—the victim or the victim's family is allowed to punish a criminal or directly receive goods or money as compensation for a crime. Before Western influence altered their customs, an "eye for an eye" approach to punishment characterized such cultures as the Comanche Indians, the Ifugao people of Luzon in the northern Philippines, the Eskimos, and the Nuer of Africa. Although anthropologists such as E. Adamson Hoebel believe that the feud— revenge killing—was a right more in theory than in practice, carrying out that right was not condemned. Yet even in primitive cultures, a "go-between," known by varying names such as the *monka-lun* by the Ifugaos and Priest of the Earth by the Nuer, was called upon to help settle grievances between victim or victim's kin and the criminal.

Examples of how crime and punishment were handled by these primitive peoples show that a belief in justice for the victim was deeply ingrained in their unwritten legal codes. Anthropologist R. F. Barton lived with the Ifugaos of the northern Philippines at the beginning of the twentieth century. These people, known throughout the world for their fifty-foot-high rice terraces, have an intricate natural irrigation system of springs and waterfalls. Strong family ties characterize this culture, and if someone is deliberately murdered, it is the collective responsibility of the victim's family to take revenge on the murderer and, even, the murderer's kin.

For the Ifugaos, as for other primitive cultures, prisons did not exist. Therefore, the choices for punishing a serious offender were the death penalty, a fine, or exile. The victim and his kin executed the offender; if another method of punishment was taken, a neutral person would decide on the correct fine based upon the class of the offender and the victim as well as the seriousness of the crime. In the Ifugao culture, an upper-class person who stole was fined more heavily than the middle- or lower-class thief since the higher-status offender was supposed to set an example for the community.

From the writings of explorers who lived with the Eskimos before Western influences distorted their culture, it seems the Eskimos took a strict approach to punishing criminals. A murderer could be killed by the nearest blood relative of his victim. The family might also accept material support in lieu of blood revenge, although it was not uncommon for the victim's son, when he came of age, to invoke his right to retaliation and kill the murderer.

The following legend is a good example of the Eskimos' belief in retribution and their faith that, if human revenge fails, a higher spiritual law will eventually punish a criminal:

Pâtussorssuaq, Who Killed His Uncle

There lived a woman at Kûgkat, and she was very beautiful, and Alátaq was he who had her to wife. And at the same place lived Pâtussorssuaq, and Alátaq was his uncle. He also had a wife, but was yet fonder of his uncle's wife than of his own.

But one day in the spring, Alátaq was going out on a long hunting journey, and made up his mind to take his wife with him. They were standing at the edge of the ice, ready to start, when Pâtussorssuaq came down to them.

"Are you going away?" he asked.

"Yes, both of us," answered Alátaq.

But when Pâtussorssuaq heard this, he fell upon his uncle and killed him at once, for he could not bear to see the woman go away.

When Pâtussorssuaq's wife saw this, she snatched up her needle and sewing ring, and fled away, following the shadow of the tent, over the hills to the place where her parents lived. She had not even time to put on her skin stockings, and therefore her feet grew sore with treading the hills. On her way up inland she saw people running about with their hoods loose on their heads, as is the manner of the inland folk, but she had no dealings with them, for they fled away.

Then, coming near at last to her own place, she saw an old man, and running up, she found it was her father, who was out in search of birds. And the two went gladly back to his tent.

Now when Pâtussorssuaq had killed his uncle, he at once went up to his own tent, thinking to kill his own wife, for he was already weary of her. But she had fled away.

Inside the tent sat a boy, and Pâtussorssuaq fell upon him crying: "Where is she? Where is she gone?"

"I have seen nothing, for I was asleep," cried the boy, speaking falsely because of his great fear. And so Pâtussorssuaq was forced to desist from seeking out his wife.

And now he went down and took Alátaq's wife and lived with her. But after a little time, she died, And thus he had but little joy of the woman he had won by misdeed. And he himself was soon to suffer in another way.

At the beginning of the summer, many people were gathered at Natsivilik, and among them was Pâtussorssuaq, One day a strange thing happened to him, while he was out hunting: a fox snapped at the fringe of his coat, and he, thinking it to be but a common fox, struck out at it, but did not hit, And afterwards it was revealed that this was the soul of dead Alátaq, playing with him a little before killing him outright. For Alátaq's amulet was a fox.

And a little time after, he was bitten to death by the ghost of Alátaq, coming upon him in the shape of a bear, His daughter, who was outside at that time, heard the cries, and went in to tell of what she had heard, but just as she came into the house, behold, she had quite forgotten all that she wished to say. And this was because that vengeful spirit had by magic means called down forgetfulness upon her.

Afterwards she remembered it, but then it was too late. They found Pâtussorssuaq torn to pieces, torn limb from limb; he had tried to defend himself with great pieces of ice, as they could see, but all in vain.

Thus punishment falls upon the man who kills.

Peter Freuchen, an explorer who married an Eskimo woman and lived with her people in the 1920s, also recorded Eskimo folk tales. Another tale that illustrates the Eskimos' sense of retribution is that of Kayuk, a man who enjoyed eating newborn puppies.

Kayuk would get hold of a newborn puppy, pretend to admire it, and drop it, "accidentally" killing it. He would then offer to remove it to avoid distressing further the hunter and owner of the litter. Once alone, he would cook and eat the puppy. But one winter, according to Freuchen, justice was finally done:

> . . . He [Kayuk] had a weakness for frozen liver. He himself went out hunting very little, but when somebody else brought home game and reported his catch, Kayuk immediately went to visit that particular house. And when the people had seal liver lying on the meat rack to be frozen and served as a special delicacy when they had guests, lie would often make himself comfortable upon the meat rack and devour every bite.
>
> One of the hunters got fed up with that. He had a dog that was getting old and useless, so he killed it and placed his liver on the meat rack. It was dark, and liver looks like liver. But the dog liver is poisonous, unfit for human consumption. Kayuk suspected nothing, he had been out to look at his traps, and the very same evening he was up there eating away lustily. The other villagers invented excuses to go out and watch him and—for once—enjoy his gluttony.
>
> The next morning he was sick and suffered terribly. He became almost paralyzed, his skin peeled off, and his eyes were very weak for months after. But he didn't die in this round. The next year, when Kayuk drowned, it was naturally considered to be a punishment from Silarssuaq, the great spirit of justice, who hits all offenders.
>
> Here a modern society would find that death for having eaten too much seal liver was too hard a sentence. [But] Kayuk had brought shame upon his family and had been a bad example, so they found it better to get rid of him.

2.

IN ancient societies, property crime victims had the right to monetary compensation by the offender or, if none was caught, by the state. Victims of violent crimes such as murder were revenged by the victim's family—a life for a life. Both of these customs must have been satisfying to the victim and the victim's family. If they were not, the victim had the right to negotiate with the offender (or the offender's family) for another alternative.

For example, it is recorded in Homer's *Iliad* that blood revenge could be replaced with "blood money"—a fine in lieu of killing the offender. Permanent exile was usually also necessary.

The Code of Hammurabi *(c.* 1728-1686 B.C.), instituted by the king of ancient Babylonia, is one of the oldest legal codes and also one of the most generous in compensating the victim. It was the victim who was considered first, not the offender. In Babylon, a theft victim was not repaid with goods of like value; rather, each crime carried different restitution. The theft of goods while they were being transported was punishable by a fivefold restitution; the embezzlement of a merchant's money by one of his employees required a threefold payment; and stealing from the priesthood or state, a more serious offense, could only be repaid by the death of the offender. If a thief was not apprehended, the Babylonian state replaced all of the victim's stolen property, but only after the victim had itemized his property "in the presence of God."

Criminals were treated harshly in Babylon. The severity of a criminal's punishment and the amount of compensation he had to pay depended on the victim's status. But every victim was avenged and compensated. The theory of an eye for an eye had certain qualifications. If a criminal blinded a slave in one eye, for example, he had to pay the slave a compensation of half a mina of silver. A commoner who suffered a similar injury received an entire mina. If this same crime was committed against an aristocrat, the criminal himself was blinded in one eye.

Babylonian laws had considerable influence on the Canaanites in Palestine, and there are similarities between the Code of Hammurabi and the restitution of the Old Testament. Restitution and vengeance are themes that recur throughout the Bible—"eye for eye, tooth for tooth, hand for hand, foot for foot, burning for burning, wound for wound, and stripe for stripe." If a thief could not afford to compensate a victim, he became the victim's property and could be sold as a slave. The victim kept the proceeds as compensation. There is no discussion in the Bible of rehabilitation. Instead, theft was discouraged by imposing a severe burden of restitution on the offender: by making him return four or five times the value of stolen property.

Ancient Rome and Greece gradually eliminated the right of the victim to conduct a personal vendetta against the criminal and replaced it with a system under which the state fined and punished the criminal.

In 621 B.C., Draco codified the existing oral Greek laws. The Draconian code was known for its harshness: practically all offenses, from stealing a piece of bread to killing a merchant, were punishable by death. But Draco's code shifted the responsibility for meting out punishment from the victim to the state.

The Draconian laws foiled to bring law and order to Athens, and twenty-five years later they were revised by a chief magistrate named Solon. Under Solon's code *any* citizen, not just victims or their closest kin, could bring an indictment against a criminal for any offense but a capital one (here the right of prosecution and punishment was still vested in the relatives). This was another significant step in transferring control over retribution and restitution away from the victim.

The Romans also endorsed the governmental administration of punishment and compensation. As in Greece, a public prosecutor did not exist; instead, any citizen had the right to bring criminal charges against another. As a result, many of the Roman criminal suits were frivolous, motivated by the large rewards, including a share of confiscated property, that were given to successful prosecutors. Also, as in Greece, some of the penalties provided by Roman law now seem particularly harsh. For example, if a debtor failed to fulfill an obligation, his creditor could haul him into a public square and proclaim the particulars of the bad debt. He could then bring the debtor before a magistrate who confined him for sixty days while the creditor continued to announce the debtor's bad faith. If the debtor, or his family and friends, had not discharged the obligation after sixty days, the creditor had the right either to kill him or to sell him as a slave and keep the proceeds. Usually the debtor was allowed to work off his obligation.

The Code of the Twelve Tables, the codification of Roman oral law written by a ten-man commission in 451 B.C., perpetuated the Roman tradition of restitution. Under the code a thief had to pay four times the value of what he stole if he used violence or a threat of violence, three times its value if the stolen property was discovered during a search of the thief's house, or twice its value if the thief was apprehended long after the crime.

The Germanic tribes that overran Rome modified the rights that victims had enjoyed under Roman law. By the ninth century A.D. and the time of Alfred and his so-called "Dooms of Alfred," the blood feud was invoked only if the victim's request for monetary compensation was denied. But payment was still made entirely to the victim or his family. As in the Hammurabi Code, each crime had a price dependent upon the type of crime committed as well as the victim's status, age, sex, in the case of a woman whether she was of or past childbearing age, and so forth. Anyone who refused to pay the set fine was ostracized as an outlaw and any member of that community could legitimately kill the criminal.

Gradually, however, the power of the community exceeded the strength of the individual, and the community began receiving part of the victim's compensation. Thus one part of compensation went to the victim—*Wergeld*—and another part went to the community—*Friedensgeld*. In Saxon England, compensation for criminal offenses consisted of two payments: one to the victim's family *(Wer* for homicide, *Bot* for injuries) and one to the ruler or king *(Wite)*.

The next step was for the state to claim *all* monetary compensation due a victim. The Anglo-Saxons adopted the Germanic system of splitting fines between victim and ruler, but whenever a crime was termed a "breach of the king's peace," the king received the entire amount. Originally for a crime to breach the king's peace it had to affect the king's household and property directly. By the twelfth century, however, the breach of the king's peace included many private wrongs. Soon practically all major criminal acts were decided in the criminal court. Fines were remitted to the royal treasury and punishment administered by the king's officers. The victim was stripped of financial compensation and of the psychological satisfaction of avenging the crime.

This was the turning point for victim and criminal alike, for the criminal forfeited the opportunity to make a private peace with the victim or his relatives. Crime became a public affair and the victim could neither punish the criminal nor absolve him of guilt.

The body of common law that emerged from these developments not only made it difficult for the victim to receive restitution but made it criminal for him to try. It became illegal for a victim to retrieve his stolen goods from the offender or to make a deal with the criminal that he would drop prosecution if restitution was prompt.

For hundreds of years following this displacement of the victim's rights, adjusting the type and severity of punishment to the type and severity of the *victims* injury or status was replaced by an emphasis on meting out punishment determined either by the criminal's character or chances of rehabilitation or by what crimes the *state* considered most reprehensible.

Civilized society, then, has taken the right to punish or to negotiate directly or receive restitution away from the (private) victim and transferred it to the (public) state. A philosophical basis for this transferral was described in the seventeenth century by John Locke. He explained that it was in the belief that life, liberty, and property would be better guarded by a collective force that the right to personal revenge was given up. Yet today, the treatment of offenders by the state frequently enrages victims, their families, and the public.

After seeing the movie *Death Wish,* in which the hero randomly kills muggers after his wife is raped and killed, a man whose teenage son was murdered said, "You really go along with what he [the hero of the movie] does. I have heard many people who saw the movie say that they can understand that it is hard to be civilized because we need to strike back."

Even those who have not lost a member of their family are outraged at the light punishment meted out to violent criminals by the modern state. A letter to the editor of a New York newspaper about the fatal 1975 Christmas bombings at LaGuardia Airport said, "There is only one answer and that is the swift execution of these terrorists upon their conviction. In the names of the victims and their families, justice demands nothing less."

Besides denying victims and their families the psychological compensation of retribution, the modern state has also made it difficult for them to receive monetary compensation. It is now the state that levies fines against criminals. It is also the state that keeps these fines and, instead of passing them along to the victim, applies them to the care and attempted rehabilitation of the offender.

Belgian criminologist Adolphe Prins wrote in the late nineteenth century about the inequitable treatment accorded the offender and his victim: ". . . The guilty man lodged, fed, clothed, warned, lighted, entertained, at the expense of the state in a model cell, issued from it with a sum of money lawfully earned, has paid his debt to society. . . . But his victim has his own consolation; he can think that by taxes he pays to the treasury, he has contributed towards the paternal care which has guarded the criminal during his stay in prison. "

In March 1977 a photograph of a convicted and confessed murderer-rapist appeared in a New York newspaper. Under the photo was an article describing how this man, who was a prisoner in a maximum security prison, had just been awarded his bachelor of arts degree at the expense of the state and how he was now ready to pursue his master's degree—also on public funds.

While the offender is being educated, housed, and fed at the expense of the taxpayers, the victim is left to pay his own medical expenses, perhaps to adjust to a permanent physical handicap, and to replace essential possessions that have been stolen and will never be recovered.

3.

THERE are four basic recourses open to crime victims today: some form of insurance, a civil suit brought by the victim, restitution paid by the criminal as a requirement of the state, and compensation with public funds. None of these options properly meets the needs of the victim; all are inadequate.

Insurance

THE need for some type of insurance against property losses due to robbery or burglary was dramatically illustrated when thousands of store merchants were literally impoverished by looting thefts that occurred during the New York City blackout in July 1977. Those who had *crime* insurance policies, however, were soon reimbursed with funds that prevented *total* dissolution of their businesses. Federal crime insurance is available in those states where local governments do not provide similar low-cost insurance against crime-related losses *regardless* of how crime-ridden the neighborhood the store is in. Federal crime insurance is administered by the United States Department of Housing and Urban Development (HUD) and is available in the following states: Arkansas, Colorado, Connecticut, Delaware, Florida, Georgia, Illinois, Kansas, Maryland, Massachusetts, Minnesota, Missouri, New Jersey, New York, Ohio, Pennsylvania, Rhode Island, and Tennessee, as well as the District of Columbia.

Residential policies are available in amounts of $1,000 to $10,000, covering burglary and robbery losses. Commercial policies are available for businesses in amounts from $1,000 to $15,000, covering the same crime losses. Any licensed insurance agent or broker in these states will sell a federal crime insurance policy in the same way as fire or auto insurance; the commission goes to the agents as brokers. Annual rates vary, but in most urban areas residential policies range from $30, for $1,000 coverage, to $70, for $10,000 coverage.

To be eligible, all participants must equip their doors with dead-bolt locks and all windows with window locks or bars. In addition, police must be notified if a home or an apartment is burglarized, and signs of forced entry must be visible, Repeated claims cannot raise a policy's rates.

Some victims who are injured in a violent robbery may have enough health and hospital insurance to pay their medical expenses; most do not. Those persons, unless they live in a state that provides government crime compensation (for which they need to be *eligible* for benefits), have to rely upon unemployment insurance, welfare payments, food stamps, or loans from private or business sources. According to a spokesman for the New York State Crime Compensation Board, most awards go toward medical expenses of victims.

Most medical insurance policies, however, are still not designed to fulfill all of a crime victim's needs. Fees for psychological counseling arising out of a victimization may amount to thousands of dollars; plastic surgery to repair facial disfigurements from bullets or knives is costly. A report issued in August 1977 indicated that about 18 million Americans lack a health plan of any sort. Many of these uninsured Americans are either the poverty-level or unemployed people whom the FBI identifies as the most likely victims of violent personal crime.

Civil Actions against Offenders

THE state prosecutes in criminal cases, but in civil suits, the victim (plaintiff) may directly sue his or her attacker (defendant) and, if successful, win damages awarded by the court.

Civil court, ideally, would be one place for victims to get proper restitution since almost every crime has a corresponding civil tort. The crime of assault, for example, is also the civil tort of battery; the crime of attempted assault is both the criminal and civil act of assault. A person who attempts or commits the crime of rape, robbery, or assault has probably also violated the civil torts of assault or battery. Other torts that victims may sue for are false imprisonment, the infliction of mental distress, negligence, wrongful death, libel and slander, invasion of privacy, and arrest without a warrant.

A victim usually sues his attacker if he has sustained physical injuries or grave psychological distress. It is not necessary for the state to press criminal charges against the offender for a victim to initiate, or to win, a civil suit. In a civil suit, the victim-plaintiff only has to prove his or her case by a *preponderance of evidence*— the victim's case need only be more convincing to a judge and jury than that of the attacker-defendant. Hence it is considerably easier to win a civil case than a criminal one in which severe rules of evidence require that the state prove a defendant's guilt "beyond a reasonable doubt." Furthermore, since the jury is deciding only whether the defendant (criminal) should pay the plaintiff (victim) a monetary award—and not whether the defendant should go to prison—juries do not have the same reluctance to convict as they often do in criminal cases.

Yet few victims of violent crimes consider initiating a civil suit, as shown in a study undertaken by the Osgoode Hall Law School in Canada of 431 crime victims in Toronto in 1966. Of 167 crime victims surveyed by mail and telephone, only 14.9 percent considered suing; 5.4 percent consulted a lawyer; 4.8 percent had tried to collect damages from their attackers; and only 1.8 percent (or 3 out of the 167 respondents) actually collected damages.

Those last statistics indicate why the alternative of a civil suit is pursued by so few victims; although it may be easier for a victim to win a civil case, it may be impossible to collect from the defendant the damages set by the court. One reason is that violent-crime offenders are "judgment-proof," too poor to pay any damages. Others may have money but do not have it stored in legal, accessible places such as banks or bonds but instead have it "hidden" under someone else's name or buried somewhere. Frequently, juvenile offenders—who account for almost half of all arrests for robbery, burglary, larceny, auto theft, rape, murder, and assault—appear impoverished, but have parents who are solvent and capable of paying damages to the victim. William Hyland, the New Jersey attorney general, testified as follows before a committee of the House of Representatives, Ninety-fourth Congress, on victims of crime compensation legislation: "Private lawsuits against the criminals themselves are, in the main, futile gestures. Most scoundrels are judgment-proof. And so, what is needed is a system of governmental indemnification against actual losses."

Besides the inability or reluctance of the criminal to fulfill the court's restitution decision, the victim may be unable to afford a lawyer in the first place, although the recent surplus of lawyers has necessitated that some take on cases on a "contingency fee" basis— only if their client wins is the payment of a fee necessary. The Lawyer Referral Services of the American Bar Association provide assistance in finding local representation around the country. Another possibility for crime victims is to consult one of the 300 local legal aid societies that are federally funded by the Legal Services Corporation in Washington, D.C. Although the requirements vary from program to program, if someone makes two unsuccessful tries to get a private attorney to take his or her case, free legal representation may be available in civil matters for low-income citizens.

A victim may also fail to sue a criminal because he or she fears retaliation or harassment by the defendant. Victims may also feel guilty about collecting damages—however justified and necessary because of hospital and medical costs—because it might be misinterpreted by their peers as "profiting" from their victimization. Occasionally a victim may feel the criminal has "learned his lesson" because a police officer reprimanded him at the station house, and the victim, unaware of subsequent expenses arising from the crime, reluctantly drops the charges.

There are, however, victims who do sue their attackers, and noteworthy cases are publicized or find their way into law texts. One recent example of victims bringing civil suit was found on "Page Six," the gossip sheet of the *New York Post,* In November 1977, the headline "Fists Fly on News Front" began a story of a reporter for a New Jersey newspaper who was suing a TV newscaster for assault and battery following an alleged fight. The assailant, the victim recalled, " 'grabbed me by the lapels and shoved me around. I got scared and started apologizing, and he let go. But when I got into my car, I felt a fist in my face.' "

In other cases victims sue agencies they feel were negligent in protecting them. For example, in *Schuster* v. *City of New York* (1958) New York City was found responsible for failing to provide proper police protection for Schuster after he cooperated as an informer and was later murdered by persons unknown. Other, more recent, "third-party" suits have included the payment of damages by hotel chains, furniture delivery companies, or universities for failing to provide proper lock systems that would have protected the victim against the criminal assault or for not screening employees properly to uncover prior convictions for violent crimes.

Restitution

RESTITUTION programs in the United States generally require the apprehension of the criminal. The criminal, rather than the victim, is the consistent variable in restitution programs; he or she makes restitution to the victim *or* to a "substitute victim," such as a charitable institution, if the victim is unable or unwilling to participate in the program. Restitution may be made in the form of money or services. Most restitution programs are restricted to nonviolent property crimes such as burglary and larceny.

Many restitution programs are motivated by the idealistic concept that the criminal's rehabilitation is aided by involving him with the victim (consequence) of his illegal actions. In some states, restitution is used as a "substitute" for prisons, as a necessary condition for probation or, later, early parole. Often some of the earnings of inmate work-release programs go directly to victims.

British philosopher Jeremy Bentham (1748-1832) advocated restitution when he said: "What is paid by the offender as a fine, is a punishment, and nothing more; what he pays as a satisfaction is also a punishment, and a punishment even more than ordinarily strong, besides this, it is a satisfaction for the party injured; that is to say, a good."

Advocates of modern restitution programs, such as Professor Burt Galaway and corrections specialists Joe Hudson and Robert Mowatt, cite four principal purposes and benefits of restitution: it offers the offender a method of circumventing more severe but permissible means of punishment such as a prison term; it helps to restore the offender's self-respect; it is less costly than keeping an offender in prison; and it gives the victim psychological and material satisfaction. In Multnomah County, Oregon, for example, a new restitution program repaid $480,000 to victims within eighteen months. In 1975, inmates on parole in Colorado paid $518,000 in restitution to their victims. One restitution program in Minnesota had eighty-seven paroled men participating between 1972 and 1975. Each man made an average payment of $400 to his victim, and after the convicts' release, only 8 percent committed new felonies. (A nationwide follow-up study of 78,143 offenders released during 1972 indicated that by 1976, 81 percent of all burglars and 74 percent of all types of criminals had been rearrested.)

In the Minnesota program, offender and victim sign a legal agreement stating how much compensation will be paid and how. Once this agreement is signed, the offender is paroled. He takes a job arranged by the program and repays the victim simultaneously working toward financial independence. The paroled offenders live in a minimum-security facility until they have completed their payments. Violent criminals or those with more than three felony convictions are ineligible for the program.

Even violent offenders would prefer restitution to prison. In a survey conducted by this author of more than 100 violent offenders who responded to this researcher's query in a leading offender newsletter, forty-two of the violent offenders who completed the detailed questionnaire whose crimes ranged from burglary, aggravated assault, robbery, rape, and attempted murder to manslaughter and murder were asked, "Except for murder, do you think a person convicted of a crime should pay the victim rather than go to prison?" Twenty-six wrote *yes;* six replied *no*, four had no reply, and six provided other responses. When asked what they should pay the victim for, inmates were divided over whether they should pay for property loss, psychological damages, or loss in work pay. A majority agreed they should reimburse their victims for medical costs. Exact tallies follow:

Property loss	Yes 17	No 19	No reply 4	Other 2
Medical expenses	Yes 22	No 13	No reply 4	Other 3
Psychological damages	Yes 17	No 17	No reply 4	Other 4
Loss in work pay	Yes 17	No 18	No reply 4	Other 3

Those who were unwilling to give restitution to the victim offered such answers as "I should be paid," "Nothing at all," or "I prefer prison." Responses to other questions were also interesting. Only three of the forty-two respondents claimed that they were innocent of the crime for which they had been imprisoned. Twenty-five out of the forty-two men had themselves been victims of violent personal or property crimes. Many indicated that they considered the violent crimes they had committed to be retribution for the crimes committed against them.

Compensation

FROM about 1728 to 1686 B.C. the Babylonian Code of Hammurabi recognized the commitment of the city and governor "to pay compensation to a victim's family if someone is killed."

In A.D. 1917, Italian criminologist Enrico Ferri described what had been the crime victim's plight for hundreds of years: "The State cannot prevent crime, cannot repress it, except in a small number of cases, and consequently fails in its duty for the accomplishment of which it receives taxes from its citizens, and then, after all that, it accepts a reward; and over and above this, it condemns every ten years some 3,230,000 individuals, the greater part of whom it imprisons, putting the expense of their maintenance on the back of the honest citizen whom it has neither protected from nor indemnified for the harm done by the crime; and all this in the name of the eternal principles of absolute and retributive justice. It is evident that this manner of administering justice must undergo a radical change."

Now, almost 4,000 years after Hammurabi, modern states are beginning to compensate some crime victims and some of their families.

Mr. and Mrs. Walker were shopping at their local grocery store in Brooklyn on December 14, 1974. Suddenly a thirty-year-old man entered the store, pulled out a revolver, and demanded that Mr. Walker "give it over." He then shot Mr. Walker in the stomach; Walker died before reaching the hospital.

At the time of his murder, Mr. Walker, a construction worker, was earning $1,000 a month. His life insurance policy benefits and small savings left his forty-four-year-old widow and nine-year-old daughter only $11,000.

Almost two years later, the New York State Crime Victims Compensation Board awarded Mrs. Walker $15,000 for the loss of her husband's earnings and as reimbursement for the funeral expenses, which amounted to $1,626.50. Mrs. Walker would receive no further crime-related benefits, and her $200-a-month Social Security benefits from the federal government barely covered her rent. She worked as a practical nurse to supplement that income.

The defendant was tried and convicted of manslaughter. He was sentenced to serve twenty years to life in a state prison. By the time of his release, the murderer would have cost the state of New York a minimum of $220,000, based on the 1976-77 cost of $10,537 to imprison each of the 10,020 incarcerated felons in New York State. The state corrections budget for 1976-77 was $240 million. In that same year, the crime compensation board was appropriated $3 million to give to victims.

As noted elsewhere in this chapter, all fifty states now have a state crime victim compensation board. Its necessity is best expressed by victims, such as Mrs. Walker, who have received even minimal financial benefits:

It would have been impossible without the crime compensation. I didn't know anything about it until a social worker at the hospital told me about it about a month afterwards.

My husband was a very nice, quiet man. He never was no trou-ble. It [his murder] set my daughter back in school nine months. She don't want to talk about it. She don't want to hear noth-ing about it. She breaks down. It would have helped her to have talked to a counselor when it happened. It would have helped me too.

Next month it will be a year since the trial. The trial was very bad for me because I had to see him [the murderer] again. After the trial, I got sick; very very sick. I went to bed for a week and I've been under a doctor's care for nerves and depression ever since. The doctor says he can't cure my mind. He sent me to another and he said my heart isn't too good because I'm in a very deep depression. I have nightmares about what happened. The doctor told me it takes time. Things like that take time.

It's hard to start a new life. It's not that easy at all. Maybe if I wasn't there [when he was killed], But I was right there. The man stood over him with a gun.

I've thought of moving away from the city since it happened but this is where we settled when we came here from Cuba, because it's better to get a job here.

Juan moved to Westchester, New York, from Puerto Rico twenty years ago. He had never missed work until February 1974 when he tried to stop an argument and was stabbed in the kidneys and intestines by a nineteen-year-old stranger. Juan has had to have three operations since then and has had to stay in the hospital a total of sixty-one days. The medical bills immediately after the stabbing were over $10,000. At that time, Juan was employed as a chauffeur for a Wall Street firm. His employer paid his salary while he was hospitalized and also lent him the money for his medical bills. But the New York State Crime Compensation Board award enabled Juan to pay back his employer.

I found out about crime compensation through the police department. A police officer told me about it when I told him about the expenses I was going to have when t was a victim. About a year after I was stabbed, they [the compensation board] sent me a check so I could repay my boss. Paying my hospital bills was a wonderful thing they [the compensation board] did for me. Oh, I tell you, I'm so happy. After thinking about the knife, and then I have to lose my health too with the money I owe, It was very bad for me, very bad. Also anytime I need a doctor because of what happened, they [the compensation board] will pay for that.

It was very bad. It [the stabbing] shocked everybody. The funny part of it is the guy that stabbed me didn't even go to jail. They caught him. He got three years' probation.

Since then, sometimes I've been very nervous. Very nervous. Any little thing I get so excited and nervous. I don't sleep very good. I've been going to the doctor now, but I'm still very nervous. Sometimes it gets so bad I take the sleeping pills he gave me, but just for a while. It cools me down a bit. Then I stop it because I don't like them.

Thank God, every day go by I feel better, Every time I drink liquor, it hurt me. But I don't need that. The only thing he told me is I can't lift no weight. He wanted me to report that I'm too disabled to work, and go on my Social Security benefits. I told him no. I want to be doing something, What I did was to get a second mortgage on my house and with the money I opened up a tavern, so now I'm self-employed.

British penal reformer Margery Fry was most directly responsible for the enactment of modern crime victim compensation programs. In the 1950s Fry, herself a purse-snatching victim, wrote passionate arguments favoring government assistance. For example, in "Justice for Victims," which appeared in the *Journal of Public Lato,* Fry wrote:

> A man was blinded as the result of an assault in 1951, and awarded compensation of 11,500 pounds. His two assailants, now out of prison, have been ordered to pay five shillings a week each. The victim will need to live another 442 years to collect the last installment. A bitter mockery! Have we no better help to offer to the victims of violent crime?

By 1964 the arguments made by Fry and other pro-victim criminologists began to yield results. New Zealand became the first modern state to provide government-funded crime compensation and to guarantee that a victim would not have to join the welfare rolls or rely solely on the generosity of friends and relatives. In 1965, Great Britain, Australia, and the state of California passed similar laws.

In 1966, state-by-state compensation in the United States began, perhaps as a result of the influential support of former Supreme Court Justice Arthur Goldberg. In a 1964 *New York University Law Review* article, Goldberg wrote:

> *Whenever the government considers extending a needed service to those accused of crime, the question arises: But what about the victim? We should confront the problem of the victim directly; his burden is not alleviated by denying necessary services to the accused. Many countries throughout the world, recogniz-ing that crime is a community problem, have designed systems for government compensation of victims of crime. Serious con-sideration of this approach is long overdue here. The victim of a robbery or an assault has been denied the "protection" of the laws in a very real sense, and society should assume some responsibil-ity for making him whole.*

In all state compensation plans, funds are reserved for personal injuries resulting from a violent personal crime, such as rape, robbery, or assault, or, in the case of homicide, for loss of support and, in some states, for funeral expenses. The largest compensation awards, which range from a low of $10,000 to as high as $190,000 as the maximum amount for a claim (in the state of Washington), usually go to victims who have suffered physical disabilities that will permanently damage their earning power. In most states, Good Samaritans—those injured while coming to the aid of a victim or the police—are also eligible. Compensation for property losses is not available although in most states, although those under the age of 18 and over the age of 60 who had items stolen necessary to their well-being, such as eye glasses, prosthetics, clothing, or hearing aids, may be reimbursed. (It is expected that property loss claims are filed with home or apartment insurance, companies.) One exceptions is the state of Florida. As stated at their state compensation program website, one of the eligible victims includes "Any elderly or disabled adult who lost property as a result of a crime."

An excellent way to learn more about eligibility requirements as well as the reimbursements or payments after all sources for reimbursement are contacted is from the National Association of crime victim compensation Boards (NACVB). At their website, https://nacvcb.org, you will find a state-by-state listing, with links to that state's program. It is an easy and convenient way to learn about that information which is unique to each state. There are some eligibility considerations, however, that can be highlighted such as:

- Reporting the crime to police is usually a requirement but how long someone has to do that varies greatly. New York State requires reporting the crime to police or another agency within just one week.
- Time limit to file claim also varies from within a year of the crime to within 7 years.
- You cannot have been involved in the commission of the crime.
- Other insurance must be factored into the claim and used first before any awards, such as medical or dental insurance, life insurance, in the case of homicide victims.
- Some states cover crime scene cleanup (up to $2,500).

- Who is covered such as the direct victim, the person who was the actual crime victim, and/or what some states refer to as a derivative victim (also known as a secondary victim) which could include the spouse, parent, sibling, child, or grandparent of the victim.

As noted above, most compensation statutes also stipulate that victims must have notified the police within a certain time after the crime and that they must have been cooperative with the police. For example, refusing to look through police mug shots might disqualify a victim for crime compensation.

In most states, a victim must also show financial need. what follows are two examples of crime victims who were disqualified by state compensation boards:

> Victim, male, age 24 . . . filed for reimbursement for medical and hospital expenses as a result of being jumped and assaulted which caused him to sustain broken nose and an injured upper lip. Although the Board felt that the claimant was an innocent victim of a violent crime, they were unable to reimburse the claimant due to the fact that no report to a law enforcement agency could be found on this case.

> Victim, male, age 29 . . . Claimant filed for reimbursement of medical and hospital expenditures as well as loss of income as a result of being injured when he was stabbed in the left shoulder by a knife or a sharp object which pierced his lung. The assailant was a female who committed this act without warning and who claimed that the claimant had mistreated her daughter. Claimant was uncooperative with the police in pressing for arrest and conviction of the woman who assaulted him, and, therefore, an important element of the statute was not fulfilled.

The federal and state governments in the United States have made strides in compensating victims. The federal government gives funds to the states who can use it for reimbursing eligible victims. some victims, such as victims of terrorism including 911, received federal funding. *Worth* is the 2021 movie starring Michael Keaton, who plays Kenneth Feinberg, who was put in charge of the controversial 911 Compensation Fund.

At their website, PrisonPolicy.org, the Prison Policy Initiative notes that spending on public jails and prisons in the U.S. is estimated at $80.7 billion. On July 22, 2021, President Biden signed the VOCA Fix to Sustain the Crime Victims Fund Act of 2021 with the goal of stabilizing the Crime Victims Fund which was set up as part of the 1984 victims of Crime (VOCA) Act. Previously the funding cap for 2021 for fiscal years 2021 had been set at $2.015 billion.

Even in states with long-standing compensation programs, relatively few victims are adequately compensated for their physical and emotional or psychological and certainly for their property losses. since that is rarely covered/ Consider New York State for 2021 according to the statistics shared at the https://www.criminaljustice.ny.gov site. In 2021, if you add up the number of reported victims in New York State and New York City for 2021, it totals 129,593 for the four violent crimes that they tracked: Murder (880 and 488 victims respectively), Rape (6,213 and 2,460, respectively), Robbery (18,050 and 13,909) and Aggravated Assault (51,086 and 36,507).

Now consider that the New York State Crime Victim Compensation Board reports that for 2020-2021, they accepted 7,058 claims from victims and paid out $18,696,108 to individual victims and $91,476,066 to victim witness assistance programs, If you divide the number of claims into that total amount, you can see how small each individual claim was although the amount awarded would vary depending upon the medical or other approved costs to reimburse. Since there were 129,593 reported violent crime victims in New York in 2021. The total accepted claims and the total payouts are relatively small.

If someone in New York State is murdered, all that is available to a spouse or eligible family member for that lifetime of lost earnings: $30,000. That is generally only paid out after any other sources like life insurance are unavailable.

If approved, the New York State Crime Victims Board will reimburse up to $6,000 for a funeral. However, the Legal Referral Service for the New York City Bar at their website (nycbar.org) notes "The average price of a funeral in New York is $10,000." (Retrieved February 3, 2023). You can see why so many crime victims try other sources for funding, such the crowdfunding site gofundme.com. The states and federal government have made strides since the late 1970s in offering compensation to some crime victims and their families, but there is still so much more that needs to be done.

7

Summing Up

It is impossible to undo a victimization. At the least, help for victims should include the promise that they will not be violated again, but that pledge is equally impossible. Wendy, whose recollection of her boyfriend's murder began Chapter One, was a secondary victim of homicide when she was in her teens, living in a California suburb. Over ten years later, on the other side of the country, she was again a witness to a crime. For her—and for another victim of this incident—the fear she had for a decade—that she could be victimized twice—was realized. Luckily she was unhurt:

The first day I was back in New York [after being away for about eight months] I had a marvelous lunch with my friend at a nice little French restaurant. Then I went to Fifth Avenue in the fifties to return an airline ticket and get a cash refund. I walked in and a robbery was going on. The guy apparently jumped over the counter and pulled out a gun. I watched him order the attendants behind the counter to open the drawers faster. This guy started stuffing his pockets with all the money. The clerk kept telling us to be cairn and the guy was reiterating it.

Then, finally, the guy runs around the counter, walks out past us, and the clerk unlocks the door and the police come. This was on a Monday, and on the previous Wednesday they had been similarly robbed. Prior to that, they had been at that location for ten years without an incident.

I had been talking to an architect from Rome. After this thing [the robbery] and after the police came, people were really failling apart. There was one woman who had to go into the back room. None of us were really threatened at all, but people were so shook up that to watch everybody I was still a little bit shaken.

I couldn't believe what had happened, and what I had been through. I was going to Bloomingdale's, so he [the architect] and I walked together. We couldn't stop talking because of this anxiety. He had an appointment and he was already late, but he practically forced me to have coffee. We talked about anything except what happened. About communism, about what's happening in Italy, what my husband and I had done in Tanzania. We had a lot to talk about but that wasn't the point. He was about an hour and a half late and he was just shaken. He told me that he had lived in New York and he was robbed [his home was burglarized] but he said he didn't feel bad because they took possessions—radio, stereo, and so forth—things that could be replaced and are nothing. But he said, "This time I feel different. I feel trespassed." And I said, "Sort of like rape." And he said, "Yes, I feel that." And it was so odd because I had a tragic experience in my life [Alan's murder] and therefore I may be responding differently than a lot of people because I was very nervous. But yet even this man, who to my knowledge has not had such an incident happen to him, was visibly shaken and white.

I left him at the corner and I started to call a good friend of mine in New York just to talk to him because I was really nervous. That's when I really fell apart. When I couldn't reach my friend, I was frantic and I walked into Bloomingdale's and someone bumped into me and I almost jumped out of my skin. I stopped at another phone booth to call my friend. It was one of those booths without a door and I had my back turned. Someone was waiting to make a call and when I turned around I just looked into his chest—it was a large man—and I screamed.

In the years since Alan's brutal murder in 1965 the chances of becoming a victim for everyone—not just Wendy—have increased. Serious crime is more common than ever before. Now it is not only urban dwellers who can say they know at least one person who has been burglarized, robbed, raped, murdered, or beaten; rural communities are finding these crimes afflicting their neighborhoods as well. Six children in Birmingham, Michigan (population 28,000), were killed in 1976/77; a sniper murdered six persons and then killed himself in Hackettstown, New Jersey (population 10,000). In January 2023, a father shot and killed seven immediate and extended family members, and then committed suicide, allegedly two weeks after his wife in Enoch, Utah (population 8,016) filed for divorce .

"Crime," wrote sociologist Daniel Bell, "in many ways, is a Coney Island mirror, caricaturing the morals and manners of a society. ... As a society changes, so does, in lagging fashion, its type of crime."

Sadly, in addition to America's amazing contributions in technology and film, it has developed an international reputation as a violent county. Consider that 31-year-old Dr. Matthew Wilson, an astrophysicist from the UK who was visiting his girlfriend in Atlanta, Georgia, was killed by a stray bullet that hit him in the head. (*The Guardian* online, Jan 22, 2022.)

Europeans continue to be shocked by the level of violence that Americans seem to tolerate. Even going back to 1974, for example, Serge Chauvel-Leroux, a reporter for *Le Figaro* in Paris, wrote in a three-part series about his trip to Manhattan:

> There were as many murders committed in 1973 in New York City as there were in the entire nation of France. And as for crimes of less importance, the U.S. federal services themselves counseled us to take with a grain of salt the statistics put out by the New York City Police Department. In U.S. cities, they told us, it is a common practice to juggle crime figures in order to furnish one's own city with a better public image. Not only that, but there are many crimes committed in which the victims never bring charges: rape, for example; or various burglaries in which the person robbed feels it is self-defeating or too much of a hassle to report it to the police department. Therefore, according to these men with whom I spoke in the federal government, one should multiply the official city figures by two, at the very least; and some believe that ten times would be a more accurate count.

Most nonvictims who read Chauvel-Leroux's reports would either deny that the crime problem is as bad as he says or deny that it could ever happen to them. They would never categorize Atlanta with Belfast, or Cleveland with Derry, even though a person is more likely to be killed in those American cities.

Many blame the police for failing to protect victims of crime. Aren't the police an arm of the criminal justice system that reflects the people themselves? Sir Robert Mark, former head of London's Scotland Yard, explained in an interview with this author in London in July 1975:

> In a free society, or a supposedly free society, the police are necessarily the most accurate reflection of its standards. By that I mean that we are tired in Great Britain of being used as a stick to beat the American police over the head with. That if in fact the American people have got complaints about the American police, the fault is not that of the American police, the fault is theirs; because *the people* determine the numbers of police, *they* determine the limitation of police powers under the ¡aw, *they* determine their accountability, *they* determine the social conditions in which the police have to work, and, in particular, *the people* determine the system of criminal justice which governs the effectiveness of the police.
>
> I trust you won't think me offensive when I say that I regard [the American] system of criminal justice as being in some respects unsatisfactory . . . that [the American criminal justice system] represents almost the bottom. . . . Justice in the United States seems to be almost completely dominated by the lawyers and their vested interests. For example, the New York City Police arrested 94,071 people for felony in 1971, and of those only 552 persons went on trial for a felony. Now, in a society where you permit that to happen, is it surprising that the police should resort to violence themselves or to improper methods to obtain convictions or to deal with wrongdoers? If the police, who are there to protect the people, are frustrated by a system of justice which they think is corrupt, self-interested, and so on, how can you blame them for adopting methods which we condemn over

here as being unacceptable, especially considering the extent to which violence is used against the police?

If change is to occur, we must assess the high level of crime in the U.S. and the reasons for it. Our goal should be threefold: (1) an awareness that the criminal justice system must change, (2) programs offering help for victims of crime whether or not the criminal is caught, (3) the growth of community-based crime-prevention groups and activities. In many communities, programs have already been initiated to achieve these goals. But for today's crime victims—and tomorrow's potential ones—these changes are not fast enough. Rhetoric needs to be replaced with real and dramatic improvements. And the implementation of these programs must have the support of the entire community.

In 1976 F. Emmett Fitzpatrick, Philadelphia's district attorney, tried to find out what changes the people wanted in the criminal justice system. More than 700 persons attended a series of fifteen public hearings. The focus was on pretrial detention and sentencing of convicted offenders. What was apparent from the Public Hearings Report issued in November 1976 was that Philadelphians are determined "to be protected from the 'revolving door' criminal justice system that persists in returning dangerous defendants to their communities time and time again." The major recommendations by those citizens to accomplish that aim were:

1. Amending bail statutes so that an arrestee's psychiatric evaluation will be a determining factor in his or her being released before trial. (Practically anyone may now be released before trial if he or she puts up the required amount of bail.)

2. If there is any indication that an arrestee out on bail would commit another violent act, bail should be denied.

3. Police officers should become more visible in their assigned communities.

4. The role of the probation officer in rehabilitation has to become a more authentic one.

5. "The plight of victims and witnesses" should receive "even more widespread attention."

What is the tangible help available *now* to victims of crime? The government has provided meager financial aid but has generally ignored, for example, a victim's need for counseling for the predictable trauma caused by a crime, or a victim's right to pertinent information about his case. Help for victims seems to fall into a few major categories—those funded by federal, state, or city sources and usually operated through the district attorney's office or the police department; and those privately supported by donations or contributions, usually run through a neutral office or in the victim advocate's home.

Two examples of these programs are telephone, videoconferencing, and text services and walk-in counseling for individual sessions or groups. Experienced social workers, psychiatrists, psychologists, trained staff or volunteer victim advocates, nurses, police officers, psychologists, and other victim service provides must be educated in the needs of crime victims. They also must learn how to prevent the unnecessary secondary victimizations by the criminal justice system or the institutionalization of crime, a new "sub-specialty" with all the bureaucratic trappings that go with such a designation. Instead, those who counsel crime victims in clinics or in private offices should understand that crime victimization is another dynamic of restoring any individual to the point where he or she can cope. Those who advise victims should know the differences among the three basic ways of talking to someone who needs help: interviewing, investigating, and interrogating. Although the first one, interviewing, is preferred, it is the last one that is too often used. Victims are often left weak and defenseless, and unlike the demanding criminal, they may be grateful for whatever help they are given, no matter how minor, no matter how unsuitable.

The first major effort by the federal government was the grants given to the National District Attorneys Association (NDAA) in October 1974. That money was used to implement victim-witness assistance programs at select district attorneys' offices throughout the country. From an initial field unit core of eight such offices, it has grown to have a presence in practically every district attorney's office. Helping victims cope is one of the goals of these programs but the main goal is to train victims to be better witnesses if their case goes to trial. Today, however, only 2 or 3 percent of all criminal cases at the state or federal level go to trial. The rest are plea bargained.

Since the district attorney does not see a citizen until he or she has already been a victim, the various projects emphasize post-victimization concerns such as:

- Information: explanations of the criminal justice system and each facet of the system with which the victim or witness will become involved, in layman's language.

- Notification: telephone or mail contact to advise the witness of the need to appear or recent developments in the case (plea bargaining, dismissal, etc.) and of the final adjudication of the case.

- Telephone alert: the unit contacts a witness to determine if he can be reached by telephone on the scheduled trial date. If the witness qualifies, he may then be placed on "alert" and telephoned to come into court only if his testimony is needed.

- Escort/page: witnesses are met at the entrance to the courthouse and thereafter escorted to the assistant district attorney's office, courtroom, cafeteria, and the like.

- Social service referral: when a need is apparent for social services, victims and witnesses are referred to the appropriate agency. When possible the victim will be escorted to that agency.

- Reception: a host or hostess greets witnesses and sees to their needs while they await their turn to testify. The waiting area or witness reception center is attractively decorated and such comforts as coffee, newspapers, magazines, television, and telephones can he provided.

- Employer intervention: contact is made with the witness's employer when requested by the witness, to officially request the employer's cooperation with the district attorney's office by granting time off with pay to the witness.

- Property return: field offices help to have personal property returned to victims as soon as legally possible.

But too often these programs, because of their locations within the district attorneys' offices, are unavailable to victims who do not report the crime, or do not become involved in the system because the criminal is not caught, or do not wish to become involved in "the system." The same holds true of programs run through the police departments. Even many independent programs have found it necessary to attach themselves to some arm of the criminal justice system to get the funding necessary for victim-related activities.

The Commission on Victim Witness Assistance has been distributing a victim rights card that they designed; statewide programs, such as the New York State Crime Victims Compensation Board (now referred to as the Office of Victim Services) have revised it for their own localities. The card might be called a victim's counterpart of the Miranda warning—the notification to arrested persons that they have the right to remain silent and the right to have counsel present.

NATIONAL DISTRICT ATTORNEYS ASSOCIATION COMMISSION ON VICTIM WITNESS ASSISTANCE

We've all been giving Miranda warnings since 1966. How many of us read victims and witnesses their rights?

They have rights too. Will you take time to tell them where they can get help? It could be a pleasant experience . . . refer victims and witnesses to the District Attorney's Special Witness Assistance Unit.

You have the right as a crime victim or witness:
- to be free from intimidation;
- to be told about compensation available to victims for their injuries;
- to be told about social service agencies which can help you;
- to be assisted by your criminal justice agency.

Your **District Attorney** operates a special **Witness Assistance Unit**. If you need help, call:
914-682-2827

This card is designed to be handed out by police officers to victims who seem to be in need of services furnished by the victims assistance program.

The second leading crime victim efforts today in the United States are the nonprofits who offer training for victim service providers, such as NOVA (National Organization of Victim Assistance) and the National Center for Victims of Crime, as well as the free information they provide the public through their websites and NOVA's annual conference.

There are many questions raised about any program. Should victims participate in a program or should they seek out private counseling instead? What help is available for victims who choose not to report the crime to the police? Should the police and district attorney programs be limited only to victims of violent personal crimes as most commonly are? If correctional officers are paid employees, as well as those involved in reentry programs for the formerly incarcerated, and not volunteers, are there funds available to start paying trained volunteers who are helping victims?

The third change—the expansion of community-based crime-prevention programs—is perhaps the most valuable source of aid for victims and non victims alike. Although each program's liaison with the police, courts, or correctional facilities differs widely, the programs are far less closely con-trolled by "the system" than the crime victim advocate groups now operat-ing. Many crime prevention programs also include privately funded crime victim assistance programs. Through such programs as CLASP in Philadel-phia, the Women's Crusade Against Crime in St. Louis, and Citizens' Crime Watch in Miami, citizens are implementing crime-fighting programs and watchdog controls on *their* criminal justice system. Some of their efforts include court watching; one-to-one victim counseling; marking personal property; reporting possible illegal fencing operations; locking car doors and securing homes; and volunteer citizen police patrols known by such terms as "block watchers," "auxiliary police," "posses," and "crime watches."

As these efforts expand, change will spread. The St. Louis, Missouri, Women's Crusade Against Crime now numbers three thousand active members. In just seven years their educational and practical programs have resulted in a reduced number of crime victims in their community, an increase in the property value of homes that would otherwise have been abandoned as tenants moved to the suburbs, and the creation of an inte-grated inner-city neighborhood with all the advantages of urban living while reducing the blight of high-crime victimization.

If the government and the criminal justice system fail victims, the citi-zens must find a way to right those wrongs and prevent more victimization. If those efforts are ignored rather than encouraged, a return to vigilantism is not simply possible—it is probable.

In April 1977 a pistol and rifle group in New York City announced that it was offering a $200 award and citation to any victim of a robbery or an assault who killed his or her attacker. It was also announced that three businessmen who had shot their assailants the week before were soon to be "honored" at a ceremony arranged by that pistol and rifle group. The award was quickly withdrawn—probably because of pressure from civil lib-erties and religious organizations—but it set an ugly, up-to-date example of the counter-violence reaction predicted by violence expert Richard Maxwell Brown, history professor at the College of William and Mary, in his essay "The American Vigilante Tradition," published in 1969:

> *Whether or not the crime rate is really rising or declining is currently being debated by experts, but in one way the question is beside the point. Must urban Americans, particularly in the largest cities, are firm in their belief that there is too much crime, that their persons or property are in danger, and that regular law enforcement is not coping with the problem. The same feelings in earlier times led Americans to resort to vigilantism.*

There is nothing pleasant about being a crime victim. Crime can be traumatic, horrifying, financially damaging, shocking, frightening, and unfair; it is not something anyone should want to experience.

What will it take to stop romanticizing the criminal? Forty thousand homicide victims a year? Ten more slain political leaders? A hundred thousand more rape victims? The total decay and depletion of the inner cities because of fear and vandalism?

Everyone must answer those questions for himself or herself. Each person must decide how much time and effort he or she is willing to contribute to reversing the epidemic of violence and property crime today. But as a secondary victim of the homicide of my 23-year-old brother Seth Alan Barkas, as well as the primary victim of several larceny-thefts, and other crimes, if not for my brother's senseless murder, I would have accepted my own victimizations as I considered violent crime something "out there" that "couldn't happen to me." Sadly, for me and for millions of others, that myth has proven false.

There is no one answer but we know from the examples of other countries around the world, including Britain, Australia, Canada, New Zealand, and Norway, that following a mass murder, tighter gun laws led to a dramatic reduction in gun-related deaths. (Max Fisher, "Other Countries Had Mass Shootings. Then They Changed Their Gun Laws." *The New York Times*, May 25, 2022)

Our gun death rate of 10.6 per 100,000 persons in 2016 is dramatically higher than the 2.1 rate of Canada or 1.0 of Australia. Small comfort that our rate is much lower than the rate of 38.7 in Venezuela or 39.2 per 100,000 in El Salvador. (Gramlich, "What the Data Says About Gun Deaths in the U.S.," Pew Research Group, February 3, 2022.)

We also know that the mentally ill, especially those with severe disorders including schizophrenia or psychotic disorders, are more likely to be a victim of crime than a perpetrator. But it has been pointed out that 5% of mass shooters have severe mental illness; another 25% have non-psychotic neurological illnesses and depression, and another 23% have substance use issues. This is pointed out in an interview with Ragy Girgis, M.D., an associate professor of clinical psychiatry, in his interview in *Columbia Psychiatry News*. ("Is There a Link Between Mental Health and Mass Shootings?" July 6, 2022) There had been more than 300 mass shootings in the U.S. in 2022 by July, when that interview was published. If Dr. Girgis' percentages are accurate, just by dealing more effectively with the severely mentally ill could prevent 15 mass shootings a year.

We need to teach children as young as possible, and reinforce those teachings with teens, and adults too, that they need to know the facts about crime, not the myths. Yes, teaching "stranger danger" has its benefits. "Don't take candy from strangers" and do not let someone lure you into a van with the promise of showing you their new puppies. But we know from victimology and criminology research, and police reports, that infants under one are more likely to be killed by a parent, usually the mother, than by a stranger. And that other than robbery, perpetrators are more likely to be someone known to the victim: an acquaintance, family member, friend, or a trusted authority figure like a babysitter, coach, or religious leader. Teaching children, teens, and adults about the red flags and warning signs to watch for, whether it is someone known to that individual or a stranger, and how to call 9-1-1 for help, will go further than just teaching "stranger danger."

Finally, since someone can bleed out in just a few minutes, and police cor emergency medical help an take a couple of minutes to ten minutes or longer, depending on traffic and other factors, learning how to Stop the Bleed® just might save a life impacted by violent crime.

NOTES AND ACKNOWLEDGMENTS

Please note that the updated references throughout the original Scribner text have not been added to this section. Instead, those citations are included, usually in a parentheses, right after the statement or quotation that was referred to. In other words, these notes and acknowledgments have not been edited. The crime scene picture before the Preface is courtesy of Shutterstock.

The citations for each chapter that follow are intended to pinpoint specific unpublished or published references for key concepts; they are by no means complete. Many references appear in shortened form if complete entries are provided in the bibliography.

Nor could all the individuals who were of help be listed. One obvious reason is the request for anonymity from victims and offenders. The other is that the persons who answered questions or supplied information number in the thousands. I trust they know that my debt for their assistance is just as great without specific notation, and I humbly acknowledge all anonymous and highlighted sources for their contribution to this book.

I was fortunate to have had portions of this manuscript criticized by Deans Norval Morris and Herbert W. Edwards, Professors Victor Barnouw, Edwin Cur-ley, Marvin E. Wolfgang, and Arthur N. Niederhoffer, Frederic Wertham, M.D., Richard B. Hoffman, Rabbi Irwin Isaacson, Mary M. Innes, Charlotte Greene, Mary Sherry, Jim Wade, Doc Coover, Barbara Wood, Thurston Clarke, Patricia Cristol, Stuart Johnson, and James DeMarse.

PREFACE

From the first draft to the final version, this section profited from the careful readings and suggestions of James DeMarse, Doe Coover, Dean H. W. Edwards, my parents, Dr. William and Gladys Barkas, Batja Cates, Clarence Dowthard, Carol Shookhoff, and Maxine Wallach.

Barbara Gordon wrote and directed the television program that helped inspire this book; "Eye On 'Victims of Violent Crimes,' " broadcast on WCBS-TV. Barbara Gordon and I later spoke about the program, and she kindly arranged for George Dessert of WCBS-TV to send me its transcript.

Hundreds of persons spoke to me during my various trips to Europe, but Brian Southam of Concord Books, Norman Franklin and Peter Hopkins of Routledge & Kegan Paul, Ltd., and Mary Tierney were particularly generous in arranging introductions. Some of the fundamental meetings and follow-up correspondence were with Sir Robert Mark of Scotland Yard; Erin Pizzey of the Chiswick Women's Aid; Professors Roger Hood, Ian Taylor, Terence Morris, and Stan Cohen; psychiatrists Anthony Storr, T. C. N. Gibbens, and John Gums; and journalists and writers Peter Evans, Alvin Schuster, Heno Magee, Nicholas and Aideen Coffey, Khushwant Singh, and Woodrow Wyatt.

1. WHO ARE THE VICTIMS OF CRIME?

Official crime statistics are gathered by the FBI Uniform Crime Reports and appear annually in a series entitled *Crime in the United States,* published by the U.S. Government Printing Office in Washington, D.C. Individual reports are usually published and provided by police departments around the country as well. The President's Commission on Law Enforcement and the Administration of Justice, published in various formats including the Avon paperback book *The Challenge of Crime in a Free Society* (1968), provided statistics on the economic costs of crime. Victim studies as noted in the bibliography were useful in estimating unreported crimes. Professor Wesley Skogan of Northwestern University first alerted me that his estimates of the actual reported crime victims were also in the thirty millions; he sent me his useful articles, including "The Victims of Crime: Some National Survey Findings," in *Criminal Behavior and Social Systems,* 2nd ed., edited by Anthony L. Guenther (Chicago: Rand McNally, 1976), pp. 135-37, and "Dimensions of the Dark Figure of Unrepealed Crime," in the Jan. 1977 *Crime & Delinquency.*

The view of crime victims as a minority group developed from Gordon All-port's *The Nature of Prejudice;* the labeling of the poor was noted by William Ryan in *Blaming the Victim.* Richard Quinney, Howard Zinn, and Paul Tappan contributed to my reexamination of the fundamental questions about who victims and criminals are. Basic background texts in criminology included Sutherland and Cressey's *Criminology;* collected articles edited by Wolfgang, Savitz, and Johnston in *The Sociology of Crime and. Delinquency;* Cressey and Ward's *Delinquency, Crime, and Social Process;* Reid's *Crime & Criminology;* and the works of others, including Garofalo Raffaele, Enrico Ferri, William L. Prosser, Richard A. Cloward and Lloyd E. Ohlin, Alfred Adler, and Thorsten Sellin. On international crime conferences, see Alper and Boren, *Crime International Agenda* (Lexington, Mass.: D. C. Heath, 1972).

Karen Riedel, a friend who is a speech pathologist, first pointed out to me that the physical disabilities caused by crime are often overlooked. John Gunn, author of *On Violence* (New York: Praeger, 1974), shared his unpublished manuscripts on crime victims with me that included references to surveys on disaster victim survivors. Professor Martin Symonds also devoted a lecture in his graduate course "The Psychology of Victims" to disaster victims as well as the stages of reactions experienced by crime victims. Elisabeth Kübler-Ross's *On Death and. Dying,* Robert T. Flint's extensive correspondence and published pamphlet "The Psychology of Victims: Student Monograph," and Ann Wolbert Burgess's article "Family Reaction to Homicide" also stressed these similar victim responses.

The revenge quotations compiled by criminologist Gets are published in "Victims of Crimes of Violence and the Criminal Justice System," by G. Geis, chap. 5 in Chappell and Monahan, *Violence and Criminal Justice.*

The victim quotes were published in "What Now for the Grieving Families of 'Son of Sam's' Victims?" by Joan Kron *(New York Times,* Aug. 15, 1977, p. 22); "Victim's Relatives Are 'Relieved,' Hope Suspect Is 'the Right Guy,' " by Robert McG. Thomas, Jr. *(New York Times,* Aug. 11, 1977, p. D-17); the editorial extract is from "The Added Danger of a Savage Week" *(New York Times,* Aug. 3, 1977, p. A-20).

How mourners resolve their grief according to Larry A. Rugen appears in his article "Human Grief: A Model for Prediction and Intervention," in *American Journal of Orthopsychiatry,* vol. 47, Apr. 1977, pp. 196-206.

Ebba Lewis kindly allowed me to capsulize the story of the real John and Laurie based upon her interviews with his family from her unpublished paper. Sociologist William F, McDonald has discussed the concept of victims hiring their own lawyers in criminal cases and sent me a copy of his unpublished papers and published article, "Toward a Bicentennial Revolution in Criminal Justice: The Return of the Victim."

After reading "Children's Reactions to Innocent Victims" by Gerald M. Stein in *Child Development* (vol. 44, Dec. 1973, pp, 805-10) I wrote to Dr. Stein. His reply suggested that, among others, I should first contact Professor Melvin J. Lerner. Within a few months, I received from him an enormous package of his writings explaining and experimenting with the "just-world hypothesis."

Psychologist Albert Ellis included his comments on crime victims in a Sept. 14, 1976, letter to me; since our first meeting in 1973, he has always been concerned about my research.

The concept of fight or flight, and the physiological changes that accompany fear or rage, evolved from Erich Fromm, *The Anatomy of Human Destructiveness;* Konrad Lorenz, *On Aggression;* Gregory A. Kimble and Norman Garmezy, *Principles of General Psychology,* 2nd ed. (New York: Ronald Press Company, 1963), pp. 386-99; D. H. Funkenstein, "The Physiology of Fear and Anger," *Scientific American,* May 1955; and Walter B. Cannon, *The Wisdom of the Body* (1932).

"Identification with the aggressor" is discussed in Anna Freud's classic work, *The Ego and Mechanisms of Defense.* Other developments of this concept are in Brenner's *Elementary Textbook of Psychoanalysis* and Freedman, Kaplan, and Sadock (eds.), *Comprehensive Textbook of Psychiatry—H,* 2nd ed., pp. 530-33.

The quotation from Arthur Bremer's diary is reprinted by permission of *Harper's* magazine; it appeared in the Jan. 1973 issue. Other reports of real crimes committed in imitation of fictional ones include Aaron Latham's "The Columbia Murder That Gave Birth to the Beats"; Richard Gooding, "Film's Maker Would Burn It" *(New York Post,* Mar. 19, 1977, p. 35); and Darryl D'Monte, "Can Violence Be Justified?" The example of the San Francisco broomstick "rape" was reported by John J. O'Connor in "Warning: Violence on TV Is Dangerous to Your Health" (*New York Times,* Nov. 3, 1974, p. D-29).

In addition to the original writings of those authors discussed in the section on literature—Dreiser, Christie, Capote, Dostoevsky, and Rossner—I also read background biographical material, critical studies, and major works not mentioned. The conclusions about those authors' interpretations of victims, however, I arrived at on my own; afterward, I discovered Professor Kress's unpublished paper "Doubly Abused: The Plight of Crime Victims in Literature" as well as Colin MacInnes's provocative essay "Does the Realty Exist?" a review of Gay Talese's *Honor Thy Father* in the *New York Times Book Review* (Oct. 31, 1971, pp. 2, 18). How Agatha Christie and Georges Simenon viewed the crime victim emerged in John Leonard's essay written at Christie's death, "An Etiquette of Murder; Dame Agatha Made Mystery Story an Enjoyable Middle-class Virtue," in the *New York Times*, and in Anatole Broyard's review of Simenon's *Maigret and the Black Sheep*, "Criminal Etiquette," in the Jan. 23, 1976, *New York Times.*

Theodore Dreiser's quotation reversing victim and criminal roles appeared in his *Mystery Magazine* series, June 1935, p, 73. The excerpt from *The Prophet* is reprinted by permission of Alfred A. Knopf (New York, copyright 1923).

For views on *Looking for Mr. Goodbar* I read Aljean Harmetz, "Will 'Mr. Goodbar' Make Voyeurs of Us All?" *New York Times,* July 24, 1977, and Judy Klemesrud, "Diane Keaton: From Mr. Allen to 'Mr. Goodbar,' " *New York Times,* Apr. 17, 1977.

My understanding of victimology evolved from interviews with Professors Marvin E. Wolfgang, Ian Taylor, Arthur Niederhoffer, Marshall B. Clinard, aided by comments from Crown Attorney Peter Rickaby of Toronto, Canada, Richard Quinney, Howard Zinn, Ann Wolbert Burgess, Mary Sherry, and extensive letters from founder Beniamin Mendelsohn. The volumes edited by Israel Drapkin and Emilio Viano, *Victimology* (Lexington, Mass.: Lexington Books, D. C. Heath, 1974) and *Victimology: A New Focus,* vols. 1-5 (Lexington, Mass,: Lexington Books, D. C. Heath, 1975), anthologize the key founding articles as well as later commentary.

Whenever possible, I read the original sources, such as Stephen Shafer's *The Victim and His Criminal* and von Hentig's *The Criminal and His Victim.* Other references are to Walter Reckless's textbook, *The Crime Problem,* 2nd ed. (New York: Appleton-Century-Crofts, 1955), pp. 23-24; M. Hunt's *The Mugging;* B. Gelb's *On the Track of Murder;* M. Wolfgang's "Victim-Precipitated Criminal Homicide," reprinted in dozens of criminological anthologies including M. Wolfgang (ed.), *Studies in Homicide* (New York: Harper & Row, 1967); Joseph D. McNamara, "FBI Statistics," *Washington Post,* Aug. 6, 1976; and Robert A. Silverman, "Victim Precipitation; An Examination of the Concept," chap. 10 in Drapkin and Viano (eds.), *Victimology*, vol. 1, pp. 99-109.

2. THE SILENCED VICTIMS

Drs. Fredric Wertham, Michael Baden, and David Abrahamsen assisted me in learning about the murderer and the homicide victim. Dr. Wertham's writings, the letters we exchanged, and our telephone interviews continue to be fruitful in my education; novelist Richard Condon originally suggested that I contact him. Mike Baden has been a patient and sympathetic instructor as well; I appreciate his trust in letting me observe in the waiting room, autopsy lab, and museum of the city morgue. Jean-Pierre Lahary taught me much in the morgue museum, where he is curator, and in our talks. Lawyers Robert Burstein, Steven Cooper, Hugh Levine, Louis Aidala, and Bruce Kelton; Sgt. Joseph Cordes; and author Lucy Freeman also helped. Drafts of this chapter were read by Joyce Bronstein, Maria Andreacchi, Jan Van Meter, Fredric Wertham, and Anthony Storr, M.D.

The L.A. morgue television screen was also noted by Donald Carroll in "Conversation with Dr. Thomas Noguchi," *Out*, vol. 5 (Feb. 1976), p. 120.

Stages of family response to death were developed from Elisabeth Kübler-Ross, *On Death and Dying* (New York: Macmillan, 1976; 1969), and contrasted to victim interviews and to Ann Wolbert Burgess, "Family Reaction to Homicide," *American Journal of Orthopsychiatry*, vol. 45 (Apr. 1975), pp. 391-98; Larry A. Bugen, "Human Grief: A Model for Prediction," *American Journal of Orthopsychiatry*, vol. 47 (Apr. 1977), pp. 196-206; and Gilbert Geis, "Victims of Crimes of Violence and the Criminal Justice System," in *Violence and Justice*, edited by Duncan Chappell and John Monahan (Lexington, Mass.; D. C. Heath, 1975), pp. 69-71.

Psychologist Glen Boles suggested I speak with attorney and victim activist Peter Schneider. His article "In Memory of Seymour Schneider" appeared in the *New York Times*, Oct. 16, 1971, p. 29.

The preferential treatment of a certain type of murder victim was the theme in Clinton Cox's "Meanwhile in Bedford-Stuyvesant . . ." in *More*, vol. 6 (Apr. 1976), pp. 18, 20, 21.

Quotations by Brown and Benoy on capital punishment are from Nick Di-Spoldo, "Ex-Convict Looks at Supreme Court," *Fortune News*, June-July 1976, the "Death Penalty" issue, p. 4. Sarat and Vidmar's public opinion poll was capsulized in "Newsline," Patrice Horn, editor, *Psychology Today,* Sept. 1976, p. 16. There is a vast literature on the death penalty and alternatives to punishment, but I was most stimulated by Ernest van den Haag, *Punishing Criminals* (New York: Basic Books, 1975); Richard J. Gelles and M. A. Straus, "Family Experience and Public Support of the Death Penalty," *American Journal of Orthopsychiatry*, vol. 45 (July 1975), pp. 596-613; T. E. Gaddis and J. O. *Long, Killer: A Journal of Murder* (New York; Fawcett, 1970); and Albert Camus, "Reflections on the Guillotine," in *Evergreen Review Reader,* edited by Barney Rosset (New York; Grove Press, 1968), p. 91.

Statistics on the number of homicide victims are from a variety of sources, including the FBI Uniform Crime Reports, *The World Almanac and Book of Facta, 1977,* the annual reports of the metropolitan police force in England, kindly supplied by Sir Robert Mark, police commissioner, Police Chief Harold Adamson, and Crown Attorney Peter Riekaby of Toronto, Canada; D. R. Bates, "Practising Science in Northern Ireland," London *Nature,* vol. 250 (Aug. 30, 1974), pp. 754-57, sent by Dr. Bates but originally suggested by Tom Hadden, editor of the Belfast *Fortnightly;* Arnold Burnett, J. Kleitman, and R. C. Larson, "On Urban Homicide,'. A Statistical Analysis," *Journal of Criminal Justice,* vol. 3 (1975), pp. 85-100; Donald T. Lunde, "Our Murder Boom," *Psychology Today,* July 1975, p. 35; A. Joan Kiebba, "Homicide Trends in the United States, 1900-74," *Public Health Reports,* vol. 90 (May-June 1975), p. 195.

In *Murder Followed by Suicide* (London: Heinemann, 19G5) D. J. West discusses the phenomenon of murderers who kill themselves.

Material on how homicide is changing is based on numerous original and published sources, including Selvvyn Raab's articles—"33% Slain in New York Don't Know Killer," *Neto York Times,* June 13, 1976, pp. 1, 60; " 'Deliberate' Slayiugs on Increase Here," New *York Times,* Feb. 27, I.976, pp. 1, 14; "Felony Murder Hose Here Sharply in "74," *New York Times,* Mar. 23, 1975, pp. .1, 41—Sir Thomas More, *Utopia,* translated by Paul Turner (Hannoudsworth, Middlesex, England: Penguin. 1972; 1816), p.. 50 ("There's no distinction in law between theft and murder, though in equity the two things are so completely different"); Ted Morgan, "They Think, "I Can Kill Because I'm 14,' " *New York Times Magazine,* Jan. 19,

1975, p. 9; and Thomas Plate, "Investigation of a Murder," *New York,* vol. 7 (Aug. 12, 1974), pp. 34-36.

Stories about well-known victims sell newspapers and quickly become the focus of books; the reference material is voluminous. Some pertinent sources are Vincent Bugliosi with Curt Gentry, *Heller Skelter: The True Story of the Manson Murders* (New York: Norton, 1975); Tracy Kidder, *The Road to Yuba City: A Journey into the Juan Corona Murders* (Garden City, N.Y.: Doubleday, 1974); William Allen, *Starkweather: A Chronicle of Mass Murder in the Fifties* (Boston: Houghton Mifflin, 1976); "Woman Accused in 11 Deaths Paroled," *New York Times,* June 9, 1976, p. 16; "John Knight 3d Slain in Robbery; Member of Newspaper Family," *New York Times,* Dec. 8, 1975, p. 27; Arthur Bell, "The Fatal Consequences of the Secret Life," *Village Voice,* Jan. 26, 1976; "Sal Mineo Slain Near L.A. Home," *New York Post,* Feb. 13, 1976, p. I; "250 Attend Sal Mineo Funeral; Actor Is Called "Gentle Person,' " *New York Times,* Feb. 18, 1976, p. 4.1; "Barbara Colby, James Kiernan in Fatal Shooting," *Vegetarian World,* no. 4 (1975), p. 20; "Ex-Editor of Holiday, a Woman, 28, Beaten to Death on Coast," *New York Times,* Sept. 9, 1975, p. 24; and Ninette Beaver, B. K. Ripley, and Patrick Trese, *Caril* (New York: Bantam Books, 1976; 1974).

The homicide victim-offender profile was based on Lynn A. Curtis, *Criminal Violence: National Patterns and Behavior* (Lexington, Mass.; D. C. Heath, 1974), pp. 28, 48, 50.

The interviews of the Salt Lake City murderers were televised on WNBC News on July 28, 1972, in "Thou Shalt Not Kill," produced and written by Peter Jeffries, based on interviews filmed by television station KUTV in Salt Lake City. I saw a reference to the show in Frank Carrington's *The Victims* (New Rochelle, N.Y.: Arlington House, 1975), pp. 8, 198-99, and josh Kane, general program executive for NBC in New York, kindly provided me with a transcript.

Robert J. diGrazia, former Boston police commissioner, has been helpful through our meetings, letters, and telephone conversations since I first met with him in 1975, and I thank him for his comments on "crimes of passion."

There is extensive literature on guns; Jan Van Meter made suggestions and also sent me B. Bruee-Briggs, "The Great American Gun War," *The Public Interest,* no. 45 (Fall 1976), pp. 37-62; and David II. Bayley,

"Learning about Crime— The Japanese Experience," *The Public Interest,* no. 44 (Summer 1976), pp. 54-68. Other important sources are Robert Sherrill, *The Saturday Night Special* (New York: *Charterhouse* Books, 1973); Polly Toynbee, "Shooting Down Some Myths about Gun Control," the *Washington Monthly,* vol. 5 (Dec. 1973), pp. 24-31; James M. Perry, "The Gun Lobby Is Armed and Dangerous," *New Times,* vol. 5 (Oct. 17, 1975), pp. 28-29, 32-33; Hillary Johnson, "The Friendly Persuaders," in *New York Sunday News Magazine,* June 6, 1976, pp. 16-17, 18-19; Rafael Abra-movitz and Carl Stern, "A Shooting Gallery Called America?" NBC News Presents Broadcast, April 27, 1975, produced by Lucy Jarvis; and Joseph B. Treaster, "Gun Group Offers a $200 Reward to Victims Who Kill Assailants," *New York Times,* Apr. 14, 1977, p. B-2. Deputy Chief Arthur F. Di Gennaro of the Washington, D.C., Police Department provided statistics as well.

3. "IT MIGHT HAVE BEEN MURDER" VICTIMS

Dr. Robert T. Flint was helpful in his careful reading of an early draft of this chapter; research needs were facilitated by reporter Terry Zintl, author Joseph Goulden, Erin Pizzey, Ellen Berliner, *Dr.* Selwyn Smith, Murray Straus, Richard Celles, David Gil, Kathleen Fojtik, Carole Ciasen, the women of the Rainbow Retreat in Phoenix, Arixona, former Inspector Robert Houlihan of Manhattan's Ninth Precinct, police officers Bill Cutter, Don Muldoon, Tom Cimier, Chris Moran, Bill Fenty, Dan Daley, Rocco San Philippo, Phil Smith, Frank Farrelley, Charley Hall, James G. Carolan, Jr., and Sgt. Bob Wilson.

Statistics are from all sources previously listed for crime in general, especially the FBI Uniform Crime Reports and the Murder Analysis of Chicago, New York, and other cities, as well as Alex D. Pokorny's "Human Violence; A Comparison of Homicide, Aggravated Assault, Suicide, and Attempted Suicide," *Research Reports,* vol. 56 (1965), p. 497.

The extract from Edward Albee's *The Zoo Story* appeared in Lee Strasberg's collection, *Famous Plays of the 1950s* (New York: Dell Publishing Co., 1962), and is reprinted with the kind permission of Edward Albee, the William Morris Agency, Inc., and Coward, MeCann & Geoghegao, Inc.

The San Jose-Dayton crime victim survey is a U.S. Department of Justice, National Criminal justice Information and Statistics Service publication: *Crimes and Victims: A Report on the Dayton-San Jose Pilot Suroey of*

Victimization, June 1974. Other surveys and published assault victim references ave: *Criminal Victimization Surveys in the Nation's Five Largest Cities,* p. 14; Joyce Maynard, "5 Men Begin Jail Sentences in 1971 Beating of Yonkers Immigrant," *New York Times,* Aug. 17, 1976, p. 38; and Jan Hodenfield, "A Stabbing Victim's Pain and Suffering," *New York Post,* Apr. 17, 1976, pp. 2, 45.

On a victim's failure to report a crime, see Richard Block, "Why Notify the Police: The Victim's Decision to Notify the Police of an Assault," *Criminology,* vol. 11, no. 4 (1974); Edward Edelson, "Family Violence or Love? Even Steven," *Daily News,* Feb. 24, 1976, That interfering in family "squabbles" is dangerous is also noted by Leslie Maitland in "Courts Easy on Rising Family Violence," *Neto York Times,* June 14, 1976, pp. 1, 36.

The statistics on how many violent episodes occur each year between husbands and wives, siblings, and parents and children are based on a *New York Times* article, "Violence Is Occurring in the Best of Families" (Mar, 20, 1977, p. 6), summarizing the results of a study conducted by sociologists Richard Gelles, Murray Straus, and Susan Steinmetz.

Judge Jack Crawford's unique approach to wife abuse was noted in a *New York Times* article and in a follow-up interview in Feb. 1978.

Other key sources on wife beating included the August 1976 issue of *Ms.* magazine, entitled "Battered Wives: Help for the Secret Victim Next Door"; Judith Weinraub,"The Battered Wives of England: A Place to Heal Their Wounds," *New York Times,* Nov. 29, 1975, p. 17; Erin Pizzey, John Gayford, with Peter Evans, "Patterns of Violence," *New Behaviour* (London), June 5, 1975, pp. 312-13; Bowen Northrup, "Battered Women; Wife-Beating Persists but British Established Refuges to Aid Victims," *Wall Street Journal,* Aug. 20, 1976, pp. 1, 22; and Elizabeth Jean Pascoe, "Shelters for Battered Wives" *(McCall's,* Oct. 1976, p. 51).

Florence Rush read an earlier version of the child abuse section, as did Robert T. Flint, Ph.D. Statistics on child abuse are from "Child Abuse Rate Called 'Epidemic,' " *New York Times,* Nov. 30, 1975, p. 44; Judith Ramsey, "My Husband Broke the Ultimate Taboo," *Family Circle,* Mar. 8, 1977, pp. 42, 184, 186, 188-89; Fredric Wertham, M. D., "BatteredChildren and Baffled Adults,*"Bulletin of the New York Academy of Medicine,* 2nd ser., vol. 48 (Aug. 1972), p. 888; Vincent De Francis and Carrol L. Lucht, *Child Abuse Legislation in the 1970s,* rev. ed. (Denver: American Humane

Association, 1974); "1M Kids Mistreated in Year; U.S. Study," *Daily News,* Nov. 30, 1975, p. 159.

Autobiographical accounts of child abuse by adult ex-offenders are reprinted from *Fortune News,* December 1974, with the permission of its editor, David Rothenberg.

Charlotte Lackner Doyle's lecture "On Being a Woman and Becoming a Psychologist" was kindly provided to me by Dr. Doyle; Leinward's quotation on the police is from Christopher Wren's "Two Policemen Talk: Let Rizzo Do the Thinking," in the *Washington Monthly,* vol. 5 (Dec. 1973), pp. 36-37.

4. VICTIMS OF RAPE

Various early versions of this chapter benefited from readings and comments by Drs. Malkah T. Notnan, Robert T, Flint, Jeffrey Rovins, former assistant district attorney, and Florence Rush, all of whom kindly permitted quoting from their letters, original writings, or interviews.

Rape as the ultimate invasion—short of homicide, but greater than burglary, robbery, or assault—is developed by Morton Bart and Katherine Ellison in "Crisis Intervention and Investigation of Forcible Rape," *Police Chief,* vol. 41 (May 1974), pp. 70-71.

Rape as a violent, not a sexual, crime was stressed by Dr, Martin Symonds in his lectures at John Jay College of Criminal Justice and his paper presented at Seminar on Rape at John Jay, Apr. 10, 1975, "The Psychological Response of Victims to Rape," as well as in Susan Griffin's classic essay "Rape: The All-American Crime," *Ramparts,* vol. 10 (Sept. 1971), pp. 26-35, and in issues of two very useful newsletters, *Warstle* (Champaign Illinois Women Against Rape Center) and *FAAR* (Feminist Alliance Against Rape, Washington, D.C.).

Statistics, as well as general background on profiles of rape victims and offenders, are from Susan Brownmiller, Against *Our Will: Men, Women, and Rape* (New York: Simon & Schuster, 1975), p. 190; *UCR—1976,* pp. 15-17; *VCR—1975,* pp. 22-24; *1972-73 Report of the New York State Select Committee on Crime; Its Causes, Control and Effect on Society,* pp. 28-29, 34, 36-37, 39, 41-47; letters and statistical sheets from police departments around the country including New York City, Chicago, Los Angeles, San Antonio, Gainesville, and Trenton; Sarah Crichton, "The Most

Misunderstood Crime," *East Side Express,* Sept. 9, 1976, p. 3; "Revolt against Rape," *Time,* July 22, 1974, p. 85; "Rape Crisis Center of Syracuse, Inc. Quarterly Report—October, 1976," unpublished, received Nov. 1976; Menachem Amir, "Forcible Rape," *Federal Probation,* vol. 31 (Mar. 1967), pp. 51-58; and from leaflets, booklets, and questionnaires that I received during 1976-77 from several hundred rape crisis centers throughout the United States, Canada, and England, including "Rape: A Statistical Profile" (Houston Rape Crisis Coalition); "Statistics" in *Sexual Assault Handbook* (Kansas Community Rape Prevention and Victim Support Project); "Statistical Report" (Rape Treatment Center, Jackson Memorial Hospital, Miami, Florida," Recap 1975, Jan., Feb., Mar., Apr., May 1976); Dade County Rape Awareness Public Education Program; "Summary of Report on Rape in New Orleans" (Dr. Lou Hicks of the YWCA Rape Crisis Center in New Orleans, Louisiana); and "Rape Statistics, May 20, 1976" (HARCC, Harrisburg Area Rape Crisis Center, Pennsylvania),

The quotation from Barbara Howar, "It Couldn't Happen to Her, but It Did," review of *First, You Cry* by Betty Roltin (Philadelphia: J. B. Lippincott, 1976) in the *New York Times Book Review,* Sept. 26, 1976, p. 10, is reprinted with permission of the New York Times Company.

Myths about the rape victim are discussed in Menachem Amir, *Patterns in Forcible Rape* (Chicago: University of Chicago Press, 1971), and "Forcible Rape" in *Federal Probation* (Mar. 1967), pp. 51-58, reprinted in Marvin E. Wolfgang, Leonard Savitz, and Norman Johnson (eds.), *The Sociology of Crime and Delinquency,* 2nd ed. (New York: John Wiley & Sons, 1970; 1962), chap. 61, pp. 644-53.

Critiques of Amir's methodology and conclusions by Kurt Weis and Sandra S. Borges appear in their "Victimology and Rape; The Case of the Legitimate Victim," *Issues in Criminology,* vol. 8 (Fall 1973), pp, 71-115, and "Victimology and the Justification of Rape" in Drapkin and Viano (eds.), *Victimology,* vol. 5, chap. 1, pp. 3-28.

Eldridge Cleaver's confession about his rape attacks is reprinted with permission of his publisher from *Soul on Ice* {New York: McGraw-Hill, and London: Jonathan Cape, Ltd., 1968).

Susan Griffin quoted the California parole officer on the sanity of rapists in "Rape: . . ."; psychiatrist John Gunn and others have expressed similar views.

An instructor at the New York City Police Academy provided the investigative categories in looking for rape offenders.

The original interviews and perceptions about rape derived from this work were supplemented by interviews, correspondence, reprints, and readings of Russell's *The Politics of Rape: The Victim's Perspective,* Hillberman's *The Rape Victim,* Macdonald's *Rape: Offenders and Their Victims,* Burgess and Holmstrom's articles on rape victims and *Rape: Victims of Crisis,* Sutherland and Scherl, "Patterns of Response among Victims of Rape," Footlick and Howard, and others, "Rape Alert," *Newsweek,* Nov. 10, 1975.

Houston's successful implementation of a physical evidence kit is described by Linda Cryer in "Rape Examination: A Prescription for Medico-Legal Procedures," *Victimology,* vol. I (Summer 1976), pp. 337-41 and follow-up correspondence, Mar. 22, 1977.

Sarah Crichton kindly permitted reprinting the opening paragraph from her article "The Most Misunderstood Crime," which appeared in the New York *East Side Express,* Sept. 9, 1976, p, 3.

Treatment by the police was the focus of an early article stressing the victim by Rhoda J. Milliken, "The Sex Offender's Victim," *Federal Probation,* vol. 14 (Sept. 1950), pp, 22-26. The story about the rapist acquitted because of the victim's possession of a diklo is from Roy Mokrzycki, "The Nifty and the Gross," *Juris Doctor,* Oct. 1976, p. 22, and Audrey Blumberg and Carol Bohmer, "The Rape Victim and Due Process," *Case and Comment,* Nov.-Dec. 1975, pp. 3-16.

The quotations of rape victim responses are from the Dade County, Florida, study "After the Rape . . ." reprinted with the kind permission of director Muriel Solomon.

Frederic Storaska's extract appeared in *New Woman,* vol. 6 (May-June 1976), beginning p. 46, and is reprinted from *How to Say No to a Rapist and Survive* (New York: Random House, 1975) with the permission of the publisher.

Statistics on sexually abused children are from Judy Ramsey, "My Husband Broke the Ultimate Taboo," *Family Circle,* Mar. 8, 1977, pp. 42, 184-86, 188-89; "Fact Sheet on the Sexually Abused Child," by M. Solomon, issued by Rape Awareness Public Education Program, Miami, Florida. Terms are defined by Burgess and Holmstrom in "The Rape Victim in the Emergency Ward," *American Journal of Nursing,* vol, 73 (Oct. 1973), pp. 1741-43, and their other writings on rape victims, and *J.* E. Hall Williams, "The Neglect of Incest: A Criminologist's View," in *Victimology: A New Focus,* vol. 4, pp. 191-96.

The quotation from Drs. Renée S. T. Brant and Veronica B. Tisza is reprinted with their kind permission from "The Sexually Misused Child," *American Journal of Orthopsychiatry,* vol. 47 {Jan. 1977), pp. 80-90.

5. "I WANT WHAT YOU'VE GOT" VICTIMS

Assistant Professor Hugh D. Barlow, psychologist Robert T. Flint, and sociologist Marshall B. Clinard provided useful comments on an early draft of this chapter.

The quote that begins "On July 23, I was mugged ..." began an LEAA, U.S. Department of Justice, Public Information Office, press release, dated Sept. 19, 1976, about crime against the elderly. George Sunderland, director of the National Association of Retired Persons crime prevention program, was said to have received that letter from an elderly man hospitalized in Long Island Jewish Hospital for crime-related injuries.

Information on youth crime appeared in an article in *Time,* July 11, 1977.

Psychiatrist John M. Macdonald provided the groundwork for the robber as hero in his chapter "The Robin Hood Tradition" in *Armed Robbery: Offenders and Their Victims* (Springfield, Ill.: Charles C. Thomas, 1975), pp. 3-34. Maurice Keen's quote from *The Outlaws of Medieval Legend* (Toronto: University of Toronto Press, 1961) was quoted on page 5 of Macdonald's study. John Toland's quotation comparing the real Bonnie and Clyde with the Hollywood characters is reprinted by permission of the New York Times Company, Inc. from the *New York Times Magazine,* Feb. 18, 1968, beginning p. 26.

The increase in bank robberies is noted in the 1975 Uniform Crime Reports and in Macdonald's *Armed Robbery*. In addition to letters from and interviews with unnamed inmates on what makes a person a likely victim, advice is offered by Beth Fallon in her summary of the ex-offender conference in New York as reported in "Mugged? Give In, Say Ex-Thugs," New York *Daily News,* June 3, 1975, p. 31, and by M. Symonds in "Victims of Violence," *American Journal of Psychoanalysis,* p. 20, noting: "Most of them [muggers he interviewed] are surprised at victim cooperation and yet would beat the victims senseless if they didn't cooperate."

The Feb. 1976 issue of *The Police Chief*, "Crime against the Elderly," vol. 43, was entirely devoted to all aspects of the subject, including "Senior Citizen Crime Prevention Program," "Police and the Older Victim," and "Law Enforcement and the Senior Citizen." Phone interviews with Philip J. Gross were also helpful in studying this subject.

Lois Gould's response is reprinted by permission of the New York Times Company; it appeared in "Follow-up, 1974," by David C. Anderson and Holcomb B. Noble in the *New York Times Magazine*, Dec. 29, 1974, p. 39. Lois Gould's concern for my work over the years is also appreciated.

Victim retaliation is noted in Macdonald, *Armed Robbery*, "Victims Who Kill," pp. 203-8, and in Rita Mauser's comments at the conclusion of the WNBC-TV three-hour special on violence, broadcast on Jan. 5, 1977, 11:30 P.M.-midnight.

Dr. Symonds noted the burglary victim's feeling of being invaded, as did Bard and Ellison's article on the victim's reaction to rape as well as Robert T. Flint's booklets to accompany victim-sensitivity training for police officers. Victim accounts include Albin Krebs, "Burglary, to the Victim, Is a Kind of Rape of the Home," *New York Times*, Apr. 10, 1977, sec. 8, pp. 1-2; J. Berendt's "I Catch a Burglar" and Mort Weisinger's "We've Been Robbed!" in *Long Island*, Jan. 4, 1976, pp. 5, 8-9, 18.

The South Carolina study, "The Decision to Call the Police: Reactions to Burglary," was completed by A, Emerson Smith and Dal Maness, Jr., and appears as chap, 3 in McDonald (ed.), *Criminal Justice and the Victim*,

The cost of preventing each subway robbery was reported in *Crime and Delinquency Literature*, vol. 7 (Mar. 1975), p. 1.

6. CONSIDERING THE VICTIMS

Early drafts of various sections of this chapter were commented on by Professors Arthur H. Niederhoffer, Dean Norval Morris, Mary Sherry, Paul Rothstein, Victor Barnouw, Rabbi Irwin Isaacson, Mary M. Innes, James O'Shea Wade, Edwin Curley, Edward Morrison, Joe Hudson, and Richard B. Hoffman. Correspondence with numerous lawyers, scholars, and crime victim specialists was helpful, especially E. Adamson Hoebel, T. R. Fehrenbach, Robert L. Carneiro, Tom Hutchinson, Senator Edward Kennedy and his staff, Gilbert Geis, LeRoy L. Lamborn, James Brooks, Winsor C. Schmidt, Wilfred S. Pang, Richard J. Gross, Martin I, Moylan, the late

Samuel L. Scheiner, George Nicholson, Abe Simon, Harry Benkert, Richare A. Godegast, Joseph Pinkus, the Reverend Robert A. Denston, John P, J, Dussich, George Hamilton, Ian Hill, Margaret Fates, C. O. Huggard, and others.

Primary sources for material on the victim in primitive societies included Barton's "Ifugao Law"; Malinowski's *Crime and Custom in Savage Society;* E. Adam-son Hoebel's *The Law of Primitive Man;* Boas, *The Central Eskimo;* E. E. Evans-Pritchard, "The Nuer of the Southern Sudan," in *African Political Systems,* edited by M. Fortes and E. E. Evans-Pritchard (London; Oxford University Press, 1940); Ernest Wallace and E. Adamson Hoebel, *The Comanches: Lords of the South Plains;* and Paul Bohanmm (ed.), *Law and Warfare.*

"Pâtussorssuaq, Who Killed His Uncle" is reprinted from Knud Rasmussen, *Eskimo Folk-Tales,* edited and translated by W. Worster (London: Gyldendal, 1921), and Kayuk's story is reprinted from Peter Freuchen, *Book of the Eskimos* (New York; Fawcett, 1961), with permission of his estate.

Other primary sources used for this chapter included the Code of Hammurabi as reprinted in James B. Pritchard (ed.), *The Ancient Near East,* vol. 1, translated by Theophile J. Meek (Englewood Cliffs, N.J.: Prentice-Hall, 1958); Alexander Jones (ed.), *The Jerusalem Bible;* Homer, *The Iliad* and *The Odyssey; The Laws of Manu,* translated by Georg Bühler; Cicero, *Murder Trials,* translated by Michael Grant; Kathleen Freeman (ed. and trans.), *The Murder of H erodes and Other Trials from the Athenian Law Courts;* and the Constitution and Bill of Rights of the United States.

Secondary sources included Maine, *Ancient Law;* Russell, *History of Western Philosophy;* Wormser, *Story of the Law;* McDonald, "Towards a Bicentennial Revolution in Criminal Justice: The Return of the Victim," *American Criminal Law Review;*Morison, *Oxford History of the American People;* Schafer, *The Victim and His Criminal* and *Restitution to Victims of Crime;* Gordon, *Hammurabi's Code: Quaint or Forward-looking?;* R. R. Cherry, *The Growth of Criminal Law in Ancient Communities;* Basham, *The Wonder That Was India;* Maine, *Dissertations on Early Law and Custom;* Thorn, Lockyer, and Smith, A *History of England;* Las-ter, "Criminal Restitution" in *Considering the Victim,* edited by Hudson and Galaway; Lloyd, *The Year of the* who was kind enough to mail me his thesis on crime victims, initiated his 1965 study because he had been in the audience when Goldberg first delivered that address.)

Claimant reports were taken from the hundreds sent by all the crime victim compensation boards,

Statistics on government expenditures in 1974 for criminal justice activities appeared in the June 1976 *Federal Probation,* p. 86.

The chart on crime victim compensation evolved from my own initial draft, which was then compared with Richard J. Gross's more extensive version that originally appeared in the *North Dakota Lato Review,* vof. 53 (1976), and Ann Rule's "At Last—Help for Innocent Victims of Crime" in *Good Housekeeping,* July 1977. Steve Sanders assisted in telephone checks on missing figures or discrepancies.

7. SUMMING UP

Nonurban killings were cited from "The Town That Lives in Terror," by Bill Davidson *(Good Housekeeping,* Sept. 1977); "Grim Turn in Trial of Child Killings" *(New York Post,* Mar. 23, 1977); "Sniper Slays 6 in Jersey and Then Takes Own Life" *(New York Times,* Aug. 28, 1977); "Suspect in Jersey Sniper Killings Had Extensive Psychiatric Record," by Pranay Gupte *(New York Times,* Aug. 30, 1977); "Mother, 7 Children and a Niece Found Slain in Connecticut Fire," by Diane Henry *(New York Times,* July 23, 1977); and "Mother and 7 Children Are Buried," by Diane Henry *(New York Times,* Jnly 28, 1977).

People magazine, Jan. 1977, p. Ill, noted *that Helter Skelter* (nitrated everything in 1976 except for the old movie *Gone with the Wind,*

Serge Chauvel-Leroux's series, "Stop au Crime; New York Contre-Attaque . , , ," appeared in Paris, *Le Figaro,* June 26, 27, 28, 1974. (Sam Flores provided a translation.)

The differences among interviewing, investigating, and interrogating were discussed in a lecture by Dr. Martin Symonds at the Karen Homey Clinic in New York, Jan. 1976.

Information on NDAA, Call for Action, and other programs cited was drawn from booklets, reports, leaflets, and correspondence, including the July 1976 NDAA narrative, and interviews with Richard P. Lynch, Commission on Victim Witness Assistance; Sandra J. Brown of Call for Action,

Washington, D.C., headquarters; Joseph P. Mueller, Carol Viddard, Ann Slaughter of Aid to Victims of Crime, Inc., St. Louis; Col. SaLees Seddon, Delphine McClellan, Mary Fetch, Berneice Page, Lyn Sikolnik, and numerous others of Women's Crusade Against Crime; Jim Walsh of Victims Information Bureau of Suffolk; Catherine Lynch, Muriel Solomon, Ellie Wigner, Harvey C. Jacobs, editor of the *Indianapolis News;* Betty Ann Good of the Miami Citizens' Crime Watch; and numerous others.

BIBLIOGRAPHY

1. BOOKS

Abraham, Henry J. *The Judicial Process,* 3rd ed. New York; Oxford University Press, 1975.

Abrahamsen, David. *Crime and the Human Mind.* New York: Columbia University Press, 1944.

_____. *The Murdering Mind.* New York: Harper & Row, 1973.

_____. *The Psychology of Crime.* New York; Columbia University Press, 1960.

Adler, Freda. *Sisters in Crime: The Rise of the New Female Criminal.* New York: McGraw-Hill, 1975,

Aeschylus. *Orestela: Agamemnon, The Libation Bearers, The Eumenides.* Translated by Richard Lattimore. Chicago: University of Chicago Press, 1973; 1953.

Allport, Gordon W. *The Nature of Prejudice.* Abridged. Garden City, N.Y.; Doubleday/Anchor Books, 1958; 1954.

Alvarez, A. *The Savage God: A Study of Suicide.* New York: Bantam Books, 1973.

Amir, Menachem. *Patterns in Forcible Rape.* Chicago: University of Chicago Press, 1971.

Arendt, Hannah. *Eichmann in Jerusalem: A Report on the Banality of Evil.* Rev. ed. New York: Viking Press, 1965; 1963.

_____. *On Violence.* New York: Harcourt Brace Jovanovich, 1970; 1969.

Aries, Philippe. *Western Attitudes toward Death: From the Middle Ages to the Present.* Translated by Patricia M. Ranum, Baltimore, Md.: Johns Hopkins University Press, 1974.

Astor, Gerald. *The Charge Is Rape.* Chicago: Playboy Press, 1974.

Balikci, Asen. *The Netsilik Eskimo.* Garden City, N.Y,: Natural History Press, 1970.

Basham, A. L. *The Wonder That Was India: A Survey of the Culture of the Indian Suh-Continent before the Coming of the Muslims.* New York: Grove Press, 1954.

Becker, Howard S. *Outsiders: Studies in the Sociology of Deviance.* Rev. ed. New York: Free Press, 1973; 1963.

Berne, Eric. *Games People Play: The Psychology of Human Relationships.* New York: Grove Press, 1964.

Black, Charles L., Jr. *Capital Punishment: The Inevitability of Caprice and Mistake.* New York: W. W. Norton, 1974.

Black, Henry Campbell, ed. *Black's Law Dictionary,* 4th rev. ed. St. Paul, Minn.: West Publishing Co., 1968; 1891.

Blumberg, Abraham S. *Criminal Justice.* New York: Franklin Watts, 1974,

_____. ed. *Current Perspectives on Criminal Behavior.* New York: Alfred A. Knopf, 1974.

Boas, Franz. *The Central Eskimo.* Lincoln, Nebr.; University of Nebraska Press, 1964; 1888.

Bohannan, Paul, ed. Law *&- Warfare.* Austin; University of Texas Press, 1967.

Brenner, Charles. An *Elementary Textbook of Psychoanalysis.* Rev. ed. Garden City, N.Y.: Doubleday/Anchor Books, 1974; 1955.

Brownmiller, Susan. *Against Our Will: Men, Women and Rape.* New York: Simon & Schuster, 1975.

Bugliosi, Vincent, with Gentry, Curt. *Heller Skelter: The True Story of the Manson Murders.* New York-, W. W. Norton, 1974.

Burgess, Ann, and Holmstrom, Lynda Lytic. *Rape: Victims of Crisis.* Bowie, Md.: Robert J. Brady, 1974.

Burgess, Anthony. *A Clockwork Orange.* New York: W. VV. Norton, 1963.

Cameron, Mary O. *The Booster and the Snitch.* Glencoe, Ill.: Free Press, 1964.

Camus, Albert. *The Rebel: An Essay on Man in Revolt.* Translated and edited by Anthony Bower. New York: Vintage Books, 1956; 1951.

_____. *The Stranger.* Translated by Stuart Gilbert. New York: Vintage Books, 1954; 1942.

Capote, Truman. *In Cold Blood: A True Account of a Multiple Murder and Its Consequences.* New York: New American Library, 1965.

Carrington, Frank G. *The Victims.* New Rochelle, N.Y.: Arlington House, 1975.

The Challenge of Crime in a Free Society: A Report by the President's Commission on Law Enforcement and Administration of Justice. New York: Avon Books, 1968; 1967.

Chappcll, Duncan, and Monahan, John, eds. *Violence and Criminal Justice.* Lexington, Mass.: Lexington Books, D. C. Heath, 1975.

Christie, Agatha. *Evil under the Sun.* New York: Pocket Books, 1975; 1945.

Cicero. *Murder Trials, (c.* 80-60 B.C.) Translated by Michael Grant. Harmonds-worth, Middlesex, England; Penguin Books, 1975.

Clark, Ramsey. *Crime in America.* New York: Simon & Schuster, 1970.

Clark, Tim, and Penyeate, John. *Psychopath: The Case of Patrick Mackay.* London: Routledge & Kegan Paul, 1976.

Cleaver, Eldridge. *Soul on Ice.* New York: Dell, 1968.

Clinard, Marshall B. *Sociology of Deviant Behavior.* 4th ed. New York: Holt, Rinehart and Winston, 1974; 1957.

Cloward, Richard A., and Ohlin, Lloyd E. *Delinquency and Opportunity: A Theory of Delinquent Gangs.* New York: Free Press, 1960.

Cohen, Stanley, and Taylor, Laurie. *Psychological Survival: The Experience of Long-Term Imprisonment.* Harmonds worth, Middlesex, England: Penguin Books, 1972.

Collins, Philip. *Dickens and Crime.* Bloomington, Ind.: Indiana University Press, 1968; 1962.

Comprehensive Textbook of Psychiatry—II. 2nd ed. 2 vols. Edited by Drs. Alfred M. Freedman, Harold I. Kaplan, and Benjamin J. Sadock. Baltimore, Md.: Williams & Wilkins, 1975; 1967.

Conklin, John E. *Robbery and the Criminal Justice System.* Philadelphia; J. B. Lippincott, 1972.

Curtis, Lynn A. *Criminal Violence: National Patterns and Behavior.* Lexington, Mass.; Lexington Books, D. C. Heath, 1974.

The Dartmouth Bible: An Abridgment of the King James Version, with Aids to Its Understanding as History and Literature, and as a Source of Religious Experience. Edited by Roy B. Chamberlin and Herman Feldman. Boston; Houghton Mifflin, 1965.

Dawdley, David. *A Nation of Lords: The Autobiography of the Vice Lords.* Garden City, N.Y.: Doubleday/Anchor Books, 1973.

De Quincey, Thomas. *Miscellaneous Essays.* Boston; Ticknor, Reed, and Fields, 1851.

de Wit, Jan, and Hartup, Willard W., eds. *Determinants and Origins of Aggressive Behavior.* The Hague, The Netherlands: Mouton, 1974.

Dickens, Charles. *Oliver Twist.* New York: Books, Inc., 1930; 1838.

Dostoevsky, Fyodor. *Crime and Punishment.* Translated by Michael Scammell. New York: Washington Square Press, 1972; 1866.

Drapkin, Israel, and Viano, Emilio, eds. *Victimology.* Lexington, Mass,; Lexington Books, D. C. Heath, 1974.

_____ and _____, eds. *Victimology: A New Focus. Volume I—Theoretical Issues in Victimology.* Lexington, Mass.: Lexington Books, D. C. Heath, 1975.

_____ and _____, eds, *Victimology: A New Focus. Volume II—Society's Reaction to Victimization.* Lexington, Mass.; Lexington Books, D. C. Heath, 1975.

_____ and _____, eds. *Victimology: A New Focus. Volume III—Crimes, Victims, and Justice.* Lexington, Mass.: Lexington Books, D, C. Heath, 1975.

_____ and _____, eds. *Victimology: A New Focus. Volume IV—Violence and Its Victims.* Lexington, Mass.: Lexington Books, D. C. Heath, 1975.

_____ and _____, eds. *Victimology: A New Focus- Volume V—Exploiters and Exploited.* Lexington, Mass.: Lexington Books, D. C. Heath, 1975.

Dreiser, Theodore. *An American Tragedy.* New York: New American Library, 1964; 1925.

Durkheim, Emile. *The Rules of Sociological Method.* 8th ed. Translated by Sarah A. Solovay and John H. Mueller. Edited by George E. G. Catlin. New York: Free Press, 1964; 1895.

Edelhertz, Herbert, and Geis, Gilbert. *Public Compensation to Victims of Crime.* New York: Praeger, 1974.

Ellis, Albert, and Harper, Robert A. *A New Guide to Rational Living.* Englewood Cliffs, N.J.: Prentice-Hall, 1975; 1961.

Erikson, Erik H. *Childhood and Society.* New York: W. W. Norton, 1950.

Evans-Pritchard, E. E, *The Niter. A Description of the Modes of Livelihood and Political Institutions of a Nilotic People.* London: Oxford University Press, 1940.

Eysenck, H. J. *Crime and Personality.* Boston: Houghton Mifflin, 1964.

Faulkner, William. *The Faulkner Reader.* New York: Random House, 1959.

Ferri, Enrico. *Criminal Sociology.* Boston: Little, Brown, 1917.

Fortes, M., and Evans-Pritchard, E. E., eds. *African Political Systems.* London: Oxford University Press, 1940.

Frank, Ceroid. *The Boston Strangler:* New York: Signet Classics, 1966.

Frankel, Marvin E. *Criminal Sentences: Law without Order.* New York: Hill & Wang, 1973.

Fraser, Morris, *Children in Conflict.* Harmondsworth, Middlesex, England: Penguin Books, 1974.

Freeman, Kathleen. *The Murder of Herodes and Other Trials from the Athenian Law Courts.* New York: W. W. Norton, 1963.

Freeman, Lucy, and Hulse, Wilfred C. *Children Who Kill.* New York: Berkley, 1962.

Freuchen, Peter. *Book of the Eskimos.* New York: Fawcett, 1961.

Freud, Anna. *The Ego and the Mechanisms of Defense.* New York: International Universities Press, 1946; 1936.

_____. *Psychoanalytic Study of the Child.* New York: International Universities Press, 1958.

Freud, Sigmund. *Totem and Taboo.* Translated by James Strachey. New York: W. W. Norton, 1950.

Fromm, Erich. *The Anatomy of Human Destructiveness.* New York: Fawcett, 1975; 1973.

Fry, Margery. *Arms of the Law.* London: Victor Gollancz, 1951.

Caddis, Thomas E., and Long, James O. *Killer: A Journal of Murder* (based on the papers of Henry Lesser). Greenwich, Conn.: Fawcett Premier Books, 1973; 1970.

Garofalo, Raffaele. *Criminology.* Boston: Little, Brown, 1914.

Gelb, Barbara. *On the Track of Murder.* New York: William Morrow, 1975.

Gelles, Richard J. *The Violent Home: A Study of Physical Aggression between Husbands and Wives.* Vol. 13. Beverly Hills, Calif.: Sage Publications, 1974.

Gibran, Kahlil. *The Prophet.* New York: Alfred A. Knopf, 1963; 1923.

Graham, Hugh Davis, and Gurr, Ted Robert, eds. *Violence in America: Historical and Comparative Perspectives.* New York: Bantam Books, 1969.

Gunn, John. *Violence.* New York: Praeger, 1973.

Hall, Jerome. *Theft, Law and Society.* Indianapolis, Ind.: Bobbs-Merrill, 1935.

Haskins, James. *Street Gangs: Yesterday and Today.* New York: Hastings House, 1974.

Heifer, Ray E., and Kempe, C. Henry, eds. *The Battered Child.* Rev. ed. Chicago: University of Chicago Press, 1974; 1968.

Hilberman, Elaine. *The Rape Victim.* Washington, D.C.: American Psychiatric Association, 1976.

Hobbes, Thomas. *Leviathan.* Edited by C. B. Macpherson. London: Everyman's Library, 1965; 1651.

Hoebel, E. Adamson. *Anthropology: The Study of Man.* 4th ed. New York: McGraw-Hill, 1972; 1949.

_____. *The Law of Primitive Man: A Study in Comparative Legal Dynamics.* Cambridge, Mass.: Harvard University Press, 1961; 1954.

Hofstadter, Richard, and Wallace, Michael, eds. *American Violence: A Documentary History.* New York: Vintage Books, 1971.

Holmes, Oliver Wendell. *The Common Law.* Edited by M. DeWolfe Howe. Boston: Little, Brown, 1963; 1881.

Homer. *The Iliad,* (sixth century B.C.) Translated by William Cowper. New York: C. P. Putnam's Sons, 1850.

_____. *The Odyssey,* (sixth century B.C.) Translated by W. H. D. Rouse. New York: New American Library, 1963.

Hudson, Joe, and Galaway, Burt, eds. *Considering the Victim: Readings in Restitution and Victim Compensation.* Springfield, Ill, ; Charles C. Thomas, 1975.

Hunt, Morton. *The Mugging.* Harmondsworth, Middlesex, England: Penguin Books, 1975; 1972.

James, Howard. *The Little Victims: How America Treats Its Children.* New York: David McKay, 1975.

Kübler-Ross, Elisabeth. *On Death and Dying.* New York: Macmillan, 1976; 1969.

The Laws of Manu. Translated by Georg Biihler. New York: Dover Publications, 1969; 1886.

Lefkowitz, Bernard, and Gross, Kenneth G. *The Victims: The Wylie-Hoffert Murder Case—and Its Strange Aftermath.* New York: G. P. Putnam's Sons, 1969.

Locke, John. *Two Treatises of Government.* Rev. ed. Edited by Peter Laslett. New York: New American Library, 1963; 1678.

Lockhart, William B.; Kamisar, Yale; and Choper, Jesse H. *Constitutional Rights and Liberties: Cases and Materials.* 4th ed. St. Paul, Minn.: West Publishing Co., 1975; 1964.

Lorenz, Konrad. *On Aggression.* Translated by Marjorie Kerr Wilson, New York: Harcourt Brace Jovanovich, 1974; 1966.

Maas, Peter. *The Valachi Papers.* New York: G. P. Putnam's Sons, 1968.

Macdonald, John M. *Armed Robbery: Offenders and Their Victims.* Springfield, Ill.: Charles C, Thomas, 1975.

_____.*Rape: Offenders and Their Victims.* Springfield, Ill.: Charles C. Thomas, 1971.

McDonald, William F., ed. *Criminal Justice and the Victim.* Beverly Hills, Calif,: Sage Publications, 1976.

Maine, Henry Sumner. *Ancient Law: Its Connection with the Early History of Society, and Its Relations to Modern Ideas.* New York: Charles Scribner's Sons, 1871; 1861.

Malcolm X. *The Autobiography of Malcolm X.* Edited by Alex Haley. New York: Grove Press, 1964.

Malinowski, Bronislaw, *Crime and Custom in Savage Society.* Totowa, N.J.: Little field, Adams, 1972; 1926.

Malory, Thomas. *Le Morte D'Arthur: King Arthur and, the Legends of the Round Table.* Translated by Keith Baines. New York: New American Library, 1962; 1485.

Milgram, Stanley. *Obedience to Authority: An Experimental View.* New York: Harper & Row, 1975; 1974.

Mitford, Jessica. *Kind and Usual Punishment: The Prison Business.* New York: Vintage Books, 1974; 1971.

More, Thomas. *Utopia.* Translated by Paul Turner. Harmonds worth, Middlesex, England: Penguin Books, 1965; 1516.

Morris, Ed. *Bom to Lose.* New York: Mason & Lipscomb, 1974.

Morris, Norval, and Hawkins, Gordon, *The Honest Politician's Guide to Crime Control.* Chicago: University of Chicago Press, 1970.

Mulvihill, Donald J,; Curtis, Lynn A.; and Tumin, Melvin M. *Crimes of Violence. Vol. II: A Staff Report to the National Commission on the Causes and Prevention of Violence.* Washington, D.C.: U.S. Government Printing Office, December 1969. See esp. chap. 5, "The Offender and His Victim," pp. 207-58.

Mushanga, Tibamanya. *Crime and. Deviance.* Nairobi, Kenya: East African Literature Bureau, 1976.

Nettler, Gwynn. *Explaining Crime.* New York: McGraw-Hill, 1974.

New York Penal Law Criminal Procedure Law, Criminal Lawn 1975-76 Grayhook. New York: Matthew Bender, 1975.

Nicholson, George; Gondii, Thomas W,; and Greenbaum, Stuart. *Forgotten Vic-tims: An Advocate's Anthology.* Sacramento, Calif.: California District Attorneys Association, 1977.

Niederhoffer, Arthur. *Behind the Shield: The Police in Urban Society.* Garden City, N.Y.: Doubleday/Anchor Books, 1969; 1967.

_____ and Blumberg, Abraham S., eds. *The Ambivalent Force: Perspectives on the Police.* Waltham, Mass.; Ginn, 1970.

Pasternack, Stefan A., ed. *Violence and Victims.* New York: Spectrum Publications, 1975.

Paton, Alan. *Too Late the Phalarope.* New York: Charles Scribner's Sons, 1953.

Pckkanen, John. *Victims: An Account of Rape.* New York: Dial Press, 1976.

Phillips, William, ed. *The Short Stories of Dostoevskij.* Translated by Constance Garnett New York: Dial Press, 1946.

Pinkney, Alphonso. *The American Way of Violence,* New York: Random House, 1972.

Pizzey, Erin. *Scream Quietly or the Neighbours Will Hear,* Edited by A. Forbes. Harmondsworth, Middlesex, England: Penguin Books, 1974.

Plato, *The Last Days of Socrates: Euthyphro, The Apology, Crito, Phaedo.* (c. fifth century B.C.) Translated by Hugh Tredennick. Baltimore, Md: Penguin Books, 1969.

Pritchard, James B., ed. *The Ancient Near East; An Anthology of Texts and Pictures,* Vol. 1. Princeton, N.J.: Princeton University Press, 1973; 1958.

Presser, William L. *Handbook of the Law of Torts.* 4th ed. St. Paul, Minn.: West Publishing Co., 1971; 1941.

Quinney, Richard. *The Social Reality of Crime.* Boston: Little, Brown, 1970.

_____ and Wilde man, John. *The Problem of Crime: A Critical Introduction to Criminology.* 2nd ed. New York: Harper & Row, 1977.

Radzinowicz, Leon, and Hood, Roger. *Criminology and the Administration of Criminal Justice.* London: Mansen Information Publishers Ltd., 1976.

_____ and Wolfgang, Marvin, eds. *Crime and Justice.* 3 vols. New York: Basic Books, 1971.

Rasmussen, Knud. *Across Arctic America: Narrative of the Fifth Thule Expedition,* New York: Greenwood Press, 1969; 1927.

_____, collector. *Eskimo Folk-Tales.* Edited by W, Worster. London; Gyldendal, 1921.

Reasons, Charles E. *The Criminologist: Crime and the Criminal.* Pacific Palisades, Calif.: Goodyear Publishing Co., 1974.

Reckless, Walter C. *The Crime Problem.* 2nd ed. New York: Appleton-Century-Crofts, 1955; 1950.

Reid, Sue Titus. Crime *and Criminology.* Hinsdale, Ill.: Dryden Press, 1976.

Rose, Thomas, ed. *Violence in America: A Historical and Contemporary Reader.* New York: Vintage Books, 1970; 1969.

Rosenbaum, H, J., and Sederberg, P. C, eds. *Vigilante Politics.* Philadelphia: University of Pennsylvania Press, 1976.

Rossner, Judith. *Looking for Mr. Coodhar.* New York: Simon & Schuster, 1975.

Rubinstein, Jonathan. *City Police.* New York: Farrar, Straus & Giroux, 1973.

Russell, Bertrand. *A History of Western Philosophy.* New York: Simon & Schuster, 1945.

Russell, Diana E, II. *The Politics of Rape: The Victims Perspective.* New York: Stein & Day, 1975.

Ryan, William. *Blaming the Victim.* Rev. ed. New York: Vintage Books, 1976; 1971.

Schafer, Stephen. *Restitution to Victims of Crime.* London: Stevens and Sons, 1960.

_____. *The Victim and His Criminal: A Study in Functional Responsibility.* New York: Random House, 1968.

Schiff, Harriet Sarnoff. *The Bereaved Parent.* New York: Crown Publishers, 1977.

Schultz, Leroy G., ed. *Rape Victimology.* Springfield, Ill.: Charles C. Thomas, 1975.

Schur, Edwin M. *Crimes without Victims: Deviant Behavior and Public Policy.* Englewood Cliffs, N.J.: Prentice-Hall, 1965.

Sellin, Thorsten, ed. *Capital Punishment.* New York: Harper & Row, 1967.

Simenon, Georges. *Maigret and the Black Sheep*. Translated by Helen Thomson. New York: Harcourt Brace Jovanovich, 1976; 1962.

Steinmetz, Suzanne K., and Straus, Murray A., eds. *Violence in the Family*. New York: Dodd, Mead, 1974.

Stendhal. *The Red and the Black: A Chronicle of the Nineteenth Century*. Translated by Lloyd C. Parks. New York: New American Library, 1970; 1830.

Storr, Anthony. *Human Aggression*. New York: Bantam Books, 1970; 1968.

Strasberg, Lee, ed. *Famous American Plays of the 1950s*. New York: Dell Publishing Co., 1962.

Sutherland, Edwin H. *White-Collar Crime*. New York: Dryden Press, 1949.

————, ed. *The Professional Thief* Chicago: University of Chicago Press, 1937.

———— and Cressey, Donald R. *Criminology*. 9th ed. Philadelphia: Lippincott, 1974; 1924.

Sykes, Gresham M. *Crime and Society*. New York: Random House, 1956.

Taylor, Ian; Walton, Paul; and Young, Jock. *The New Criminology: For a Social Theory of Deviance*. London: Routledge & Kegan Paul, 1973.

Thomas, Piri. *Down These Mean Streets*. New York: Vintage Books, 1974; 1967.

Toch, Hans. *Violent Men: An inquiry into the Psychology of Violence*. Harmonds-worth, Middlesex, England: Penguin Books, 1972; 1969.

Viano, Emilio C, ed. *Victims and Society*. Washington, D.C.: Visage Press, 1976.

von Hentig, Hans. *The Criminal and His Victim: Studies in the Socio-biology of Crime*. New Haven, Conn.: Yale University Press, 1948.

Werfel, Franz. *Twilight of a World*. Translated by H. T. Lowe-Porter. New York: Viking Press, 1937.

Wertham, Fredric. *Seduction of the Innocent*. New York: Holt, Rinehart and Winston, 1954.

————. *The Show of Violence*. Garden City, N.Y.: Doubleday, 1967; 1948.

————. *A Sign for Cain: An Exploration of Human Violence*. New York: Warner Books, 1973; 1966.

West, D. J. *Murder Followed by Suicide*. London: Heinemann, 1965.

Willwerth, James. *Jones: Portrait of a Mugger*. New York: M. Evans, 1974.

Wilson, James Q. *Thinking about Crime*. New York: Basic Books, 1975.

Wolfgang, Marvin E. *Patterns of Criminal Homicide.* Philadelphia: University of Pennsylvania Press, 1958.

_____, ed. *Studies in Homicide.* New York: Harper & Row, 1967.

_____ and Ferracuti, Franco. *The Subculture of Violence: Towards an Integrated Theory in Criminology.* London: Tavistock, 1967.

_____; Savitz, Leonard; and Johnston, Norman, eds. *The Sociology of Crime and Delinquency.* 2nd ed. New York: Wiley, 1970; 1962.

Wormser, René A. *The Story of the Law and the Men Who Made It—From the Earliest Times to the Present.* Rev. ed. New York: Simon & Schuster, 1962; 1949.

Yablonsky, Lewis. *The Violent Gang.* Rev. ed. Baltimore, Md.: Penguin Books, 1970; 1962.

Zinn, Howard, ed. *Justice in Everyday Life: The Way It Really Works.* New York: William Morrow, 1974.

2. MAGAZINE, NEWSPAPER, AND JOURNAL ARTICLES

Abrahamsen, David. "Study of 102 Sex Offenders at Sing Sing." *Federal Probation,* vol. 14 (Sept. 1950), pp. 26-32.

"Aid to Victims of Crimes: Something Being Done at Last." *U.S. News & World Report,* vol. 79 (Dec. 8, 1975), pp. 42-44.

Amir, Menachem. "Forcible Rape." *Federal Probation,* vol. 31 (Mar. 1967), pp. 51-58.

_____, "Victim Precipitated Forcible Rape." *Journal of Criminal Law, Criminology and Police Science,* voi. 58 (1967), pp, 493-502.

Artz, George. "Reporter Meets Muggers on a Quiet Street. " *New York Post,* Sept. 30, 1974, p. 2.

"Assault on Crime: Criminals and Victims Bear Witness." *Harper's Weekly,* May 9, 1975, pp. 7-9.

Astor, Gerald. "Crime Doesn't Pay Its Victims Very Well, Either." *New York Times,* May 30, 1976, p, E-9.

Avison, Neville H., "Victims of Homicide." London *International Journal of Criminology and Penology,* vol. 2, no. 3 (1974), pp. 225-37.

Baden, Michael M. "Homicide, Suicide, and Accidental Death among Narcotic Addicts." *Human Pathology,* vol. 3 (Mar. 1972), pp. 91-95.

Bard, Morton, and Ellison, Katherine. "Crisis Intervention and Investigation of Forcible Rape." *Police Chief,* vol. 16 (May 1974), pp. 68-73.

Barkas, J. L. "Adapting to Violence." *The New Leader,* vol. 59 (Mar, 15, 1976), pp. 3-4.

_____. "From Crime to Corrections." Review of *Crime & Criminology* by Sue Titus Reid. *Federal Probation,* vol. 41 (June 1977), pp. 71-72.

Barkas, Seth. "Movies." *Baltimore,* vol. 61 (Sept, 1968), pp. 46-47; vol. 61 (Dec. 1968), pp. 15-16; vol. 62 (Jan. 1969), pp. 14-15; vol. 62 (Mar. 1969), pp. 6-7.

_____. "The Real Issue" (Letter to the Editor). "Movie Mailbag." *New York Times,* Nov. 17, 1968, p. D-18.

Barton, R. F. "Ifugao Law." *American Archaeology and Ethnology,* vol. 15 (Feb. 15, 1919), pp. 1-186.

Bell, Daniel. "Crime as an American Way of Life." *The Antioch Review,* vol. 13 (June 1953), pp. 131-54.

Berendt, John. "I Catch a Burglar." *New York,* vol. 9 (Sept. 27, 1976), pp. 39-42.

Berman, Claire. "What Youngsters Need to Know about How to Deal with Muggers." *New York Times,* July 23, 1976, p. A-9.

Bignami, Louis V. "Spend Two Hours and $20 to Make Your Place Secure." *Apartment Life,* July 1976, pp. 82-83.

Blakeslee, Sandra, "To Increase Police Sensitivity on the Plight of Rape Victims." *New York Times,* Jan. 8, 1976, p. 39.

"The Blind Taught Art of Self-Defense." *New York Times,* Sept. 19, 1976, p. 22.

Blumberg, Audrey, and Bohmer, Carol. "The Rape Victim and Due Process." *Case & Comment,* Nov.-Dec. 1975, pp. 3-16.

Brant, Renee S. T., M.D., and Tisza, Veronica B., M.D. "The Sexually Misused Child." *American Journal of Orthopsychiatry,* vol. 47 (Jan. 1977), pp, 80-90.

Bremer, Arthur H. "An Assassin's Diary." *Harper's,* vol. 246 (Jan. 1973), pp. 52-56, 61, 62, 64-66.

Brooks, James. ,:The Case for Creating Compensation Programs to Aid Victims of Violent Crimes." *University of Tulsa Law Journal,* vol. 11 (1976), pp. 477-503.

_____. "Compensating Victims of Crime: The Recommendations of Program Administrators." *Law & Society Review,* Spring 1973, pp. 445-71.

Brownmiller, Susan. "Do You Believe the Myths about Rape?" *Family Circle,* vol 87 (Oct. 1975), pp. 38, 40, 42, 178.

_____. "Under Law, Rape Was at First a Crime Only against a Father's Property. But That Has Changed." *New York Times,* Op-Ed, Oct. 1, 1975, p. 45.

Broyard, Anatole. "Criminal Etiquette." *New York Times,* Jan. 23, 1976, p. 29.

Burgess, Ann Wolbert "Family Reaction to Homicide." *American Journal of Orthopsychiatry,* vol. 45 (Apr, 1975), pp. 391-98.

_____, "The Rape Victim in the Emergency *Ward." American Journal of Nursing,* vol. 73 (Oct, 1973), pp. 1741-43.

_____, and Holmstrom, Lynda Lytle. "Rape Trauma Syndrome." *American Journal of Nursing,* vol. 131 (1974), pp. 981-86.

Carroll, Donald. "Conversation with Doctor Thomas Noguchi." *Oui,* vol. 5 (Feb. 1976), pp. 67-68, 74, 118, 120.

Chappell, Duncan, and Walsh, Marilyn. " 'No Questions Asked': A Consideration of the Crime of Criminal Receiving." *Crime and Delinquency,* Apr, 1974, pp. 157-68.

Costikyan, Edward N. "Assault with Intent to Maim." *New York,* vol. 9 (May 31, 1976), pp. 7-8.

Cox, Clinton. "Meanwhile in Bedford-Stuyvesant . . ." *More,* vol. 6 (Apr. 1976), pp. 18, 20, 21.

Coyne, Barry L. "Letter to the Editor—Protecting the Victims." *New York Post,* Sept. 3, 1975, p. 3.

Crichton, Sarah. "The Most Misunderstood Crime." *East Side Express,* Manhattan, Sept. 9, 1976, p. 3.

"Crime against the Elderly." *Police Chief,* vol. 18 (Feb. 1976).

Cunningham, Barry. "Murder Victim's Family: A Year Later." *Neto York Post,* Sept. 12, 1974, pp. 2, 54.

Darley, John M.; Teger, Allan I.; and Lewis, Lawrence D. "Do Groups Always Inhibit Individuals' Responses to Potential Emergencies?" *Journal of Personality and Social Psychology,* vol. 26 (1973), pp. 395-99.

Dershowitz, Alan. "The Special Victim Is Not New in the Law." *New York Times,* "The Week in Review," Mar. 27, 1977, p. E-6.

D'Monte, Darryl. "Can Violence Be Justified?" *Illustrated Weekly of India,* vol. 51 (Dec. 21, 1975), pp. 8-11, 13.

Dreiser, Theodore. "I Find the Real American Tragedy." *Mystery Magazine,* Feb. 1935, pp. 9-11, 88-90; Mar. 1935, pp. 22-23, 77-79; Apr. 1935, pp. 24-26, 90-93; May 1935, pp. 22-24, 83-84, 86; June 1935, pp. 20-21, 68-73.

Ellenberger, Henri. "Psychological Relationships between the Criminal and His Victim." *Revue Internationale de Criminologie et de Police Technique,* vol. 2 (1954), pp. 103-21.

Fallon, Beth. "Mugged? Give In, Say Ex-Thugs." New York *Daily News,* June 3, 1975, p. 31.

Fattali, Ezzat Abdel. "Quelques problèmes posés À la justice pénale par la victimologies' *International Annals of Criminology,* 2nd sem., 1966, pp. 335-61.

Fields, Sidney. "Only Human: The Birth of Shock." New York *Daily News,* Feb. 24, 1976, p. 53.

"First Crime Reparation Goes to Widow Injured in Mugging." *Minneapolis Star,* Oct. 11, 1974, p. 5-A.

Fry, Margery. "Justice for Victims." *Journal of Public Law,* vol. 8 (1959), pp. 191-94.

Galaway, Burt. "The Use of Restitution." *Crime & Delinquency,* vol. 23 (Jan. 1977), pp. 57-67.

Gayford, J. J. "Wife Battering: A Preliminary Survey of 100 Cases." *British Medical Journal,* Jan. 25, 1975, pp. 194-97.

Geis, Gilbert; Huston, Ted. L.; and Wright, Richard. "Compensating Good Samaritans." *Crime Prevention Review,* vol. 3 (Apr. 1976), pp. 28-35.

Gelb, Barbara. "Who Killed Beatrice Anderson? Solving a Real Murder Mystery, in the Post-Miranda Era." *New York Times Magazine,* Oct. 5, 1975, pp. 24-25, 28-30, 34, 36, 38, 40.

Gelles, Richard J. "Child Abuse as Psychopathology: A Sociological Critique and Reformulation." *American Journal of Orthopsychiatry,* vol. 43 (July 1973), pp. 611-21.

Gibbens, T. C. N. "Sane and Insane *Homicide.*" *Journal of Criminal Law, Criminology and Police Science,* vol. 49 (July-Aug. 1958), pp. 110-15.

Gittelson, Natalie. "Parents as Kidnappers." *McCall's,* Aug. 1976, p. 39.

Goldstein, Tom. "Large Number of Crime Suspects Knew Their Victims, Study Says," *New York Times,* Dec. 4, 1976, p. 30.

Gooding, Richard, and Walder, Joyce. "For Victims' Families, Bitterness and Pity," *New York Post,* Nov. 27, 1976, p. 31.

Gould, Lois. "Letter to a Robber." *Neto York Times Magazine,* Mar. 10, 1974, pp. 38-40, 42.

Green berg, Bernard. "School Vandalism: Its Effects and Paradoxical Solutions." *Crime Prevention Review,* vol. I (Jan. 1974), pp. 11-18.

Griffin, Susan. "Rape: The Ail-American Crime." *Ramparts,* vol. 10 (Sept. 1971), pp. 26-35.

Gross, Richard J. "Crime Victim Compensation in North Dakota: A Year of Trial and Error." *North Dakota Law Review,* vol. 53 (1976-77), pp. 7-49.

Gupte, Pranay. "Politicians and Judges Criticized at Rally Decrying Rise in Crime." *New York Times,* Feb. 23, 1977, p. 3.

Hall, Stuart. "Mugging: A Case Study in the Media." London *Listener,* May I, 1975, pp. 571-72.

Hallas, Clark. "Face-to-Face with Their Son's Killer." Detroit *Sunday Netos,* Jan. 12, 1975, pp. 1, 16-A.

Howar, Barbara. "It Couldn't Happen to Her, but It Did." *New York Times Book Review,* Sept. 26, 1976, pp. 8, 10.

Jenkins, Brian M. "Do What They Ask. And Don't Worry. They May Kill Me but They Are Not Evil Men." *New York Times,* Op-Ed, Oct. 3, 1975, p. 35.

"Kin of 3 Slain Men Unite Here to Fight Crime across U.S." *New York Times,* Dec. 30, 1971, p. 18.

Klebba, A. Joan. "Homicide Trends in the United States, 1900-74." *Public Health Reports,* vol. 90 (May-June 1975), pp. 195-204.

Krebs, Albia. "Burglary, to the Victim, Is a Kind of Rape of the Home." *New York Times,* Apr. 10, 1977, sect. 8, pp. 1-2.

Luster, Richard E. "Criminal Restitution: A Survey of Its Past History and an Analysis of Its Present Usefulness," *University of Richmond Law Review,* vol. 5 (1970), pp. 71-98.

Latham, Aaron. "The Columbia Murder That Gave Birth to the Beats." *New York,* vol. 9 (Apr. 19, 1976), pp. 41-53.

Leonard, John. "An Etiquette of Murder: Dame Agatha Made Mystery Story an Enjoyable Middle-Class Virtue." *New York Times,* Jan. 13, 1976, p. 40.

_____. "The Victim as Hero," review of John Barthel's *A Death in Canaan* in *New York Times,* Dec. 6, 1976, p. 31.

Lerner, Melvin J. "All the World Loathes a Loser." *Psychology Today,* June 1971, pp. 51-54, 66.

_____. "Evaluation of Performance as a Function of Performer's Reward and *Attractiveness." Journal of Personality and Social Psychology,* vol. I (Apr. 1965), pp. 355-60.

_____ and Simmons, Carolyn H. "Observer's Reaction to the 'Innocent Victim': Compassion or Rejection." *Journal of Personality and Social Psychology,* vol. 4 (1966), pp. 203-10.

Levine, Seymour. "Stress and Behavior." *Scientific American,* vol. 224 (Jan. 1971), pp. 26-31.

Lingeman, Richard R. "Writer Is Mugged, Denies Being 'Victim.' " *New York Times Magazine,* Oct. 22, 1972, pp. 11, 16, 20.

Lopez, Barry. "Wolf Kill." *Harper's,* vol. 253 (Aug. 1976), pp. 25-27.

McDonald, William F. "Towards a Bicentennial Revolution in Criminal justice: The Return of the Victim." *American Criminal Law Review,* vol. 13 (Spring 1976), pp. 649-73.

McKay, Andrew. "Compensation Board Leaves Crime Victims Holding Bag." *New York Post,* Mar. 23, 1977, p, 22.

McMillan, Penelope. "The Victims of One Crime." New York *Sunday News,* Mar. 21, 1976, pp. 11-15.

McNamara, Joseph D. "FBI Statistics." *Washington Post,* Aug. 6, 1976.

Maitland, Leslie. "Good Samaritan or Victim? A Perplexing Question." *New York Times,* Aug. 18, 1976, p. 41

Maltz, Michael D, "Crime Statistics: A Historical Perspective." *Crime & Delinquency,* vol. 23 (Jan. 1977), pp. 32-40.

Malvik, Ethel. "Society Blames the Victim of the Crime." *Science Digest,* vol. 77 (Mar. 1975), pp. 64-69.

Mark, Sir Robert. "The Rights of Wrongdoers." London *The Guardian,* May 18, 1965.

_____. "Striking a Balance." *The Police Journal* (London), Nov. 1965, pp. 503-6.

Marks, Jane. "Burglaries, Car Accidents, Rape and Other Crises—How to Help the Victims." *Glamour,* May 1977, pp. 244-45, 298.

Mendelsohn, Benjamin. "Method to Be Used by Counsel for the Defense in the Researches Made into the Personality of the Criminal. " *Revue de Droit Pénal et de Criminologie* (Aug.-Oct. 1937), p. 877.

_____. "The Origin of the Doctrine of Victimology." *Excerpta Criminologica,* vol. 3 (May-June .1963), pp. 239-44.

Milliken, Rhoda J. "The Sex Offender's Victim." *Federal Probation,* vol. 14 (Sept. 1950), pp. 22-26.

Mokrzycki, Roy. "The Nifty and the *Gross.*" *Juris Doctor,* Oct. 1976, pp. 21-22.

Monis, Terence, "The Social Toleration of Crime." In *Changing Concepts of Crime and Its Treatment.* Edited by Hugh J. Klare. Oxford: Pergamon Press, 1966, pp. 13-34.

Mowatt, Robert M. "The Minnesota Restitution Center: Paying Off the Ripped Off." In *Restitution in Criminal Justice.* Edited by Joe Hudson. St. Paul. Minn.: Mimeo. report, 1976, pp. 191-215.

Nagel, Willem H. "The Notion of Victimology in Criminology." *Excerpta Criminologica,* vol. 3 (May-June 1963), pp. 245-47.

Newton, Anne. "Aid to the Victim—Part 1; Compensation and Restitution." *Crime & Delinquency Literature,* vol. 8 {Sept. 1976), pp. 368-90.

Normandeau, A. "Patterns in Robbery." *Criminological* (Nov. 1968), pp. 2-15.

Northrup, Bowen. "Battered Women: Wife-Beating Persists, but British Establish Refuges to Aid Victims; More Than 60 Centers Help Women Fleeing Homes; Some Myths Are Fading; Why the Law Isn't Effective." *Wall Street Journal,* Aug. 20, 1976, pp. 1, 22.

Pascoe, Elizabeth Jean. "Shelters for Battered Wives." *McCall's,* vol. 105 (Oct. 1976), p. 51.

Peters, Joseph J. "Children Who Are Victims of Sexual Assault and the Psychology of Offenders." *American Journal of Psychotherapy,* vol. 30 (July 1976), pp. 398-421.

Pokorny, Alex D. "Human Violence: A Comparison of Homicide, Aggravated Assault, Suicide, and Attempted Suicide." *Research Reports,* vol. 56 (1965), pp. 489-92.

Porter, Katherine Anne. "Theft" (1930). In *50 Great Short Stories*. Edited by Milton Crane, New York: Bantam Books, 1952, pp. 182-88.

Quinney, Richard, "Who Is the Victim?" *Criminology,* vol, 10 (1972), pp. 314-23.

Raab, Selwyn. " 'Deliberate' Slaymgs on Increase Here." *New York Times,* Feb. 27, 1976, pp. 1, 14.

_____. "Felony Murder Rose Here Sharply in '74." *New York Times,* Mar, 23, 1975, pp. 1, 41.

_____. "33% Slain in New York Don't Know Killer." *New York Times,* June 13, 1976, pp. 1, 60.

_____. "Violent Crimes Drop 0.4%, Latest Police Data Indicate." *New York Times,* Apr. 24, 1976, p. 56.

Ramsey, Judith. "My Husband Broke the Ultimate Taboo." *Family Circle,* March 8, 1977, pp. 42, 184-86, 188-89.

Rapoport, Roger. "L.A.'s Indomitable Coroner: The Ultimate Sleuth." *Cosmopolitan,* Oct. 1975, pp. 214-18.

Robin, Gerald. "Forcible Rape: Institutionalized Sexism in the Criminal Justice System." *Crime 6 Delinquency,* vol. 23 (Apr. 1977), pp. 136-53.

Rothstein, Paul F. "How the Uniform Crime Victims Reparation Act Works." *American Bar Association Journal,* vol. 60 (Dec. 1974), pp. 1531-35.

Rule, Ann. "At Last—Help for Innocent Victims of Crime." *Good Housekeeping,* July 1977, pp. 84, 86, 88-90, 93.

Rush, Florence. "The Sexual Abuse of Children; A Feminist Point of View." Radi *cal Therapist,* vol. 2 (Dec. 1971), Reprinted as mimeo. by KNOW, INC., for the Rape Conference, New York Radical Feminists, Apr. 17, 1971.

Sachar, Edward J. "Behavioral Science and Criminal Law." *Scientific American,* Nov. 1963, reprint.

Sehafer, Stephen. "Restitution to Victims of Crime: An Old Correctional Aim Modernized." *Minnesota Law Review,* vol. 50 (1965), pp. 243-54.

Skogan, Wesley G. "Citizen Reporting of Crime: Some National Panel Data." *Criminology,* vol. 13 (Feb. 1976), pp. 535-49.

_____. "Dimension of the Dark Figure of Unreported Crime." *Crime & Delinquency,* vol. 23 (Jan. 1977), pp. 41-50.

Smith, Selwyn M., and Hanson, Ruth. "134 Battered Children; A Medical and Psychological Study." *British Medical Journal*, Sept. 14, 1974, pp. 666-70.

_____; _____; and Noble, Sheila. "Social Aspects of the Battered Baby Syndrome." *British Journal of Psychiatry*, vol, 125 (Dec, 1974), pp. 568-82.

Steele, Ned. "Most Murder Victims Done in by Strangers." *Long Island Press*, Nov. 22, 1976, p. 4.

Stein, Gerald M. "Children's Reactions to Innocent Victims." *Child Development*, vol. 44 (Dec. 1973), pp. 805-10.

Sutherland, Sandra, and Seherl, Donald J. "Patterns of Response among Victims of Rape." *American Journal of Orthopsychiatry*, vol. 3 (Apr, 1970), pp. 503-11.

Symonds, Martin. "Victims of Violence: Psychological Effects and Aftereffects." *American Journal of Psychoanalysis*, vol. 35 (Spring 1975), pp. 19-26.

Tappan, Paul. "Who Is the Criminal?" *American Sociological Review*, vol. 12 (Feb. 1947), pp. 96-102.

Toland, John. "Sad Ballad of the Real Bonnie and Clyde," *New York Times Magazine*, Feb. 18, 1968, pp. 26-29, 82-85.

Victimology: An International Journal, quarterly, beg, vol, 1, no. 1, Spring 1976. Washington, D.C.: Visage Press.

"The Victims of Crime." *New York Times*, Editorial, Feb. 23, 1976, p. 24.

"Villains: Who's to Blame?" *Harper's Wraparound*, vol. 250 (Jan. 1975), pp. 5-12, 98.

von Hentig, Hans. "Remarks on the Interaction of Perpetrator and Victim." *Journal of the American Institute of Criminal Law and Criminology*, vol. 31 (Mar.-Apr. 1941), pp. 303-9.

Weinraub, Bernard. "The Violence in Ulster Never Ends." *New York Titnes*, July 25, 1976, p. E-3.

Weis, Kurt, and Borges, Sandra S. "Victimology and Rape: The Case of the Legitimate Victim." *Issues in Criminology*, vol. 8 (Fall 1973), pp. 71-115.

Wertham, Fredric. "Battered Children and Baffled Adults." *Bulletin of the New York Academy of Medicine*, 2nd series, vol. 48 (Aug. 1972), pp. 887-98.

_____. "The Malignancy of Violence." *Bulletin of the New York Academy of Medicine,* 2nd series, vol. 50 (Apr. 1974), pp, 545-58.

White, Glenn. "Where Citizens Help Control Crime." *Dynamic Maturity,* vol. 10 (July 1975), pp. 10-14.

Wilson, Edward O. "Human Decency Is Animal," *New York Times Magazine,* Oct. 12, 1975, pp. 38-46, 48, 50.

Wolfgang, Marvin E. "Victim Compensation in Crimes of Personal Violence." *Minnesota Law Review,* vol. 50 (1965), pp. 223-41.

_____. "Victim-Precipitated Criminal Homicide." *Journal of Criminal Law, Criminology and Police Science,* vol. 48 (May-June 1957), pp. 1-11.

Wren, Christopher. "Two Policemen Talk: Letting Rizzo Do the Thinking." *The Washington Monthly,* vol. 5 (Dec. 1973), pp. 33-43.

Wyatt, Woodrow. Review of *Turning Points: The Memoirs of Lord Wolfenden.* London *Times,* Apr. 11, 1976.

Zahn, Margaret A. "The Female Homicide Victim." *Criminology,* vol. 13 (1975), pp. 400-415.

Zimbardo, Philip G. "Vandalism: An Act in Search of a Cause." *Bell Telephone Magazine,* July-Aug. 1972.

Zintl, Terry. "Wife Abuse: Our Almost-Hidden Social Problem." *Detroit Free Press,* Jan. 25, 1976, pp. 1, 8.

3. MISCELLANEOUS REPORTS, BOOKLETS, PAMPHLETS, PAPERS, PLAYS, FILMS, HEARINGS, SEMINARS, CONFERENCES, FACT SHEETS

Abramovitz, Rafael, and Stern, Carl. "A Shooting Gallery Called America?" Lucy Jarvis, producer; Carl Stern, narrator; Tom Priestly, director. NBC News, broadcast Apr. 27, 1975. Transcript.

After the Rape: A Report Based on Responses from Victims of Sexual Assault Treated at the Rape Treatment Center, Jackson Memorial Hospital, Miami, Florida, during the Year 1974. Miami: Metro's Rape Awareness Education Program, 1975.

Baluss, Mary E. *integrated Services for Victims of Crime: A County Based Approach.* Washington, D.C.: The National Association of Counties Research Foundation, 1975.

Barlow, Hugh D. "Crime Victims and the Sentencing Process." Paper presented at the Second International Symposium on Victimology, Boston, Mass., Sept. 5-11, 1975.

Brecht, Bertolt, and Weill, Kurt, *Threepenny Opera.* Translated by Ralph Man-heim and John Willett. At the Vivien Beaumont Theater, New York City, Nov. 5, 1976.

Brodyaga, Lisa; Gates, Margaret; Singer, Susan; Tucker, Mama; and White, Richardson. *Rape and Its Victims: A Report for Citizens, Health Facilities, and Criminal Justice Agencies.* Washington, D.C.: U.S. Department of justice, Nov. 1975.

Burgess, Ann Wolbert. "Counseling the Rape Victim." Paper presented at the New York City Conference on Health Care for Rape Victims, Oct. 23, 1975.

Camus, Albert. *Neither Victims nor Executioners.* Translated by Dwight Mac-Donald. New York: Liberation Press, 1963.

The Clockmaker. Adapted by Bertrand Tavernier from novel by Georges Simenon. Actors; Philippe Noiret and Jean Rochefort. At the Paris Theatre, New York City, Aug. 31, 1976.

Community Crime Prevention. National Advisory Commission on Criminal Justice Standards and Goals, Washington, D.C., Jan. 1973.

Compensation for Victims of Crimes of Violence. Home Office White Paper, London; Her Majesty's Stationery Office, June 1961,

Cordes, Joseph G. "The Psychology of Stranger Homicides." Term paper, John Jay College of Criminal Justice, City University of New York, Spring 1975.

Crime in the United States—1972. Uniform Crime Reports, Federal Bureau of Investigation, Washington, D.C. : released Aug. 8, 1973.

Crime in the United States—1974. Uniform Crime Reports, Federal Bureau of Investigation, Washington, D.C: released Nov. 17, 1975.

Crime in the United States—1975. Uniform Crime Reports, Federal Bureau of Investigation, Washington, D.C: released Aug. 25, 1976.

Crime in the United States—1976. Uniform Crime Reports, Federal Bureau of Investigation, Washington, D.C: released September 28, 1977.

Crime Victim Compensation. Hearing before the Subcommittee on Criminal Justice of the Committee on the Judiciary, House of Representatives, Ninety-fourth Congress, First and Second Sessions on Victims of

Crime Compensation Legislation, Nov. 4, 18; Dec. 9, 15, 1975; Feb. 7, 13, 27, 1976. Serial no. 39. Washington, D.C: U.S. Government Printing Office, 1976.

"Crime Victims—Juvenile Offenders and Constructive Suggestions for Change," Women's League of Brooklyn Psychiatric Centers, Inc. Speakers included Richard Cody, John Oliver, and J. L. Barkas. Brooklyn, N.Y., Feb. 7, 1976.

Criminal Victimization in the United States: A Comparison of 1973 and 1974 Findings: A National Crime Panel Survey Report. U.S. National Criminal Justice Information and Statistics Service, Washington, D.C, May 1976.

Criminal Victimization in the United States, 1973 Advance Report, Vol. 1: A National Crime Panel Survey Report. U.S. National Criminal Justice Information and Statistics Service, Washington, D.C., May 1975.

Criminal Victimization in the United States, January-June 1973, Vol. 1: A National Crime Panel Survey Report. U.S. National Criminal Justice Information and Statistics Service, Washington, D.C., Nov. 1974.

Criminal Victimization Surveys in the Nation's Five Largest Cities: National Crime Panel Surveys of Chicago, Detroit, Los Angeles, New York, and Philadelphia. U.S. National Criminal Justice Information and Statistics Service, Washington, D.C., Apr. 1975.

Criminal Victimization Surveys in 13 American Cities: National Crime Panel Surveys in Boston, Buffalo, Cincinnati, Houston, Miami, Milwaukee, Minneapolis, New Orleans, Oakland, Pittsburgh, San Diego, San Francisco, Washington, D.C. U.S. National Criminal Justice Information and Statistics Service, Washington, D.C, June 1975.

Death Wish. From the novel by Brian Garfield. Produced by Dino De Laurentiis, starring Charles Bronson, 1972; on WNBC-TV, Nov. 9, 1976.

Doyle, Charlotte Lackner. "On Being a Woman and Becoming a Psychologist." Lecture delivered at East Stroudsburg State College, East Stroudsburg, Pa., May 2, 1975.

Edelhertz, Herbert, and Geis, Gilbert. *State Compensation to Crime Victims in New York.* Seattle, Wash.: Battello Memorial Institute, Human Affairs Research Centers, Aug. 10, 1972.

Ennis, Philip H. *Criminal Victimization in the United States: A Report of a National Survey: Report of a Research Study Submitted to the President's*

Commission on Law Enforcement and Administration of Justice, Field Survey II. Washington, D.C: U.S. Government Printing Office, 1967.

The Federal Crime Insurance Program: Questions and Answers. HUD News (no. 76-293). Washington, D.C: U.S. Department of Housing and Urban Development, Aug. 16, 1976.

Feminist Alliance Against Rape Newsletter (F.A.A.R.). Monthly. Washington, D.C.

"Film and the Permissive Society: Cause or Effect?" A symposium and public dialogue sponsored by the Department of English and the Interdisciplinary Film Studies Committee, Arizona State University, Tempe, Ariz. Co-chairmen Nicholas A. Salerno and R. Paul Murphy, Fourth Session, "Violence," guest speakers: R. A. Heinman, J. L. Barkas, P. Patton, J. Vergis, and T. Alexander Votichenko, Oct. 13, 1976,

Fitzpatrick, F. Emmett, District Attorney. *Victims Are People: Philadelphia District Attorney's Office Commission on Victim Witness Assistance, A Report on Activities, October 1974-October 1975.* Mimeo. Philadelphia, 1975.

Flint, Robert T. *Instructors' Manual for Someone Else's Crisis.* Schiller Park, Ill.: Motorola Teleprograms, 1975.

_____, *The Psychology of Victims: Student Monograph.* Schiller Park, Ill.; Motorola Teleprograms, 1975.

Flynn, John; Anderson, Patrick; Coleman, Beverly; Finn, Mary; Moeller, Cindy; Nodel, Helena; Novara, Rosalie; Turner, Christie; and Weiss, Harry. "Spouse Assault: Its Dimensions and Characteristics in Kalamazoo County, Michigan." Mimeo. School of Social Work, Western Michigan University, Kalamazoo, Mich., June 1975.

Fojtik, Kathleen M. *Wife Beating: How to Develop a Wife Assault Task Force and Project.* 2nd ed. Ann Arbor-Washtenaw National Organization of Women, Ann Arbor, Mich.: Wife Assault Task Force, n.d.

Galvin, Patrick. *We Do It for Love.* At Lyric Players Theatre, Belfast, Northern Ireland, June 18, 1975.

Geib, Frederick A. *The Ultimate Victim: Life-Cycle of a Corpse.* Paper presented at the Second International Symposium on Victimology, Boston, Mass., Sept. 6, 1976.

Gordon, Barbara, writer and producer. "Eye on Victims of Violent Crimes," Anthony P. Hatch, exec, producer; Eric Shapiro, director. WCBS-TV,

Channel 2, New York, broadcast Feb. 24, 1975, 7:30-8:00 P.M. Transcript.

Gordon, Cyrus H. *Hammurabi's Code: Quaint or Forward-Looking?* Source Problems in World Civilization series. New York: Holt, Rinehart and Winston, 1957.

Gunn, John. "Sexual Offenders." Ms. of chapter that appeared in an article published in *British journal of Medicine,* 1975,

Haas, Harl. "Multnomah County District Attorney, Victim Assistance Project, LEAA Grant Application." Ms. duplicate. Portland, Oreg., Mar. 24, 1975.

Hardyck, Jane Allyn; Piliavin, Irving M.; and Vadum, Arlene C. "Reactions to the Victim in a Just or Non-Just World." Paper presented at the meeting of the Society of Experimental Social Psychology, Bethesda, Md., Fall 1971.

Hudson, Joe, ed. *Restitution in Criminal Justice: Based on Papers Presented at the First International Symposium on Restitution.* Spiral-bound mimeo. St. Paul, Minn., Winter 1976.

Jeffries, Peter, writer and producer. "Thou Shalt Not Kill." NBC News, broadcast Friday, July 28, 1972, 9:30 P.M. EST, Transcript.

Kress, Susan. "Doubly Abused: The Plight of Crime Victims in Literature." Paper presented at Second International Symposium on Victimology, Boston, Mass., Sept. 8, 1976.

Lamborn, LeRoy L. "Crime Victim Compensation: Theory and Practice in the Second Decade. " Paper prepared for the Second International Symposium on Victimology, Boston, Mass., July 9, 1976.

Laszlo, Anna T. "Intake Screening as a Concept in Victim Assistance: A Prosecutorial Model," Paper prepared for the Second International Symposium on Victimology, Boston, Mass., Sept. 1976.

Lerner, Melvin J. "Just World Research and the Attribution Process: Looking Back and Ahead." 96-page ms. copy printout, n.d.

_____; Miller, Dale T.; and Holmes, John G. "Deserving Versus Justice: A Contemporary Dilemma." To appear in *Advances in Experimental. Social Psychology.*

McDonald, William F. "Notes on the Victim's Role in the Prosecutorial and Dispositional Stages of the American Criminal Justice Process." Paper prepared for presentation on Sept. 8, 1976, at the Second International Symposium on Victimology, Boston, Mass.

Mark, Sir Robert. "The Compellable Witness." Speech given before the National Press Club, Washington, D.C., 1976.

Miller, J. P., scriptwriter. *Heller Skelter,* based on the book by Vincent Bugliosi and Curt Gentry. WCBS-TV, broadcast in two parts, Jan. 26, 1977, 9:00-11:00 P.M.

National Communication Network for the Elimination of Violence Against Women. Newsletter. Women's Advocates-NCN-St. Paul, Minn., beg. Winter 1977.

National District Attorneys Association Commission on Victim Witness Assistance. *Help for Victims and Witnesses: An Annual Report.* Washington, D.C., Feb. 1976.

_____. *Keep Them Informed.* Washington, D.C., n.d.

_____. *16 Ideas to Help District Attorneys Help the Victims and Witnesses of Crime.* 2nd Printing. Washington, D.C., n.d.

_____. *The Victim Advocate.* Washington, D.C., July 1977.

_____. *What Happens Now? A District Attorneys' Guide to Aid the Families of Homicide Victims.* Washington, D.C., n.d.

N.O.V.A. Newsletter. Publication of the National Organization for Victim Assistance, Akron, Ohio, beg. Sept. 1976.

Oringer, David G. *Compensation for Victims of Crimes of Violence.* Condensed and updated from a dissertation submitted as a partial requirement for the degree of Doctor of Juridical Science at the New York Law School, June 1965.

Orton, Joe. *Loot.* At the Royal Court Theatre, London, June 23, 1975.

Piñero, Miguel. *Short Eyes.* At the Vivian Beaumont Theater, New York City, June 14, 1974.

The President's Commission on Law Enforcement and Administration of Justice, Task Force on Assessment. *Task Force Report: Crime and Its Impact—An Assessment.* Washington, D.C: U.S. Government Printing Office, 1967.

Remboff, Randa. "The Ninth Precinct: A Tale of Frustration in the Urban Jungle." M.A. thesis, Graduate School of Journalism, Columbia University, New York City, 1976.

Response to Intrafamily Violence and Sexual Assault. Newsletter. Center for Women Policy Studies, Washington, D.C, beg. Oct. 1976.

Schmidt, Winsor C. *Legal Issues in Compensating Victims of Violent Crime.* Raleigh, N.C: The National Association of Attorneys General, May 1976.

Schur, Edwin M. "Victimless Crime." Paper presented at the annual meeting of American Association for the Advancement of Science, Boston, Mass., Feb. 23, 1976. Mimeo.

Simons, Carolyn W., and Piliavin, Jane Allyn. "The Effect of Deception on Reactions to a Victim." Unpublished paper, received 1976, n.d.

Solomon, Muriel, director. Metro's Rape Awareness Public Education Program. "Sexual Abuse—A Primer for Parents; The Sexually Abused Child— Guidelines for Professionals; Sexual Abuse—Guidelines for Teenagers." Duplicated fact sheets. Miami, n.d.

Straus, Murray A.; Gelles, Richard J.; and Stemmetz, Suzanne K. "Violence in the Family: An Assessment of Knowledge and Research Needs." Paper presented at the annual meeting of the American Association for the Advancement of Science, Boston, Mass., Feb. 23, 1976.

Symonds, Martin. "The Psychological Patterns of Response of Victims to Rape." Paper presented at Seminar on Rape, John Jay College of Criminal Justice and American Academy of Professional Law Enforcement, New York City, Apr, 10, 1975.

Taylor, Ian. "Victimology: An Account and a Critique." Chapter from *Encyclopaedia du Crime et de Criminologie,* Geneva, Switzerland. Duplicate ms. received from author, Sheffield, England, June 1975.

Thompson, Ronald G. "Bank Robbers' Perceptions Concerning Bank Security." M.A. thesis, Southern Illinois University, Sept. 1975.

United States Senate. Victims of Crime: Hearing before the Subcommittee on Criminal Laws and Procedures of the Committee on the Judiciary, United States Senate, Ninety-second Congress, First Session, Sept. 29; Nov, 30, 1971; and Mar. 27, 1972. Washington, D.C.: U.S. Government Printing Office, 1972.

"Victims," segment of "Sixty Minutes." Vol. 9, no. 1, CBS-TV. Broadcast Dec. 5, 1976. Irme Horvath, producer.

Victims of Crime. Ninety-second Congress, First Session. United States Senate, Committee on the Judiciary, Subcommittee on Criminal Laws and Procedures, 1972.

The Victim's Perspective on American Criminal Justice. A report prepared by the Minnesota Department of Corrections for the Governor's Commission on Crime and Prevention and Control. Mimeo. St, Paul, Minn., June 1, 1976.

"Violence in America." NBC News Reports, Edwin Newman, moderator; Stuart Schulberg, executive producer. Broadcast Jan. 5, 1977, 8:00-11:30 P.M. EST.

Warrior, Betsy. *Working on Wife Abuse.* Mimeo. Apr, 1976; rev. July 1976.

"Why Steal to Live: The History of a Young Burglar." Term paper, New School for Social Research, New York City, May 10, 1976.

Wilt, C. Marie, and Bannon, James, *A Comprehensive Analysis of Conflict-Motivated Homicides and Assaults—Detroit, 1972-1973.* Unpublished report, mimeo. Mav 1974.

ADDITIONAL REFERENCES

Updated July 2015

Acker, James R. and David R. Karp, editors. *Wounds That Do Not Bind: Victim-Based Perspectives on the Death Penalty*. Durham, North Carolina: Carolina Academic Press, 2006.

AFL-CIO. *Death on the job: The toll of neglect*. Washington, DC: AFL-CIO, 2007. (Twentieth edition, 2011)

Agnich, Laura E. "A Cross-National Study of School Violence." Ph.D. Dissertation, Doctor of Philosophy in Sociology, Virginia Polytechnic Institute and State University (Virginia Tech), May 11, 2011, Blacksburg, Virginia.

Barkan, Steve. "Sociology: Understanding and Changing the Social World." Chapter 7, Section C, "Crime and Criminals." Modified 10-06-2013. Posted at http://www.peoi.org/Courses/Coursesen/socfwk/contents/frame7c.html

Barkas, J.L. *See also* Jan Yager

Barkas, J.L. "Let's Give Crime's Victims their Due." *Newsday*, September 10, 1978, pages 1, 10.

_____. "Reflections on Murder, Criminals, Handguns…" *Newsday*, December 12, 1980.

BBC, "Pakistan Taliban: Peshawar School Attack Leaves 132 Dead." December 16, 2014. Posted at http://www.bbc.com/news/world-asia-30491435

Benbenishty, Rami and Ron Avi Astor. "School Violence in An International Context: A Call for Global Collaboration in Research and Prevention." International Journal of Violence and School, December 2008, pages 59-80. Posted at: http://www.ijvs.org/files/Revue-07/04.-Benbenishty-Ijvs-7.pdf

Burstein, Patricia. "Her Brother's Murder Drove Janet Barkas to Investigate the Sorry Plight of Crime Victims." (In Her Own Words) *People* magazine, pages 60-62, April 30, 1979, Vol. 11, No. 17. (Selected portions of the article including the interview with Burstein posted at: http://www.people.com/people/article/0,,20073516,00.html

CNN Library. "September 11 Fast Facts." Posted on August 28, 2014 at http://www.cnn.com/2013/07/27/us/september-11-anniversary-fast-facts/

Doerner, William J. and Steven P. Lab. *Victimology*.7th edition. New York: Anderson (Routledge), 2014.

Field, Peter. "Remembering September 11 the Day I'll Never Forget." Posted at   http://www.risk.net/risk-magazine/feature/1506589/remembering-september-the-day-i-ll-never-forget(Written September 18, 2001. Revised and edited, August 2002.)

Frosch, Dan and Kirk Jonson. "Gunman Kills 12 in Colorad, Reviving Gun Debate." Published at the *New York Times*, July 20, 2012. Posted at: http://www.nytimes.com/2012/07/21/us/shooting-at-colorado-theater-showing-batman-movie.html?pagewanted=all&_r=0

Ganzini, Linda, M.D.; Bentson McFarland, M.D., Ph.D.; and Joseph Bloom, M.D. "Victims of Fraud: Comparing Victims of White Collar and Violent Crime." *The Bulletin of the American Academy of Psychiatry and the Law*. Volume 18, No. 1, 1990, pages 55-63.

Greer, Desmond S. "A Transatlantic Perspective on the Compensation of Crime Victims in the United States." *Journal of Criminal Law and Criminology*. Volume 85, Issue 2, Article 2, 1994-1995, pages 333-401.

Howard, Russell D. and James J.F. Forest. *Weapons of Mass Destruction and Terrorism*. New York: McGraw-Hill/Contemporary Learning Series, 2008.

Information Please® Database. "Timeline of Worldwide School and Mass Shootings." Pearson Education © 2012. Posted at http://www.infoplease.com/ipa/A0777958.html

Karmen, Andrew. *Crime Victims: An Introduction to Victimology*. 9th edition. Independence, Kentucky: Cengage Learning, 2016.

Maguire, Mike; Rod Morgan; and Robert Reiner, editors. *The Oxford Handbook of Criminology*. Third edition. Oxford, UK: Oxford University Press, 2002.

McCoy, Kevin. "Estimate of Madoff Victims Grows." Posted at 4:16 PM EDT on May 14, 2014 at http://www.usatoday.com/story/money/business/2014/05/13/more-madoff-victims-estimated/9042383/

Moriarty, Lauren. *Controversies in Victimology.* 2nd edition. New York: Anderson (now part of Taylor & Francis), 2008.

National Crime Victims Rights Week (NCVRW). "Section 5: Landmarks in Victims' Rights & Services: An Historical Overview." Posted at: http://ovc.ncjrs.gov/ncvrw2014/pdf/Landmarks.pdf

New York County District Attorney's Office. Press release. "Western Express Cybercriminals Convicted at Trial Sentenced to Significant State Prison Time." August 8, 2013. Posted at http://manhattanda.org/press-release/western-express-cybercriminals-convicted-trial-sentenced-significant-state-prison-time

OVC (Office of Victims of Crime). "Good Samaritans: Volunteers Helping Victims Program Handbook and Training Guide." Publication date: April 2009. Posted at http://www.ovc.gov/publications/infores/Good_Samaritans/crime.html

Quinn, Elizabeth and Sara Brightman. *Crime Victimization: A Comprehensive Overview.* Durham, North Carolina: Carolina Academic Press, 2015.

RAND Corporation. "Compensating the Victims of 9/11." Research report. 2004. Posted at http://www.rand.org/pubs/research_briefs/RB9087/index1.html

Ripley, Amanda. "WTC Victims: What's a Life Worth?" Posted at Time.com on February 6, 2002 at http://content.time.com/time/nation/article/0,8599,198866,00.html

Sharp, Debra Puglisi. *Shattered: Reclaiming a Life Torn Apart by Violence.* New York: Simon & Schuster/Atria, 2004. Schwartz, Emma. "Giving Crime Victims More of Their Say." *U.S. News & World Report.* December 13, 2007. Posted at http://www.usnews.com/news/national/articles/2007/12/13/giving-crime-victims-more-of-their-say

Strom, Chris. "Cybercrime Remains Growth Industry With $445 Billion Lost." June 9, 2014, posted at http://www.bloomberg.com/news/articles/2014-06-09/cybercrime-remains -growth-industry- with-445-billion-lost

United Nations Office on Drugs and Crime (UNODC). "Comprehensive Study on Cybercrime." Vienna, Austria: United Nations, 2013.

Walklate, Professor Sandra. "Who is the Victim of Crime? Paying Homage to the Work of Richard Quinney." 22-page paper.

Walklate, Sandra; Gabe Mythen; and Ross McGarry. "Trauma, Visual Victimology, and the Poetics of Justice."

Yager, Jan. "How to Avoid Ponzi Schemes" Posted at consumeraffairs.com, 7/11/2010 http://www.consumeraffairs.com/boomerific/2010/018_avoiding_ponzi_schemes.html

_____. *Productive Relationships: 57 Strategies for Building Stronger Business Connections.* Stamford, CT: Hannacroix Creek Books, Inc., 2011. (See especially: Strategy #49: Becoming More Aware of Workplace Violence.")

RESOURCES

http://www.crimevictims.gov
From the website:
"As part of an integrated campaign to increase awareness about victims' rights, educate the public about the impact of crime, and promote crime victim resources, the Office for Victims of Crime (OVC) launched crimevictims.gov in 2005. At the time of its launch, the site was tied directly to the release of seven public service announcements (PSAs) that began to air nationally during National Crime Victims' Rights Week, an annual commemoration that promotes victims' rights and services in all sectors of society.

"Designed for three audiences—crime victims, volunteers, and victim service providers—crimevictims.gov provides a wealth of resources for each, including links to Web sites, publications, databases, and hotlines. The site intentionally mirrors the look and feel of the PSAs, "giving a face" to crime victims, volunteers, and providers through photos and brief testimonials."

Directory of Crime Victim Services
http://ovc.ncjrs.gov/findvictimservices/
National Association of Crime Victims Compensation Boards

http://www.NACVCB.org
From the website:
"The mission of the National Association of Crime Victim Compensation Boards is to provide leadership, professional development, and collaborative opportunities to our members to strengthen their capacity to improve services to crime victims and survivors. We share a vision of working together so that every victim compensation program is fully funded, optimally staffed, and functioning effectively to help victims cope with the costs of crime."

At this page you can find information about each state's crime victim compensation program:

http://nacvcb.org/index.asp?sid=5
National Center for Missing and Exploited Children
http://www.missingkids.com
Founded in 1984 as a private non-profit organization, working in partnership with the U.S. Department of Justice, to find missing children as well as to stop the sexual exploitation of minors.

National Organization of Victim Assistance (NOVA)
http://www.trynova.org/
Founded in 1975, information and advocacy non-profit organization with an annual conference related to rights and services for victims. Also offers a training program and certification for those going through a crisis.

National Association of Parents of Murdered Children, Inc.®
http://www.pomc.org/
National membership association, with one or more chapters in many states, for those who have lost a family member because of violence as well as for professionals who help crime victims.

National Institute of Justice (NIJ)
http://www.nij.gov/
From the website:
"NIJ was created in 1969 and has been in the forefront of nearly every innovation in criminal justice research and policy ever since. Understanding the nature of criminal careers, the effects of sanctions, the ways technology can improve practice, and the operations of the criminal justice system have all been deeply influenced by NIJ research findings."
Victim Support Services (Formerly Families and Friends of Violent Crime Victims)

Everett, WA
http://www.seattlefoundation.org/npos/Pages/FamiliesFriendsofMissing-PersonsViolentCrime.aspx

Founded in 1975, this is a local advocacy group for violent crime victims and their families and friends.

About the Author

Jan Yager, Ph.D., the former J.L. Barkas, has a Ph.D. in sociology from The City University of New York Graduate Center. Dr. Yager also did a year of graduate work in art therapy at Hahnemann Medical College. Her initial interest in crime victims began when she was 20, after the tragic death of her 23-year-old brother, Seth Barkas, from a mugging. To research *Victims*, in addition to obtaining her M.A. in criminal justice from Goddard College, under the mentorship of Dr. Arthur Niederhoffer, sociology professor at John Jay College of Criminal Justice, Jan conducted scores of interviews and traveled throughout the U.S. and globally including to Belfast, London, Paris, Toronto, and Amsterdam. Her master's thesis was on "Victims of Crime and Social Change." She volunteered at a Brooklyn-based crime victim hotline and at Bedford Hills Correctional Facility. For two years, she developed and ran a crime prevention resource center in New York City.

Dr. Yager has taught at The New School, Temple University, the University of Connecticut, and, since 2014, at John Jay College of Criminal Justice, where she teaches Victimology as well as Criminology, International Criminology, Penology, and Introduction to Sociology. In 2020, 2019, and 2016, the Department of Sociology at John Jay awarded her the Adjunct Excellence Award in Mentoring and, in 2017, she was awarded the Adjunct Excellence in Teaching. Dr. Yager has also taught criminology, sociology of corrections, and other courses at other colleges including William Paterson University and Kean University.

For more on the author, go to: https://www.drjanyager.com

OTHER BOOKS BY DR. JAN YAGER THAT YOU MIGHT FIND OF INTEREST

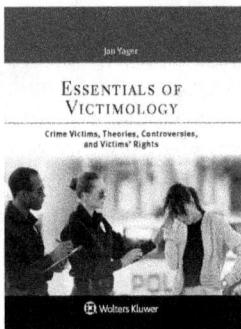

**Essentials of Victimology:
Crime Victimization, Theories,
Controversies, and Victims' Rights**
Aspen Publishing, 2022.

https://www.aspenpublishing.com

A 16-chapter textbook covering the foundations of victimology as well as such controversies as victim blame, addressing victims of violent and property crimes

Praise for *Essentials of Victimology*:
"I read Dr. Jan Yager's required textbook *ESSENTIALS OF VICTIMOLOGY* from cover to cover, and thought it was very readable, informative, and interesting! The Victimology course went well. *ESSENTIALS OF VICTIMOLOGY* was definitely a great resource I'd use again."
-- Colleen P. Eren, Ph.D., Criminology Director, William Paterson University

Contents

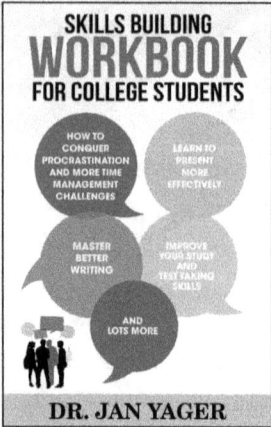

Skills Building Workbook for College Students

Hannacroix Creek Books, Inc.

Copyright year 2022

Standalone workbook or companion guide to *Time Management and Other Essential Skills for College Students.*

Covering the basics about key issues that college students need to master to succeed along with fill-in pages to complete related activities and exercises. Topics covered include:

- time management basics
- presenting with ease
- better writing skills
- making the most of remote learning
- becoming a lifelong learner
- and more

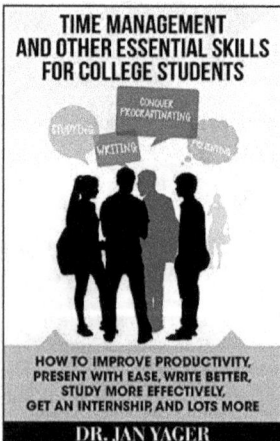

Time Management and Other Essential Skills for College Students

Hannacroix Creek Books, Inc.

How do you juggle 4 or 5 courses as well as a social life and possibly even working part-time or full-time? College makes so many demands on students that learning principles of time management just might be what is needed to get more done in less time. Other study skills tips will help too!

This book, filled with sound advice, is an outgrowth of the popular and unique SKILLS BUILDING WORKSHOP that author/sociologist/criminologist

Dr. Jan Yager has been offering every semester since 2016 at John Jay College of Criminal Justice (CUNY) where she is an award-winning Adjunct Associate Professor. In this book, you will learn to overcome procrastination, write better, speak with greater ease, improving your performance in online courses and distance learning, improving your people skills, landing an internship, making the most of winter and summer breaks, turning a professor into a mentor, and lots more.

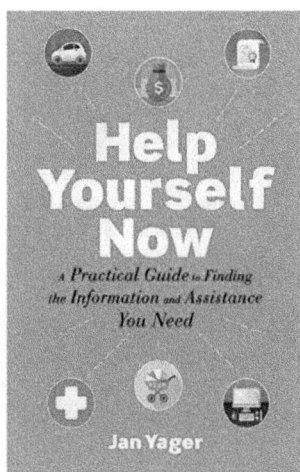

Help Yourself Now
A Practical Guide to Finding the Information and Assistance You Need
Allworth Press (an imprint of Skyhorse Publishing)

How to Find Help for Any Situation

Although we live in the age of information and everyone is bombarded with potential sources of help, sifting through those possibilities can be a chore. This is where *Help Yourself* comes in! With this useful reference, author Jan Yager provides an overview of the various situations that most people have to navigate, from calling customer service or reporting a crime to finding credible and reliable information about a business, health, or legal concern.

Each chapter of the 30 chapters includes a brief discussion of an issue, potential scenarios, and listings of relevant national and international organizations. Yager also instructs readers on researching state agencies, so they can contact appropriate organizations closer to home. Important topics of discussion include:
- Free or low-cost counseling

- Personal finances
- Housing assistance
- Employment services such as finding a job
- Family planning
- K–12 education
- College selection and funding
- Small business development
- Legal services
- Crime victim resources
- Substance abuse including alcohol and drugs
- Emergency preparedness
- and more

Chapters that may be of special interest to readers of *Victims* include: Chapter 10,"Courts and Dispute Resolution," Chapter 11, "Crime: Victims, Witnesses, and Prevention," Chapter 12, "Criminal Justice: Law Enforcement, Corrections, and Alternatives to Prison," Chapter 23, "Offenders, Inmates, and the Formerly Incarcerated"

"Yager (*When Friendship Hurts*) asserts that there is direct help available for every kind of life issue, if one only knows where to seek it out. This reference gives readers a head start on that search, listing more than 100 agencies that deal with everything from addiction and financial assistance to pregnancy and eating disorders. In a more positive vein, Yager lists resources for people interested in volunteerism and travel. The entries in all 30 categories are annotated with informative descriptions, contact information, and instructions on how to handle an immediate situation. VERDICT An excellent reference for all libraries and counseling centers." —*Library Journal* **starred review**

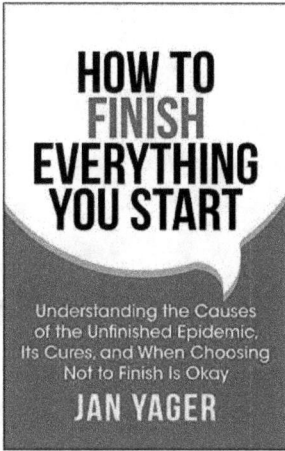

How to Finish Everything You Start
Hannacroix Creek Books, Inc. , 2019

Available in e-book, print, and audiobook versions, narrated by Gale Cruz
This practical business book will help you understand why you might not be finishing a task or project, and what to do about it. But it also goes beyond a "do this, not that" approach to help you develop a deeper insight into what you should be committing to in the first place! Divided into three parts, Part 1, "Causes," begins with a provocative chapter entitled "The Epidemic of Unfinished Everything and Its Consequences." Chapter 2 explores 21 behaviors, beliefs, and bad habits that might be at the root of not finishing. The remaining chapters in this part explore specific causes of unfinished tasks including "Having Too Much to Do at One;" "Dealing with Procrastination" and "Having an Unrealistic or No Deadline."

Part 2, "Cures," probes such remedies as "Using F-I-N-I-S-H;" "To-Do Lists that Work;" Learning to Say "No"; and more.

Part 3, "Additional Thoughts and a Conclusion," includes a chapter entitled, "The Exception That Proves the Rule: When Failing to Finish is a Good Thing" as well as the chapter, "Summing Up," with pivotal information to help you finish everything you start.

Praise for *How to Finish Everything You Start*:
"Unfinished tasks are truly an epidemic. I was inspired by reading Jan Yager's *HOW TO FINISH EVERYTHING YOU START*, and I also experienced deep introspection in doing the exercises."-
-Ajeet Khurana, CEO

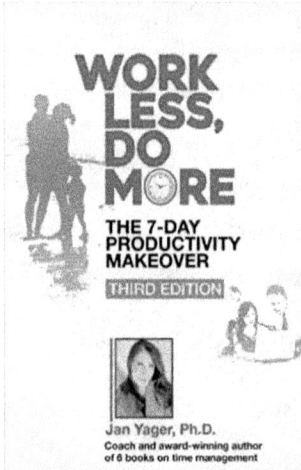

Work Less, Do More
The 7-Day Productivity Makeover
Hannacroix Creek Books, Inc.

WORK
LESS,
DO
M⊙RE

THE 7-DAY
PRODUCTIVITY
MAKEOVER

THIRD EDITION

Jan Yager, Ph.D.
Coach and award-winning author
of 6 books on time management

In this third edition of this international hit title, translated into a dozen languages, sociologist/productivity and relationship coach and expert Dr. Jan Yager offers a 7-day plan to get more done in less time. This revised and updated book covers everything from assessing how productive you are right now, goal setting, prioritizing, to getting over procrastination, perfectionism, poor planning, poor pacing, decluttering, work-life balance, and lots more.

Filled with anecdotes, examples, self-quizzes and worksheets, Dr. Yager also shares the results of her original time management surveys of more than 250 men and women on their time challenges, strengths, and preferred productivity tools.

The three editions of Work Less, Do More have been translated into a dozen languages.
The English language edition available from Hannacroix Creek Books, Inc. is available in e-book, print, and audiobook versions. There is a version available for the subcontinent of India from Jaico Publishing Company.

EFFECTIVE BUSINESS AND NONFICTION WRITING
THIRD EDITION

Learn how to improve your e-mails, letters, proposals, reports, and blogs with tips for getting your articles, blogs, or books published

JAN YAGER

Author of 38 award-winning books translated into 32 languages

Effective Business and Nonfiction Writing

Hannacroix Creek Books, Inc.

Transform your nonfiction writing NOW! Through concrete examples and clear guidelines, seasoned and prolific writer, teacher, and coach Jan Yager gives solid advice on how to create business and nonfiction writing that will help you to get ahead in your career. Originally published by Arco with the title "How to Write Like a Professional," this practical and extremely useful book provides guidelines for improved nonfiction writing including a self-evaluation to access your current writing skills; a discussion of the four basic steps to effective business writing; how to overcome writer's block; how to craft a style that's right for you and your audience; how to get your writing published; time management tips for writing; exercises to hone your writing skills; and lots more.

This 3rd edition has a new cover and Preface, which discusses the nonfiction writing demands of blogging, as well as an additional section at the back of the book entitled "Some Additional Thoughts on Nonfiction Writing" which covers
•The impact of the Internet and Internet-based reference tools on nonfiction writing
•The current state of business writing skills
•How globalization is impacting on nonfiction or business writing
•The current improved perception of using a ghostwriter or relying on editors for help
•The consequences of the rush to publish.
• and more

When Friendship Hurts:
How to Deal with Friends Who Betray, Abandon, or Wound You

Simon & Schuster, Inc., Touchstone, U.S. and Canada T
he rest of the world in English is available from Hannacroix Creek Booskc

We have all had friendships that have gone bad. Whether it takes the form of a simple yet inexplicable estrangement or a devastating betrayal, a failed friendship can make your life miserable, threaten your success at work or school, and even undermine your romantic relationships. Finally there is help. In *When Friendship Hurts,* Jan Yager, recognized internationally as a leading expert on friendship, explores what causes friendships to falter and explains how to mend them -- or end them. In this straightforward, illuminating book filled with dozens of quizzes and real-life examples, Yager covers all the bases, including:

—The twenty-one types of negative friends -- a rogues' gallery featuring such familiar types as the Blood-sucker, the Fault-finder, the Promise Breaker, and the Copycat
—How to recognize destructive friends as well as how to find ideal ones

—The e-mail effect -- how electronic communication has changed friendships for both the better and the worse
—The misuse of friendship at work -- how to deal with a co-worker's lies, deceit, or attempts at revenge
—How to stop obsessing about a failed friendship
—and much more

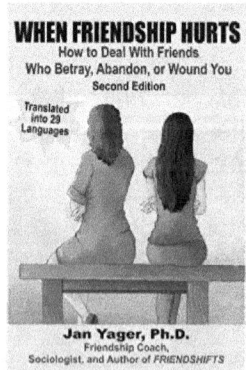

LOOKING BACKWARD, GOING FORWARD

Reflections on a Writer's Life

JAN YAGER

*Award-winning author of 50+ books,
in 35 languages, including When Friendship Hurts,
How to Finish Everything You Start,
Untimely Death (novel) and Victims*

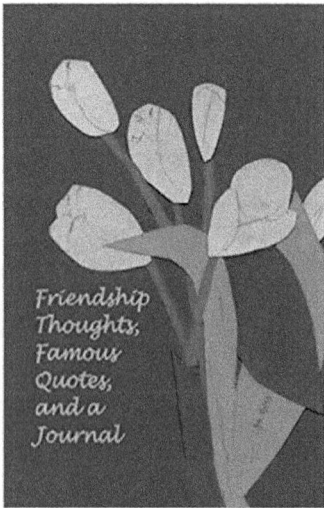

Friendship Thoughts, Famous Quotes, and a Journal

A unique 176-page friendship journal that includes an introduction about friendship and journal followed by 140 quotes on friendship from philosophers, essayists, poets, playwrights, celebrities, psychologists, sociologists, authors, and leaders that friendship expert Dr. Jan Yager has been gathering for decades. Each quote is reprinted at the top of a blank lined page where you can journal. After the quotes/lined blank pages, there are 4 more pages to add your own or other friendship quotes plus 2 blank pages for drawings or photos. Excerpts follow from several of Dr. Yager's six books on friendship and work relationships including the seven top ways to make time for your friends. Included in this journal is a contact directory for you to fill out as well as Resources for online friendship sites and a Bibliography. Use this friendship journal for yourself or give it to a friend.

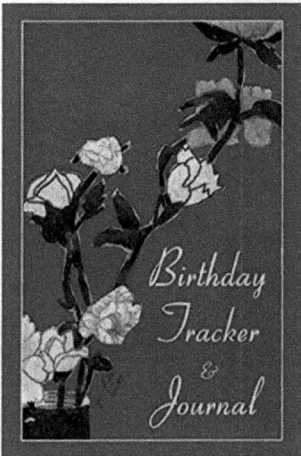

Birthday Tracker & Journal

Available in hardcover or paperback

Birthday Tracker and Journal is a special place to record important birthdays for family, friends, and others, month by month. It includes an informative introduction on birthday celebration traditions and lists birthday birthstones and flowers by month for gift-giving considerations. There is also a place to keep track of birthday cards or presents that you send, or receive, lined blank pages for your birthday reflections, and a place for birthday photos. Color illustrations by author/artist Jan Yager appear throughout. This unique book is the perfect gift or use it yourself to organize birthday (or other special occasions, like anniversaries) information.

Fiction (Novels)

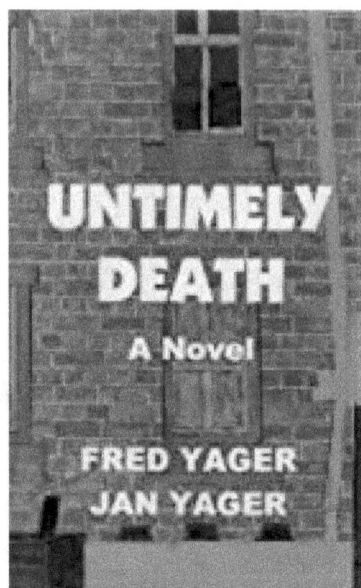

UNTIMELY DEATH

A Novel

FRED YAGER
JAN YAGER

the Pretty One

A Novel

Jan Yager

www.ingramcontent.com/pod-product-compliance
Lightning Source LLC
Chambersburg PA
CBHW072108270326
41931CB00010B/1489